Handbook of United States Economic and Financial Indicators

Recent Titles in
Bibliographies and Indexes in Economics and Economic History

International Real Estate Valuation, Investment, and Development
Valerie J. Nurcombe

Japanese Direct Foreign Investments: An Annotated Bibliography
Karl Boger, compiler

Economic Methodology: A Bibliography with References to Works in the Philosophy of
Science, 1860–1988
Deborah A. Redman, compiler

A Literature Guide to the Hospitality Industry
*Philip Sawin, Denise Madland, Mary K. Richards, and Jana Reeg
Steidinger, compilers*

Successful Industrial Product Innovation: An Integrative Literature Review
Roger J. Calantone and C. Anthony di Benedetto, compilers

The Social Dimensions of International Business: An Annotated Bibliography
Jon P. Alston, compiler

The Savings and Loan Crisis: An Annotated Bibliography
Pat L. Talley, compiler

The Japanese Automobile Industry: An Annotated Bibliography
Sheau-yueh J. Chao, compiler

Rural Economic Development, 1975–1993: An Annotated Bibliography
F. Larry Leistritz and Rita R. Hamm, compilers

Wetland Economics, 1989–1993: A Selected, Annotated Bibliography
Jay A. Leitch and Herbert R. Ludwig, Jr., compilers

A NAFTA Bibliography
Allan Metz, compiler

Handbook of United States Economic and Financial Indicators

Revised Edition

F. M. O'Hara, Jr.
and F. M. O'Hara, III

Bibliographies and Indexes in Economics and Economic History,
Number 20

Greenwood Press
Westport, Connecticut • London

Library of Congress Cataloging-in-Publication Data

O'Hara, Frederick M.
    Handbook of United States economic and financial indicators / F. M. O'Hara, Jr. and
F. M. O'Hara, III.—Rev. ed.
       p. cm.—(Bibliographies and indexes in economics and economic history, ISSN
0749–1786 ; 20)
    Includes bibliographical references and index.
    ISBN 0–313–27450–9 (alk. paper)
    1. Economic indicators—United States—Handbooks, manuals, etc. I. O'Hara, F. M.,
1968–. II. Title. III. Series.
HC106.8.O47 2000
330.973—dc21   99–054281

British Library Cataloguing in Publication Data is available.

Library of Congress Catalog Card Number: 99–054281
ISBN: 0–313–27450–9
ISSN: 0749–1786

First published in 2000

Greenwood Press, 88 Post Road West, Westport, CT 06881
An imprint of Greenwood Publishing Group, Inc.
www.greenwood.com

Printed in the United States of America

The paper used in this book complies with the
Permanent Paper Standard issued by the National
Information Standards Organization (Z39.48–1984).

10 9 8 7 6 5 4 3 2

Contents

Introduction

This book is designed to answer questions about the makeup, purposes, use, and availability of economic indicators in a broad sense of the term. This version of the *Handbook* includes 284 indicators, of which 137 are new to this edition. The entries are ordered alphabetically. "See" references are employed to overcome the difficulties produced by different agencies referring to the same indicator by different names. In addition, numerous "See also" references will lead the reader to additional entries with similar names or subject matters. These finding aids are supplemented by a subject index.

Each entry provides a brief description of the indicator; a depiction of how it is derived or calculated; a characterization of its use; an attribution of its publisher and place of announcement; a table of sources that furnish values for the indicator; and a bibliography of works that provide additional information about its origination, derivation, or use.

The source tables give the title of the publication where values for the indicator can be found, the frequency with which that publication appears, the extent of data that is provided, the format in which the data are presented, and the medium in which the publication appears. Each publication title appears in Appendix C with its address; electronic publications appear in Appendix D with their electronic addresses. The frequency of publication of values for a given indicator is denoted with a code:

h	hourly
d	daily
w	weekly
bw	biweekly
sw	semiweekly
m	monthly
q	quarterly
a	annually
i	intermittently

These codes refer specifically to the value of the indicator published (i.e., whether it is a daily value, the week's end value, the end-of-month value, etc.). Where frequencies are multiples of a unit (e.g., 20 minutes), the next-largest unit is indicated (for this example, hours). These frequency-of-publication values usually coincide with the frequency of publication of the source in which they appear; after all, the publication wants to announce the most recent value available. Occasionally, the frequency of the publication may be different from the frequency of the values cited. For example, the daily values of an indicator may be compiled and reported in a weekly or monthly publication. The user should constantly bear in mind that the "Frequency" describes the data presented.

Similarly, the extent of data is denoted with a code:

c   current (within the past year)

h   historic [extending beyond a year (or a month for daily measurements)]

f   forecast (projections for the future)

The format is indicated with a t for text or tabular presentation and g for graphic. The medium is designated as p for print or paper and e for electronic (computer files, Web sites, television programs, or similar sources). Note that the letter h is used to denote a frequency (hourly) and an extent (historic); the distinction in meaning must be made on the basis of the column in which it occurs.

Where parallel sources exist (e.g., print and electronic editions of the same publication) but contain different data (e.g., the data in the electronic version may be updated more frequently than that in the print version), parentheses are used to indicate which values go together:

USA Today   d (h)   c   t   p (e)

Here, the print version gives daily values, and the electronic version gives hourly data.

The indicators included constitute a sampling of the many indicators in use. Selection was guided by several principles. The indicators had to refer to aspects of the U.S. economy; indicators describing foreign or international economic systems were generally excluded as were indicators with only regional scopes. Technical indicators were generally excluded because of their narrow applications and the lack of published data. Polls and surveys were largely avoided because of their subjective nature. Ready access to current and historical values was important; the indicators had to be easily available to the public through publication on the World Wide Web, by national newspapers or periodicals, as part of library collections, or in government publications; indicators for which data are available only on a commercial (fee) basis were not included.

Indeed, public availability was a major determinant in selecting items for inclusion. Many brokerage houses produce indexes of different sectors of the stock market. However, only a few of these indexes are noted in mass-marketed business or financial publications. Moreover, the multiple indexes produced by a given organization often are derived in the same manner and differ only subtly in treatment of the subject matter. In such cases, one or a few such indexes were included to represent the full range of indexes, and public attention (e.g., the posting of values for specific indexes in a national newspaper like *Barron's* or *The Wall Street Journal*) was a criterion for the selection of the representative indicator(s).

In reviews of the previous edition of the *Handbook*, numerous comments were made about the "nonquantitative" indicators included in an appendix. These comments were mostly elicited by the lighthearted nature of these entries in an otherwise humorless and predictable collection of writeups. However, references to some of these indicators show up in the media like clockwork (e.g., The Superbowl Indicator), and curious readers are often led to inquire about the nature or history of such indicators. In other cases, the nonquantitative (for want of a better term) indicator might not have a high level of precision but might intuitively convey an economic principle to the reader. For example, comparative variations in the cost of living from region to region or across national boundaries might not be clear to a reader, but the Big Mac Index (which compares the cost of a Big Mac at McDonald's outlets in different locations) can bring that concept into sharp focus. As a result, this section of the book has been enlarged and enhanced along with the rest of the text. A particular favorite of the authors is The Darts Average, which is regularly published in *The Wall Street Journal* and which tracks the success of a group of pundits throwing darts at the stock pages to pick winning stocks, regularly outperforming market analysts.

In addition, four other appendixes provide supplemental information to the text. Appendix B lists the compilers of the various indicators, Appendix C gives the addresses of the printed sources of the indicators, Appendix D names the universal resource locators (URLs) of the Web-based resources cited, and Appendix E compiles the sources of information used to prepare this publication along with some supplemental sources that the reader can go to for further information about economic indicators in general or about a specific indicator.

During the compilation of this edition of the *Handbook*, many changes took place in the preparation and publication of economic indicators. Budgetary pressures forced government agencies to combine or eliminate the preparation of many indicators or the publications in which those indicators were announced and archived for public use. The long-running publication *Business Conditions Digest*, which published hundreds of indicators and provided long-term series of comparative data, ceased publication. Privatization occurred with several indicators (such as the Leading Indicators Composite Index) and publications (such as *Business Statistics*, formerly published by the Bureau of Economic Analysis). And corporate sales and takeovers altered ownership patterns: The Telerate service of Dow-Jones was sold to Bridge Communications in late 1998, and the Business Payment Index ceased publication after the 1996 sale of TRW Information Systems and Services to Experian. Such transitions caused discontinuities in the production and publication of the indicators and, in some cases, basic changes in the ways the indicators were calculated. On the other hand, the computer has made the publication and retrieval of values for economic indicators easier and faster. During the past decade, many indicator data sets moved to (or were replicated on) computerized databases, which were easy to update and readily accessible. With the advent of the World Wide Web, another migration took place. One effect of the advent of the WWW is the multitude of Web sites that post current values of the most common indicators, such as the Dow Jones averages, the S&P 500, and the 30-Year Treasury Bond price and yield. Hundreds of Web sites that post these and a few other indicators were ignored in compiling the tables of data sources. For these indicators, only the most common and accessible sites were listed. Another effect is that, because Web sites are relatively simple and inexpensive to establish, they are transitory. Sites with economic data can exist one day and be gone (or have moved to a new site) the next. Moreover, new insights and analyses in the form of new indicators can be readily brought before the public (and can just as readily disappear). Such instability on the Web is typified by the Bloomberg Year 2000 Index and Bloomberg Color of Money Business Index, each of which appeared for a few months on the Bloomberg Website and then disappeared.

This impermanence of electronic data will affect how the reader uses this work. In many cases, the data sought reside on Web pages that are hidden by the intricate structure of the site. To help the reader find those pages, detailed URLs have frequently been supplied. However, if the structure or organization of the site is altered, those URLs may no longer be valid. In such cases, the reader is urged to go to the site's home page and to search through the new structure to find the desired information.

All of these influences have made the selection of entries for this handbook problematic. We have tried to reflect the great diversity of information obtainable without citing information that will not be available when the reader wants to use it. We hope that we have chosen judiciously and, at the end of this task, do not look forward to having to cope with this constant change in a future edition.

We wish to thank the many institutions whose resources we used in compiling this volume, among which are the libraries of The University of Tennessee, the University of Arizona, Arizona State University West, the University of California at Berkeley, Northern Arizona University, Tennessee Technological University, Florida State University, and Vanderbilt University. We also wish to thank Albert Sindlinger and individuals at The Conference Board, Lipper Analytical Services, Bloomberg Information Services, Experian, the Federal Reserve Bank of San Francisco, and TheStreet.com, among many others, for their help and guidance. We especially wish to thank Linda O'Hara, our wife and mother, for her support throughout this project and her help in proofreading and indexing the final copy.

MAIN ENTRIES

A

Advance Durable Goods
[See Durable Goods]

Advisory Sentiment Index
[Also called Sentiment Index of the Leading Services]

The percentage of investment advisory services or stock-investment news-letters that are bearish (i.e., expect interest rates to fall and bond prices to rise).

This index is determined by surveying about 100 of the leading stock advisory services' publications each week and classifying their recommendations as bullish or bearish. The results of the survey are tabulated as the percentages of the services that are bullish and bearish. The percentage of services expressing bearish sentiments is then graphed alongside the Dow-Jones Industrial Average.

When inverted, the bearish sentiment follows the major stock price averages very closely. The index, therefore, is used as a contrary indicator of market behavior. Used as an intermediate-term trend indicator. Often used with a moving-average system to detect sell signals.

Published weekly by Chartcraft, Inc., in *Investors Intelligence.*

Source	Frequency	Extent	Form	Medium
Barron's	w	c	t	p

Bibliography

Colby, Robert W., and Thomas A. Meyers, *The Encyclopedia of Technical Market Indicators*, Dow Jones-Irwin, Homewood, Ill., 1988, pp. 82-86.

Pring, M. J., *Technical Analysis Explained, An Illustrated Guide for the Investor*, McGraw-Hill, New York, 1980, pp. 212-214.

Smith, Gary, "Using Sentiment Indicators in Decisions to Buy or Sell," *Financial Managers' Statement* **11**, 38-40 (Mar./Apr. 1989).

Solt, Michael E., "How Useful Is the Sentiment Index?" *Financial Analysts Journal* **44**, 45-55 (Sept./Oct. 1988).

Advisory Service Index
[See Advisory Sentiment Index]

Aerospace Vehicles, New Orders

The dollar value of the new orders placed in a given month with U.S. developers or producers of airplanes, missiles, spacecraft, and engines for such vehicles.

This indicator is compiled by surveying companies in the target industry monthly and asking them to report their new orders (including backlog) received for prime contracts and subcontracts less terminations during the period. All orders and backlog reported must be supported by binding legal documents. Data are also provided for conversions, modifications, site activation, other aerospace products and services (including drones), and research and development.

Used to gauge the employment activity of heavy industry and to form projections of the gross national product.

Published annually by the Aerospace Industries Association of America and the U.S. Department of Commerce, Bureau of the Census, in *Aerospace Industry (Orders, Sales, and Backlog)*, Current Industrial Reports Series MA-37D.

Source	Frequency	Extent	Form	Medium
Aerospace Facts and Figures	a	h	t	p
Aerospace Industry	a	h	t	p
Business Statistics	i	h	t	p
Statistical Abstract	a	h	t	p

Bibliography

Slater, Courtenay M., Ed., Business Statistics of the United States, 1995 ed., Bernan Press, Lanham, Md., 1996, pp. 257-258.

U.S. Department of Commerce, Bureau of Economic Analysis, *Business Statistics, 1963-91*, USGPO, Washington, D.C., 1992, pp. 190-191.

After-Tax Corporate Profits
[See Corporate Profits]

Agricultural Employment
[See also Farm Employment]

An estimate of the number of persons in the United States for whom the practice of agriculture is the principal employment.

The statistics for this indicator are derived from the data of the Current Population Survey conducted monthly by the Bureau of the Census. The Survey covers about 60,000 occupied households and has a response rate of about 97.5%. The Agricultural Employment data count the number of responders whose primary employment is in agriculture and who are age 16 or older. It comprises the self-employed, persons who work for wages or salaries, and those who put in 15 hours or more per week as unpaid workers on family farms. Inmates of institutions (such as penal farms) are not included. The data are adjusted to compensate for the number of nonrespondents, to reflect the known distribution of characteristics of the U.S. population, and to reflect the expected changes in each item between the preceding month's value and the current month's value (an estimate based on the part of the sample common to both months). The data are seasonally adjusted.

Used to assess the productivity of the agricultural labor force. About 4% of the population produces most of the country's food needs as well as the food exports that, taken together, are among the nation's largest foreign exchange earners. It is also used to detect and evaluate the effects on the agricultural industry of structural and technological changes. This productivity and these effects have additional importance in expectations about future food supply, consumer prices, real estate prices, and several other aspects of the national economy. Such measures of employment serve as indicators of overall economic activity.

Published monthly by the U.S. Department of Labor, Bureau of Labor Statistics, in *Employment and Earnings*.

Source	Frequency	Extent	Form	Medium
Business Statistics	i	h	t	p
Economic Indicators	m	c, h	t	p, e
Employment & Earnings	m	c	t	p
Federal Reserve Bulletin	m	c, h	t	p
Handbook of International Economic Statistics (CIA)	a	h	t	p
S&P Basic Statistics - Production Indexes and Labor Statistics	i	h	t	p
S&P Current Statistics	i	h	t	p
Statistical Abstract	a	h	t	p
Survey of Current Business	m	c	t	p, e

Bibliography
Carnes, W. Stansbury, and Stephen D. Slifer, *The Atlas of Economic Indicators: A Visual Guide to Market Forces and the Federal Reserve*, Harper Business, New York, 1991, pp. 59-72.
Daly, P. A., "Agricultural Employment: Has the Decline Ended?," *Monthly Labor Review*, 11-17 (Nov. 1981).

Ilg, Randy E., "The Changing Face of Farm Employment," *Monthly Labor Review* **118**, 3-12 (Apr. 1995).

Koretz, Gene, "State Employment Gains Are Outpacing the Official Tally," *Business Week*, p. 20 (Feb. 1, 1993).

"Labor Force, Employment, and Unemployment from the Current Population Survey," pp. 3-13 in *BLS Handbook of Methods*, U.S. Department of Labor, Bureau of Labor Statistics, Washington, D.C., 1992.

Lavin, Vance, and James Heitman, "Employment and Unemployment Data: Dramatic Changes of Key Indicators," *Government Finance Review* **10**, 35 (1994).

Miller, Glenn H., Jr., "Employment Indicators of Economic Activity," *Economic Review of the Federal Reserve Bank of Kansas City* **72** (7), 42-62 (July/Aug. 1987).

Moore, Geoffrey, "Employment: The Neglected Indicator," *Wall Street Journal*, 10 (Feb. 3, 1972).

Moore, Geoffrey Hoyt, *Improving the Presentation of Employment and Unemployment Statistics*, National Commission on Employment and Unemployment Statistics Background Paper No. 22, USGPO, Washington, D.C., 1978.

Moore, G. H., and J. Shiskin, "Why the Leading Indicators Really Do Lead," *Across the Board*, 71-75 (May 1978).

Plocek, Joseph E., *Economic Indicators: How America Reads Its Financial Health*, New York Institute of Finance, New York, 1991, 53-97.

Ruggles, Richard, *Employment and Unemployment Statistics as Indexes of Economic Activity and Capacity Utilization*, National Commission on Employment and Unemployment Statistics Background Paper No. 28, USGPO, Washington, D.C., 1979.

Shiskin, Julius, "Employment and Unemployment: The Doughnut or the Hole," *Monthly Labor Review*, 3-10 (Feb. 1976).

U.S. Department of Labor, Bureau of Labor Statistics, *BLS Handbook of Methods*, Bull. 2490, USGPO, Washington, D.C., 1997, pp. 4-14.

U.S. Department of Labor, Bureau of Labor Statistics, *Workers, Jobs, and Statistics*, Rept. 698, U.S. Department of Labor, Washington, D.C., 1983.

U.S. Department of Labor, Bureau of Labor Statistics, *A Guide to Seasonal Adjustment of Labor Force Data*, Bull. 2114, U.S. Department of Labor, Washington, D.C., 1982.

U.S. Department of Labor, Bureau of Labor Statistics and Bureau of the Census, *Concepts and Methods Used in Labor Force Statistics Derived from the Current Population Survey*, BLS Rept. 463 and Current Pop. Rept. (Ser. P-23) 62, U.S. Department of Labor and U.S. Department of Commerce, Washington, D.C., 1976.

Air Carriers

[See Revenue Passenger Miles]

Aircraft, New Orders
[See Aerospace Vehicles, New Orders]

Aircraft Shipments
The number and dollar value of the complete civilian aircraft and foreign-customer nonmilitary aircraft, engines, and components shipped by reporting U.S. aircraft manufacturers in a given month.

For this indicator, manufacturers are surveyed monthly and asked to report the number of aircraft shipped, the dollar value of the shipments, and the airframe weight shipped. The number of shipments and dollar values are totaled and published. Dollar values do not include the values of the spare parts shipped with the aircraft but include engines. Airframe weight does not include aircraft's load, engine, propellers, wheels, or other accessories.

Used as an indicator of activity in the heavy-industry sector of the economy.

Published monthly by the U.S. Department of Commerce, Bureau of the Census in *Civil Aircraft and Aircraft Engines*, Current Industrial Reports, Series M37G.

Source	Frequency	Extent	Form	Medium
Aerospace Facts and Figures	a	h	t	p
Business Statistics	i	h	t	p
FAA Statistical Handbook	a	h	t	p
Statistical Abstract	a	h	t	p

Airline Passenger Miles
[See Revenue Passenger Miles]

American Appraisal Company Indexes
[See Boeckh Building Cost Index]

American Customer Satisfaction Index
A national, cross-industry measure of quality of and customer satisfaction with a wide range of products and services.

Since 1994, the National Quality Research Center at the University of Michigan has been conducting telephone interviews with a national sample of almost 50,000 customers per year. Respondents are selected on the basis of having recently bought or used a company's product or service. For most companies, interviews are conducted with about 250 of their customers. The products and services of about 200 companies and major government services are assessed. Companies are selected on the basis of total sales, with preference to those for which financial data are publicly available. The government services selected are ones with which a majority of household consumers can be expected to have had some recent first-hand contact and experience (such as solid-waste disposal, the U.S. Postal Service, the Army & Air Force Exchange Service, the Internal Revenue Service, and police protection). Specific companies are included or excluded from the index as their market position changes. The company/agency scores are used in a multiequation econometric model to sequentially produce industry scores, economic-sector scores, and a national customer satisfaction index, each based on a scale of 0 to 100.

Used to review customer satisfaction, to analyze quality trends, to predict the effect of improved quality, and to evaluate the financial impact of improved quality.

Updated quarterly by the National Quality Research Center and the American Society for Quality, the index is published annually in *Fortune* magazine.

Source	Frequency	Extent	Form	Medium
Fortune	a	c	t	p, e

Bibliography
"American Customer Satisfaction Index," http://acsi.asq.org/, visited Feb. 20, 1998.

Anderson, Eugene W.; Barbara Bryant; Jaesung Cha; Claes Fornell; and Michael D. Johnson, *American Customer Satisfaction Index Methodology Report*, American Society for Quality Control, Milwaukee, 1994.

Bryant, Barbara, "The American Customer Satisfaction Index: Description, Findings, and Implications," *Journal of Marketing* **60** (4), 7-18 (1996).

"Finally, a Way to Make Your Corporate Vision 20/20," http://acsi.asqc.org/acsisoft.html, visited Feb. 20, 1998.

American Stock Exchange Big Block Activity

The number of transactions on the American Stock Exchange that exceed 10,000 shares during a day.

American Stock Exchange members report all large-block buy and sell orders electronically. The orders are transmitted to the Exchange floor, where they are tallied daily.

Because such large transactions are almost always the actions of institutional investors, these statistics are taken to indicate the gross market activity of traders with large and sophisticated analytical resources. This statistic is a coincident indicator that generally confirms movements in other stock-market indicators.

Published daily as a news release from the American Stock Exchange.

Source	Frequency	Extent	Form	Medium
AMEX Fact Book	a	h	t	p
Barron's	w	c	t	p
New York Times	d	c	t	p

Bibliography

Bohlen, Dudley R., "Large Block Transactions: A Premier Contrary Indicator," pp. 42-1 to 42-5 in *The Encyclopedia of Stock Market Techniques*, Investors Intelligence, Larchmont, N.Y., 1983.

Pring, Martin J., *Technical Analysis Explained, An Illustrated Guide for the Investor*, McGraw-Hill, New York, 1980, pp. 158-159.

Zweig, Martin E., "Trusty Market Indicator, Bring the Record of the Big-Block Index up to Date," *Barron's*, 11-12 (Jan. 24, 1983).

American Stock Exchange Composite Index
[Replaced the American Stock Exchange Market Value Index]

A measure of the change in the aggregate market value of outstanding issues on the American Stock Exchange.

This indicator is calculated by multiplying the share price for common shares, American Depositary Receipts, real estate investment trusts, master limited partnerships, and closed-end investment vehicles listed on the American Stock Exchange. Rights, preferred stocks, and when-issued stocks are not included. This calculated value is then indexed to the value of 550 for Dec. 29, 1995. Because the index is capitalization weighted, it is not affected by new listings, delistings, splits, suspensions or halts of trading, or distributions of dividends.

Used as a measure of the overall stock market strength and of speculative activity.

Issued daily as a press release by the American Stock Exchange.

Source	Frequency	Extent	Form	Medium
AMEX Fact Book	m, a	h	t, g	p
Annual Statistical Digest (FRB)	a	c	t	p
Barron's	w	c	t	p
CBS	h	c	t	e
CNN	h	c	t	e
Federal Reserve Bulletin	m	c, h	t	p
Investor's Business Daily	d	c	t	p
Media General	d	c	t	e
Moody's Handbook of Common Stocks	a	h	t	p
Mutual Funds Update	m	c	t	p
New York Times	d (h)	c	t	p (e)
Securities Industry Trends	m	c, h	t	p
Securities Industry Yearbook	a	h	t	p
Statistical Abstract	a	h	t	p

Source	Frequency	Extent	Form	Medium
USA Today	d (h)	c	t	p (e)
Value Line Investment Survey, Part 2: Selection and Opinion	w	c	t	p
Wall Street Journal	d	c	t	p

Bibliography
"Introduction of the New AMEX Composite Index," AMEX Fact Book, American Stock Exchange, New York, 1997, p. 14.

American Stock Exchange Computer Technology Index

A measure of the change in the aggregate market value of the stocks of 30 computer-related firms.

This indicator is capitalization weighted and is calculated by multiplying the share price for common shares of the 30 selected stocks by the number of shares outstanding for each issue. This value is then indexed to the value for July 29, 1983, which was assigned an index value of 100.00. Because it is capitalization weighted, the index is not affected by new listings, delistings, splits, suspensions or halts of trading, or distributions of dividends. IBM, Hewlett-Packard, and Digital Equipment Corp. account for about 60% of the index's value.

Used as an indicator of the strength within this sector of the market and by the American Stock Exchange as the basis of cash-settled index-option contracts.

Published daily as a news release from the American Stock Exchange.

Source	Frequency	Extent	Form	Medium
AMEX Fact Book	a	h	t, g	p
Bloomberg	h	c	t	e

Bibliography
Berlin, Howard M., *The Handbook of Financial Market Indexes, Averages, and Indicators*, Dow Jones-Irwin, Homewood, Ill., 1990, pp. 24-25.

American Stock Exchange Institutional Index

A measure of the change in the aggregate market value of the stocks of 75 companies selected as being the most widely held as equity investments by the nation's largest institutional investors (as determined from those institutions' 13(f) reports filed with the Securities and Exchange Commission).

This indicator is capitalization weighted and is calculated by multiplying the share price for common shares of the 75 selected stocks by the number of shares outstanding for each issue. This value is then indexed to the value for June 24, 1986, which was assigned an index value of 25. The list of 75 stocks is reviewed quarterly and substitutions of comparable holdings are made when needed. Stocks to be included in the index must be held by at least 200 large institutional investors and have had at least 7 million shares traded during each of the previous two quarters.

Used as a measure of the overall stock market strength and of speculative activity by the largest and most influential traders in the market. Also used by the American Stock Exchange and the Chicago Board of Trade as the basis for cash-settled index-option contracts.

Published daily as a news release from the American Stock Exchange.

Source	Frequency	Extent	Form	Medium
AMEX Fact Book	a	h	t, g	p
Bloomberg	h	c	t	e

Bibliography
Berlin, Howard M., *The Handbook of Financial Market Indexes, Averages, and Indicators*, Dow Jones-Irwin, Homewood, Ill., 1990, pp. 24-28.

American Stock Exchange Major Market Index

A measure of the market-price movement of the stocks of 20 blue-chip companies listed on the New York Stock Exchange.

To calculate the value of the Index, the concurrent share prices of the 20 selected stocks are arithmetically summed and divided by the current index divisor, which reflects the effects of stock splits, spinoffs, mergers, and other such influences. For the sake of comparison, the current value can be compared with the value of the index of 200 in 1983; but it is not indexed to that historic value.

Used to track stock-market cycles (although limited in this regard by the small number of largely unrepresentative stocks that make up the index) and as the basis for cash-settled index-option contracts traded on the American Stock Exchange, Chicago Board of Trade, and European Options Exchange.

Calculated continually throughout the trading day and reported on the American Stock Exchange quotation system.

Source	Frequency	Extent	Form	Medium
AMEX Fact Book	a	h	t	p
Barron's	w	c	t	p
Bloomberg	h	c	t	e
Business Week	h	c	t	e
CBS	h	c	t	e
StockMaster	d	c, h	g, t	e
USA Today	h	c	t	e

Bibliography
Berlin, Howard M. *The Handbook of Financial Market Indexes, Averages, and Indicators*, Dow Jones-Irwin, Homewood, Ill., 1990, pp. 28-29.

American Stock Exchange Market Value Index

[Replaced the American Stock Exchange Price-Change Index; replaced by the American Stock Exchange Composite Index]

A measure of the change in the aggregate market value of outstanding common shares, American Depositary Receipts, and warrants on the American Stock Exchange.

This indicator was calculated by multiplying the share price for common shares, American Depositary Receipts, and warrants by the number of shares outstanding for all of the corporations listed on the American Stock Exchange. The calculation included reinvestment of dividends. Rights, preferred stocks, and when-issued stocks were not included. This calculation was then indexed to the value for Sept. 4, 1973, which was assigned an index value of 100.00. In July 1983, the base level was adjusted to 50. Because the market value was capitalization weighted, the index was not affected by new listings, delistings, splits, suspensions or halts of trading, or distributions of dividends. Subsidiary indexes for nine industrial groupings and eight geographic areas were also calculated.

Used as a measure of the overall stock market strength and of speculative activity.

The major measure of the activity of the American Stock Exchange since 1973, this index was discontinued on Dec. 31, 1996. It was replaced by the American Stock Exchange Composite Index. Because calculation of the two indexes is different, values should not be compared.

Bibliography

Berlin, Howard M., *The Handbook of Financial Market Indexes, Averages, and Indicators*, Dow Jones-Irwin, Homewood, Ill., 1990, pp. 23-24.

Bosworth, Barry, "The Stock Market and the Economy," *Brookings Papers on Economic Activity* **2**, 257-290 (1975).

Frumkin, Norman, *Guide to Economic Indicators*, 2nd ed., M. E. Sharpe, Armonk, N.Y., 1994, p. 77.

Kirk, John, "American Exchange's Market Indicators Explained," *Banking* **59**, 4 (Sept. 1966).

"Market Guides," *Barron's*, 9+ (Sept. 26, 1966).

Schoomer, B. A., Jr., "The American Stock Exchange Index System," *Fin. Anal. J.* **20**, 57-61 (May-June 1967).

American Stock Exchange Members' Short Sales

[See also New York Stock Exchange Members' Short Sales]

The total shares sold short for the accounts of AMEX members during a given week.

A short sale is the selling of shares that are not owned by the seller but rather are borrowed from another account. The borrowed shares are sold at the current share price in anticipation of the seller's being able to purchase replacement shares at a lower price in the future and returning them to the account from which they were borrowed. The practice is followed when a declining market is expected. The Exchange's specialists total up the number of shares sold short each day by different classes of traders, and the Exchange reports those totals each week.

Used to predict peaks and troughs in stock-market activity. The theory is that when the members of the Exchange, who are regarded as knowledgeable and insightful about the workings of the market, are selling short, they are anticipating a decline in the market. When few of the trades of the members are short sales, they are collectively anticipating an upturn in the market in the near term.

Published weekly by the American Stock Exchange in a news release.

Source	Frequency	Extent	Form	Medium
Barron's	w	c	t	p
Wall Street Journal	w	c	t	p

Bibliography

Berlin, Howard M. *The Handbook of Financial Market Indexes, Averages, and Indicators*, Dow Jones-Irwin, Homewood, Ill., 1990, pp. 226-227.

Colby, Robert W., and Thomas A. Meyers, *The Encyclopedia of Technical Market Indicators*, Dow Jones-Irwin, Homewood, Ill., 1988, pp. 450-451.

Müller, Thomas, and Harold Nietzer, *Das Grosse Buch der Technischen Indikatoren: Alles über Oszillatoren, Trendfolger, Zyklentechnik*, Thomas Müller, Börsenverlag, Rosenheim, Germany, 1995, p. 447.

Pring, Martin J., *Technical Analysis Explained, An Illustrated Guide for the Investor*, McGraw-Hill, New York, 1980, pp. 210-212.

American Stock Exchange Odd-Lot Index
[See also New York Stock Exchange Odd-Lot Sales]

A measure of the portion of the daily or weekly sales on the American Stock Exchange that are made up of 100 shares or less.

The daily or weekly total of odd-lot transactions on the Exchange is divided by the total number of transactions occurring on the Exchange during that period.

Used to predict future movements in stock market activity. Because small sales such as these are considered to be made largely by individual investors with relatively little sophistication and few informational resources, this value is considered to be and is commonly used as a contrary indicator of market activity.

Published daily as a news release from the American Stock Exchange.

Source	Frequency	Extent	Form	Medium
AMEX Fact Book	a	h	t	p
Barron's	w	c	t	p

Bibliography

Aby, Carroll A., Jr., "The Odd Lot Short Sales Index and Market Bottoms, 1960-1973," *University of Michigan Business Review*, 10-13 (Nov. 1974).

Colby, Robert W., and Thomas A. Meyers, *The Encyclopedia of Technical Market Indicators*, Dow Jones-Irwin, Homewood, Ill., 1988, pp. 333-336.

Dyl, Edward A., and Edwin D. Maberly, "Odd-Lot Transactions Around the Turn of the Year and the January Effect," *Journal of Financial and Quantitative Analysis* **27** (4), 591-604 (1992).

Gordon, William, *The Stock Market Indicators as a Guide to Market Timing*, Investors Press, Palisades Park, N. J., 1968, pp. 61-71.

Hayes, Michael, *The Dow Jones - Irwin Guide to Stock Market Cycles*, Dow Jones - Irwin, Homewood, Ill., 1977, pp. 168-172.

Norris, Floyd, "Odd-Lot Short Sales," *Barron's* **66** (34), 21 and 36 (Aug. 25, 1986).

American Stock Exchange Oil Index
[Formerly the Oil and Gas Index]

A measure of the change in the aggregate market value of the stocks of 16 major integrated firms involved in various phases of the oil industry (i.e., companies involved in producing petroleum or exploring for and/or developing petroleum resources).

This indicator is price weighted and is calculated by multiplying the share price for common shares of the 16 selected stocks by the number of shares outstanding for each issue. This value is then indexed to the value for Aug. 27, 1984, which was assigned an index value of 125. Because of the method of calculating the market value, the index is not affected by new listings, delistings, splits, suspensions or halts of trading, or distributions of dividends. British Petroleum accounts for about 60% of the index's value.

Used as an indicator of the strength within this sector of the market. Also used as the basis of cash-settled index-option contracts that are traded on the American Stock Exchange.

Published daily as a news release from the American Stock Exchange.

Source	Frequency	Extent	Form	Medium
AMEX Fact Book	a	h	t, g	p
Bloomberg	h	c	t	e

Bibliography
Berlin, Howard M., *The Handbook of Financial Market Indexes, Averages, and Indicators*, Dow Jones-Irwin, Homewood, Ill., 1990, pp. 28-30.

American Stock Exchange Price-Change Index
[See American Stock Exchange Market Value Index]

American Stock Exchange Price-Level Index
[See American Stock Exchange Market Value Index]

American Stock Exchange Seat Sales

The price paid in dollars for one seat on or membership in the American Stock Exchange; such membership is required to actively trade on the Exchange, and the number of seats is limited. Prices paid are determined by supply and demand, and the sales are private ones between individuals.

Seats on the American Stock Exchange can be transferred by an auction system. The price paid for a seat is determined by prevailing stock-market conditions and by supply and demand. Brokers involved in these sales report them and the prices to the Exchange; AMEX then averages these seat prices each month and reports that average value.

An indicator of expected future profitability of the exchange; used mostly for historical comparisons of stock-market activity and current strength of the market.

The average values are published monthly as a news release from the American Stock Exchange. The latest quote is posted on the AMEX market line at 212-306-2243.

Source	Frequency	Extent	Form	Medium
AMEX Fact Book	a	h	t	p

Bibliography

Eaton, Leslie, "No Hot Seat: Value of Exchange Memberships Plunges," *Barron's* **70** (4), 36 (Jan. 22, 1990)

"Exchanges: Members and Seats on AMEX," http://invest-faq.com/articles/exch-seats-amex.html, visited Jan. 12, 1998.

American Stock Exchange Short Interest Ratio

[See also New York Stock Exchange Members Short Sales and New York Stock Exchange Nonmembers Short Sales]

The portion of the American Stock Exchange's volume made up of short selling.

This indicator is calculated by dividing the monthly uncovered short positions on the American Stock Exchange (expressed in shares) by the average daily volume for each day of the preceding month.

Used as a buy or sell signal because it is considered to be a measure of the demand for future trading and of traders' opinions on stocks. Short sellers eventually have to cover their positions. In a rising market, this necessity increases the demand for the shorted stocks, increasing their prices. In a declining market, no such immediate demand for the stocks exists, and their values are likely to decline. However, trading strategies like arbitrage between two stocks in a takeover and arbitrage to profit from the prices among a large group of investments have undermined the theoretical foundations of this indicator.

Published monthly (midmonth) as a news release from the American Stock Exchange.

Source	Frequency	Extent	Form	Medium
AMEX Fact Book	a, m	h	t	p

Bibliography

Colby, Robert W., and Thomas A. Meyers, *The Encyclopedia of Technical Market Indicators*, Dow Jones-Irwin, Homewood, Ill., 1988, pp. 450-451.

Gordon, William, *The Stock Market Indicators as a Guide to Market Timing*, Investors Press, Palisades Park, N. J., 1968, pp. 93-110.

Hayes, Michael, *The Dow Jones - Irwin Guide to Stock Market Cycles*, Dow Jones - Irwin, Homewood, Ill., 1977, pp. 147-150.

Kerrigan, Thomas J., "The Short Interest Ratio and Its Component Parts," *Financial Analysts Journal*, 45-49 (Nov./Dec. 1974).

Kerwin, Kathleen, "Bearish on the Short Interest: It's Been a Faulty Technical Indicator," *Barron's* **64**, 24 (Dec. 24, 1984).

Smith, Randall O., "Short Interest and Stock Market Prices," *Financial Analysts Journal*, 151-154 (Nov./Dec, 1968).

American Stock Exchange TICK
[See TICK]

American Stock Exchange Volume

The total number of common and preferred stock shares bought and sold daily on the American Stock Exchange.

Records of sales are used to tally and sum the number of individual shares traded during each day.

Used as an indicator of market interest and activity (demand for stocks) and in conjunction with price trends to determine market advances and declines.

Published daily as a news release from the American Stock Exchange.

Source	Frequency	Extent	Form	Medium
AMEX Fact Book	a	h	t	p
Annual Statistical Digest (FRB)	a	c	t	p
Federal Reserve Bulletin	m	c, h	t	p
Moody's Handbook of Common Stocks	a	h	g	p
New York Times	d	c	t	p
SEC Annual Report	a	c	t	p
Securities Industry Trends	m	c, h	t	p
Securities Industry Yearbook	a	h	t	p
Value Line Investment Survey, Part 2: Selection and Opinion	w	c	t	p

Bibliography
Colby, Robert W., and Thomas A. Meyers, *The Encyclopedia of Technical Market Indicators*, Dow Jones-Irwin, Homewood, Ill., 1988, p. 515.
Kirk, John, "American Exchange's Market Indicators Explained," *Banking* **59**, 4 (Sept. 1966).

American Stock Exchange Volume Momentum

A measure of the current performance of the American Stock Exchange in comparison with its performance during the recent past.

This indicator is calculated by dividing the average volume per day of shares bought and sold on the American Stock Exchange for the past month by the monthly volume of shares on that exchange averaged over the past six months.

Used to determine trends in market activity; used in conjunction with the Price Momentum. Total volume usually falls prior to declines and rises before advances.

Published monthly in *Media General Financial Weekly*.

Source	Frequency	Extent	Form	Medium
AMEX Fact Book	a	h	t	p

Bibliography
Kirk, John, "American Exchange's Market Indicators Explained," *Banking* **59**, 4 (Sept. 1966).

AMEX Index
[See American Stock Exchange Composite Index]

Annual Capital Expenditures
[See Capital Expenditures]

Appliance Factory Sales
[Also called Appliance Factory Shipments]

Number of units shipped during a given month by the major appliance manufacturing industry, including exports.

To compile this statistic, manufacturers are surveyed monthly. Reports are classified by type of product, and totals are calculated for the different classifications. Totals by class are then summed. The grand total may differ from the numerical sum of the class data because of overlapping of the categories. In addition, different appliances have been included in the survey at different times, making year-to-year values less comparable.

Used as a leading indicator of consumer sentiment, indicating whether consumers are and will be buying more or less than they have been in the past. Closely tied to and responsive to interest rates and housing starts.

Published monthly by the Association of Home Appliance Manufacturers in *Home Appliance Newsline.*

Source	Frequency	Extent	Form	Medium
AHAM Fact Book	a	h	t	p
Home Appliance Newsline	m	c	t	p
Major Household Appliances	a	c	t	p

Arms Index
[See Short-Term Trading Index]

Auto and Light Truck Production

An enumeration of the lightweight motor vehicles manufactured in the United States each month.

Manufacturers of motor vehicles tally the number of vehicles they assemble each week and cumulate these values each month. Variations occur from manufacturer to manufacturer in the types of vehicles included in the tallies. Generally, automobiles, vans, and light trucks are included; heavy trucks (defined by gross vehicle weight class) and busses are excluded. Many trade organizations, publishers, and financial firms collect and cumulate these data [notably Ward's Communications (which covers North American production and imports from Asia and Europe) and the American Automobile Manufacturers Association (AAMA, which is made up of Chrysler, Ford, and General Motors)]. Variation in geographic coverage of the data occurs among the organizations collecting the data. Frequently, vehicles manufactured in Canada, the United States, and Mexico for the U.S. market are included. The Federal Reserve Bank of Chicago uses the Ward's data to compile monthly U.S. production data, which it then indexes to the 1992 annual average as adjusted for seasonal variations.

Used as a leading indicator of economic activity, as a leading indicator of demand for durable goods, and as a forecasting tool for predicting future employment and production in the automotive-parts industry.

The U.S. unit-production values are published monthly in an AAMA report on production; they are also summarized quarterly on the AAMA World Wide Web home page at www.aama.com/data/table1.html. Production values for U.S. and other North American vehicles are given monthly by Ward's Communications on the World Wide Web at www.wardsauto.com/statistics/wards_psumm.htm; weekly production data are published in *Ward's Automotive Reports* and in Crain Automotive Group's *Automotive News*. The index of motor-vehicle production is published monthly by the Federal Reserve Bank of Chicago on the World Wide Web at www.frbchi.org/econinfo/midwest_econ/mvprod.html.

Source	Frequency	Extent	Form	Medium
Automotive News Market Data Book	a	h, f	t, g	p
Business Week	w	c	t	p
Handbook of International Economic Statistics (CIA)	a	h	t	p
National Transportation Statistics	a	h	t	p
S&P Basic Statistics - Transportation	i	c, h	t	p
Statistical Abstract	a	h	t	p
Stat-USA	m	c	t	e
The US Automobile Industry	m	c	t	p
World Motor Vehicle Data	a	h	t	p

Bibliography

Aley, James, "Why Autos Aren't a Good Economic Indicator," *Fortune* **132**, 38 (July 10, 1995).

Harris, Ethan S., and Joann Martens, "Two Capsules on the Auto Sector ... Forecasting Automobile Output ... Projecting Consumer Expenditures on Automobiles," *Federal Reserve Bank of New York Quarterly Review* **10**, 40-44 (Winter 1985/1986).

Auto and Light Truck Sales

An enumeration of the lightweight motor vehicles sold in the United States each month.

Manufacturers of motor vehicles tally the number of vehicles sold each week and cumulate these values each month. Many of them publish the data in press releases during the first week of the following month. Variations occur from manufacturer to manufacturer in the types of vehicles included in the tallies. Generally, automobiles, vans, and light trucks are included; heavy trucks (defined by gross vehicle weight class) and busses are excluded. Many trade organizations, publishers, and financial firms collect and cumulate these data, and many of these firms publish reports of the numbers of units sold. The U.S. Department of Commerce's Bureau of Economic Analysis (BEA) collects data from a variety of these firms [notably Ward's Communications (which covers North American production and imports from Asia and Europe), the American Automobile Manufacturers Association (AAMA, which is made up of Chrysler, Ford, and General Motors), Autofacts, and Source News & Reports], seasonally adjusts the figures, and converts them to dollar values based on the manufacturers' suggested retail prices of the vehicles. The resulting values (in billions of dollars) are used in the National Income and Product Accounts (NIPA). The Federal Reserve Bank of

New York uses the Ward's and AAMA data and the BEA adjustment factors to track sales each month in millions of units.

Used as an input to the NIPA, as a leading indicator of economic activity, as a leading indicator of demand for durable goods, and as a forecasting tool for predicting employment and production requirements for the automotive and automotive parts industries.

Published each month by the Federal Reserve Bank of New York on the World Wide Web at www.ny.frb.org/pihome/statistics/indicators/. Factory sales of motor vehicles to dealers are published monthly by Crain Automotive Group in *Automotive News*.

Source	Frequency	Extent	Form	Medium
Automotive News Market Data Book	a	h, f	t, g	p
Bank of America	m	c, h	t	e
Bank of Tokyo-Mitsubishi	m	c, h	t	e
Barron's	w	c	t	p
Business Statistics	i	h	t	p
Chemical Week	w	c	t	p
Economic Handbook of the Machine Tool Industry	a	h	g	p
First Union	m	c, h	t	e
FRB New York	m	c, h	g	e
FRED	m	c, h	t	e
Industry, Trade, and Technology Review	q	c	t	p
National Transportation Statistics	a	h	t	p
Stat-USA	m	c	t	e
The US Automobile Industry	m	c	t	p
Value Line Investment Survey, Part 2: Selection and Opinion	w	c, h, f	t	p
World Motor Vehicle Data	a	h	t	p

Bibliography

Aley, James, "Why Autos Aren't a Good Economic Indicator," *Fortune* **132**, 38 (July 10, 1995).

Carnes, W. Stansbury, and Stephen D. Slifer, *The Atlas of Economic Indicators: A Visual Guide to Market Forces and the Federal Reserve*, Harper Business, New York, 1991, pp. 45-50.

Grant, John, 1938- *A Handbook of Economic Indicators*, University of Toronto Press, Toronto, 1992, pp. 146-147.

Harris, Ethan S., and Joann Martens, "Two Capsules on the Auto Sector ... Forecasting Automobile Output ... Projecting Consumer Expenditures on Automobiles," *Federal Reserve Bank of New York Quarterly Review* **10**, 40-44 (Winter 1985/1986).

Niemira, Michael P., and Gerald F. Zukowski, *Trading the Fundamentals: The Trader's Guide to Interpreting Economic Indicators and Monetary Policy*, McGraw-Hill, New York, 1998, pp. 25-30.

Plocek, Joseph E., *Economic Indicators: How America Reads Its Financial Health*, New York Institute of Finance, New York, 1991, pp. 115-119.

Rogers, R. Mark, *Handbook of Key Economic Indicators*, Irwin Professional Pub., Burr Ridge, Ill., 1994, 75-81.

Santini, Danilo J., "Watch Auto Technology, Fuel Prices to Forecast Slumps," *Journal of Business Forecasting* **3**, 18-22 ff. (1984).

Slater, Courtenay M., Ed., Business Statistics of the United States, 1995 ed., Bernan Press, Lanham, Md., 1996, p. 271.

U.S. Department of Commerce, Bureau of Economic Analysis, *Business Statistics 1963-1993*, USGPO, Washington, D.C., 1994, pp. 191-192.

Average Daily Volume

[See American Stock Exchange Volume and New York Stock Exchange Average Daily Volume]

Average Hourly and Weekly Earnings

[See also Employment Cost Index and Real Earnings]

The average gross hourly earnings of workers (1) in manufacturing and (2) all private nonagricultural industries and the average gross weekly earnings of workers in the (1) wholesale and retail trade, (2) construction, (3) manufacturing, and (4) all private nonagricultural industries. "Workers" include all production and nonsupervisory personnel in the mining; construction; manufacturing; transportation and public utilities; trade, finance, insurance, and real estate; and service industries.

The Bureau of Labor Statistics compiles this indicator by collecting monthly payroll figures from a sampling of employers. These figures include all pay before any deductions are taken out. Total payrolls are divided by total hours reported for each industry. Real earnings are calculated by dividing these values by the Consumer Price Index for Urban Wage Earners and Clerical Workers for the current month and multiplying by 100. A stratified estimating procedure is used to avoid bias toward large industries or certain regions.

Widely used in collective bargaining, in escalating the costs of labor covered by long-term contracts, and in general economic analyses.

Published monthly by the U.S. Department of Labor, Bureau of Labor Statistics in a Bureau of Labor Statistics press release entitled "The Employment Situation."

Source	Frequency	Extent	Form	Medium
BCI	m	h	g	e
BLS	m	c, h	t	e
Business Statistics	i	h	t	p
Economic Indicators	m	c, h	t	p, e
Employment & Earnings	m	c, h	t	p
The Employment Situation	m	c	t	p
International Financial Statistics	a	h	t	p
Monthly Labor Review	m	c, h	t	p
Quote.com	m	c	t	e
Real Earnings	m	c	t	p
S&P Basic Statistics - Production Indexes and Labor Statistics	i	h	t	p
S&P Current Statistics	i	h	t	p
Statistical Abstract	a	h	t	p

Bibliography

Frumkin, Norman, *Guide to Economic Indicators*, 2nd ed., M. E. Sharpe, Armonk, N.Y., 1994, pp. 26-29.

Hoel, Arline Alchian; Kenneth W. Clarkson; and Roger LeRoy Miller, *Economics Sourcebook of Government Statistics*, Lexington Books, Lexington, Mass., 1983, pp. 183-186.

Joint Economic Committee, *1980 Supplement to Economic Indicators, Historical and Descriptive Background*, USGPO, Washington, D.C., 1980, pp. 48-50.

"Reconciliation and Other Special Tables: A Look at How BEA Presents the NIPAs," *Survey of Current Business* **73**, 29-32 (Feb. 1993).

Rogers, R. Mark, *Handbook of Key Economic Indicators*, Irwin Professional Pub., Burr Ridge, Ill., 1994, pp. 23-24.

Slater, Courtenay M., Ed., Business Statistics of the United States, 1995 ed., Bernan Press, Lanham, Md., 1996, pp. 241-242.

Tainer, Evelina M., *Using Economic Indicators to Improve Investment Analysis*, John Wiley & Sons, New York, 1993, pp. 184-186.

U.S. Department of Commerce, Bureau of Economic Analysis, *Business Statistics, 1963-91*, USGPO, Washington, D.C., 1992, pp. 155-157.

U.S. Department of Labor, Bureau of Labor Statistics, *BLS Handbook of Methods*, Bull. 2490, USGPO, Washington, D.C., 1997, pp. 15-31.

U.S. Department of Labor, Bureau of Labor Statistics, *BLS Measures of Compensation*, USGPO, Washington, D.C., 1986, pp. 22-33.

U.S. Department of Labor, Bureau of Labor Statistics, *Major Programs of the Bureau of Labor Statistics*, USGPO, Washington, D.C., 1994, pp. 17-18.

U.S. Department of Labor, Bureau of Labor Statistics, *Workers, Jobs, and Statistics*, Rept. 698, U.S. Department of Labor, Washington, D.C., 1983.

Average Manufacturing Workweek

An estimation of the average number of hours each production worker in manufacturing industries worked during the given week.

The Bureau of Labor Statistics collects employment figures each month from a sample of employers for a specific pay period. The total hours of work paid for by each industry for a week is divided by the number of manufacturing and related workers for that industry. The resulting values are then seasonally adjusted.

Used as one of the components of the Leading Indicators Composite Index. The number of hours worked is also used to indicate future employment levels. After a recession, a rise in the number of hours worked indicates increased business activity and often precedes a rise in the number of employed persons. During a peak in the business cycle, a drop in the number of hours worked indicates a possible slowdown in the economy.

Published monthly by the U.S. Department of Labor, Bureau of Labor Statistics, in *Employment and Earnings*.

Source	Frequency	Extent	Form	Medium
Business Statistics	i	h	t	p

Bibliography

Bluestone, Abraham, "Overtime Hours as an Economic Indicator," *Monthly Labor Review* **79** (9), 1024-1028 (1956).

Bry, Gerhard, *The Average Workweek as an Economic Indicator*, Occasional Paper No. 69, National Bureau of Economic Research, New York, 1959.

Mendelssohn, R. C., "Three BLS Series as Business Cycle Turn Signals," *Monthly Labor Review* **82** (9), 973-976 (1959).

Moore, Geoffrey Hoyt, and Melita H. Moore, *International Economic Indicators: A Sourcebook*, Greenwood Press, Westport, Conn., 1985, pp. 27-28.

Moore, G. H., and J. Shiskin, "Why the Leading Indicators Really Do Lead," *Across the Board*, 71-75 (May 1978).

Rogers, R. Mark, *Handbook of Key Economic Indicators*, Irwin Professional Pub., Burr Ridge, Ill., 1994, pp. 23-24.

Tainer, Evelina M., *Using Economic Indicators to Improve Investment Analysis*, John Wiley & Sons, New York, 1993, p. 218.

U.S. Department of Labor, Bureau of Labor Statistics, *A Guide to Seasonal Adjustment of Labor Force Data*, Bull. 2114, U.S. Department of Labor, Washington, D.C., 1982.

U.S. Department of Labor, Bureau of Labor Statistics, *Workers, Jobs, and Statistics*, Rept. 698, U.S. Department of Labor, Washington, D.C., 1983.

U.S. Department of Labor, Bureau of Labor Statistics, and Bureau of the Census, *Concepts and Methods Used in Labor Force Statistics Derived from the Current Population Survey*, BLS Rept. 463 and Current Pop. Rept. (Ser.

P-23) 62, U.S. Department of Labor and U.S. Department of Commerce, Washington, D.C., 1976.

Willacy, Hazel M., "Changes in Factory Workweek as an Economic Indicator," *Monthly Labor Review* **93** (10), 25-32 (1970).

Average Prime Rate Charged by Banks

The interest rate that banks charge their most-credit-worthy business customers on short-term loans and the base on which those banks determine the rates they will charge to other business customers averaged nationwide.

The prime rate charged by the majority of 30 large money-market banks on each day of the month is multiplied by the number of days that rate was in effect. Those values are summed, and the total is divided by the number of days. The average is expressed in percentage points and is not seasonally adjusted.

Used to determine an estimated national base for the cost of money and to note trends in that cost; used as a benchmark for setting interest rates on a variety of corporate and consumer borrowings (including bonds). It is a component of the Lagging Indicators Composite Index.

Published monthly by the Board of Governors of the Federal Reserve System in *Selected Interest Rates*, Statistical Release H.15 (519).

Source	Frequency	Extent	Form	Medium
Annual Statistical Digest (FRB)	a	c	t	p
Bank Rate Monitor	w	c, h	t	e
Barron's	w	c	t	p
BCI	m	h	g	e
Business Statistics	i	h	t	p
Business Week	w	c	t	p
Commodity Yearbook	a	c, h	t	p
Conference Board/BCI	m	c	t	e
Construction Review	m	c, h	t	p
Economic Indicators	m	c, h	t	p, e
Federal Reserve Board	d	c, h	t	e
Federal Reserve Bulletin	m	c, h	t	p
Financial Data	w	c	g, t	p
First Union	m	c, h	t	e
Forecast	a	c, f	t	p
FRB Dallas	m	c, h	t	e
FRB New York	d	c, h	t	e
Industry Week	w	f	t	p

Source	Frequency	Extent	Form	Medium
International Financial Statistics	a	h	t	p
Investor's Business Daily	d	c, h	g, t	p
Moody's Bond Record	m	c	g	p
New York Times	d	c	t	p
Northeast Louisiana University	w, m	c, h	t	e
Real Estate Outlook	m	c, h	t	p
Securities Industry Yearbook	a	h	t	p
Selected Interest Rates	m	c	t	p
S&P Basic Statistics - Banking and Finance	i	h	t	p
S&P Current Statistics	i	h	t	p
Statistical Abstract	a	h	t	p
Survey of Current Business	m	c	t	p, e
USA Today	d	c	t	p, e
Value Line Investment Survey, Part 2: Selection and Opinion	w	c, h, f	t	p
Wall Street Journal	d	c	t	p

Bibliography

Frumkin, Norman, *Guide to Economic Indicators*, 2nd ed., M. E. Sharpe, Armonk, N.Y., 1994, pp. 146, 149-151.

Hoel, Arline Alchian; Kenneth W. Clarkson; and Roger LeRoy Miller, *Economics Sourcebook of Government Statistics*, Lexington Books, Lexington, Mass., 1983, pp. 146-148.

Joint Economic Committee, *1980 Supplement to Economic Indicators, Historical and Descriptive Background*, USGPO, Washington, D.C., 1980, p. 111.

Moore, Geoffrey Hoyt, and Melita H. Moore, *International Economic Indicators: A Sourcebook*, Greenwood Press, Westport, Conn., 1985, pp. 46-47.

Renshaw, Edward, Ed., *The Practical Forecasters' Almanac: 137 Reliable Indicators for Investors, Hedgers, and Speculators*, Business One Irwin, Homewood, Ill., 1992, p. 51.

Average Retail Food Prices
[See Retail Food Prices]

Average Weekly Earnings
[See Average Hourly and Weekly Earnings]

Average Weekly Hours

The average number of hours spent working each week by American workers. "Workers" include all production and nonsupervisory personnel in the mining; construction; manufacturing; transportation and public utilities; trade, finance, insurance, and real estate; and service industries. Includes all time for which the employees are paid.

The Bureau of Labor Statistics collects employment figures each month from a sample of employers for a specific pay period. The total hours of work paid for by each industry is divided by the number of production and related workers for that industry. The resulting values are then seasonally adjusted by multiplying them by an adjustment factor.

Used as a leading indicator of the effects of changes in economic activity in the manufacturing sector of the U.S. economy because the cutting back of overtime and of the workweek is frequently an initial response by manufacturers to decreased demand for products. These data are also used in compiling other indicators, such as average earnings and current production estimates.

Published monthly by the U.S. Department of Labor, Bureau of Labor Statistics, in *Employment and Earnings*.

Source	Frequency	Extent	Form	Medium
BCI	m	h	g	e
BLS	m	c, h	t	e
Business Statistics	i	h	t	p
Conference Board/BCI	m	c	t	e
Economic Indicators	m	c, h	t	p, e
Employment & Earnings	m	c, h	t	p
The Employment Situation	m	c	t	p
FRED	m	c, h	t	e
Monthly Labor Review	m	c, h	t	p
Quote.com	m	c	t	e
Real Earnings	m	c	t	p
Recession Recovery Watch	m	g	g	p
S&P Basic Statistics - Income and Trade	i	h	t	p
S&P Basic Statistics - Production Indexes and Labor Statistics	i	h	t	p
S&P Current Statistics	i	c, h	t	p
Statistical Abstract	a	c	t	p
Survey of Current Business	m	c	t, g	p, e

Bibliography

Bry, Gerhard, *The Average Workweek as an Economic Indicator*, Occasional Paper No. 69, National Bureau of Economic Research, New York, 1959.

Frumkin, Norman, *Guide to Economic Indicators*, 2nd ed., M. E. Sharpe, Armonk, N.Y., 1994, pp. 30-33.

Joint Economic Committee, *1980 Supplement to Economic Indicators, Historical and Descriptive Background*, USGPO, Washington, D.C., 1980, p. 51.

"Official Indicators: What Are They? Can They Predict the Future?" *U.S. News and World Report*, 66-67 (Aug.16, 1976).

Tainer, Evelina M., *Using Economic Indicators to Improve Investment Analysis*, John Wiley & Sons, New York, 1993, p. 218.

U.S. Department of Labor, Bureau of Labor Statistics, *A Guide to Seasonal Adjustment of Labor Force Data*, Bull. 2114, U.S. Department of Labor, Washington, D.C., 1982.

U.S. Department of Labor, Bureau of Labor Statistics, *BLS Handbook of Methods*, Bull. 2490, USGPO, Washington, D.C., 1997, pp. 15-31.

U.S. Department of Labor, Bureau of Labor Statistics, *Major Programs of the Bureau of Labor Statistics*, USGPO, Washington, D.C., 1994, pp. 4-5.

U.S. Department of Labor, Bureau of Labor Statistics, and U.S. Department of Commerce, Bureau of the Census, *Concepts and Methods Used in Labor Force Statistics Derived from the Current Population Survey*, BLS Rept. 463 and Current Pop. Rept. (Ser. P-23) 62, U.S. Department of Labor and U.S. Department of Commerce, Washington, D.C., 1976.

U.S. Department of Labor, Bureau of Labor Statistics, *Workers, Jobs, and Statistics*, Rept. 698, U.S. Department of Labor, Washington, D.C., 1983.

Wrightsman, Dwayne, "Three Leading Indicators of Changes in Inflation," *Journal of Business Forecasting* 9 (3), 11-14.

B

Bad Guess Theorem
[See Appendix A. Nonquantitative Indicators]

Balance of Payments, Current Account
[See also Balance of Trade]

The difference in the dollar values of the goods and services that are exported from the United States and those that are imported into the United States.

The Balance of Payments is the sum of several other measures: the Balance of Trade (including imports and exports of nonmonetary gold and adjustments in U.S. trade with Canada, the United States' largest trading partner) plus the current accounts of services (such as travel and tourism) plus foreign aid to other governments plus monetary transactions of central banks plus direct investment abroad (such as in real estate) plus assets held in foreign banks.

Used as an indicator of how the United States fares in international trade competition and of the magnitude of the country's international debt.

Published monthly by the U.S. Department of Commerce, Bureau of Economic Analysis, in *Survey of Current Business*.

Source	Frequency	Extent	Form	Medium
Balance of Payments Statistics Yearbook (IMF)	a	h	t	p
Barron's	w	c	t	p
BEA	q	c, h	t	e
Economic Report of the President	a	h	t	p, e
Forecast	a	c, f	t	p
FRED	m	c, h	t	e

Source	Frequency	Extent	Form	Medium
International Financial Statistics	a	h	t	p
Statistical Abstract	a	h	t	p
Survey of Current Business	m	c, h	t	p, e
World Financial Markets	m	c, h	t	p

Bibliography
Frumkin, Norman, *Guide to Economic Indicators*, 2nd ed., M. E. Sharpe, Armonk, N.Y., 1994, pp. 34-40.

Hoel, Arline Alchian; Kenneth W. Clarkson; and Roger LeRoy Miller, *Economics Sourcebook of Government Statistics*, Lexington Books, Lexington, Mass., 1983, pp. 207-209.

Joint Economic Committee, *1980 Supplement to Economic Indicators, Historical and Descriptive Background*, USGPO, Washington, D.C., 1980, pp. 133-136.

Lavin, Michael R., *Business Information: How to Find It, How to Use It*, Oryx Press, Phoenix, Ariz., 1992, pp. 334-335.

Niemira, Michael P., and Gerald F. Zukowski, *Trading the Fundamentals: The Trader's Guide to Interpreting Economic Indicators and Monetary Policy*, McGraw-Hill, New York, 1998, pp.155-162.

Rogers, R. Mark, *Handbook of Key Economic Indicators*, Irwin Professional Pub., Burr Ridge, Ill., 1994, pp. 172-190.

Stratford, Jean S., and Juri Stratford, *Major U.S. Statistical Series: Definitions, Publications, Limitations*, American Library Association, Chicago, 1992, pp. 79-93.

U.S. Department of Commerce, Bureau of Economic Analysis, *The Balance of Payments of the United States: Concepts, Data Sources, and Estimating Procedures*, USGPO, Washington, D.C., 1990.

Balance of Trade
[Also called the Merchandise Trade Balance]

The difference in the dollar values of the goods that are exported from the United States and the goods that are imported into the United States.

United States Merchandise Imports is subtracted from United States Merchandise Exports to give a net balance. Data exclude military grants and are derived from census data adjusted for differences in valuation, coverage, and timing.

Used to assess the performance of the nation's international transactions, including gold movements, foreign trade, and foreign exchange. Domestic employment is often linked with this indicator with the rationale that goods imported from other countries represent jobs exported to those countries.

Published monthly by the U.S. Department of Commerce, Bureau of Economic Analysis, in *Survey of Current Business* and also reported in *U.S. Export and Import Merchandise Trade*, FT900, published by the Bureau of the Census.

Source	Frequency	Extent	Form	Medium
Agricultural Outlook	m	c, h	t	p
Annual Statistical Digest (FRB)	a	c	t	p
Barron's	w	c	t	p
BCI	m	h	g	e
Business Statistics	i	h	t	p
Economic Indicators	m	c, h	t, g	p, e
Federal Reserve Bulletin	m	c, h	t	p
Financial Digest	bw	c	t	p
First Union	m	c, h	t	e
Forecast	a	c, f	t	p
Handbook of International Economic Statistics (CIA)	a	h	t	p
International Economic Review	q	c, h	t	p
National Income and Product Accounts of the US	a	h	t	p
S&P Basic Statistics - Income and Trade	i	h	t	p
S&P Current Statistics	i	h	t	p
Statistical Abstract	a	h	t	p
Stat-USA	m	c	t	e
Survey of Current Business	m	c, h	t	p, e
US Foreign Trade Highlights	a	h	t, g	p
Value Line Investment Survey, Part 2: Selection and Opinion	w	h	g	p
World Financial Markets	m	c, h	t	p

Bibliography

Amuzegar, Jahangir, "The U.S. External Debt in Perspective," *Finance and Development* **25** (2), 18-19 (June 1988).

Carnes, W. Stansbury, and Stephen D. Slifer, *The Atlas of Economic Indicators: A Visual Guide to Market Forces and the Federal Reserve*, Harper Business, New York, 1991, pp. 169-178.

Frumkin, Norman, *Guide to Economic Indicators*, 2nd ed., M. E. Sharpe, Armonk, N.Y., 1994, pp. 41-48.

Hoel, Arline Alchian; Kenneth W. Clarkson; and Roger LeRoy Miller, *Economics Sourcebook of Government Statistics*, Lexington Books, Lexington, Mass., 1983, pp. 207-209.

Joint Economic Committee, *1980 Supplement to Economic Indicators, Historical and Descriptive Background*, USGPO, Washington, D.C., 1980 pp. 129-132.

Lavin, Michael R., *Business Information: How to Find It, How to Use It*, Oryx Press, Phoenix, Ariz., 1992, p. 362.

Niemira, Michael P., and Gerald F. Zukowski, *Trading the Fundamentals: The Trader's Guide to Interpreting Economic Indicators and Monetary Policy*, McGraw-Hill, New York, 1998, pp. 155-162.

Rogers, R. Mark, *Handbook of Key Economic Indicators*, Irwin Professional Pub., Burr Ridge, Ill., 1994, pp. 172-190.

Stratford, Jean S., and Juri Stratford, *Major U.S. Statistical Series: Definitions, Publications, Limitations*, American Library Association, Chicago, 1992, pp. 79-93.

Tainer, Evelina M., *Using Economic Indicators to Improve Investment Analysis*, John Wiley & Sons, New York, 1993, pp. 129-136.

Bank Debits

The dollar value of all the checks that depositors write on their bank accounts during a specified period.

To calculate this value, the Federal Reserve System regularly surveys about 1600 banks in more than 200 centers of financial activity across the country. New York City is not included because of the effects on banking transactions there by the heavy trading of securities. Respondents provide dollar amounts of bank debits and demand deposits less debits to U.S. Government accounts and interbank transactions. Withdrawal slips are not included among the debits.

Used as an indicator of current business activity.

Published monthly by the Board of Governors of the Federal Reserve System in *Federal Reserve Bulletin*.

Source	Frequency	Extent	Form	Medium
Annual Statistical Digest (FRB)	a	c	t	p
Debits and Deposit Turnover at Commercial Banks	m	c	t	p
Federal Reserve Bulletin	m	c, h	t	p
S&P Basic Statistics - Banking and Finance	i	h	t	p
S&P Current Statistics	i	h	t	p
Statistical Abstract	a	h	t	p

Bibliography

Garvy, George, *Debits and Clearings Statistics and Their Use*, Greenwood Press, Westport, Conn., 1982; reprint of George Garvy, *Debits and Clearings Statistics and Their Use*, Board of Governors of the Federal Reserve System, Washington, D.C., 1959.

Bank Failures

The number of banks that fail to maintain adequate reserves to cover their liabilities and deposits during a given reporting period and are forced into receivership or required to sell their assets, loans, and deposits to another bank.

The Federal Deposit Insurance Corp. (FDIC) monitors the financial condition of its more than 14,000 participating institutions and maintains standards of performance. When a bank fails to meet those criteria, it can be forced to be absorbed by a stronger institution or to liquidate its assets and cease operation. The FDIC tallies the number of such failures quarterly and cumulates it annually.

Used as a broad indicator of the health of the banking industry, of the financial markets, and of regional and national business conditions. It also reflects a cost of doing business for banks because high rates of failure require healthy banks to pay higher rates for deposit insurance, thus cutting into their profit margins at times when business conditions are suboptimal.

Published quarterly by the Federal Deposit Insurance Corp. in *The FDIC Quarterly Bank Profile* and annually in *Statistics on Banking*.

Source	Frequency	Extent	Form	Medium
Bankinfo	a	c, h	t	e
FDIC Annual Report	a	h	t	p
FDIC Quarterly Banking Profile	q	c, h	t	p

Bibliography

Smith, Stephen D., and Larry D. Wall, "Financial Panics, Bank Failures, and the Role of Regulatory Policy," *Economic Review, Federal Reserve Bank of Atlanta* **77** (1), 1-11 (Jan./Feb. 1992).

James, Christopher, "The Losses Realized in Bank Failures," *Journal of Finance* **46**, 1223-1242 (1991).

Bank Interest Rates on Business Loans
[See **Average Prime Rate Charged by Banks**]

Bank Loans
[See **Commercial and Industrial Loans Outstanding, Weekly Reporting Large Commercial Banks; see also Change in Business Loans**]

Bank Loans, Investments, and Reserves
[See **Loans and Investments and Reserves and Borrowings**]

Bank of Tokyo–Mitsubishi/Chain Store Age Weekly Leading Indicator of Chain Store Sales

An appraisal of near-term future sales by chain stores in the United States.

Each week, the Bank of Tokyo–Mitsubishi and *Chain Store Age* combine the ABC News/Money Magazine Buying Plans Index, a selected long-term government interest rate, the MBA Home Purchase Index, and initial jobless claims and index the result to a value of 100 for 1977.

Used as an indicator of future retail-store performance with a lead time of about seven months.

Published weekly on the Internet by the Bank of Tokyo–Mitsubishi and *Chain Store Age* at www.chainstoreage.com/financial_desk/weekly_sales/indicator.htm.

Source	Frequency	Extent	Form	Medium
Bank of Tokyo-Mitsubishi	w	c, h	t, g	e
Chain Store Age	w	c, h	t, g	e

Bibliography

Harris, Ethan S., and Clara Vega, *What Do Chain Store Sales Tell Us about Consumer Spending?*, Research Paper 9614, Federal Reserve Bank of New York, New York, 1996.

Bank of Tokyo–Mitsubishi Chain Store Sales Index

A measure of the sales volume of consumer goods by multiple-outlet department stores in the United States.

Each month, the Bank of Tokyo–Mitsubishi polls major retail chains for same-store data on sales. The values received are compared with previous-month data and to year-ago data, and are reported as percentages of increase or decrease. The data are also broken down by size of chain, by region of the country, and by consumer-good class (e.g., electronics, household goods, and apparel). Finally, the data for 80 to 90 major retailers are normalized to a value of 100 for 1977 to determine the index value and are seasonally adjusted.

Although week-to-week volatility in the data is a problem, it is used as a gauge of the strength of the consumer market, the sector that drives more than 60% of the U.S. economy.

Published monthly by Bank of Tokyo–Mitsubishi as a news release and on its Web site at www.btmny.com/reports/research/comment/Chain_Store_Sales.htm.

Source	Frequency	Extent	Form	Medium
Bank of Tokyo-Mitsubishi	m	c, h	t	e
Cents	m	c, h	t, g	e
Chain Store Age	m	c, h	t	p
ICSC	m	c, h	t	e
Retail Trends	w	c, h	g	e

Bibliography

Harris, Ethan S., and Clara Vega, *What Do Chain Store Sales Tell Us about*

Consumer Spending?, Research Paper 9614, Federal Reserve Bank of New York, New York, 1996.

Tainer, Evelina M., *Using Economic Indicators to Improve Investment Analysis*, John Wiley & Sons, New York, 1993, pp. 68-70.

Bank of Tokyo–Mitsubishi/Schroders Weekly U.S. Retail Chain Store Sales Index

An indicator of the current sales performance of U.S. chain stores.

Reports of the week's sales are received from major retail chains across the country. These data from (roughly) the same stores each week data are compiled, and the result is divided by a comparable value derived in 1977 and then multiplied by 100.

Used to assess the current performance of the retail-sales sector and as a major gauge of current consumer spending, which accounts for almost two-thirds of the economy.

Published weekly on the Internet by the Bank of Tokyo–Mitsubishi and Schroders Wertheim at www.chainstoreage.com/financial_desk/weekly_sales/snapshot.htm.

Source	Frequency	Extent	Form	Medium
Cents	w	c, h	t, g	e

Bibliography

"BTM/SW Chain Store Sales," www.econoday.com/market_events/standard/not_available/mit_stor_sale.shtml, visited July 16, 1999.

Harris, Ethan S., and Clara Vega, *What Do Chain Store Sales Tell Us about Consumer Spending?*, Research Paper 9614, Federal Reserve Bank of New York, New York, 1996.

Bank Rate Monitor Index

The average interest rate paid by banks on fixed-rate certificates of deposit and money-market accounts.

Each week, *Bank Rate Monitor* surveys more than 2500 banks and other financial institutions. Among the data gathered are the current yields those institutions offer on a variety of certificates of deposit and money-market accounts. These rates are then averaged and tabulated for the different types of deposit and terms of maturity.

Used as a point of comparison for yields offered by financial institutions on a variety of money-market and certificate-of-deposit accounts and as a general indicator of investment yields, the cost of money, and inflation. All interest rates tend to move higher as the economy heats up or as inflation increases. On the other hand, lower U.S. interest rates generally reduce the demand for the dollar by hurting returns on many interest-bearing investments.

Published each Wednesday in the weekly *Bank Rate Monitor*; daily data are available on the Bank Rate Monitor's site on the World Wide Web.

Source	Frequency	Extent	Form	Medium
Wall Street Journal	d	c	t	p

Bibliography
"About Bank Rate Monitor," www.bankrate.com/bankrate/Publ/about.htm, visited Aug. 14, 1997.
Lehmann, Michael B., *The Irwin Guide to Using the Wall Street Journal*, 5th ed., Irwin, Chicago, 1996, p. 261.

Bankers Acceptances
A typical interest rate charged by banks on credit extended to commercial customers.

When a customer presents a bank with a letter of credit, the bank may extend an offer of a draft or order that bears a specific amount and date of maturity (usually 30 to 180 days from the date of acceptance). The draft (the acceptance) is then a liability of the issuing institution, usually a large bank. These acceptances are frequently used to finance foreign trade. Bankers acceptances are negotiable and can be sold or discounted to other individuals or institutions. In the United States, an over-the-counter market exists for bankers acceptances among a dozen or so dealers. Each week, the Federal Reserve System estimates the most-representative rate quoted by these dealers for bankers acceptances of top-rated banks.

Used as an indicator of the cost of money, the availability of capital, and inflation.

Issued monthly as Statistical Release G.13(415), *Selected Interest Rates*, by the Board of Governors of the Federal Reserve System.

Source	Frequency	Extent	Form	Medium
Annual Statistical Digest (FRB)	a	c	t	p
Barron's	w	c	t	p
Business Statistics	i	h	t	p
Federal Reserve Board	d	c, h	t	e
Federal Reserve Bulletin	m	c, h	t	p
Financial Digest	bw	c	t	p
FRED	d, w, m	c, h	t	e
Investor's Business Daily	d	c	t	p
New York Times	d	c	t	p
Northeast Louisiana University	w, m	c, h	t	e

Source	Frequency	Extent	Form	Medium
Securities Industry Yearbook	a	h	t	p
Selected Interest Rates	m	c	t	p
S&P Basic Statistics - Banking and Finance	i	h	t	p
S&P Current Statistics	i	h	t	p
Statistical Abstract	a	h	t	p
Wall Street Journal	d	c	t	p

Bibliography

Currier, Chet, *The Investor's Encyclopedia*, Franklin Watts, New York, 1987, pp. 6-9.

Duffield, Jeremy, and Bruce Summers, "Bankers Acceptances," pp. 114-122 in *Instruments of the Money Market*, Federal Reserve Bank of Richmond, Richmond, Va., 1981.

Frumkin, Norman, *Guide to Economic Indicators*, 2nd ed., M. E. Sharpe, Armonk, N.Y., 1994, p. 50.

Harton, H. Lynn, "Developing Rational Policies for Letters of Credit," *Journal of Commercial Lending* **74** (9), 14-25 (May 1992).

Hoel, Arline Alchian; Kenneth W. Clarkson; and Roger LeRoy Miller, *Economics Sourcebook of Government Statistics*, Lexington Books, Lexington, Mass., 1983, pp. 105-106.

LaRoche, Robert K., "Bankers Acceptances," *Economic Quarterly, Federal Reserve Bank of Richmond* **79** (1), 75-85 (Winter 1993).

BanxQuote Index
[Also called the BanxQuote Major Banks Index]

The average interest rate paid by banks on fixed-rate certificates of deposit and money-market accounts.

Masterfund, Inc., has identified 18 leading banks, three each in New York, Pennsylvania, Florida, Illinois, Texas, and California. Each week, these banks are polled for their current interest rates on different fixed-rate certificates of deposit and money-market accounts. These rates are averaged to produce the index, which is expressed as a percentage yield for regular money-market accounts and certificates of deposit with maturities of one, two, three, and six months and for jumbo (greater than $100,000) accounts and deposits with maturities of one, two, and five years.

Used to compare yields offered by financial institutions on a variety of money-market and certificate-of-deposit accounts and as a general indicator of investment yields, the cost of money, and inflation. All interest rates tend to move higher as the economy heats up or as inflation increases. Lower rates generally reduce the demand for the dollar by hurting returns on interest-bearing investments.

Issued daily on the World Wide Web at www.banxquote.com/bloomberg/ rates.asp and each Tuesday as a report from BanxQuote of Wilmington, Del.

Source	Frequency	Extent	Form	Medium
Wall Street Journal	d	c	t	p

Bibliography
"BanxQuote," banx.com/about.asp, visited July 16, 1999.
Berlin, Howard M., *The Handbook of Financial Market Indexes, Averages, and Indicators*, Dow Jones-Irwin, Homewood, Ill., 1990, p. 114.
Lehmann, Michael B., *The Irwin Guide to Using the Wall Street Journal*, 5th ed., Irwin, Chicago, 1996, p. 261.

Barron's Confidence Index

A comparison of the yields of higher- and lower-grade bonds.

This index is calculated by dividing the average yield on Barron's ten best-grade [AAA (Aaa) or AA (Aa)] corporate bonds by the average yield on ten intermediate-grade [BBB (Baa)] bonds. The ratio has a high value when investors are confidently buying corporate-debt issues that are below top grade and has a low value when they are taking refuge by purchasing top-grade issues.

Used to forecast movements in the corporate-bond markets. The higher the Index, the more confident one might be in the markets and the more likely one might be to purchase lower-grade bonds. Conversely, the lower the Index, the less confidence might be placed in the corporate-bond markets, and the riskier it might be to purchase lower-grade bonds. Bond prices react to interest rates; the rate of economic growth; and costs for goods, services, and commodities. Increasing interest rates, rapid economic growth, and rising prices are signs of inflation that erodes the value of bonds.

Published weekly by Dow Jones and Co. in *Barron's National Business and Financial Weekly*.

Source	Frequency	Extent	Form	Medium
Barron's	w	c	t	p

Bibliography
Amling, F., *Investments, An Introduction to Analysis and Management*, Prentice Hall, Englewood Cliffs, N.J., 1974.
Berlin, Howard M., *The Handbook of Financial Market Indexes, Averages, and Indicators*, Dow Jones-Irwin, Homewood, Ill., 1990, pp. 75-77.
Colby, Robert W., and Thomas A. Meyers, *The Encyclopedia of Technical Market Indicators*, Dow Jones-Irwin, Homewood, Ill., 1988, p. 135.
Gaumnitz, Jack E., and Carlos A. Salabar, "The Barron's Confidence Index, An Examination of Its Value as a Market Indicator," *Financial Analysts J.* **22**, 16 (Sept.-Oct. 1969).

Gordon, William, *The Stock Market Indicators as a Guide to Market Timing*, Investors Press, Palisades Park, N. J., 1968, pp. 79-90.

Granville, Joseph E., "Market Forecaster? Barron's Confidence Index Has Compiled an Uncanny Record," *Barron's*, pp. 9+ (Sept. 7, 1959).

Pierce, Phyllis S. (Ed.), *The Irwin Investor's Handbook*, Irwin Professional Publishing, Burr Ridge, Ill, 1995, p. 70.

Barron's Fifty-Stock Average

A weighted average of the price of 50 selected stocks.

Fifty leading New York Stock Exchange-listed stocks are selected: 42 industrials, 5 transportations, and 3 public utilities. A $100 investment in each is assumed. The average price per share for the collective investment is then calculated from their closing prices each Thursday. As a result, equal percentage movements of different stocks have the same effect on the calculated average even though those stocks may have radically different prices per share. The issues included are changed periodically to compensate for the effects of market movements on the weighting of the selected portfolio.

Used as an overall indicator of stock-price activity.

Published weekly by Dow Jones and Co. in *Barron's National Business and Financial Weekly*.

Source	Frequency	Extent	Form	Medium
Barron's	w	c	t	p

Bibliography

Berlin, Howard M., *The Handbook of Financial Market Indexes, Averages, and Indicators*, Dow Jones-Irwin, Homewood, Ill., 1990, pp. 30-32.

Barron's Gold Mining Index

A weighted average of the prices of four selected stocks of gold-mining companies. One of the Barron's group stock averages.

At the close of business each Thursday, the prices of four gold-mining stocks are noted; each is factored by a multiplier calculated to account for stock splits, dividend payments, etc. and to produce the four weighted prices; the weighted prices are summed; and the total is divided by 4. The resulting figure is published as the index, although the number is not indexed to any other value.

Used as an indicator of the strength of this sector of the market and for the demand for gold as opposed to other investments.

Published weekly by Dow Jones and Co. in *Barron's National Business and Financial Weekly*.

Source	Frequency	Extent	Form	Medium
Barron's	w	c	t	p

Bibliography
Berlin, Howard M., *The Handbook of Financial Market Indexes, Averages, and Indicators*, Dow Jones-Irwin, Homewood, Ill., 1990, pp. 32, 34.

Barron's Group Stock Averages

The average price of a selected group of stocks.

Several hundred stocks are selected to represent various sectors of the stock market (aircraft manufacturers, pharmaceutical firms, banks, etc.). The closing prices for each of these stocks is noted on each Thursday, and a simple arithmetic average is calculated. Adjustments to the data are made to compensate for splits, large dividend payments, and other anomalies.

Used as a price indicator of stocks in key-industry market sectors.

Published weekly by Dow Jones and Co. in *Barron's National Business and Financial Weekly*.

Source	Frequency	Extent	Form	Medium
Barron's	w	c	t	p

Barron's Twenty Low-Priced Stocks Index

The average price of 20 selected low-priced stocks listed on major exchanges.

In July of 1960, twenty stocks were selected that met four criteria: a price of $15 or less, a ratio of current assets to current liabilities of 2 to 1 or better, a satisfactory earnings record, and a price substantially below the 1959 high. These stocks have been changed as issues disappeared from the market or their prices became too large. The values of these stocks as of Thursday are totaled up to calculate the index. The index is adjusted for stock splits by multiplying the previous week's value of a stock that has been split by a compensating factor.

A measure of speculative activity on the stock market; a lagging indicator of market price trends.

Published weekly by Dow Jones and Co. in *Barron's National Business and Financial Weekly*.

Source	Frequency	Extent	Form	Medium
Barron's	w	c	t	p

Bibliography
Berlin, Howard M., *The Handbook of Financial Market Indexes, Averages, and Indicators*, Dow Jones-Irwin, Homewood, Ill., 1990, pp. 32-33.
Merjos, A., "Swinging Index," *Barron's*, 9+, Nov. 23, 1970.

Betzold-Berg Investment Portfolio Index

An indicator of the aggregate performance of the investments in the average bank's portfolio.

A hypothetical portfolio is constructed to accurately reflect the average bank's holdings in six sectors of the fixed-income cash market: treasury bonds, federal-agency bonds, adjustable-rate securities, fixed-rate mortgage-backed securities and/or CMO/REMICs, municipal bonds, and "other" securities as defined in the call-report data. The "average bank" is defined as one with holdings between $10 million and $1 billion. The portfolio is weighted the same as the most recent call-report data and is rebalanced monthly.

Used to gauge how a bank's portfolio has performed for the latest month. Published monthly in *ABA Banking Journal*.

Source	Frequency	Extent	Form	Medium
ABA Banking Journal	m	c, h	g, t	p

Bibliography
Betzold, Nicholas, and Richard Berg, "There Ought to Be an Investment Portfolio Index," *ABA Banking Journal* **89**, 65-66 (April 1997).

Big Block Activity
[See American Stock Exchange Big Block Activity and New York Stock Exchange Big Block Activity]

Big Mac Index
[See Appendix A. Nonquantitative Indicators]

BLS Railroad Freight Price Index
A measure of the rise or fall of the prices for shipping a fixed set of commodities in the United States by rail under specified conditions.

Each month, the Interstate Commerce Commission samples 1% of the waybills of Class 1 railroads (those having annual revenues of at least $94.4 million in 1990). The Bureau of Labor Statistics examines a sample of these waybills to identify shipments of specific quantities of specific commodities under specific conditions between specific points on the 15th of the month. They then note the prices charged for these shipments and special services (derived from the published tariffs of the carriers), aggregate the prices charged, and index these prices to the charges for identical earlier shipments. Monthly price indexes are calculated for 11 commodity groups as well as for rail freight in general.

Used as a general indicator of the cost of doing business and of inflation.

Released as a monthly report by the U.S. Department of Labor, Bureau of Labor Statistics, and published in *Business Statistics*.

Source	Frequency	Extent	Form	Medium
Business Statistics	i	h	t	p
S&P Current Statistics	i	h	t	p

Source	Frequency	Extent	Form	Medium
Statistical Abstract	a	h	t	p

Bibliography

Fehd, Carolyn S., "Introducing Price Indexes for Railroad Freight," *Monthly Labor Review* **98** (6), 19-24 (June 1975).

U.S. Department of Commerce, Bureau of Economic Analysis, *Business Statistics, 1963-91*, USGPO, Washington, D.C., 1992, p. 167.

Boeckh Building Cost Index

[See also Building Cost Index, Construction Cost Index, and Composite Construction Price Index]

A measure of the combined effect of wage and price changes on the value of the construction dollar.

For 20 cities across the United States, costs are determined for 115 elements of materials, labor, insurance and tax rates. These costs, along with uniform allowances for contractor overhead and profits, are used to determine the costs of constructing four representative types of buildings (frame, brick, concrete, and steel). These costs are then indexed to earlier values (originally, 1926-1929 = 100; values reported by the U.S. Department of Commerce are indexed to 1987 = 100) and used to construct indexes for total construction; residential construction costs; construction costs for apartments, hotels, and office buildings; and construction costs for commercial buildings and factories.

Used as a measure of inflation, as a price inflator in calculating construction cost estimates, and as component of the Department of Commerce's Construction Cost Indexes.

Published bimonthly by E. H. Boeckh and Associates, an operating unit of American Appraisal Associates.

Source	Frequency	Extent	Form	Medium
Construction Review	m	c, h	t	p
Statistical Abstract	a	h	t	p

Bibliography

Hoel, Arline Alchian; Kenneth W. Clarkson; and Roger LeRoy Miller, *Economics Sourcebook of Government Statistics*, Lexington Books, Lexington, Mass., 1983, pp. 27-30.

Levy, Elliot, "Construction Cost Indexes, 1915-1976," *Construction Review*, 4-17 (June/July 1977).

U.S. Department of Commerce, Bureau of Economic Analysis, *Business Statistics, 1963-91*, USGPO, Washington, D.C., 1992, pp. 151-152.

Bond Buyer Eleven-Bond Index

The yield of a representative, high-grade, general-obligation municipal bond having a maturity of about 20 years and selling at a price close to par.

A component of the Bond Buyer Twenty-Bond Index, only limited to high-grade general-obligation municipal bonds with ratings of AA or Aa and with maturities of about 20 years. Calculated each Thursday (or Wednesday, if Thursday is a holiday). The yield for each bond is divided by a bond-specific conversion factor, and the converted yields are then summed, divided by 11, and multiplied by a coefficient that makes the index comparable through day-to-day changes in the makeup of the sample of bonds. The list of bonds included in the sample is changed regularly so the sample reflects bonds selling near par with nearly 20 years to maturity.

Used as an indicator of the general condition of the market for general-obligation municipal bonds, being representative of the rates for such bonds.

Published weekly in *The Bond Buyer* (the week's value appears in each issue).

Source	Frequency	Extent	Form	Medium
The Bond Buyer	w	c, h	t, g	p, e

Bibliography
Berlin, Howard M., *The Handbook of Financial Market Indexes, Averages, and Indicators*, Dow Jones-Irwin, Homewood, Ill., 1990, pp. 79-80.

Bond Buyer Forty Municipal Bond Index

A general measure of the current market for municipal bonds.

At noon and 3:00 pm each trading day, *The Bond Buyer* polls five principal municipal-bond dealers to get these brokers' assessments of the prices at which $100,000 of face value of 40 specified bonds would trade. The 40 selected securities are actively traded, tax-exempt revenue and general-obligation municipal bonds, all of which meet specified criteria related to size, quality, maturity and other characteristics. The highest and lowest of the price assessments for each bond are dropped, and the remaining three prices are averaged. The average prices are each divided by a bond-specific conversion factor, and the converted prices are then summed, divided by 40, and multiplied by a coefficient that makes the index comparable through day-to-day changes in the makeup of the sample of bonds. The index is reported in units and thirty-seconds. It is also calculated and reported on the basis of average yield to maturity. The list of bonds included in the sample is changed regularly so the sample reflects bonds selling near par with 19 to 20 years to maturity.

Used as an indicator of the general condition of the municipal-bond market, being representative of the prices and rates for such bonds.

Published daily in *The Bond Buyer*; historical data appear in the Friday edition.

Source	Frequency	Extent	Form	Medium
Barron's	w	c	t	p
The Bond Buyer	d	c, h	t, g	p, e
First Union	m	c, h	t	e
New York Times	d	c	t	p
Wall Street Journal	d	c	t	p

Bibliography

Berlin, Howard M., *The Handbook of Financial Market Indexes, Averages, and Indicators*, Dow Jones-Irwin, Homewood, Ill., 1990, pp. 77-79.

Granito, Michael P., "The Problem with Bond Index Funds," *Journal of Portfolio Management* **13** (4), 41-47 (1987).

Bond Buyer Twenty-Bond Index

The yield of a representative general-obligation municipal bond having a maturity of about 20 years and selling at a price close to par.

Originally, the bonds of the 20 largest cities were selected, but substitutions have been made as cities paid off their debts or had no debt outstanding with a sufficiently long maturity. Calculated each Thursday (or Wednesday, if Thursday is a holiday). The yields of the bonds on each Thursday are noted and averaged.

Used as a yardstick to compare the yields of various municipal bonds and as a general measure of inflation. Bond yields generally react to interest rates and inflation because inflation erodes the value of all fixed-income investments and it influences the Federal Reserve to raise interest rates. In addition, these rates reflect the price that cities and other bond-issuing organizations are going to have to pay to borrow money from the public; these interest rates, in turn, affect tax rates, municipal services, and purchases.

Published weekly in *The Bond Buyer* (the week's value appears in each issue).

Source	Frequency	Extent	Form	Medium
Annual Statistical Digest (FRB)	a	c	t	p
Bank Rate Monitor	w	c, h	t	e
Barron's	w	c	t	p
The Bond Buyer	w	c, h	t, g	p, e
Business Statistics	i	h	t	p
Federal Reserve Bulletin	m	c, h	t	p
Financial Digest	bw	c	t	p
New York Times	w	c, h	g	p
Northeast Louisiana University	w, m	c, h	t	e
Selected Interest Rates	m	c	t	p

Source	Frequency	Extent	Form	Medium
Statistical Abstract	a	c, h	t	p
Value Line Investment Survey, Part 2: Selection and Opinion	w	c	t	p

Bibliography

Berlin, Howard M., *The Handbook of Financial Market Indexes, Averages, and Indicators*, Dow Jones-Irwin, Homewood, Ill., 1990, pp. 79-80.

Hoel, Arline Alchian; Kenneth W. Clarkson; and Roger LeRoy Miller, *Economics Sourcebook of Government Statistics*, Lexington Books, Lexington, Mass., 1983, p. 104.

Bond Buyer Twenty-Five Revenue Bond Index

A general measure of the current market for revenue municipal bonds.

Each Thursday, *The Bond Buyer* determines the prices at which 25 specific revenue municipal bonds are trading and calculates the yields. The 25 selected securities are actively traded, tax-exempt revenue municipal bonds, all of which meet specified criteria related to size, quality, maturity and other characteristics. The yield for each bond is divided by a bond-specific conversion factor, and the converted yields are then summed, divided by 25, and multiplied by a coefficient that makes the index comparable through day-to-day changes in the makeup of the sample of bonds. The list of bonds included in the sample is changed regularly so the sample reflects bonds selling near par with nearly 30 years to maturity.

Used as an indicator of the general condition of the revenue-municipal-bond market, being representative of the rates for such bonds.

Published weekly in *The Bond Buyer* (the week's value appears in each issue).

Source	Frequency	Extent	Form	Medium
The Bond Buyer	w	c. h	t, g	p, e
New York Times	w	c, h	g	p
Value Line Investment Survey, Part 2: Selection and Opinion	w	c	t	p

Bibliography

Berlin, Howard M., *The Handbook of Financial Market Indexes, Averages, and Indicators*, Dow Jones-Irwin, Homewood, Ill., 1990, pp. 79-80.

Bridge-CRB Futures Price Index

[Also called the KR-CRB Futures Price Index, Knight-Ridder Commodity Research Bureau Futures Price Index, the KR-CRB Index, the KR-CRB Futures Index, and the CRB Futures Index; see also the Bridge-CRB Index]

A broad measure of the prices for futures options on foodstuffs and industrial raw materials.

A weighted index of 21 futures contracts covering grains, fibers, industrial products, livestock, meats, precious metals, petroleum, imports, wood, and energy. Specific contract sizes for particular commodities on specified exchanges are used to calculate the index, each contract being subject to a daily minimum movement and a daily maximum limit. The price for each commodity is calculated by averaging the futures prices for the contract months occurring during the next nine months. (Some futures contracts are not let for every month.) These unweighted average price relatives are then geometrically averaged, and the result is (1) divided by 53.0615 (the value for 1967), (2) multiplied by 0.95035 (a constant adjustment factor related to a historic change in the components of the index), and (3) multiplied by 100. Do not confuse this with the KR-CRB Index, which is an index of spot-market prices; both are frequently referred to as the KR-CRB Index. The index is also broken down into six components (industrials, grains, oilseeds, livestock/meats, energy, and precious metals) that are reported separately.

Used as a daily gauge of inflation and as an indicator of the direction of prices in general. It is an integrative indicator in that commodity prices are subject to not only the pressures of supply and demand but also the influences of weather, crop failures, trading cycles, politics, and governmental actions. Also used as the basis for cash-settled futures contracts traded on the New York Futures Exchange.

Computed and distributed every 15 seconds of the trading day by Bridge Communications, and the daily closing value is reported by Bridge Communications' Commodity Research Bureau.

Source	Frequency	Extent	Form	Medium
Barron's	q	c	g	p
Bridge	d	c	t	e
Commodity Yearbook	a, m	h	t	p
Investor's Business Daily	w	c, h	g	p
Journal of Commerce	d	c	t	p
Statistical Abstract	a	h	t	p

Bibliography
Berlin, Howard M. *The Handbook of Financial Market Indexes, Averages, and Indicators*, Dow Jones-Irwin, Homewood, Ill., 1990, pp. 99-104.
Boughton, James M., and William H. Branson, "Commodity Prices as a Leading Indicator of Inflation," pp. 305-338 in Kajal Lahiri and Moore, Geoffrey H. Moore, Eds., *Leading Economic Indicators: New Approaches and Forecasting Records,* Cambridge University Press, New York, 1991.
Commodity Research Bureau, "The CRB Futures Price Index: A Glimpse at Tomorrow Today," pp. 54T-63T in *The CRB Commodity Yearbook*, John Wiley, New York, 1996.
Frumkin, Norman, *Guide to Economic Indicators*, 2nd ed., M. E. Sharpe, Armonk, N.Y., 1994, pp. 100-103.

Segars, Alan D., "Commodities an Inflation Indicator," *Pensions and Investments* **23** (1), 20 (Jan. 9, 1995).

Siconolfi, Michael, "Reliability of CRB's Futures Price Index as Barometer of Inflation Is Questioned," *Wall Street Journal*, p. 42 (June 29, 1987).

Tainer, Evelina M., *Using Economic Indicators to Improve Investment Analysis*, John Wiley & Sons, New York, 1993, pp. 167-168.

Bridge-CRB Index

[Also called the KR-CRB Index, the Tuesday Index of Spot Market Prices, the CRB Spot Price Index, the Knight-Ridder Commodity Research Bureau Index, the CRB Index, and the CRB-BLS Spot Market Index; see also the Change in Sensitive Prices, the Bridge-CRB Futures Index, the Journal of Commerce Index, and the Change in Industrial Materials Price Index]

An indicator of the trend in costs for basic foodstuffs and industrial raw materials traded on commodity markets and organized exchanges.

Each working day, the spot-market prices (the prices for which commodities are selling for immediate delivery) of 23 commodities representing livestock, fats and oils, metals, and textiles are noted. When spot prices are not available, bid or asked prices may be used. Unweighted geometric averages of the individual prices are calculated with 1967 as the base year to produce the index value for the week. Monthly values are geometric averages of the Tuesday prices during the month. Data are not adjusted for seasonal variation.

Used as an indicator of inflation, reflecting, as it does, the costs for basic raw materials. The markets for these commodities are assumed to be among the first to be influenced by changes in economic conditions; this index is a leading indicator overall and at troughs and is unclassified at peaks.

Reported weekly by Bridge Communications in the *CRB Commodity Index Report*.

Source	Frequency	Extent	Form	Medium
Business Week	h	c	t	e
Commodity Yearbook	m	h	t	p
First Union	m	c, h	t	e
Statistical Abstract	a	h	t	p
USA Today	d	c	t	p
Wall Street Journal	m	c	g	p

Bibliography

Berlin, Howard M. *The Handbook of Financial Market Indexes, Averages, and*

Boughton, James M., and William H. Branson, "Commodity Prices as a Leading Indicator of Inflation," pp. 305-338 in Kajal Lahiri and Moore, Geoffrey H. Moore, Eds., *Leading Economic Indicators: New Approaches and Forecasting Records,* Cambridge University Press, New York, 1991.

Segars, Alan D., "Commodities an Inflation Indicator," *Pensions and Investments* **23** (1), 20 (Jan. 9, 1995). *Indicators*, Dow Jones-Irwin, Homewood, Ill., 1990, pp. 99-104.

Brokerage House Rule
[See Appendix A. Nonquantitative Indicators]

BTM
[See Bank of Tokyo–Mitsubishi]

Building Cost Index
[See also Boeckh Building Cost Index, Construction Cost Index, and Composite Construction Price Index]

A measure of the combined effect of wage and price changes on the value of the construction dollar.

Four costs are calculated, those of: 68.38 hours of skilled labor at the average rate for such labor in 20 selected cities; 25 cwt of standard structural steel shapes at the average price for such steel at three selected mills; 22.56 cwt of Portland cement at the average price for such cement in 20 selected cities; and 1088 board feet of two-by-four lumber at the average price for such lumber in 20 selected cities. These values are weighted with empirically derived statistical weights to normalize the data. These weights are adjusted periodically to reflect economic conditions. The calculated total is then indexed to the totals in 1913 and 1967, producing two series, a 1913 = 100 series and a 1967 = 100 series. Monthly indexes are the indexes calculated for the first week of the month. Annual indexes are straight mathematical averages of the component months. The skilled-labor and materials components are also broken out and published as separate indexes. A related index, the Construction Cost Index, uses much of the same data in its derivation; it uses a different labor base that only includes unskilled labor.

Used to judge underlying trends of construction costs in the United States and to estimate costs of future construction projects; one of the Department of Commerce's Construction Costs Indexes.

Published weekly (national; 1913 = 100) and monthly (city-by-city; 1967 = 100) by McGraw-Hill Information Systems Co. in *Engineering News-Record*.

Source	Frequency	Extent	Form	Medium
Business Statistics	i	h	t	p
Construction Review	m	c, h	t	p
ENR	m	c	t	p
Statistical Abstract	a	h	t	p
Value of New Construction Put in Place (CCR C30)	m	c, h	t	p

Bibliography
"Construction Costs Tracked for U.S.," *Engineering News-Record*, **210** (12), 114-121 (Mar. 24, 1983).

Building Permits
[See also Housing Permits and Value of New Construction Put in Place]
The number of building permits issued for nonresidential construction.

A mail survey by the Bureau of the Census of 8,500 of a population of 19,000 permit-issuing places requests the number of residential and nonresidential building permits issued during a quarter by local building-permit officials. The results are tallied and graphically presented along with monthly U.S. Department of Housing and Urban Development data on publicly owned housing construction.

Used as an indicator of activity within the construction industry and as a measure of construction patterns.

Published quarterly by the Department of Commerce, International Trade Administration, in *Construction Review*.

Source	Frequency	Extent	Form	Medium
BCI	m	h	g	e
Builder	m	c	t	p
Conference Board/BCI	m	c	t	e
Construction Review	m	c, h	t	p
FRB Chicago	m	c, h	t	e
Statistical Abstract	a	a	t	p
Stat-USA	m	c	t	e
US Census Bureau	m	c, h	t	e

Bibliography
MacAuley, Patrick H., "The Leading Construction Markets in the United States," *Construction Review* **39** (1), iv-vi (Winter 1993).
MacAuley, Patrick H., "Revisions in Metropolitan Statistical Areas for Building Permits Data," *Construction Review* **39** (2), xx-xxi (Spring 1993).
WEFA Group, *Guide to Economic Indicators: U.S. Macroeconomic Services*, WEFA Group, Bala Cynwyd, Pa., 1997, p. 15.

Bureau of the Census Composite Construction Price Index
[See Composite Construction Price Index]

Business Confidence Index
[See Measure of Business Confidence]

Business-Cycle Indicators
[See Leading Indicators Composite Index, Lagging Indicators Composite Index, and Coincident Indicators Composite Index]

Business Executives' Expectations
[See Measure of Business Confidence; see also Dun & Bradstreet Profits Optimism Index and Dun & Bradstreet Sales Optimism Index]

Business Failures
The number of court proceedings or voluntary actions entered into during a month that are likely to result in a loss to creditors.

Dun & Bradstreet surveys the records of the federal bankruptcy courts and tallies the number of industrial and commercial enterprises that are petitioned into those courts along with the number of concerns that are forced out of business through the actions of state courts involving foreclosure, execution, attachments with insufficient assets to cover all claims, receivership, reorganization, or rearrangement. To these numbers are added the number of voluntary discontinuances with known loss to creditors and voluntary compromises with creditors out of court, where this information can be obtained. The information is reported both as the total number of failed businesses and as an index number. The index number is the number of failed businesses per 10,000 businesses listed in the *Dun & Bradstreet Reference Book*; it shows the annual rate at which business concerns would fail if the rate of that month prevailed for the year. The index is seasonally adjusted. Data are presented in aggregate and broken down by geographic area and by industry.

Used as an indicator of overall business activity; inversely tied to the expansion and contraction of business activity. It has implications for various aspects of business and finance, such as employment level, credit costs, inflation, and earnings and profits. The lower the number of business failures, the stronger the economy. Changes in the business-failure numbers usually lag behind economic turning points (e.g., businesses continue to fail even after the economy as a whole begins to emerge from a recession).

Published monthly by Dun & Bradstreet, Inc., in *Monthly Business Failures*; quarterly in *Dun & Bradstreet Looks at Business*; and annually in the *Dun & Bradstreet's Business Failure Record*; also published as a news release that is posted on the World Wide Web at www.dnb.com.

Source	Frequency	Extent	Form	Medium
Barron's	w	c	t	p
Business Failure Record	a	h	t, g	p
Business Statistics	i	h	t	p
Economic Report of the President	a	h	t	p, e

Source	Frequency	Extent	Form	Medium
Monthly Business Failures	m	c	t	p
Quarterly Business Failures	q	c	t	p
S&P Basic Statistics - Income and Trade	i	h	t	p
S&P Current Statistics	i	c	t	p
Statistical Abstract	a	h	t	p

Bibliography

Dun & Bradstreet, Economic Analysis Department, *Business Failure Record*, Dun & Bradstreet, New York, annual.

Frumkin, Norman, *Guide to Economic Indicators*, 2nd ed., M. E. Sharpe, Armonk, N.Y., 1994, pp. 53-57.

Gearhart, Reid, "Growth Continues, but Pace Slows," *D&B Reports* **33**, 10 (Mar./Apr. 1985).

Moore, Geoffrey H., *Leading Indicators for the 1990s*, Dow Jones-Irwin, Homewood, Ill., 1990, pp. 134-136.

U.S. Department of Commerce, Bureau of Economic Analysis, *Business Statistics, 1963-91*, USGPO, Washington, D.C., 1992, p. 145.

Zannowitz, Victor, and Lionel J. Lerner, "Cyclical Changes in Business Failures and Corporate Profits," pp. 350-385 in Geoffrey H. Moore, *Business Cycle Indicators*, Princeton University Press, Princeton, N.J., 1961.

Business Incorporations
[See New Business Incorporations]

Business Inventories
[See Manufacturing and Trade Inventories]

Business Inventory-Sales Ratio
[See Manufacturers' Inventory-Sales Ratio]

Business Investment and Plans
[Formerly Contracts and Orders for Plant and Equipment]

The value of new contract awards to building contractors, public-works contractors, and public-utilities contractors and of new orders received by manufacturers in nondefense capital-goods industries.

The data for this indicator are made up of three components: data on commercial and industrial contracts (e.g., banks, office buildings, stores, warehouses, and factories); data on contracts for privately owned nonbuilding construction (such as streets, bridges, dams, parks, sewerages, power plants, airports, and pipelines); and data on manufacturers' new orders (e.g., steam turbines and communications equipment). The construction contracts data cover new construction, additions, and major alterations; maintenance work is excluded. The data are derived from Dodge reports (which represent actual construction costs exclusive of land, architects' fees, and costs for equipment) supplemented by permit-place reports. Manufacturers' new orders are compiled by the Census Bureau [see Manufacturers' New Orders for Consumer Goods and Materials]. The three components of the data are seasonally adjusted, totaled, expressed in billions of dollars, and converted to 1972 dollars.

A leading indicator of overall economic activity.

Published quarterly by the U.S. Department of Commerce, Bureau of the Census, in *Annual Capital Expenditures Survey*.

Source	Frequency	Extent	Form	Medium
Annual Capital Expenditures Survey	q	c	t	p
BCI	m	h	g	e

Bibliography

Frumkin, Norman, *Guide to Economic Indicators*, 2nd ed., M. E. Sharpe, Armonk, N.Y., 1994, pp. 240-243.

Moore, Geoffrey Hoyt, and Melita H. Moore, *International Economic Indicators: A Sourcebook*, Greenwood Press, Westport, Conn., 1985, pp. 31-32.

Nelson, C. R., *The Investor's Guide to Economic Indicators*, John Wiley & Sons, New York, 1987, pp. 189-193.

"Official Indicators: What Are They? Can They Predict the Future?" *U.S. News and World Report*, 66-67 (Aug. 16, 1976).

Business Loans
[See Commercial and Industrial Loans Outstanding, Weekly Reporting Large Commercial Banks]

Business Week Production Index
A weighted average of the production activity in nine major U.S. industrial sectors.

The weekly production of nine industrial sectors [steel production (tons), auto production (vehicles), truck production (vehicles), electric power production (millions of kilowatt-hours), crude-oil production (thousands of barrels per day), coal (thousands of net tons), lumber (millions of feet), rail freight (billions of ton-miles), and machinery and defense equipment (estimated; typically constitutes more than 40% of the index's weight)] is determined from trade organizations and other industry sources. Each of the nine values is weighted with an empirically derived statistical weighs to normalize the data; these weights are adjusted annually. Each normalized value is seasonally adjusted with weekly seasonal factors. The resulting values are summed, and the result is divided by a constant to give the index. The index is periodically revised to incorporate benchmark revisions of the underlying data. The index is expressed as a four-week moving average (with the most recent week getting the greatest weighting). The unaveraged value and a monthly average of the weekly unaveraged values are also presented.

Used as an immediate indicator of the well-being of the industrial economy; foreshadows the short-term swings and major turning points in the industrial sector that determine the direction and force of the economy as a whole.

Published weekly in *Business Week* and on the World Wide Web at www.businessweek.com.

Source	Frequency	Extent	Form	Medium
Business Week	w	c, h	t, g	p, e
Chemical Week	w	c	t	p
S&P Current Statistics	i	c	t	p

Bibliography

"A New Economic Index That Provides Early Forecasts," *Business Week*, 154-158 (Nov. 14, 1983).

Plocek, Joseph E., *Economic Indicators: How America Reads Its Financial Health*, New York Institute of Finance, New York, 1991, pp. 163-165.

Buying Plans Index

A periodic survey to determine families' appraisals of present business conditions, future business conditions, plans to make major purchases in the near future, and plans to take a vacation in the near future.

Each month, 10,000 households are surveyed and asked how they feel business conditions and employment opportunities are at the present time and how they feel those conditions and opportunities will be six months hence. They are also asked if they plan to purchase a home or automobile, buy an appliance, or take a vacation during the following six months. The panel constitutes a representative sample of the U.S. population. The responses are tallied and expressed as percentages. Data from a survey are directly comparable with the data from previous surveys. The index was originally compiled bimonthly.

Used as an indicator of future consumer-related production activity.

Published monthly by the Conference Board in *Consumer Confidence Survey*.

Source	Frequency	Extent	Form	Medium
Consumer Confidence Survey	m	c	t	p

Bibliography

"Consumer Attitudes and Buying Plans," *Conference Board Record*, 34-35 (Feb. 1968).

C

Capacity Utilization
[Also called the Capacity Utilization Rate]

The ratio of industrial output to installed capacity expressed as a percentage.

The Federal Reserve estimates productive capacity of the manufacturing, mining, and electric and gas utilities industries by deriving 75 individual production indexes from physical measurements compiled by trade associations, surveys of utilization rates and investment, and estimates of the growth of capital investment. They then divide those indexes by utilization rate data from various company surveys and smooth that data to reflect long-term production trends, business judgements about the degree of facility use, and the pattern of real investment over the course of the business cycle. Estimates cover primary- and advanced-processing industries, durable and nondurable manufacturing, as well as mining and utilities. Value-added proportions are used to weight the individual capacity indexes. The resultant capacity index is then divided into the Board's index of industrial production, and the result is multiplied by 100.

Used as an important indicator of resource use; high utilization rates are generally associated with increased levels of investment and, in certain industries, with bottlenecks and supply-side inflationary pressures. Also used by industry and government in studies of investment patterns; output per man-hour; and costs, prices, and profits.

Published monthly by the Board of Governors of the Federal Reserve System in *Capacity Utilization: Manufacturing and Materials*, Statistical Release G.3 (402).

Source	Frequency	Extent	Form	Medium
Annual Statistical Digest (FRB)	a, m	c	t	p
Barron's	m	c	t	p

Source	Frequency	Extent	Form	Medium
BCI	m	h	g	e
Commodity Yearbook	a, m	c, h	t	p
Economic Handbook of the Machine Tool Industry	a	h	g	p
Economic Indicators	a, m	c, h	t, g	p, e
Economic Report of the President	a	h	t	p, e
Federal Reserve Board	m	c	t	e
Federal Reserve Bulletin	a, q, m	c, h	t	p
First Union	m	c, h	t	e
FRB Chicago	q	c, h	t	e
FRB Dallas	m	c, h	t	e
FRED	m	c, h	t	e
Industrial Production and Capacity Utilization	m	c	t, g	p
Statistical Abstract	a	h	t	p
Stat-USA	m	c	t	e
Survey of Current Business	a, m	c, h	t, g	p, e
Value Line Investment Survey, Part 2: Selection and Opinion	a, q	c, h, f	t	p

Bibliography

Bleakley, Fred R., "Capacity Utilization Is Losing Credibility," *Wall Street Journal*, pp. A2+, Feb. 14, 1995.

Board of Governors of the Federal Reserve System, *Federal Reserve Measures of Capacity and Capacity Utilization*, Federal Reserve Board, Washington, D.C., 1978.

Board of Governors of the Federal Reserve System, *Industrial Production*, rev. ed., Federal Reserve Board, Washington, D.C., 1977.

Carnes, W. Stansbury, and Stephen D. Slifer, *The Atlas of Economic Indicators: A Visual Guide to Market Forces and the Federal Reserve*, Harper Business, New York, 1991, pp. 93-101.

DeLeeuw, Frank, *Measurement of Capacity Utilization: Problems and Tasks*, Staff Studies No. 105, Board of Governors of the Federal Reserve System, Washington, D.C., 1979.

Frumkin, Norman, *Guide to Economic Indicators*, 2nd ed., M. E. Sharpe, Armonk, N.Y., 1994, pp. 67-70.

Frumkin, Norman, *Tracking America's Economy*, 2nd ed., Sharpe, Armonk, N.Y., 1992, pp. 158-174.

Garner, C. Alan, "Capacity Utilization and U.S. Inflation," *Economic Review of the Federal Reserve Bank of Kansas City* **79** (4), 5-21 (1994).

Grant, John, *A Handbook of Economic Indicators*, University of Toronto Press, Toronto, 1992, pp. 148-149.

Hoel, Arline Alchian; Kenneth W. Clarkson; and Roger LeRoy Miller, *Economics Sourcebook of Government Statistics*, Lexington Books, Lexington, Mass., 1983, pp. 23-26.

Joint Economic Committee, *1980 Supplement to Economic Indicators, Historical and Descriptive Background*, USGPO, Washington, D.C., 1980, pp. 62-64.

Niemira, Michael P., and Gerald F. Zukowski, *Trading the Fundamentals: The Trader's Guide to Interpreting Economic Indicators and Monetary Policy*, McGraw-Hill, New York, 1998, pp. 145-153.

Plocek, Joseph E., *Economic Indicators: How America Reads Its Financial Health*, New York Institute of Finance, New York, 1991, pp. 166-169.

Raddock, Richard D., "Industrial Production, Capacity, and Capacity Utilization Since 1987," *Federal Reserve Bulletin* **79** (6), 590-605 (1993).

Raddock, Richard D., "Revised Federal Reserve Rates of Capacity Utilization," *Federal Reserve Bulletin* **71** (10), 754-766 (1985).

Rogers, R. Mark, *Handbook of Key Economic Indicators*, Irwin Professional Pub., Burr Ridge, Ill., 1994, pp. 130-143.

Ruggles, Richard, *Employment and Unemployment Statistics as Indexes of Economic Activity and Capacity Utilization*, National Commission on Employment and Unemployment Statistics Background Paper No. 28, USGPO, Washington, D.C., 1979.

Tainer, Evelina M., *Using Economic Indicators to Improve Investment Analysis*, John Wiley & Sons, New York, 1993, pp. 225-227.

WEFA Group, *Guide to Economic Indicators: U.S. Macroeconomic Services*, WEFA Group, Bala Cynwyd, Pa., 1997, p. 6.

Wrightsman, Dwayne, "Three Leading Indicators of Changes in Inflation," *Journal of Business Forecasting Methods and Systems* **9** (3), 11-14 (1990).

Capacity Utilization Rate
[See Capacity Utilization]

Capital Expenditures

An estimate of the amount American business invests in plant and equipment.

As part of the Census of Manufactures, the Bureau of the Census each year collects data on new capital expenditures. Those expenditures include (1) permanent additions and major alterations to manufacturing establishments and (2) machinery and equipment used for replacement and additions to plant capacity. The data include expenditures for both new and used buildings/structures and machinery/equipment. The sample for the annual survey includes approximately 45,000 private, nonfarm businesses with at least 5 paid employees but excludes foreign operations of U.S. businesses, businesses in U.S. territories, government operations, agricultural-production companies, and private households. For the larger firms, capital-expenditures data are published for 94 industries at 2- or 3-digit Standard Industrial Classification (SIC) code levels. Values are expressed as billions of dollars and as percent increase or decrease.

Used to identify trends in capital expenditures by businesses, to analyze business-asset depreciation, to improve estimates of capital stock for productivity analysis, and to improve quarterly estimates of the gross domestic product.

Announced annually by the Bureau of the Census as a press release and in the report *Annual Capital Expenditures*.

Source	Frequency	Extent	Form	Medium
Annual Statistical Digest (FRB)	a, q	c	t	p
Economic Handbook of the Machine Tool Industry	a	h	g	p
Financial Digest	m	c	t	p
Recession Recovery Watch	a	h	g	p
Statistical Abstract	a	c, h	t	p
S&P Basic Statistics - Income and Trade	a	h	t	p

Bibliography
"Annual Capital Expenditures Survey," www.census.gov/prod/www/abs/ace-pdf.html, visited July 14, 1999.
"County and City Data Book City Source Notes: Manufactures," www.lib.virginia.edu/socsci/ccdb/documents/sn_cif13.html, visited July 14, 1999.
"Plant and Equipment Survey," www.census.gov/econ/www/mu1000.html, visited July 14, 1999.
U.S. Department of Commerce, Bureau of the Census, *1992 Subject Series, Measures of Value Produced, Capital Expenditures, Depreciable Assets, And Operating Expenses*, RC(92)-S-2, USGPO, Washington, D.C., 1996.

Car Loadings
[Also called Freight-Car Loadings]
The total number of railroad car loadings by Class 1 railroads for all commodities.

All Class 1 railway carriers (railroads that have annual gross revenues of $50 million or more) report the number of car loadings to the Association of American Railroads weekly. The Association then totals these figures. Class 1 haulers handle 97% of the railroad traffic in the United States.

Used as a leading indicator of general business activity; it is tied closely to the manufacturing output, sales of consumer goods, and the need for raw materials by manufacturers.

Published weekly by the Association of American Railroads in *Rail News Update*.

Source	Frequency	Extent	Form	Medium
Railroad Facts	a	h	t	p
Railway Age	m	c	t	p
S&P Basic Statistics - Transportation	i	h	t	p
Statistical Abstract	a	h	t	p
Transportation Statistics in the US	a	c	t	p
Trends: Weekly Traffic of Major Railroads	w	c	t	p

CBOE 250 Stock Index
[See Chicago Board Options Exchange 250 Stock Index]

Certificate of Deposit Interest Rates

A typical interest rate offered by dealers on certificates of deposit selling on the secondary market.

Large-denominated certificates of deposits (CDs) for funds on deposit at financial institutions are negotiable and can be sold or discounted to other individuals or institutions. In the United States, an over-the-counter market exists for CDs among a dozen or so dealers. To be attractive to buyers, the yields of these secondary CDs must be higher than the yields available from the primary issuers; thus, the interest rates are higher than the original ones. At the end of each week, the Federal Reserve System polls at least five dealers to determine the interest rates at which they are selling these instruments. The responses are then arithmetically averaged. A similar average of poll results among financial institutions that are primary issuers of certificates of deposit is calculated on a daily basis.

Used as an indicator of the cost of money, the availability of capital, and inflation.

Secondary-market values issued monthly as statistical release G.13 (415), *Selected Interest Rates*, by the Board of Governors of the Federal Reserve System; values for the primary market issued daily as a press release by Banxquote and published weekly in *IBC Moneyfund Report*.

Source	Frequency	Extent	Form	Medium
Bank Rate Monitor	d	c	t	e
Barron's	w	c	t	p
Federal Reserve Board	d	c, h	t	e
First Union	m*	c, h	t	e
Forecast	q	c, f	t	p

Source	Frequency	Extent	Form	Medium
FRB Chicago	d, w	c, h	t	e
FRB New York	d	c	t	e
FRED	w, m	c, h	t	e
International Economic Review	a, m, q	c	t	p
Investor's Business Daily	d	c, h	g, t	p
New York Times	d	c	t	p
S&P Basic Statistics - Banking and Finance	a, m	h	t	p
S&P Current Statistics	m	c	t	p
Statistical Abstract	a	h	t	p
USA Today	d	c	t	p
Value Line Investment Survey, Part 2: Selection and Opinion	w	c	t	p
Wall Street Journal	d, w*	c	t	p

*Secondary market

Bibliography

Hoel, Arline Alchian; Kenneth W. Clarkson; and Roger LeRoy Miller, *Economics Sourcebook of Government Statistics*, Lexington Books, Lexington, Mass., 1983, pp. 107-108.

Chain Store Sales

[See Bank of Tokyo–Mitsubishi/Chain Store Age Weekly Leading Indicator of Chain Store Sales, Bank of Tokyo–Mitsubishi Chain Store Sales Index, and Bank of Tokyo–Mitsubishi/Schroders Weekly U.S. Retail Chain Store Sales Index]

Change in Business Loans

The actual differences during the month in the total amount of commercial and industrial loans outstanding.

About 320 banks report their outstanding loans to commercial and industrial customers to the Federal Reserve on a weekly basis (see Commercial and Industrial Loans Outstanding, Weekly Reporting Large Commercial Banks). These figures are totaled for the previous month and seasonally adjusted. The month's total is subtracted from the total for the preceding month, and the change is converted to a simple annual rate measured in billions of dollars.

Considered to be an indicator of future business activity because businesses usually finance additional inventory and borrow in anticipation of increased volume of production.

Weekly values are published monthly by the Board of Governors of the Federal Reserve System in *Federal Reserve Bulletin*.

Source	Frequency	Extent	Form	Medium
Federal Reserve Bulletin	m	c	t	p

Bibliography

Snyder, Richard M., *Measuring Business Changes*, Wiley, New York, 1955, pp. 272 ff.

Change in Hours per Unit of Output

A measure of the change during the past year in labor costs per unit of output.

Labor input is taken largely from the Hours and Employment Series of the Bureau of Labor Statistics. These data are supplemented with data from the National Income and Product Accounts compiled by the Bureau of Economic Analysis and data from the Census Population Survey conducted by the Bureau of the Census. From these data, hours of employment are estimated. Output is derived from the real Gross Domestic Product compiled by the Bureau of Economic Analysis, giving the 1992 dollar value of the goods and services produced by labor located in the United States. From these data, a value for the number of employee hours required to produce a unit of output is calculated for each quarter. The percentage change that occurs for a four-quarter interval is then calculated from these values. The resultant percentage is sometimes seasonally adjusted.

Used as an indicator of productivity and inflation.

Published quarterly by the Bureau of Labor Statistics in *Productivity and Costs*.

Source	Frequency	Extent	Form	Medium
Economic Indicators	a, q	h	t	p, e
Statistical Abstract	a	h	t	p

Bibliography

Moore, Geoffrey Hoyt, and Melita H. Moore, *International Economic Indicators: A Sourcebook*, Greenwood Press, Westport, Conn., 1985, p. 45.

Change in Industrial Materials Price Index

[Also called the Daily Price Index of Industrial Materials; see also the Change in Sensitive Prices, the Journal of Commerce Index, the Bridge-CRB Index, and the Bridge-CRB Futures Index]

A measure of trends of prices of raw materials on commodity markets and exchanges.

The prices of 17 raw materials (crude oil, benzene, burlap, cotton, print cloth, polyester, aluminum, copper scrap, lead, tin, zinc, steel scrap, hides, plywood, rubber, tallow, and hardwood lumber) are determined, and a weighted arithmetic average is calculated. Since 1982, the prices used have been the averages of figures for all working days. These monthly averages are then used to calculate a six-month smoothed annual rate based on the ratio of the current month's index to the average index for the preceding 12 months. The data are not seasonally adjusted.

Used as an indicator of emerging inflation.

Published monthly in *The Journal of Commerce* by the Center for International Business Cycle Research.

Source	Frequency	Extent	Form	Medium
Journal of Commerce	m	c	t	p

Bibliography

Moore, Geoffrey Hoyt, and Melita H. Moore, *International Economic Indicators: A Sourcebook*, Greenwood Press, Westport, Conn., 1985, p. 33-34.

Change in Inventories on Hand and on Order
[See Inventory Change Index]

Change in Sensitive Prices
[See also the Bridge-CRB Index, Bridge-CRB Futures Index, Journal of Commerce Index, and Change in Industrial Materials Price Index]

The change in an index of prices charged in primary markets for 13 specified classes of crude materials.

A sample of specified commodities from 13 classes of crude materials (hides and skins, potash, crude natural rubber, wastepaper, iron ore, iron and steel scrap, nonferrous metal scrap, sand, gravel and crushed stone, bituminous coal, anthracite coal, natural gas, and crude petroleum) are priced by reporters in a sample of primary markets in the United States. These prices are gathered for the Tuesday of the week containing the 13th of the month or are an average of prices throughout the month. The actual wholesale selling prices quoted by representative manufacturers or on organized exchanges or markets are the prices gathered. The price data are weighted based on the value of shipments and combined. The total is indexed to a value of 100 for 1967 and seasonally adjusted. The indicator is expressed as a percent change from the previous month and as a four-term weighted moving average placed at the terminal month.

A leading indicator at peaks, troughs, and overall.

Published monthly by the U.S. Department of Labor, Bureau of Labor Statistics, in a press release.

Source	Frequency	Extent	Form	Medium
BCI	m	h	g	e
S&P Basic Statistics - Income and Trade	i	h	t	p

Source	Frequency	Extent	Form	Medium
Statistical Abstract	a	h	t	p

Bibliography
"Official Indicators: What Are They? Can They Predict the Future?" *U.S. News and World Report*, 66-67 (Aug. 16, 1976).
U.S. Department of Commerce, Bureau of Economic Analysis, *Handbook of Cyclical Indicators*, U.S. Department of Commerce, Washington, D.C., 1984, p. 25.

Changes in Consumer Installment Credit
[See Consumer Installment Credit]

Chemical Industry Leading Indicator

A 3-month leading indicator of chemical industry (Standard Industrial Classification Code 28) production and employment.

Each month, government, industry, and business statistics are combined and indexed to a prior, benchmark value. The statistical components of the indicator started with overtime hours, the S&P index of stock prices for chemicals, and consumer spending on nondurables. But the components have varied over the years. For example, the overtime hours value was dropped soon after initiation of the indicator, and housing starts has become a major component in recent years. The indicator is rebenchmarked every 10 years to the average value for the most recent year ending in 7.

Used as a predictor of future activity in chemical manufacturing.

Published monthly in *Chemical Week* magazine.

Source	Frequency	Extent	Form	Medium
Chemical Week	m	c, h	g	p

Bibliography
"More on Economics," *Chemical Week*, p. 5 (Dec. 1, 1982).

Chemical Week Price Index

A measure of the aggregate change in the prices of chemicals.

To compile this index, a sample of the chemical industry is surveyed weekly to determine the current prices of a specific (unweighted) selection of chemicals. The value of this chemical marketbasket is then indexed to the cost of a similar marketbasket in 1967; the 1967 index value is fixed at 100.

Used as an indicator of the cost of doing business. Many industries are dependent on feedstock chemicals for their manufacturing processes; when the prices of those feedstocks go up, the cost of manufacturing goes up, also.

Published monthly by McGraw-Hill Economics in *Chemical Week*.

Source	Frequency	Extent	Form	Medium
Chemical Week	m	c, h	t, g	p

Chicago Board Options Exchange 250 Stock Index

A broad-based stock-price index based on the 250 highest-capitalized stocks on the New York Stock Exchange.

A joint venture of the Chicago Board of Trade and the Chicago Board Options Exchange, the index takes the stock prices of the 250 highest-capitalized firms represented on the New York Stock Exchange, weights each stock price by the company's capitalization, totals those values, and indexes the result to a value of 100 for July 29, 1983. The 250 equities represent about 70% of the total NYSE market value. The list of stocks included in the index is revised quarterly.

Used as the basis for cash-settled index-options futures contracts traded on the Chicago Board Options Exchange.

Calculated continually by the Chicago Board Options Exchange and announced in a daily news release.

Source	Frequency	Extent	Form	Medium
Barron's	w	c	t	p

Bibliography
Berlin, Howard M. *The Handbook of Financial Market Indexes, Averages, and Indicators*, Dow Jones-Irwin, Homewood, Ill., 1990, pp. 34-36.

Christmas Price Index
[See Appendix A. Nonquantitative Indicators]

Coal Production

An estimate (based on car loadings and average tonnage carried by car) of the U.S. production in tons of bituminous coal and lignite during a given month.

Weekly, the Association of American Railroads surveys the coal industry to determine the number of car loadings performed at mine mouths. This number of car loadings is then multiplied by the average coal tonnage carried per car as calculated by the Interstate Commerce Commission. The Energy Information Administration (EIA) independently surveys the industry to determine the methods of coal distribution. From its data, the EIA calculates the ratio of coal that is shipped by rail. The amount estimated to be shipped by rail is then divided by this ratio to produce an estimate of all production.

Used to determine the energy mix used to meet the country's energy requirements and as an indirect measure of industrial activity.

Published weekly by the U.S. Department of Energy, Energy Information Administration, in *Weekly Coal Production*.

Source	Frequency	Extent	Form	Medium
Annual Energy Review	a	h	t, g	p
Basic Petroleum Data Book	a	h	t	p
Business Statistics	i	h	t	p
Business Week	w	c	t	p
Handbook of International Economic Statistics (CIA)	a	h	t	p, e
Monthly Energy Review	m	h	t, g	p
Quarterly Coal Production	q	h	t, g	p
S&P Basic Statistics - Energy, Electric Power, and Fuels	i	h	t	p
Statistical Abstract	a	h	t	p
Weekly Coal Production	w	c	t, g	p

Bibliography

U.S. Department of Commerce, Bureau of Economic Analysis, *Business Statistics, 1963-91*, USGPO, Washington, D.C., 1992, pp. 183-184.

Coincident Indicators
[See Coincident Indicators Composite Index]

Coincident Indicators Composite Index

The average behavior of a group of economic indicators whose values have been noted to coincide with business-cycle turns.

Four economic indicators were selected because their values generally changed in a manner similar to changes in the business cycles and at about the same time as those business-cycle changes. Those indicators are

▸ nonagricultural employment,
▸ index of industrial production,
▸ personal income (less transfer payments), and
▸ manufacturing and trade sales.

Month-to-month percent changes or differences are calculated for each component of the composite index. The percent changes (or differences) for each component are standardized to an absolute value of one by dividing each monthly change by the average of these changes. These standardized changes are then weighted according to the economic significance, statistical adequacy, cyclical timing, conformity to business cycles, smoothness, and currency of each component. A weighted average of the standardized changes is then computed for all the components.

Indicates changes in the direction of aggregate economic activity; viewed by many as an indicator of current and future levels of economic activity.

Issued monthly as a press release by The Conference Board and on their World Wide Web home page at www.conference-board.org.

Source	Frequency	Extent	Form	Medium
Barron's	w	c	t	p
BCI	m	h	g	e
Conference Board/BCI	m	c	t	e
FRB Dallas	m	c, h	t	e
Statistical Abstract	a	h	t	p
Stat-USA	m	c	t	e

Bibliography

Beckman, Barry A., and Tracy R. Tapscott, "Composite Indexes of Leading, Coincident, and Lagging Indicators," *Survey of Current Business* **67** (11), 24-28 (1987).

Frumkin, Norman, *Guide to Economic Indicators*, 2nd ed., M. E. Sharpe, Armonk, N.Y., 1994, pp. 217-223.

Frumkin, Norman, *Tracking America's Economy*, 2nd ed., Sharpe, Armonk, N.Y., 1992, pp. 283-301.

Green, George R., and Barry A. Beckman, "Business Cycle Indicators: Upcoming Revision of the Composite Indexes," *Survey of Current Business* **73** (10), 44-51 (1993).

Green, George R., and Barry A. Beckman, "The Composite Index of Coincident Indicators and Alternative Coincident Indexes," *Survey of Current Business* **72** (6), 42-45 (1992).

Hertzberg, Marie P., and Barry A Beckman, "Business Cycle Indicators: Revised Composite Indicators," *Survey of Current Business* **69** (1), 23-28 (1989).

Hoel, Arline Alchian; Kenneth W. Clarkson; and Roger LeRoy Miller, *Economics Sourcebook of Government Statistics*, Lexington Books, Lexington, Mass., 1983, pp. 61-65.

Jun, Duk Bin, and Young Jin Joo, "Predicting Turning Points in Business Cycles by Detection of Slope Changes in the Leading Composite Index," *Journal of Forecasting* **12** (3/4), 197-213 (1993).

Moore, Geoffrey H., "Leading and Confirming Indicators of General Business Changes," pp. 45-109 in Geoffrey H. Moore, Ed., *Business Cycle Indicators*, Vol. 1, Princeton University Press, Princeton, N.J., 1961.

Niemira, Michael P., and Gerald F. Zukowski, *Trading the Fundamentals: The Trader's Guide to Interpreting Economic Indicators and Monetary Policy*, McGraw-Hill, New York, 1998, pp. 61-66.

Plocek, Joseph E., *Economic Indicators: How America Reads Its Financial Health*, New York Institute of Finance, New York, 1991, 312-315.

Renshaw, Edward, "On Measuring Economic Recessions," *Challenge* **34** (2), 58-59 (1991).

Renshaw, Edward, Ed., *The Practical Forecasters' Almanac: 137 Reliable Indicators for Investors, Hedgers, and Speculators*, Business One Irwin, Homewood, Ill., 1992, p. 23-24.

Rogers, R. Mark, *Handbook of Key Economic Indicators*, Irwin Professional Pub., Burr Ridge, Ill., 1994, 260-261.

Samuelson, Paul, "Paradise Lost & Refound: The Harvard ABC Barometers," *Journal of Portfolio Management* **13** (3), 4-9 (1987).

Color Index
[See Appendix A. Nonquantitative Indicators]

Commerce Department Composite Construction Cost Index
[See Composite Construction Price Index]

Commercial and Industrial Loans Outstanding, Weekly Reporting Large Commercial Banks
[Also called Bank Loans]

The average dollar amount of business loans outstanding in a given month.

The Federal Reserve System receives from about 320 banks reports that include data on the amount of commercial and industrial loans outstanding as of each Wednesday and the amount of loans sold outright during each week to the banks' own foreign branches, nonconsolidated nonbank affiliates, holding companies, and consolidated nonbank subsidiaries of the holding companies. All of these are summed and seasonally adjusted weekly. The arithmetic mean of the weekly values for a month is calculated for the monthly value.

Used as a lagging indicator for peaks, for troughs, and overall; a component of the Lagging Indicators Composite Index.

Published weekly by the Board of Governors of the Federal Reserve System in *Assets and Liabilities of Commercial Banks in the U.S.*

Source	Frequency	Extent	Form	Medium
Annual Statistical Digest (FRB)	a	c	t	p
BCI	m	h	g	e
Business Statistics	i	h	t	p
Conference Board/BCI	m	c	t	e
Economic Indicators	m	c, h	t, g	p, e
FDIC Quarterly Banking Profile	q	c	t	p
Federal Reserve Bulletin	m	c	t	p
Finance Companies (FRB Stat Rel G.20)	m	c	t	p
Financial Digest	bw	c	t	p

Source	Frequency	Extent	Form	Medium
First Union	m	c, h	t	e
Forecast	a	c, f	t	p
FRED	w	c, h	t	e
Statistical Abstract	a	h	t	p
Survey of Current Business	m	c, h	t	p, e

Bibliography

Chadwick, Nathaniel, "An Infallible Indicator of Stock Market Trends," *Banking*, 39+ (Mar. 1971).

Frumkin, Norman, *Guide to Economic Indicators*, 2nd ed., M. E. Sharpe, Armonk, N.Y., 1994, pp. 49-52.

Jacoby, N.; H. Neil; and R. J. Saulnier, *Business Finance and Banking*, rev. ed., National Bureau of Economic Research, New York, 1980.

Moore, Geoffrey Hoyt, and Melita H. Moore, *International Economic Indicators: A Sourcebook*, Greenwood Press, Westport, Conn., 1985, p. 46.

U.S. Department of Commerce, Bureau of Economic Analysis, *Handbook of Cyclical Indicators*, U.S. Department of Commerce, Washington, D.C., 1984, pp. 32-33.

Commercial Paper Interest Rates
[See also Prime Commercial Paper]

A typical interest rate offered by issuers of unsecured, short-term promissary notes.

Financially healthy corporations that are considered sound and whose securities are highly rated often raise short-term (60 to 270 days) cash by borrowing from investors and signing promissary notes (referred to as commercial paper) for the loan. These promissary notes are usually unsecured, and are issued on a discount basis directly to investors or through dealers who are specialists in commercial paper. Investors or dealers in commercial paper usually get the offerings reviewed by companies that rate such paper for financial quality and soundness. At the end of each week, the Federal Reserve System polls at least five of the thousand or so U.S. dealers in commercial paper to determine the interest rates at which they are selling these notes. The responses are then arithmetically averaged.

Used as an indicator of the cost of money, the availability of capital, and inflation.

Issued weekly in Statistical Release H.15 (519), *Selected Interest Rates*, by the Board of Governors of the Federal Reserve System.

Source	Frequency	Extent	Form	Medium
Annual Statistical Digest (FRB)	a	c	t	p

Source	Frequency	Extent	Form	Medium
Barron's	w	c	t	p
Business Statistics	i	h	t	p
Business Week	w	c	t	p
Federal Reserve Board	d	c, h	t	e
Federal Reserve Bulletin	m	c	t	p
First Union	m	c, h	t	e
FRB Chicago	d	c, h	t	e
FRED	d, w, m	c, h	t	e
International Financial Statistics	a	h	t	p
Moody's Bond Record	m	c	g	p
New York Times	d	c	t	p
Securities Industry Yearbook	a	h	t	p
Selected Interest Rates	m	c	t	p
S&P Basic Statistics - Banking and Finance	i	h	t	p
Statistical Abstract	a	h	t	p
US Financial Data	w	h	g	p
Wall Street Journal	d	c	t	p
Value Line Investment Survey, Part 2: Selection and Opinion	w	c	t	p

Bibliography

Hoel, Arline Alchian; Kenneth W. Clarkson; and Roger LeRoy Miller, *Economics Sourcebook of Government Statistics*, Lexington Books, Lexington, Mass., 1983, pp. 109-111.

Commodity-Based Stage-of-Processing Indexes
[See Finished Goods Price Index and Index for Intermediate Materials]

Commodity Research Bureau Futures Price Index
[See Bridge-CRB Futures Index]

Commodity Research Bureau Spot Price Index
[See Bridge-CRB Index]

Composite Coincident Indicators
[See Coincident Indicators Composite Index]

Composite Construction Cost Index
[See Composite Construction Price Index]

Composite Construction Price Index
[Formerly Composite Construction Cost Index; see also Boeckh Building Construction Index, Building Cost Index, and Construction Cost Index]

An indication of the change in prices of construction materials and activities with time.

In 1990, the Bureau of the Census replaced the Composite Construction Cost Index with the Composite Construction Price Index and an Implicit Price Deflator. The new Composite Construction Cost Index is calculated from a weighted average of several other indexes of construction costs: Single Family Houses Under Construction (covering residential, nonresidential, and military buildings); Turner Construction Company (covering nonresidential and military buildings); Federal Highway Administration Composite Index (covering selected types of highway, street, railroad, and military construction); Bureau of Reclamation (covering selected types of conservation, development, railroad, and sewer construction); and the Handy-Whitman Public Utility Indexes (covering construction for electric light and power, gas, telecommunications, petroleum pipelines, and water-supply facilities). The weights are kept constant at their 1987 values, and the components are expressed in terms of 1987 values so the index shows only changes in prices since 1987.

Used to estimate the increase in construction costs caused by inflation; also used to deflate the Value of New Construction Put in Place series of statistics.

Published as a monthly report by the Bureau of the Census in *Values of New Construction Put in Place*.

Source	Frequency	Extent	Form	Medium
Business Statistics	i	h	t	p
Construction Review	m	c, h	t	p
Statistical Abstract	a	h	t	p

Bibliography
Hoel, Arline Alchian; Kenneth W. Clarkson; and Roger LeRoy Miller, *Economics Sourcebook of Government Statistics*, Lexington Books, Lexington, Mass., 1983, pp. 27-30.

U.S. Department of Commerce, Bureau of Economic Analysis, *Business Statistics 1963-1993*, USGPO, Washington, D.C., 1994, pp. 151-152.

Composite Index of Coincident Indicators
[See Coincident Indicators Composite Index]

Composite Index of Lagging Indicators
[See Lagging Indicators Composite Index]

Composite Index of Leading Indicators
[See Leading Indicators Composite Index]

Composite Lagging Indicators
[See Lagging Indicators Composite Index]

Composite Leading Indicators
[See Leading Indicators Composite Index]

Conference Board Help Wanted Advertising Index
[See Help-Wanted Advertising Index]

Confidence Index
[See Barron's Confidence Index]

Constant Maturities Treasury Securities
An estimated yield to maturity for any Treasury security given the aggregate performance of such securities in current bond markets.

This statistic is derived by plotting the closing yields of selected outstanding Treasury securities on a graph with the date of maturity on the x-axis and the yield on the y-axis. A single, continuous yield curve is then drawn through the midst of the plotted points, allowing a yield to be interpolated for any fixed maturity (e.g., 1, 2, 3, 5, 7, 10, 20, or 30 years).

Used to estimate the yield of a Treasury security for a given time to maturity.

Published weekly by the Board of Governors of the Federal Reserve System in *Selected Interest Rates*, Statistical Release H.15 (519); weekly values are published monthly in *Selected Interest Rates*, G.13 (415).

Source	Frequency	Extent	Form	Medium
Bank Rate Monitor	w	c	t	e
Economic Indicators	w, m, a	c, h	t	p, e
Federal Reserve Board	d	c, h	t	e
FRED	d, w, m	c, h	t	e
Selected Interest Rates	m	c	t	p
Statistical Abstract	a	c, h	t	p

Bibliography
Hoel, Arline Alchian; Kenneth W. Clarkson; and Roger LeRoy Miller, *Economics Sourcebook of Government Statistics*, Lexington Books, Lexington, Mass., 1983, pp. 160-162.
Joint Economic Committee, *1980 Supplement to Economic Indicators, Historical and Descriptive Background*, USGPO, Washington, D.C., 1980, pp. 108-109.

Construction Contract Awards

The estimated total dollar value of awards for housing, industrial and commercial buildings, utilities, and public works throughout the United States for a given month.

This indicator is calculated from data from the Dodge reports, sampling, permit filings, and publications, with the majority coming from the Dodge reports. The values reflect as closely as possible the actual construction costs exclusive of land, architect's fees, and equipment that is not an integral part of the structure. The data are indexed to a value of 100 for 1977 and are seasonally adjusted. The annual indexes are based on annual data; they are not simply averages of the monthly figures.

Used as an indicator of trends in future construction activity, in the purchase and use of construction materials, in construction employment, in wages earned, and in taxable property.

Published monthly by McGraw-Hill Information Systems Co., F. W. Dodge Div., in *Engineering News Record* and by the U.S. Department of Commerce, Bureau of Economic Analysis, in *Survey of Current Business*.

Source	Frequency	Extent	Form	Medium
Barron's	w	c	t	p
BCI	m	h	g	e
Business Statistics	i	h	t	p
Construction Outlook	a	c, f	g	p
Construction Review	m	h	t	p
Economic Indicators	m	c, h	t	p, e
ENR	m	c	t	p
Federal Reserve Bulletin	m	c	t	p
Statistical Abstract	a	h	t	p
Survey of Current Business	m	c, h	t	p, e

Bibliography

Carnes, W. Stansbury, and Stephen D. Slifer, *The Atlas of Economic Indicators: A Visual Guide to Market Forces and the Federal Reserve*, Harper Business, New York, 1991, pp. 147-152.

Snyder, Richard M., *Measuring Business Changes*, Wiley, New York, 1955, p. 210.

"The Methodology Underlying the Dodge Index of Construction Contracts, Seasonally Adjusted," *Construction Review*, 5-7 (Nov. 1959).

U.S. Department of Commerce, Bureau of Economic Analysis, *Business Statistics, 1963-91*, USGPO, Washington, D.C., 1992, p. 150.

Construction Cost Index

[See also Boeckh Building Cost Index, Building Cost Index, and Composite Construction Price Index]

A measure of the combined effect of wage and price changes on the value of the construction dollar.

Four costs are calculated, those of: 200 hours of common labor at the average rate for such labor in 20 selected cities; 25 cwt of standard structural steel shapes at the average price for such steel at three selected mills; 22.56 cwt of Portland cement at the average price for such cement in 20 selected cities; and 1088 board feet of two-by-four lumber at the average price for such lumber in 20 selected cities. These values are weighted with empirically derived statistical weights to normalize the data. The calculated total is then indexed to the totals in 1913 and 1967, producing two series, a 1913 = 100 series and a 1967 = 100 series. Monthly indexes are the indexes calculated for the first week of the month. Annual indexes are straight mathematical averages of the component months. The common-labor and materials components are also broken out and published as separate indexes. A related index, the Building Cost Index, uses much of the same data in its derivation; it uses a different labor base reflecting the employment of skilled labor.

Used to judge underlying trends of construction costs in the United States and to estimate costs of future construction projects. This index has become an industry standard for tracking the escalation of construction costs and is one of the ten construction-cost indexes published by the Department of Commerce in *Business Statistics*.

Published weekly (whole United States; 1913 = 100) and monthly (city-by-city; 1967 = 100) by McGraw-Hill Information Systems Co. in *Engineering News-Record*.

Source	Frequency	Extent	Form	Medium
Business Statistics	i	h	t	p
Construction Review	m	c, h	t	p
ENR	m	c	t	p
S&P Basic Statistics - Building and Building Materials	i	h	t	p
S&P Current Statistics	i	h	t	p
Statistical Abstract	a	h	t	p
Value of New Construction Put in Place (CCR C30)	m	c, h	t	p

Bibliography

"Construction Costs Tracked for U.S.," *Engineering News-Record* **210** (12), 114-121 (Mar. 24, 1983).

Hoel, Arline Alchian; Kenneth W. Clarkson; and Roger LeRoy Miller, *Economics Sourcebook of Government Statistics*, Lexington Books, Lexington, Mass., 1983, pp. 27-30.

Koehn, Enno, "Economic and Social Factors in Construction," *Cost Engineering*
    31 (10), 15-18 (Oct. 1989).
U.S. Department of Commerce, Bureau of Economic Analysis, *Business Statistics,
    1963-91*, USGPO, Washington, D.C., 1992, pp. 151-152.

Construction Put in Place
[See Value of New Construction Put in Place]

Construction Spending
[See Value of New Construction Put in Place]

Consumer Comfort Index

A measure of consumers' confidence in their own finances and in the
economy as a whole.

Each week, *Money* magazine and ABC News conduct a random survey of
more than 1000 consumers across the country to gauge their opinions about the
current shape of the economy, their own finances, and their willingness to spend
money. The responses are expressed on a scale ranging from -100 to 100.

Used as a barometer of American public opinion about the U.S. economy and
as a predictor of near-term future retail sales.

Released each Wednesday evening as a press release by ABC News and
Money magazine.

Source	Frequency	Extent	Form	Medium
Bank of Tokyo-Mitsubishi	w	c, h	t	e

Bibliography
Niemira, Michael P., and Gerald F. Zukowski, *Trading the Fundamentals: The
    Trader's Guide to Interpreting Economic Indicators and Monetary Policy*,
    McGraw-Hill, New York, 1998, pp. 35-41.

Consumer Confidence Index
[See also Buying Plans Index]

A quantitative assessment of how consumers feel about current business
conditions and employment opportunities, how those conditions will change in the
next six months, and how their own conditions will be affected by those changes.

NFO Research, Inc., mails a questionnaire to 5000 representative sample
homes each month. These families are asked about (1) the current state of business
conditions and employment opportunities, (2) how these conditions and
opportunities will change during the following six months, and (3) how they feel
their own economic conditions will change during the same period. The fraction
of positive opinions expressed by respondents is calculated and indexed to a value
of 100 for 1985. The resulting index shows month-to-month variations in opinions
about economic outlook.

Used to foretell short-term shifts in the national economic growth rate and to guide production and marketing decision making. Closely watched by economists and financiers as a barometer of consumers' willingness to borrow and spend; such consumer spending makes up about two-thirds of the nation's economic activity. Decreases in consumer confidence can lessen spending, putting less pressure on supplies and prices.

Published monthly by The Conference Board in *Consumer Confidence Survey*; announced in a press release and on the World Wide Web at www. conference-board.org.

Source	Frequency	Extent	Form	Medium
Bank of America	m	c, h	t	e
Bank of Tokyo-Mitsubishi	m	c, h	t	e
BCI	m	h	g	e
Consumer Confidence Survey	m	h	g	p
CRB Commodity Yearbook	a	h	t	p

Bibliography

Cutler, Blayne, "The Feel-Good Index," *American Demographics* **14** (9), 56-60 (Sept. 1992).

Frumkin, Norman, *Guide to Economic Indicators*, 2nd ed., M. E. Sharpe, Armonk, N.Y., 1994, pp. 76-82.

Fuhrer, Jeffrey C., "What Role Does Consumer Sentiment Play in the U.S. Macroeconomy?" *New England Economic Review*, 32-44 (Jan./Feb. 1993).

Garner, C. Alan, "Forecasting Consumer Spending: Should Economists Pay Attention to Consumer Confidence Surveys?" *Economic Review of the Federal Reserve Bank of Kansas City* **76** (3), 57-71 (May/June 1991).

Honomichl, Jack, "'Mood of the People' Predicts What Economists Can't," *Marketing News* **25** (22), 19 (Oct. 28, 1991).

Kinsey, Jean D., "Consumer Confidence: Does It Lead or Lag the Economy?" *Fedgazette* **5** (1), 18 (Jan. 1993).

Linden, Fabian, "The Measure of Consumer Confidence," *Across the Board* **16** (4), 74-79 (April 1979).

Linden, Fabian, "What Do the Experts Know?" *Across the Board* **27** (11), 13-14 (Nov. 1990).

Niemira, Michael P., and Gerald F. Zukowski, *Trading the Fundamentals: The Trader's Guide to Interpreting Economic Indicators and Monetary Policy*, McGraw-Hill, New York, 1998, pp. 35-41.

WEFA Group, *Guide to Economic Indicators: U.S. Macroeconomic Services*, WEFA Group, Bala Cynwyd, Pa., 1997, p. 8.

Consumer Credit
[See Consumer Installment Credit]

Consumer Installment Credit

Estimates of credit extended and credit repaid and of the net change in credit debt outstanding (in 1972 dollars) for credit given to individuals through normal business channels, usually for the purchase of consumer goods.

Every five years, the Federal Reserve conducts benchmark surveys of the outstanding credit extended by finance companies. Other financial institutions (e.g., banks, savings and loan associations, and retailers) are polled annually. The benchmarks are adjusted with monthly survey data. The data are broken down into auto loans, revolving-credit credit cards, mobile-home loans, and other installment loans (e.g., truck, recreational-vehicle, and home-improvement loans). Long-term financings (e.g., mortgages), purchases made with travel and entertainment credit cards, borrowings on life-insurance policies, loans to farmers, and noninstallment credit are excluded. Typically, benchmark surveys are conducted every five years, and these benchmark values are then brought up to date by surveying a sample of the population of creditors on a monthly or annual basis. These intermediate estimates are then adjusted for season and trading day.

Consumer installment credit is used as an indicator of near-term consumer purchasing power and the market for consumer goods often bought on the installment plan. Insofar as consumers deliberately choose to alter their stock of debt with respect to their expected future incomes, consumer installment credit and other forms of consumer debt reflect the general financial position of consumers and is an important element in the demand for funds in the financial community. It is used to calculate a component of the Lagging Indicators Composite Index.

Published monthly by the Board of Governors of the Federal Reserve System in *Consumer Installment Credit*, Statistical Release.

Source	Frequency	Extent	Form	Medium
Annual Statistical Digest (FRB)	a	c	t	p
Bank of Tokyo-Mitsubishi	m	c, h	t	e
BCI	m	h	g	e
Business Statistics	i	h	t	p
Consumer Credit	m	c	t	p
Economic Indicators	m	c, h	t	p, e
Economic Report of the President	a	h	t	p, e
Federal Reserve Board	m	c	t	e
Federal Reserve Bulletin	m	c	t	p
Financial Digest	bw	c	t	p
First Union	m	c, h	t	e
S&P Basic Statistics - Income and Trade	i	h	t	p

Source	Frequency	Extent	Form	Medium
S&P Current Statistics	i	h	t	p
Statistical Abstract	a	h	t	p
Stat-USA	m	c	t	e

Bibliography

Board of Governors of the Federal Reserve System, *Banking and Monetary Statistics, 1941-1970*, Federal Reserve Board, Washington, D.C., 1971.

Dunkelberg, William C., "Analyzing Consumer Spending and Debt," *Business Economics* **24** (3), 17-22 (July 1989).

Frumkin, Norman, *Guide to Economic Indicators*, 2nd ed., M. E. Sharpe, Armonk, N.Y., 1994, pp. 83-86.

Frumkin, Norman, *Tracking America's Economy*, 2nd ed., Sharpe, Armonk, N.Y., 1992, pp. 69-72.

Grant, John, *A Handbook of Economic Indicators*, University of Toronto Press, Toronto, 1992, pp. 150-151.

Hoel, Arline Alchian; Kenneth W. Clarkson; and Roger LeRoy Miller, *Economics Sourcebook of Government Statistics*, Lexington Books, Lexington, Mass., 1983, pp. 112-114.

Joint Economic Committee, *1980 Supplement to Economic Indicators, Historical and Descriptive Background*, USGPO, Washington, D.C., 1980, pp. 98-100.

Kirk, John, "Economic Indicators: The How and the Why," *Banking*, 27-28 (Aug. 1964).

Moore, Geoffrey Hoyt, and Melita H. Moore, *International Economic Indicators: A Sourcebook*, Greenwood Press, Westport, Conn., 1985, pp. 36-37.

Niemira, Michael P., and Gerald F. Zukowski, *Trading the Fundamentals: The Trader's Guide to Interpreting Economic Indicators and Monetary Policy*, McGraw-Hill, New York, 1998, pp. 43-48.

Plocek, Joseph E., *Economic Indicators: How America Reads Its Financial Health*, New York Institute of Finance, New York, 1991, p. 126.

Silvia, John E., and Barry Whall, "Rising Consumer Debt: For Better ... Or for Worse," *Challenge* **31** (1), 55-60 (Jan./Feb. 1988).

Slater, Courtenay M., Ed., Business Statistics of the United States, 1995 ed., Bernan Press, Lanham, Md., 1996, p. 225.

Tainer, Evelina M., *Using Economic Indicators to Improve Investment Analysis*, John Wiley & Sons, New York, 1993, pp. 79-84.

U.S. Department of Commerce, Bureau of Economic Analysis, *Business Statistics, 1963-91*, USGPO, Washington, D.C., 1992, p. 160.

Consumer Price Index
[Formerly called the Cost of Living Index]

The cost for a specific mix of type and quantity of consumer goods and services as related to the cost for an equivalent mix in 1982-1984, covering the prices of everything people buy in the normal courses of their lives, such as food, clothing, transportation, fuel, household supplies, health services and materials, recreational goods and events, and shelter.

This index is calculated by observing the prices of about 400 precisely specified goods and services at points of purchase and by other means nationwide. This sample covers more than 180 classes of goods and services and is taken at about 21,000 retail and service establishments and about 60,000 households in 91 urban areas allocated around the country in such a way as to produce the most accurate national consumer price index possible. Cost data are determined by telephone surveys and personal visits and include all applicable taxes. Data for some of these areas (Chicago, Los Angeles, New York, Philadelphia, and San Francisco) are published monthly, some bimonthly, some semiannually, and some annually, although data for food, fuel, and other selected categories are collected monthly for all geographic areas. The sampling procedures are continually adjusted to reflect new consumer purchasing patterns resulting from changes in relative prices, income, tastes, demographics, technologies, and population. The costs incurred by (1) urban wage earners and clerical workers [CPI-W] (which covers about 42% of the U.S. population) and (2) all urban households [CPI-U] (which covers about 80% of the U.S. population) are then estimated by weighting, averaging, and summing the prices. The prices are then indexed to the price for an equivalent mix in 1982-1984 (1982-1984 = 100). When a statistical series is changed significantly, its new value is linked to a prior old value, and that index will then move upward or downward in accordance with subsequent changes in prices relative to that old value. A new series is based on its value on the date of its introduction. The resulting consumer price index is then broken down into components not only for the two classes of consumers nationwide noted above (CPI-W and CPI-U) but also for classes of goods and services, regions of the country, and major metropolitan areas. For most series, both seasonally adjusted and unadjusted data are published. Local-area CPIs are subject to more variability and statistical error than the national indexes, CPI-W and CPI-U. The indexes are considered to be representative of the changes in costs faced by 90% of the U.S. urban households and 50% of the urban wage and clerical workers.

Used as an escalator (cost of living allowance) or adjustment factor for 20% of union-contract wages; federal, military, and corporate pensions; Social Security, school-lunch, and food-stamp benefits; housing and education grants; rents; royalties; child-support payments; prenuptial agreements; tax computations (to exclude taxes on gains attributable to inflation); and other federal statistics (e.g., retail sales, hourly and weekly earnings, personal consumption expenditures, and the gross national product). It is a major indicator of inflation and as such is used to guide business decisions and in setting and evaluating governmental economic policies. The monthly change in the services class is a component of the Lagging Indicators Composite Index.

Published monthly by the U.S. Department of Labor, Bureau of Labor Statistics, in a press release.

Source	Frequency	Extent	Form	Medium
Agricultural Outlook	m	c	t	p
Agricultural Statistics	a	c	t	p
Annual Statistical Digest (FRB)	a	c	t	p
Bank of America	q	f	t	e
Bank of Tokyo-Mitsubishi	m	c, h	t	e
BCI	m	h	g	e
BLS	m	c, h	t	e
Blue Chip Economic Indicators	m	c, f	t	p
Business Statistics	i	h	t	p
Commodity Yearbook	a	c	t	p
Consumer Price Index	m	c	t	p
Consumer Price Index Detailed Report	m	c, h	t, g	p
Economic Handbook of the Machine Tool Industry	a	h	g	p
Economic Indicators	m	c, h	t, g	p, e
Economic Report of the President	a	h	t	p, e
Federal Reserve Bulletin	m	h	t	p
Financial Digest	bw	h	t	p
First Union	m	c, h	t	e
Forecast	a	c, f	t	p
FRB Chicago	q	c, h	t	e
FRB Dallas	m	c, h	t	e
FRB Minneapolis	m	h	t	e
FRB New York	m	c, h	g	e
FRED	m	c, h	t	e
Handbook of International Economic Statistics (CIA)	a	c	t	p, e
Industry Week	w	f	t	p
International Economic Review	i	c	t	p
International Economic Scoreboard	q	f	t	p
International Financial Statistics	a	c, h	t	p
Monthly Labor Review	m	c, h	t	p
Mortgage Banking	m	c	t	p

Source	Frequency	Extent	Form	Medium
Mutual Fund Factbook	a	h	g	p
Mutual Funds Update	m	c	t	p
Real Estate Outlook	m	c, h	t	p
Recession Recovery Watch	m	h	g	p
Securities Industry Yearbook	a	h	t	p
Social Security Bulletin	a	h	t	p
S&P Basic Statistics - Price Indexes	m	h	t	p
S&P Current Statistics	i	h	t	p
Statistical Abstract	a	h	t	p
Statistical Yearbook of the Electric Utility Industry	a	c	t	p
Stat-USA	m	c	t	e
Survey of Current Business	m	c, h	t, g	p, e
Treasury Bulletin	q	h	g	p
Value Line Investment Survey, Part 2: Selection and Opinion	w	c, h, f	t	p
World Financial Markets	m	c	t	p

Bibliography

Andelman, David A., "Consumer Price, Consumer Hype," *Management Review* **86** (7), 37-40 (July-Aug. 1997).

Bryan, Michael F., and Stephen G. Cecchetti, "The Consumer Price Index as a Measure of Inflation," *Economic Review of the Federal Reserve Bank of Cleveland* 29 (4), 15-24 (1993)

Cagan, Phillip, and Geoffrey H. Moore, *The Consumer Price Index: Issues and Alternatives*, American Enterprise Institute Studies in Economic Policy No. 325, American Enterprise Institute, Washington, D.C., 1981.

Carlson, Keith M., "Do Price Indexes Tell Us about Inflation? A Review of the Issues," *Federal Reserve Bank of St. Louis Review* **71** (6), 12-30 (1989).

Carnes, W. Stansbury, and Stephen D. Slifer, *The Atlas of Economic Indicators: A Visual Guide to Market Forces and the Federal Reserve*, Harper Business, New York, 1991, pp. 111-118.

Darnay, Arsen J., *Economic Indicators Handbook: Time Series, Conversions, Documentation*, Gale Research, Detroit, 1992, pp. 219-223.

Dentzer, Susan, "A Sneak Attack via Statistics: How the Consumer Price Index Is Calculated and Its Economic Effects," *U.S. News & World Report* **121** (23), 78 (Dec. 9, 1996).

Fixler, Dennis, "The Consumer Price Index: Underlying Concepts and Caveats," *Monthly Labor Review* **116** (12), 3-12 (1993).

Frumkin, Norman, *Guide to Economic Indicators*, 2nd ed., M. E. Sharpe, Armonk, N.Y., 1994, pp. 87-92.

Frumkin, Norman, *Tracking America's Economy*, 2nd ed., Sharpe, Armonk, N.Y., 1992, pp. 232-233.

Grant, John, *A Handbook of Economic Indicators*, University of Toronto Press, Toronto, 1992, pp. 151-155.

Hoel, Arline Alchian; Kenneth W. Clarkson; and Roger LeRoy Miller, *Economics Sourcebook of Government Statistics*, Lexington Books, Lexington, Mass., 1983, pp. 3-7.

Lavin, Michael R., *Business Information: How to Find It, How to Use It*, Oryx Press, Phoenix, Ariz., 1992, p. 333.

Marcoot, John L., and Richard C. Bahr, "The Revised Consumer Price Index: Changes in Definitions and Availability," *Monthly Labor Review* 109 (7), 15-23 (1986).

Moore, Geoffrey Hoyt, *The Anatomy of Inflation*, Bureau of Labor Statistics Report No. 373, U.S. Department of Labor, Bureau of Labor Statistics, Washington, 1969.

Moulton, Brent P., "Basic Components of the CPI: Estimation of Price Changes," *Monthly Labor Review* 116 (12), 13-24 (1993).

Nelson, C. R., *The Investor's Guide to Economic Indicators*, John Wiley & Sons, New York, 1987, pp. 23-24.

Niemira, Michael P., and Gerald F. Zukowski, *Trading the Fundamentals: The Trader's Guide to Interpreting Economic Indicators and Monetary Policy*, McGraw-Hill, New York, 1998, pp. 49-60; 112.

Nordhaus, William D., "Beyond the CPI: An Augmented Cost of Living Index (ACOLI)," *Business Economics* 32 (3), 48-53 (July 1997).

Plocek, Joseph E., *Economic Indicators: How America Reads Its Financial Health*, New York Institute of Finance, New York, 1991, pp. 283-287.

Renshaw, Edward, Ed., *The Practical Forecasters' Almanac: 137 Reliable Indicators for Investors, Hedgers, and Speculators*, Business One Irwin, Homewood, Ill., 1992, pp. 63, 66, 70-71.

Rogers, R. Mark, *Handbook of Key Economic Indicators*, Irwin Professional Pub., Burr Ridge, Ill., 1994, pp. 82-108.

Scheibla, Shirley Hobbs, "The Cost of Living: Does the CPI Accurately Measure It?" *Barron's*, pp. 16 + 46-47 (May 22, 1989).

Schmidt, Mary Lynn, "Effects of Updating the CPI Market Basket," *Monthly Labor Review* 116 (12), 59-62 (1993).

Slater, Courtenay M., Ed., *Business Statistics of the United States*, 1995 ed., Bernan Press, Lanham, Md., 1996, pp. 228-229.

Tainer, Evelina M., *Using Economic Indicators to Improve Investment Analysis*, John Wiley & Sons, New York, 1993, pp. 174-180.

U.S. Department of Commerce, Bureau of Economic Analysis, *Business Statistics, 1963-91*, USGPO, Washington, D.C., 1992, pp. 146-148.

U.S. Department of Labor, Bureau of Labor Statistics, *BLS Handbook of Methods*, Bull. 2490, USGPO, Washington, D.C., 1997, pp. 167-230.

U.S. Department of Labor, Bureau of Labor Statistics, *CPI Detailed Report*, USGPO, Washington, D.C., monthly.

U.S. Department of Labor, Bureau of Labor Statistics, *Major Programs of the Bureau of Labor Statistics*, USGPO, Washington, D.C., 1994, pp. 10-11.

U.S. Department of Labor, Bureau of Labor Statistics, *Revising the Consumer Price Index*, Bureau of Labor Statistics, Washington, D.C., 1978.

U.S. Department of Labor, Bureau of Statistics, *The Consumer Price Index: Concepts and Content over the Years*, Bureau of Labor Statistics, Washington, D.C., May 1978.

WEFA Group, *Guide to Economic Indicators: U.S. Macroeconomic Services*, WEFA Group, Bala Cynwyd, Pa., 1997, p. 9.

Wynne, Mark A., and Fiona D. Sigalla, "The Consumer Price Index," *Economic Review of the Federal Reserve Bank of Dallas* 1-22 (Second Quarter, 1994).

Consumer Prices, Major Industrial Countries

Estimated change in the average cost of living in the United States, Canada, Japan, France, Germany, Italy, and England since a given reference date.

Methods of calculating the price index vary from country to country. Generally, a particular "market basket," including rent and ordinary services is specified, and the cost for that given mix and quantity of goods and services is surveyed each month at a regular time. The weighted sum of the similar costs is then indexed to the cost found for the items some time in the past (ranging from 1970 to 1976). The sample population may or may not include rural families. The indexes are not seasonally adjusted; all are adjusted to an index value of 100 for 1967. The data for the various countries are roughly comparable, but not strictly comparable because of differences in the methods used to compile each country's values.

Used to determine changes and trends in the costs of goods and services purchased by the average wage earner in the respective foreign country.

Published monthly by the U.S. Department of Commerce, International Trade Administration, Office of Planning and Research, in *International Economic Indicators*.

Source	Frequency	Extent	Form	Medium
Economic Indicators	m	c, h	t	p, e
Handbook of International Economic Statistics (CIA)	a	c	t	p, e
International Economic Review	i	c	t	p
International Economic Scoreboard	a	f	t	p

Source	Frequency	Extent	Form	Medium
Statistical Abstract	a	h	t	p
United Nations Statistical Yearbook	a	h	t	p

Bibliography

Cagan, Phillip, and Geoffrey H. Moore, *The Consumer Price Index: Issues and Alternatives*, American Enterprise Institute Studies in Economic Policy No. 325, American Enterprise Institute, Washington, D.C., 1981.

Joint Economic Committee, *1980 Supplement to Economic Indicators, Historical and Descriptive Background*, USGPO, Washington, D.C., 1980, pp. 127-129.

Consumer Sentiment Index
[See Index of Consumer Expectations]

Consumer Spending
[See Personal Consumption Expenditures and Retail Sales]

Contract Awards
[See Construction Contract Awards]

Contracts and Orders for Plant and Equipment
[Also called Plant and Equipment Expenditures; see Business Investment and Plans]

Corporate Bond Yield Averages
[See Moody's Corporate Aaa Bond Yield Averages]

Corporate Profits
[Also called After-Tax Corporate Profits]

Profits earned by U.S. corporations before and after taxes.

Annual tabulations by the Internal Revenue Service of corporate profits reported on unaudited tax returns are adjusted to make them comparable with other measures of income and extrapolated with quarterly data from the Federal Trade Commission, from federal regulatory agencies, and from surveys and miscellaneous sources. The resulting before-taxes estimated corporate profits are then seasonally adjusted. Dividends are estimated from a survey of publicly reported dividends. Other components of profit are estimated as residuals. Undistributed profits essentially equal the change in corporate net worth produced by current operations. Data given for all domestic industries and for the financial, manufacturing, and wholesale and retail trade sectors; data include inventory valuation. Also presented as profits earned after taxes, showing the distribution among taxes, dividends, undistributed profits, and inventory.

In that it measures the contribution of corporate profits to the national income, this indicator is used to assess the state of health of a substantial part of the nation's business community and is used to assess future tax receipts and budgets.

Published by the U.S. Department of Commerce, Bureau of Economic Analysis, in *Survey of Current Business*.

Source	Frequency	Extent	Form	Medium
BCI	m	h	g	e
Economic Indicators	m	c, h	t, g	p, e
Economic Report of the President	a	h	t	p, e
Federal Reserve Bulletin	m	c	t	p
Forecast	a	c, f	t	p
FRED	m	c, h	t	e
Recession Recovery Watch	m	h	g	p
S&P Current Statistics	i	c	t	p
Statistical Abstract	a	h	t	p
Survey of Current Business	m	c	t	p, e
Value Line Investment Survey, Part 2: Selection and Opinion	w	c, h, f	t	p

Bibliography

Joint Economic Committee, *1980 Supplement to Economic Indicators, Historical and Descriptive Background*, USGPO, Washington, D.C., 1980, pp. 23-26.

Moore, Geoffrey Hoyt, and Melita H. Moore, *International Economic Indicators: A Sourcebook*, Greenwood Press, Westport, Conn., 1985, p. 35.

Office of Federal Statistical Policy and Standards, *Gross National Product Data Improvement Project Report*, U.S. Department of Commerce, Washington, D.C., 1977.

Tainer, Evelina M., *Using Economic Indicators to Improve Investment Analysis*, John Wiley & Sons, New York, 1993, pp. 47-51.

Cost of Laughing Index
[See Appendix A. Nonquantitative Indicators]

Cost of Living Index
[See Consumer Price Index]

CRB-BLS Spot Market Index
[See Bridge-CRB Index]

CRB (BLS-Formula) Spot Group Indices, Raw Industrials
[See Bridge-CRB Index]

CRB Spot Price Index
[See Bridge-CRB Index]

Crude Oil Prices
[See Oil Prices]

Current Assets and Liabilities of Nonfinancial Corporations

A measure of the net working capital (cash, U.S. Government securities, notes and accounts receivable, inventories, and other current assets less notes and accounts payable and other current liabilities) of a significant segment of U.S. business.

The data are derived primarily from the quarterly reports from corporations required by the Federal Trade Commission and various regulatory agencies. The data are directly benchmarked to annual tabulations prepared by regulatory agencies. Data on other industries are derived indirectly. The data are periodically benchmarked to the Statistics of Income prepared by the Internal Revenue Service.

Used by business and industry for investment analysis and by the government to prepare the national economic and flow-of-funds accounts.

Published quarterly by the Federal Trade Commission and the Board of Governors of the Federal Reserve System in the *Federal Reserve Bulletin*.

Source	Frequency	Extent	Form	Medium
Annual Statistical Digest (FRB)	a	c	t	p
Federal Reserve Bulletin	m	c	t	p
Statistical Abstract	a	h	t	p

Bibliography

Joint Economic Committee, *1980 Supplement to Economic Indicators, Historical and Descriptive Background*, USGPO, Washington, D.C., 1980, pp. 106-108.
"Working Capital of Nonfinancial Corporations," *Federal Reserve Bulletin* **64**, 533-537 (July 1978).

D

Daily Price Index of Industrial Materials
[See Change in Industrial Materials Price Index]

Darts Average
[See Appendix A. Nonquantitative Indicators]

Delinquency Rate on Consumer Loans
[See also Mortgage Delinquencies and Mortgage Delinquency Rate]

A measure of the ability of the borrowing public to meet its financial obligations.

The American Bankers Association surveys its member banks each quarter to determine the performance of consumer loans, including the number of consumer loans whose payments are 30 days or more past due. The delinquency rate is calculated as the percentage of those loans that are in arrears. The consumer loans are divided into eight categories: auto loans made directly by banks, auto loans purchased by banks from other loan originators, personal loans, fixed-term second mortgages, home-improvement loans, recreational-vehicle loans, mobile-home loans, and boat loans. Delinquency rates are calculated for each category as well as for the composite. Delinquency rates for credit-card debt are not included in this calculation, but are reported separately by the American Bankers Association.

Used as an indicator of the overall health of the economy under the assumption that, when business, jobs, and cash are short, individuals are unable or unwilling to make timely payments on their outstanding debt.

Announced quarterly by the American Bankers Association in *Consumer Credit Delinquency Bulletin*.

Source	Frequency	Extent	Form	Medium
Consumer Credit Delinquency Bulletin	q	c	t	p
Statistical Abstract	a	h	t	p

Department of Commerce Composite Construction Cost Index
[See Composite Construction Price Index]

Deposit Turnover

The ratio of bank debits to bank deposits.

This indicator is constructed from the total debits and deposits that are reported to the Federal Reserve System by all member banks once a month. These respective reported figures are totaled, and the total deposits are divided into the total debits.

Used as an indicator of the total velocity of money (a measure of the number of times money circulates in one year) and as an indicator of fluctuations of the business cycle.

Published monthly by the Board of Governors of the Federal Reserve System in *Federal Reserve Bulletin*.

Source	Frequency	Extent	Form	Medium
Annual Statistical Digest (FRB)	a	c	t	p
Debits and Deposit Turnover at Commercial Banks	m	c	t	p
Federal Reserve Bulletin	m	c	t	p
S&P Basic Statistics - Banking and Finance	i	h	t	p
S&P Current Statistics	i	h	t	p
Statistical Abstract	a	h	t	p

Bibliography

Garvy, George, *Debits and Clearings Statistics and Their Use*, Greenwood Press, Westport, Conn., 1982; reprint of George Garvy, *Debits and Clearings Statistics and Their Use*, Board of Governors of the Federal Reserve System, Washington, D.C., 1959.

Discomfort Index
[See Misery Index in Appendix A. Nonquantitative Indicators]

Discount Rate
[See Federal Reserve Discount Rate]

Disposable Personal Income
[See also Sources of Personal Income and Disposition of Personal Income]

The income available to persons for spending or saving.

The U.S. Department of Commerce's Bureau of Economic Analysis calculates the aggregate personal income of U.S. citizens and residents. From that estimate, all estimated personal tax and nontax payments to public agencies is subtracted; these aggregate payments include all financial obligations to governmental agencies (e.g., taxes, fees, forfeitures, tuition, and hospital bills). The individual is considered to have discretionary use of the remainder. Reported in billions of current and constant dollars; also reported on a per capita basis with midyear population estimates from the Bureau of the Census.

Used to forecast consumption expenditures for goods and services, as a component in the measurement of the nation's standard of living, and in the calculation of a component of the Coincident Indicators Composite Index.

Published monthly by the U.S. Department of Commerce, Bureau of Economic Analysis, in *Personal Income and Outlays*.

Source	Frequency	Extent	Form	Medium
Agricultural Outlook	m	c	t	p
Agricultural Statistics	a	h	t	p
Bank of America	q	c, h	t	e
Bank of Tokyo-Mitsubishi	m	c, h	t	e
BCI	m	h	g	e
BEA	q	c, h	t	e
Blue Chip Economic Indicators	m	c, f	t	p
Business Statistics	i	h	t	p
Conference Board/BCI	m	c	t	e
Economic Indicators	m	c, h	t, g	p, e
Federal Reserve Bulletin	m	c	t	p
First Union	m	c, h	t	e
FRED	m	c, h	t	e
S&P Current Statistics	i	c	t	p
Statistical Abstract	a	h	t	p
Stat-USA	m	c	t	e
Survey of Current Business	m	c	t	p, e
US Census Bureau	a	c, h	t	e
Value Line Investment Survey, Part 2: Selection and Opinion	w	c	t	p

Bibliography

Carnes, W. Stansbury, and Stephen D. Slifer, *The Atlas of Economic Indicators: A Visual Guide to Market Forces and the Federal Reserve*, Harper Business, New York, 1991, 127-134.

Frumkin, Norman, *Guide to Economic Indicators*, 2nd ed., M. E. Sharpe, Armonk, N.Y., 1994, pp. 235-239.

Hoel, Arline Alchian; Kenneth W. Clarkson; and Roger LeRoy Miller, *Economics Sourcebook of Government Statistics*, Lexington Books, Lexington, Mass., 1983, pp. 73-79.

Kirk, John, "Economic Indicators: The How and the Why," *Banking*, 27-28 (Aug. 1964).

Niemira, Michael P., and Gerald F. Zukowski, *Trading the Fundamentals: The Trader's Guide to Interpreting Economic Indicators and Monetary Policy*, McGraw-Hill, New York, 1998, pp. 187-195.

Rogers, R. Mark, *Handbook of Key Economic Indicators*, Irwin Professional Pub., Burr Ridge, Ill., 1994, pp. 41-61.

Slater, Courtenay M., Ed., Business Statistics of the United States, 1995 ed., Bernan Press, Lanham, Md., 1996, pp. 221-225.

Snyder, Richard M., *Measuring Business Changes*, Wiley, New York, 1955, p. 20 ff.

U.S. Department of Commerce, Bureau of Economic Analysis, *Business Statistics, 1963-91*, USGPO, Washington, D.C., 1992, pp. 142-143.

WEFA Group, *Guide to Economic Indicators: U.S. Macroeconomic Services*, WEFA Group, Bala Cynwyd, Pa., 1997, p. 21.

Disposition of Personal Income

[See also Disposable Personal Income and Personal Consumption Expenditures]

An analysis and tabulation of the uses to which individuals in the United States put their earnings.

This indicator is calculated by first subtracting from the U.S. aggregate total personal income the aggregate estimated personal taxes paid and nontax payments made to give the aggregate estimated disposable personal income of the United States. From this disposable personal income is subtracted the estimated personal outlays (personal consumption expenditures, interest paid by consumers to business, and personal transfer payments to foreigners) to give the amount saved by individuals, expressed both as an aggregate amount and as a percentage of disposable personal income. The personal consumption expenditures are derived for benchmark years by taking the producers' prices for goods produced and adding to them estimates of transportation charges, trade markups, and taxes. These benchmark data are updated quarterly with the Census Bureau's retail sales figures and other data. The aggregate disposable personal-income and personal-consumption-expenditure data are reduced to per capita figures by dividing them by the Census

Bureau's estimate of total population of the United States. These per capita values are then deflated to constant dollars by dividing them by an implicit deflator.

Used as an indicator of income available for spending or saving; of trends in consumer purchases; and of the division of the national output among consumer demand, business capital formation, and other expenditures.

Published quarterly by the U.S. Department of Commerce, Bureau of Economic Analysis and Bureau of the Census, in *Personal Income and Outlays*.

Source	Frequency	Extent	Form	Medium
Business Statistics	i	h	t	p
Economic Indicators	m	c, h	t	p, e
Economic Report of the President	a	h	t	p, e
Statistical Abstract	a	h	t	p
Survey of Current Business	m	c	t	p, e

Bibliography

Joint Economic Committee, *1980 Supplement to Economic Indicators, Historical and Descriptive Background*, USGPO, Washington, D.C., 1980, pp. 15-19.

Rogers, R. Mark, *Handbook of Key Economic Indicators*, Irwin Professional Pub., Burr Ridge, Ill., 1994, pp. 41-61.

Dividend-Price Ratio
[See Standard and Poor's 500 Price-Earnings Ratio]

Dollar Index
[See Federal Reserve Trade-Weighted Dollar and Morgan Guaranty Index]

Dom Perignon Champagne New Year's Celebration Index
[See Appendix A. Nonquantitative Indicators]

Domestic Crude Oil Production
[See Petroleum Production]

Donoghue's Money Fund Average
[See Money Fund Average]

Dow Jones 20-Bond Average

A daily comparison of the closing prices of ten public utilities and ten industrial issues.

Formerly called the Dow Jones 40-Bond Average when it included bonds issued by 20 railroad corporations, this indicator is now based on the selected bonds of ten public utilities and ten industrial corporations listed on the New York

Stock Exchange. The closing prices of those stocks are summed each day and arithmetically averaged. Two subindexes, the Dow Jones 10 Utility Bond Average and the Dow Jones 10 Industrial Bond Average, are also derived from the same prices and in the same manner.

Used as a yardstick to compare the yields of various bonds.

Published daily by Dow Jones & Co. in *The Wall Street Journal*.

Source	Frequency	Extent	Form	Medium
Barron's	w	c	t	p
Investor's Business Daily	d	c	t	p
Wall Street Journal	d	c	t	p

Bibliography

Berlin, Howard M. *The Handbook of Financial Market Indexes, Averages, and Indicators*, Dow Jones-Irwin, Homewood, Ill., 1990, p. 81.

Moore, Geoffrey H., *Leading Indicators for the 1990s*, Dow Jones-Irwin, Homewood, Ill., 1990, p. 133.

Pierce, Phyllis S., Ed., *The Dow Jones Averages, 1885-1995*, Professional Publishing, Chicago, 1996, pages not numbered.

"Welcome to Dow Jones Averages," averages.dowjones.com/home.html, visited July 15, 1999.

Dow Jones 65
[See Dow Jones Composite Average]

Dow Jones Average
[See Dow Jones 20-Bond Average, Dow Jones Composite Average, Dow Jones Industrial Average, Dow Jones Transportation Average, and Dow Jones Utilities Average]

Dow Jones Commodity Futures Index

A general measure of the trend in prices of contracts for the future delivery of agricultural and industrial raw materials.

Prices for futures contracts extending five months (150 days) in the future are calculated for twelve commodities (corn, soybeans, wheat, coffee, cotton, sugar, copper, gold, silver, live cattle, hogs, and lumber). The five-month contract price for each commodity is determined by taking two contract months, one expiring in fewer than 150 days and one expiring in more than 150 days. Weights are assigned to each of the two contracts based on the number of days between the expected expiration date and the 150th day. The price of each of the two contracts is multiplied by its weighting factor, the results are added, and the sum is divided by the ratio of (1) the number of days between the expiration dates of the two contracts and (2) 150. Each of those 12 five-month commodity-futures prices is divided by its price on the base date, and the results are totaled, divided by 12, and multiplied by 100. This indexes the aggregate price to a base of 100 as of Dec. 31, 1974. When the monthly value for the index is cited, the prices for the last trading day of the month are used.

Used as a general indicator of the trend in futures markets, as an indicator of future trends in the costs for foodstuffs and raw materials, and as an indicator of emerging inflation. The differences between futures and spot prices are regarded by some as indicative of future price movements.

Compiled hourly by Dow Jones, and the closing value is published daily in *The Wall Street Journal*.

Source	Frequency	Extent	Form	Medium
Wall Street Journal	d	c	t	p

Bibliography
Lehmann, Michael B., *The Irwin Guide to Using* The Wall Street Journal, 5th ed., Irwin, Chicago, 1996, pp. 223-241.
"New Indexes of Commodity Futures, Spot Prices with Broader Content Start Today at Dow Jones," *Wall Street Journal*, p. 46 (Jan. 4, 1982).
Plocek, Joseph E., *Economic Indicators: How America Reads Its Financial Health*, New York Institute of Finance, New York, 1991, pp. 273-276.

Dow Jones Commodity Spot-Price Index

A measure of prices of widely traded commodities; the average movement in prices of basic agricultural products and industrial raw materials.

The spot prices of twelve commodities (corn, soybeans, wheat, coffee, cotton, sugar, copper, gold, silver, live cattle, hogs, and lumber) are determined at the close of trading each day. Each of those commodity prices is divided by its price on the base date, and the results are totaled, divided by 12, and multiplied by 100. This indexes the aggregate price to a base of 100 as of Dec. 31, 1974. When the monthly value for the index is cited, the prices for the last trading day of the month are used.

Used as an indicator of current prices for foodstuffs and raw materials, as an indicator of inflation, and as a comparator for the prices of futures contracts for delivery of commodities at later dates. The differences between futures and spot prices are regarded by some as indicative of future price movements.

Compiled daily at the close of trading by Dow Jones and published in *The Wall Street Journal*.

Source	Frequency	Extent	Form	Medium
Wall Street Journal	d	c	t	p

Bibliography
Lehmann, Michael B., *The Irwin Guide to Using* The Wall Street Journal, 5th ed., Irwin, Chicago, 1996, pp. 223-241.

"New Indexes of Commodity Futures, Spot Prices with Broader Content Start Today at Dow Jones," *Wall Street Journal*, p. 46 (Jan. 4, 1982).

Plocek, Joseph E., *Economic Indicators: How America Reads Its Financial Health*, New York Institute of Finance, New York, 1991, pp. 273-276.

Dow Jones Composite Average

A daily comparison of the closing prices of about 65 selected securities.

Dow Jones selects the common stocks of about 65 corporations listed on the New York Stock Exchange. These corporations are those included in the industrial, utilities, and transportation averages. It then sums the closing prices of those stocks each day. The total is then divided by a constant divisor to produce the average. This is not a strict arithmetic average because the constant divisor is not the number of listings being averaged. It is, instead, a number derived from the previous day's average, taking into account the effects of stock splits, dividends, or substitutions. The constant divisor is revised by recalculating the sum of the previous day's closing prices with new values for affected stocks (e.g., with one-third of the old price for a stock that split 3:1) and dividing that new sum by the average that had originally been calculated for that day. The resulting new constant divisor is used for calculating subsequent days' averages. A new constant divisor is calculated for the Composite Average if stock splits or other changes in individual component stocks cause an appreciable distortion in the Average.

An indicator of stock-market cycles, prices, and valuation.

Published daily by Dow Jones & Co. in *The Wall Street Journal*.

Source	Frequency	Extent	Form	Medium
Barron's	w	h	t	p
Bloomberg	h	c	t	e
Business Statistics	i	c	t	p
Dow Jones	h	c	t	e
Financial Digest	a	c	t	p
Historical Statistics	i	h	t	p
New York Times	d	c	t	p
S&P Current Statistics	i	c	t	p
Statistical Abstract	a	h	t	p
Value Line Investment Survey, Part 2: Selection and Opinion	w	c	t	p
Wall Street Journal	d	c	t	p

Bibliography

Berlin, Howard M. *The Handbook of Financial Market Indexes, Averages, and Indicators*, Dow Jones-Irwin, Homewood, Ill., 1990, p. 14.

Hoel, Arline Alchian; Kenneth W. Clarkson; and Roger LeRoy Miller, *Economics Sourcebook of Government Statistics*, Lexington Books, Lexington, Mass., 1983, pp. 155-157.

Munn, Glenn G.; F. L. Garcia; and Charles J. Woelfel, *Encyclopedia of Banking and Finance*, Bankers Publishing, Rolling Meadows, Ill., 1991.

Willoughby, Jack, "The Stock Market Is a Lousy Economic Forecaster," *Forbes* **140**, 32-34 (Nov. 30, 1987).

Dow Jones Equity Market Index
[See Dow Jones Global-U.S. Index]

Dow Jones Global-U.S. Index
A broad-based indicator of the movement of the share prices of New York Stock Exchange, American Stock Exchange, and over-the-counter stocks.

More than 700 stocks are selected from those listed on the New York Stock Exchange, American Stock Exchange, and over-the-counter market to represent about 80% of the equities market. The index is capitalization weighted and indexed to a base of 100 for June 30, 1982. The index is also broken down into nine component sectors (basic materials, energy, industry, cyclical consumer goods, noncyclical consumer goods, technology, financial services, utilities, and conglomerates), and these sectors are further subdivided into 82 industry groups. Individual indexes (e.g., the Dow Jones Precious Metals Index) are calculated and published for some of these industry groups, again on a capitalization-weighted basis.

Used as a measure of overall stock-market performance.

Published daily in *The Wall Street Journal* by Dow Jones.

Source	Frequency	Extent	Form	Medium
Barron's	w	c	t	p
Wall Street Journal	d	c	t	p

Bibliography
Berlin, Howard M. *The Handbook of Financial Market Indexes, Averages, and Indicators*, Dow Jones-Irwin, Homewood, Ill., 1990, p. 14.

Dow Jones Industrial Average
A measure of the market-price movement of the securities of 30 industrial (i.e., not transportation or utility) corporations; a widely used barometer of the stock market.

The editors of *The Wall Street Journal* select 30 industrial common stocks. The closing prices of those stocks are summed, and this total is then divided by a constant divisor to produce the average. This is not a strict arithmetic average because the constant divisor is not the number of listings being averaged. It is, instead, a number derived from the previous day's average, taking into account the effects of stock splits, stock dividends, and substitutions within the list of selected stocks. The constant divisor is revised by recalculating the sum of the previous day's closing prices with new values for affected stocks (e.g., with one-third of the old price for a stock that split 3:1) and dividing that new sum by the average that had originally been calculated for that day. The resulting new constant divisor is used for calculating subsequent days' averages. A new constant divisor is calculated for the Average if a stock splits or other changes in individual component stocks cause a change in the Average of five or more points. The component stocks and the current divisor can be found in the footnotes to the Average in each issue of *The Wall Street Journal*. The Average's data series of comparable values extends from Oct. 1, 1928, to the present. As of Nov. 1, 1999, the 30 stocks were Allied Signal, Aluminum Company of America, American Express, AT&T, Boeing, Caterpillar, Citigroup, Coca Cola, Walt Disney, E. I. Du Pont De Nemours & Co., Eastman Kodak, Exxon, General Electric, General Motors, Hewlett Packard, Home Depot, Intel Corp., International Business Machines, International Paper, Johnson & Johnson, JP Morgan & Co., McDonalds, Merck & Co., Microsoft Corp., Minnesota Mining & Manufacturing, Philip Morris, Procter & Gamble, SBC Communications, United Technologies, and Wal-Mart Stores. This selection of stocks is subject to change at any time.

The Dow Jones Industrial Average (DJIA) is the most widely quoted stock market indicator and it is used to track stock-market cycles. It does have limitations, representing as it does only a small number of stocks, and those are for large companies that are generally highly capitalized. The index is licensed for use as the basis for option and futures trading.

The DJIA is compiled by Dow Jones & Co., and the value at the close of business is published the next business day in *The Wall Street Journal* and appears on nightly television network news. More frequent calculations of the Average are available on CNN Headline News, the New York Stock Exchange ticker, and various electronic stock-quotation services.

Source	Frequency	Extent	Form	Medium
Barron's	w	c	t, g	p
Bridge	d	c	t	e
Business Statistics	i	h	t	p
Business Week	w (h)	c	t	p (e)
CBS	h	c	t	e
CNN	h	c	t	e
Dow Jones	h	c	t	e
Economic Indicators	m	c, h	t	p, e
Financial Digest	bw	c	t	p

– D –

Source	Frequency	Extent	Form	Medium
First Union	m	c, h	t	e
Investor's Business Daily	d	c, h	t, g	p
Media General	d	c	t	e
Moody's Handbook of Common Stocks	q	h	g	p
Mutual Funds Update	m	c	t	p
NASDAQ Factbook	a	h	g	p
New York Times	d (h)	c	t, g	p (e)
Outlook	w	c	t	p
PCQuote	h	c	t	e
Quote.com	h	c	t	e
Securities Industry Trends	m	c, h	t	p
Securities Industry Yearbook	a	h	t	p
S&P Current Statistics	i	h	t	p
Statistical Abstract	a	h	t	p
StockMaster	d	c, h	g, t	e
USA Today	d (h)	c	t	p (e)
Value Line Investment Survey, Part 2: Selection and Opinion	w	c	t	p
Wall Street Journal	d	c	t, g	p

Bibliography

"America's Diverging Stockmarket Indices: Push-Me-Pull-You," *Economist* **314** (7643), 84 (Feb. 24, 1990).

Browning, E. S., "'New Economy' Stocks Join Industrials," *Wall Street Journal*, pp. C1 and C15 (Oct. 27, 1999).

Dreman, David, "Meaningless Signals," *Forbes* **136**, 230 (Dec. 16, 1985).

Frumkin, Norman, *Guide to Economic Indicators*, 2nd ed., M. E. Sharpe, Armonk, N.Y., 1994, pp. 275-286.

Hoel, Arline Alchian; Kenneth W. Clarkson; and Roger LeRoy Miller, *Economics Sourcebook of Government Statistics*, Lexington Books, Lexington, Mass., 1983, pp. 155-157.

Merjos, Anna, "How's the Market Doing? It Often Depends on Which Index You Use," *Barron's* **70** (34), 18-20; 27-28 (Aug. 20, 1990).

Norris, Floyd, "Dow Takes on a New, High-Technology Look," *New York Times*, pp. C1 and C15 (Oct. 27, 1999).

Penner, Karen, "Does the Market Matter? Yes, but in Surprising New Ways," *Business Week* (3131), 24-26 (Oct. 30, 1989).

Pierce, Phyllis S., Ed., *The Dow Jones Averages, 1885-1995*, Professional Publishing, Chicago, 1996, pages not numbered.

Pring, Martin J., *Technical Analysis Explained, An Illustrated Guide for the Investor*, McGraw-Hill, New York, 1980, pp. 112-119.

"Welcome to Dow Jones Averages," averages.dowjones.com/home.html, visited July 15, 1999.

Willoughby, Jack, "The Stock Market Is a Lousy Economic Forecaster," *Forbes* **140**, 32-34 (Nov. 30, 1987).

Dow Jones Railroads Average
[See Dow Jones Transportation Average]

Dow Jones Transportation Average
[Formerly Dow Jones Railroads Average]

A comparison of the prices of the securities of about 20 corporations in the transportation industry.

The editors of *The Wall Street Journal* select about 20 transportation-industry common stocks. The closing prices of those stocks are summed, and this total is then divided by a constant divisor to produce the average. This is not a strict arithmetic average because the constant divisor is not the number of listings being averaged. It is, instead, a number derived from the previous day's average, taking into account the effects of stock splits, dividends, or substitutions. The constant divisor is revised by recalculating the sum of the previous day's closing prices with new values for affected stocks (e.g., with one-third of the old price for a stock that split 3:1) and dividing that new sum by the average that had originally been calculated for that day. The resulting new constant divisor is used for calculating subsequent days' averages. A new constant divisor is calculated for the Transportation Average if stock splits or other changes in individual component stocks cause a change in the Average of two or more points.

Used as a technical indicator of stock-market cycles, as an indicator of the performance of the equities that make up the transportation sector, and as an indicator of investor confidence in the transportation sector.

Published daily by Dow Jones & Co. in *The Wall Street Journal*.

Source	Frequency	Extent	Form	Medium
Barron's	w	c	t, g	p
Bloomberg	h	c	t	e
Business Statistics	a	h	t	p
Business Week	h	c	t	e
CBS	h	c	t	e
CNN	h	c	t	e
Dow Jones	h	c	t	e

Source	Frequency	Extent	Form	Medium
Financial Digest	bw	c	t	p
Investor's Business Daily	d	c, h	t, g	p
New York Times	d	c	t	p
PCQuote	h	c	t	e
S&P Current Statistics	i	h	t	p
Statistical Abstract	a	h	t	p
USA Today	d (h)	c	t	p (e)
Value Line Investment Survey, Part 2: Selection and Opinion	w	c	t	p
Wall Street Journal	d	c	t	p

Bibliography

Berlin, Howard M. *The Handbook of Financial Market Indexes, Averages, and Indicators*, Dow Jones-Irwin, Homewood, Ill., 1990, p. 14.

Donlan, Thomas G., "Canaries in the Mine: Airlines Offer a Leading Economic Indicator," *Barron's* **77** (10), 51 (July 28, 1997).

Hoel, Arline Alchian; Kenneth W. Clarkson; and Roger LeRoy Miller, *Economics Sourcebook of Government Statistics*, Lexington Books, Lexington, Mass., 1983, pp. 155-157.

Munn, Glenn G.; F. L. Garcia; and Charles J. Woelfel, *Encyclopedia of Banking and Finance*, Bankers Publishing, Rolling Meadows, Ill., 1991.

Pierce, Phyllis S., Ed., *The Dow Jones Averages, 1885-1995*, Professional Publishing, Chicago, 1996, pages not numbered.

"Welcome to Dow Jones Averages," averages.dowjones.com/home.html, visited July 15, 1999.

Willoughby, Jack, "The Stock Market Is a Lousy Economic Forecaster," *Forbes* **140**, 32-34 (Nov. 30, 1987).

Dow Jones Utilities Average

A comparison of the prices of the securities of about 15 utility corporations.

The editors of *The Wall Street Journal* select about 15 electric or gas utilities' common stocks. The prices of those stocks are summed, and this total is then divided by a constant divisor to produce the average. This is not a strict arithmetic average because the constant divisor is not the number of listings being averaged. It is, instead, a number derived from the previous day's average, taking into account the effects of stock splits, dividends, or substitutions. The constant divisor is revised by recalculating the sum of the previous day's closing prices with new values for affected stocks (e.g., with one-third of the old price for a stock that split 3:1) and dividing that new sum by the average that had originally been calculated for that day. The resulting new constant divisor is used for calculating subsequent days' averages. A new constant divisor is calculated for the Utilities Average if stock splits or other changes in individual component stocks cause a change in the Average of one or more points.

Used as a technical indicator of stock-market cycles, as an indicator of the performance of the equities that make up the utilities sector, and as an indicator of investor confidence in the utilities sector.

Published daily by Dow Jones & Co. in *The Wall Street Journal*.

Source	Frequency	Extent	Form	Medium
Barron's	w	c	t, g	p
Bloomberg	h	c	t	e
Business Statistics	a	h	t	p
Business Week	h	c	t	e
CBS	h	c	t	e
CNN	h	c	t	e
Dow Jones	h	c	t	e
Financial Digest	bw	c	t	p
Investor's Business Daily	d	c, h	t, g	p
New York Times	d	c	t	p
PCQuote	h	c	t	e
S&P Current Statistics	i	h	t	p
Statistical Abstract	a	h	t	p
StockMaster	d	c, h	g, t	e
USA Today	d (h)	c	t	p (e)
Value Line Investment Survey, Part 2: Selection and Opinion	w	c	t	p
Wall Street Journal	d	c	t	p

Bibliography

Berlin, Howard M. *The Handbook of Financial Market Indexes, Averages, and Indicators*, Dow Jones-Irwin, Homewood, Ill., 1990, p. 14.

Hoel, Arline Alchian; Kenneth W. Clarkson; and Roger LeRoy Miller, *Economics Sourcebook of Government Statistics*, Lexington Books, Lexington, Mass., 1983, pp. 155-157.

Munn, Glenn G.; F. L. Garcia; and Charles J. Woelfel, *Encyclopedia of Banking and Finance*, Bankers Publishing, Rolling Meadows, Ill., 1991.

Pierce, Phyllis S., Ed., *The Dow Jones Averages, 1885-1995*, Professional Publishing, Chicago, 1996, pages not numbered.

"Welcome to Dow Jones Averages," averages.dowjones.com/home.html, visited July 15, 1999.

Willoughby, Jack, "The Stock Market Is a Lousy Economic Forecaster," *Forbes*
  140, 32-34 (Nov. 30, 1987).

Drinking Couple Count
[See Appendix A. Nonquantitative Indicators]

Dun & Bradstreet Number of Business Failures
[See Business Failures]

Durable Goods
[See also Manufacturers' New Orders; Manufacturers' Orders; and
Manufacturers' New Orders: Capital Goods Industries, Nondefense]
    An estimate of the new orders received during a given month (less
cancellations) by manufacturers of durable goods (manufactures that are expected
to last more than three years).
    The Durable Goods value is a subset of the Manufacturers' New Orders.
Manufacturers are surveyed monthly by the Bureau of the Census and asked to
report the sales value of orders for goods to be delivered at some future date, the
sales value of orders filled immediately during the month, and the net sales value
of contract changes that have resulted in increases or decreases in order values.
New orders are defined as orders supported by binding legal documents. The value
of any cancellations is to be deducted from the totals. Because some companies
report only backlogs of unfilled orders and in order to maintain the distinction
between orders and shipments, orders remaining unfilled at the end of the monthly
reporting period are estimated directly and separately and they are then combined
with shipments data to produce the new-orders data. Although the new-orders data
are not independently seasonally adjusted, they are derived from data that are
seasonally adjusted.
    Used as a leading indicator of the strength of the manufacturing sector and of
the general economy; a gauge of future industrial activity.
    Published monthly by the U.S. Department of Commerce, Bureau of the
Census, in *Survey of Current Business*.

Source	Frequency	Extent	Form	Medium
Bank of America	q	c, h	t	e
Bank of Tokyo-Mitsubishi	m	c, h	t	e
Barron's	w	c	t	p
Business Statistics	i	h	t	p
Economic Handbook of the Machine Tool Industry	a	h	t	p
First Union	m	c, h	t	e

Source	Frequency	Extent	Form	Medium
FRB Dallas	m	c, h	t	e
S&P Current Statistics	i	h	t	p
Stat-USA	m	c	t	e
Survey of Current Business	m	c	t	p, e

Bibliography

Carnes, W. Stansbury, and Stephen D. Slifer, *The Atlas of Economic Indicators: A Visual Guide to Market Forces and the Federal Reserve*, Harper Business, New York, 1991, pp. 119-126.

Grant, John, *A Handbook of Economic Indicators*, University of Toronto Press, Toronto, 1992, pp. 155-156.

Niemira, Michael P., and Gerald F. Zukowski, *Trading the Fundamentals: The Trader's Guide to Interpreting Economic Indicators and Monetary Policy*, McGraw-Hill, New York, 1998, pp. 67-72.

Plocek, Joseph E., *Economic Indicators: How America Reads Its Financial Health*, New York Institute of Finance, New York, 1991, p. 203.

Tainer, Evelina M., *Using Economic Indicators to Improve Investment Analysis*, John Wiley & Sons, New York, 1993, pp. 98-103.

WEFA Group, *Guide to Economic Indicators: U.S. Macroeconomic Services*, WEFA Group, Bala Cynwyd, Pa., 1997, p. 11.

Zarnowitz, Victor, "Cyclical Aspects of Incorporations and the Formation of New Business Enterprises," pp. 386-419 in Geoffrey H. Moore, Ed., *Business Cycle Indicators*, Vol. 1, Princeton University Press, Princeton, N.J., 1961.

E

e-Business 50
[See USA Today Internet 100 Index]

E-Commerce Index
[See TheStreet.com E-Commerce Index]

e-Consumer 50
[See USA Today Internet 100 Index]

E-Finance Index
[See TheStreet.com E-Finance Index]

Early Warning Barometer
[See Appendix A. Nonquantitative Indicators]

Earnings Index
[See Employment Cost Index; see also Average Hourly and Weekly Earnings]

Earnings-Price Ratio
[See Standard & Poor's 500 Price-Earnings Ratio]

Electric Power Production
The amount of electricity produced in the United States for public consumption during a given month expressed in million kilowatt-hours.

All electric supply systems in the United States producing electricity for public use are surveyed monthly, and their reported production is totaled.

Used as a general indication of the health of the U.S. economy because electricity use is so closely tied to manufacturing activity and the provision of services. For the same reason, this value is, to a certain degree, an early indicator of industrial production. It is also a leading indicator of capital appropriations by the utilities industry.

Published monthly by the U.S. Department of Energy, Energy Information Administration, in *Electric Power Monthly.*

Source	Frequency	Extent	Form	Medium
Annual Energy Review	a	h	t, g	p
Barron's	w	c	t	p
Chemical Week	w	c	t	p
Electric Power Annual	a	h	t	p
Electric Power Monthly	m	c	t	p
Electrical World	m	c	t, g	p
Handbook of International Economic Statistics (CIA)	a	h	t	p, e
Monthly Energy Review	m	c, h	t, g	p
S&P Basic Statistics - Energy, Electric Power, and Fuels	i	h	t	p
S&P Current Statistics	i	c	t	p
Statistical Abstract	a	h	t	p
Statistical Yearbook of the Electric Utility Industry	a	c, h	t	p

Bibliography

Electric Power Annual, Energy Information Administration, Washington, D.C., annually.

Electric Power Quarterly, Energy Information Administration, Washington, D.C., quarterly.

U.S. Department of Commerce, Bureau of Economic Analysis, *Business Statistics, 1963-91*, USGPO, Washington, D.C., 1992, p. 170.

Elves' Forecast
[See Appendix A. Nonquantitative Indicators]

Employee Hours in Nonagricultural Establishments

A measure of the amount of time worked each year by individuals in the industrial and service sectors.

Each month, the Bureau of Labor Statistics, operating through state employment-security offices, surveys employers and determines from the employers' payroll records the number of hours worked during a given week of that month. All work paid for is considered, including the hours of production, supervisory, and salaried individuals who worked full time or part time as temporary or permanent employees. All paid hours of those on paid leave or those who worked only part of the pay period are also counted. If someone worked two jobs, all their working hours would be counted. The only employees excluded are those on unpaid leave (including those on layoff and strike), the self-employed, unpaid volunteers, family workers, farm and domestic workers, and military personnel. The data are broken down by industry (mining; construction; manufacturing; transportation and public utilities; wholesale trade; finance, real estate, and insurance; service delivery; and local, state, and federal governments) as well as being reported in aggregate. The data are annualized by multiplying the data for the month's sample week by 52.

Used as an indicator of the onset of or recovery from recessions and as an indicator of the current behavior of and near-term prospects for the overall economy. Changes in the number of hours worked reflect demands on the labor market with consequent links to labor costs, selling prices of manufactured goods, and inflation.

Published monthly by the U.S. Department of Labor, Bureau of Labor Statistics, in a press release.

Source	Frequency	Extent	Form	Medium
BCI	m	h	g	e
Employment & Earnings	m	c	t	p

Bibliography

Kellner, Irwin L., "Are Labor Markets Really Tightening?" *Chemical Economic Report* 1-3 (Aug. 1994).

Miller, Glenn H., Jr., "Employment Indicators of Economic Activity," *Economic Review of the Federal Reserve Bank of Kansas City* **72** (7), 42-52 (1987).

Moore, Geoffrey H., *Leading Indicators for the 1990s*, Dow Jones-Irwin, Homewood, Ill., 1990, pp. 37-38.

U.S. Department of Labor, Bureau of Labor Statistics, *BLS Handbook of Methods*, Bull. 2490, USGPO, Washington, D.C., 1997, pp. 15-31.

Employees on Nonfarm Payrolls
[See Nonagricultural Employment]

Employment
[See Agricultural Employment, Farm Employment, and Nonagricultural Employment]

Employment by Industry
[See Nonagricultural Employment]

Employment Cost Index

[Formerly called the Hourly Earnings Index; see also Average Hourly and Weekly Earnings]

An indexed estimate of the hourly wages paid to production or nonsupervisory employees, full- and part-time; a comprehensive measure of labor-cost trends.

Each quarter, the Bureau of Labor Statistics surveys about 5400 employers to determine the wages (straight-time), salaries (total earnings before payroll deductions), and benefits paid to employees during a sample week. The values do include bonuses, incentive earnings, commissions, and cost-of-living adjustments but not shift differentials, overtime premiums, or nonproduction bonuses. The included benefits are paid leave, supplemental pay, severance pay, health and life insurance, pension and savings-plan contributions, social security, and unemployment insurance. Earnings of the self-employed, owner-managers, household workers, and unpaid family members are not counted. Federal workers are also excluded, but workers of state and local governments have been included since 1981. The data are derived for specific occupations and industries and the total values are divided by the corresponding hours, weighted by employment counts from the most recent decennial Census of Population, aggregated, and indexed to a value of 100 for 1989. In addition to the aggregate value, the data are also presented by business sector, region of the country, components of compensation, and bargaining status. The precursor Hourly Earnings Index was developed in 1971 and used until 1989 to approximate the national month-to-month wage-rate change from average hourly earnings determined by the Bureau's Current Employment Statistics Program.

Used as a measure of a cost of doing business and, therefore, of inflation; watched as a key element of inflation; regarded as the best measure of labor costs (which represent about two-thirds of the prices of products). It is also used as a benchmark in labor-contract negotiations; for example, it is used in the federal pay-setting process.

Reported quarterly by the U.S. Department of Labor, Bureau of Labor Statistics, in a press release entitled *Employment Cost Index*.

Source	Frequency	Extent	Form	Medium
Barron's	w	c	t	p
BLS	q	c, h	t	e
Business Statistics	i	h	t	p
Compensation and Working Conditions	q	c	t	p
Economic Indicators	m	c, h	t	p, e
Economic Report of the President	a	h	t	p, e
Employment Cost Index	q	c	t, g	p
FRB Dallas	m	c, h	t	e

Source	Frequency	Extent	Form	Medium
FRED	m	c, h	t	e
Monthly Labor Review	m	c	t	p
Statistical Abstract	a	h	t	p
Stat-USA	m	c	t	e
Value Line Investment Survey, Part 2: Selection and Opinion	w	c, h, f	t	p

Bibliography

Grant, John, *A Handbook of Economic Indicators*, University of Toronto Press, Toronto, 1992, pp. 182-183.

Lethan, Michael K., Mark A. Lowenstein, and Aaron Cushner, "Is the ECI Sensitive to the Method of Aggregation?" *Monthly Labor Review* **120** (6), 3-11 (June 1997).

Nathan, Felicia, "Analyzing Employer Costs for Wages, Salaries, and Benefits," *Monthly Labor Review* **110**, 3-11 (October 1987).

Niemira, Michael P., and Gerald F. Zukowski, *Trading the Fundamentals: The Trader's Guide to Interpreting Economic Indicators and Monetary Policy*, McGraw-Hill, New York, 1998, pp. 103-107.

Samuels, Norman J., "New Hourly Earnings Index," *Monthly Labor Review* **94** (12), 66 (Dec. 1971).

Scheifer, Victor J., "Employment Cost Index: A Measure of Change in the 'Price of Labor'," *Monthly Labor Review* **98**, 3-12 (July 1975).

Schwenk, Albert E., "Employment Cost Index Rebased to June 1988," *Monthly Labor Review* **113**, 38-39 (April 1990).

Slater, Courtenay M., Ed., Business Statistics of the United States, 1995 ed., Bernan Press, Lanham, Md., 1996, pp. 233-234.

Tainer, Evelina M., *Using Economic Indicators to Improve Investment Analysis*, John Wiley & Sons, New York, 1993, pp. 186-189.

U.S. Department of Commerce, Bureau of Economic Analysis, *Business Statistics, 1963-91*, USGPO, Washington, D.C., 1992, pp. 157-158.

U.S. Department of Labor, Bureau of Labor Statistics, *BLS Handbook of Methods*, Bull. 2490, USGPO, Washington, D.C., 1997, pp. 57-65.

U.S. Department of Labor, Bureau of Labor Statistics, *Employment Cost Indexes and Levels, 1975-1995*, Bulletin 2466, USGPO, Washington, D.C., 1995.

U.S. Department of Labor, Bureau of Labor Statistics, *Major Programs of the Bureau of Labor Statistics*, USGPO, Washington, D.C., 1994, pp. 18-19.

WEFA Group, *Guide to Economic Indicators: U.S. Macroeconomic Services*, WEFA Group, Bala Cynwyd, Pa., 1997, p. 13.

Wood, G. Donald, "Employment Cost Index to Replace Hourly Earnings Index," *Monthly Labor Review* **111** (7), 32-35 (July 1988).

Engineering News-Record Cost Index
[See Building Cost Index and Construction Cost Index]

ENR Cost Index
[See Building Cost Index and Construction Cost Index]

Eurodollar Interest Rates

A typical interest rate offered by traders in dollar-denominated deposits in banks outside the United States or in U.S.-based international banking facilities.

Eurodollars are deposits in banks outside the United States or in international banking facilities in the United States that are denominated in U.S. dollars. Generally, they are for large sums at fixed terms of six months or less. A secondary market for these deposits exists, and banks participating in the Eurodollars market trade Eurodollars much like U.S. banks trade on the Federal Funds market. At the end of each week, the Federal Reserve System determines the daily quotations of the London bid rate for Eurodollars and arithmetically averages the interest rates quoted. The average rate is published the following Monday. The rates for Eurodollars tend to track U.S. rates for deposits of similar size and maturity.

Used as an indicator of the cost of money, the availability of capital, and inflation.

Issued weekly in Statistical Release H.15 (519), *Selected Interest Rates*, by the Board of Governors of the Federal Reserve System.

Source	Frequency	Extent	Form	Medium
Annual Statistical Digest (FRB)	a	c	t	p
Bridge	d	c	t	e
Chicago Mercantile Exchange	w	c, h	g	e
Financial Digest	bw	c	t	p
Investor's Business Daily	d	c	t	p
New York Times	d	c	t	p
Northeast Louisiana University	w, m	c, h	t	e
Securities Industry Yearbook	a	h	t	p
Selected Interest Rates	m	c	t	p
Selected Interest Rates: A Weekly Series of Charts	w	c	t, g	p

Bibliography
Fabozzi, Frank J., and Frank G. Zarb, Eds., *Handbook of Financial Markets: Securities, Options, and Futures*, 2nd ed., Dow Jones-Irwin, Homewood, Ill., 1986, pp. 122-123.

Goodfriend, Norman, "Eurodollars," pp. 134-145 in Timothy Q. Cook and
    Timothy D. Rowe, *Instruments of the Money Market*, 6th ed., Federal Reserve
    Bank of Richmond, Richmond, Va., 1986.
Hoel, Arline Alchian; Kenneth W. Clarkson; and Roger LeRoy Miller, *Economics
    Sourcebook of Government Statistics*, Lexington Books, Lexington, Mass.,
    1983, pp. 122-123.
Publication Services, *The Federal Reserve System: Purposes and Functions*, Board
    of Governors of the Federal Reserve System, Washington, D.C., 1994, p. 69.

Existing Home Sales
[See also New Home Sales]

The number of single-family previously owned homes that are resold during
a given month.

The National Association of Realtors polls its members each month to
determine how many previously owned homes were sold in the United States. The
sum total is seasonally adjusted and then expressed as an annualized rate of sales
in millions of units. Upon release, that number is also expressed as a percentage of
the value for the previous month. Data are broken down by region and state, with
seasonally adjusted annual rates being calculated for each geographic region. The
median sales price is also reported by metropolitan area.

Used as a general indicator of the strength of the economy; new home sales
often reflect consumer purchasing power (resulting from current business activity)
and the general demand for consumer goods and services. Houses (and the
materials and labor that go into building them) represent a major portion of the
consumer purchases that dominate and drive the national economy. These values
are very sensitive to interest rates, particularly mortgage rates, and are also
sensitive to the prices of new homes, which in turn reflect inflation.

Published monthly as a report by the National Association of Realtors,
entitled *Real Estate Outlook: Market Trends and Insights*.

Source	Frequency	Extent	Form	Medium
Annual Statistical Digest (FRB)*	a	c	t	p
Bank of America	q	c, h	t	e
Bank of Tokyo-Mitsubishi	m	c, h	t	e
Construction Review	m	c, h	t	p
Federal Reserve Bulletin	m	c	t	p
FRB Chicago	m	c, h	t	e
Mortgage Banking	m	c	t	p
Real Estate Outlook*	m	c, h	t	p
Statistical Abstract*	a	h	t	p

*With mean and median sales prices.

Bibliography

Niemira, Michael P., and Gerald F. Zukowski, *Trading the Fundamentals: The Trader's Guide to Interpreting Economic Indicators and Monetary Policy*, McGraw-Hill, New York, 1998, pp. 134-138.

Tainer, Evelina M., *Using Economic Indicators to Improve Investment Analysis*, John Wiley & Sons, New York, 1993, pp. 113-117.

Expenditures for New Plant and Equipment
[See Capital Expenditures]

Exports
[More properly referred to as United States Merchandise Exports]

The dollar value of the goods exported from the United States, reported on a free-alongside-ship basis.

Export statistics are obtained from the Shipper's Export Declaration filed with U.S. Customs and forwarded by them to the Bureau of the Census. Aggregate values of very-low-valued shipments (e.g., $250 or less; limits vary with country of destination) are estimated with factors derived from statistical analyses of each country's importing history. Low-valued shipments are sampled, and an estimate derived from the results. All other shipments are considered individually. The figures reflect both government and nongovernment exports of domestic and foreign merchandise with the exceptions of in-transit merchandise shipped through the United States, goods for the U.S. armed forces or diplomatic missions, fuel and supplies for transporting vessels, nonmonetary gold and silver, monetary coins, and items of small statistical significance. Information on the export of military equipment and supplies under the Military Assistance Program is compiled from the records of the Department of Defense and is adjusted to show the value at the U.S. port of exportation. Three classes of domestic exports of manufactured goods; crude materials and fuels; and food, beverages, and tobacco are reported separately and as a total. Total domestic and foreign (goods imported and re-exported) exports are also reported. The value reported is the value at the U.S. port of export, based on the selling price or cost, including inland freight, insurance, and other associated charges. A merchandise trade balance is calculated and presented. The data are adjusted for seasonal and working-day variation, where appropriate.

Used as an indicator of the movement of merchandise, a large portion of the international payments comprising the balance of payments.

Published monthly by the U.S. Department of Commerce, Bureau of the Census, in *United States Foreign Trade*.

Source	Frequency	Extent	Form	Medium
Annual Statistical Digest (FRB)	a	c	t	p
Bank of Tokyo-Mitsubishi	m	c, h	t	e
Barron's	w	c	t	p

Source	Frequency	Extent	Form	Medium
BCI	m	h	g	e
BEA	q	c, h	t	e
BLS	m	c, h	t	e
Business Statistics	i	h	t	p
Economic Indicators	m	c, h	t	p, e
Economic Report of the President	a	h	t	p, e
Federal Reserve Bulletin	m	c, h	t	p
First Union	q	c, h	t	e
Forecast	a	c, f	t	p
FRB Dallas	q	c, h	t	e
FRED	m	c, h	t	e
Handbook of International Economic Statistics (CIA)	a	h	t	p, e
International Financial Statistics	a	c, h	t	p
International Trade Statistics Yearbook	a	h	t	p
National Income and Product Accounts of the US	a	h	t	p
S&P Basic Statistics - Income and Trade	i	h	t	p
S&P Current Statistics	i	h	t	p
Stat-USA	m	c	t	e
Survey of Current Business	m	c	t	p, e
US Foreign Trade Highlights	a	h	t, g	p
Value Line Investment Survey, Part 2: Selection and Opinion	w	h	g	p

Bibliography

Carnes, W. Stansbury, and Stephen D. Slifer, *The Atlas of Economic Indicators: A Visual Guide to Market Forces and the Federal Reserve*, Harper Business, New York, 1991, pp. 169-178.

Denison, Edward F., "International Transactions in Measures of the Nation's Production," *Survey of Current Business* **61**, 17-28 (May 1981).

Frumkin, Norman, *Guide to Economic Indicators*, 2nd ed., M. E. Sharpe, Armonk, N.Y., 1994, pp. 42-47.

Grant, John, *A Handbook of Economic Indicators*, University of Toronto Press, Toronto, 1992, pp. 168-170.

Joint Economic Committee, *1980 Supplement to Economic Indicators, Historical and Descriptive Background*, USGPO, Washington, D.C., 1980, pp. 129-132.

Kirk, John, "Economic Indicators: The How and the Why," *Banking*, 25-26 (July 1964).

Niemira, Michael P., and Gerald F. Zukowski, *Trading the Fundamentals: The Trader's Guide to Interpreting Economic Indicators and Monetary Policy*, McGraw-Hill, New York, 1998, pp. 155-162.

Plocek, Joseph E., *Economic Indicators: How America Reads Its Financial Health*, New York Institute of Finance, New York, 1991, pp. 239-240.

Rogers, R. Mark, *Handbook of Key Economic Indicators*, Irwin Professional Pub., Burr Ridge, Ill., 1994, pp. 172-190.

Slater, Courtenay M., Ed., Business Statistics of the United States, 1995 ed., Bernan Press, Lanham, Md., 1996, pp. 247-249.

Stratford, Jean S., and Juri Stratford, *Major U.S. Statistical Series: Definitions, Publications, Limitations*, American Library Association, Chicago, 1992, pp. 74-93.

U.S. Department of Commerce, Bureau of Economic Analysis, *Business Statistics, 1963-91*, USGPO, Washington, D.C., 1992, pp. 165-166.

F

Factory Orders
[See Manufacturers' Orders]

Factory Shipments
[See Manufacturers' Shipments]

Failure Index
[See Business Failures]

Family Income
[See Earnings of Workers and Their Families]

Farm Employment
[See also Agricultural Employment]

An estimate of the number of people who work on farms in the United States, irrespective of whether they are paid or unpaid and whether farmwork is their principal employment.

This statistic is determined by the U.S. Department of Agriculture through an annual survey of a sample of farm operators, including a subset of farm operators that hire workers. Since July 1984, data for actual employment have been gathered quarterly; previously, the statistics had been collected monthly or only annually. From the results of this survey, farm employment is estimated based on the number of self-employed farmers, unpaid farm workers, and hired farm workers identified by the survey. Estimates are not adjusted for primary and secondary employment nor are they seasonally adjusted.

Used by the Department of Agriculture for computing labor-productivity estimates. Wage data collected in association with the employment data are used by the U.S. Department of Labor in setting wages of foreign nationals employed in farm labor. The Bureau of Economic Analysis of the Department of Commerce also uses that wage data in its National Income Account series. Employment data are often used to assess current economic conditions and the short-run prospects of the economy. Measures of employment (like Farm Employment) and estimates of changes in employment serve as indicators of the current behavior of and the near-term prospects for overall economic activity.

Published quarterly by the U.S. Department of Agriculture, Agricultural Statistics Board, National Agricultural Statistics Service, in *Farm Labor*.

Source	Frequency	Extent	Form	Medium
Agricultural Statistics	a	h	t	p
Farm Labor	q	c	t	p
Historical Statistics	i	h	t	p
Statistical Abstract	a	h	t	p
US Farm and Farm-Related Employment	a	c	t	p

Bibliography

Daberkow, S. G., and L. A. Whitener, *Agricultural Labor Data Sources: An Update*, Agricultural Handbook 658, USDA Economic Research Service, Washington, D.C., 1986.

Farm Employment and Wage Rates: 1910 to 1990, NAAS Statistical Bulletin 822, 1991.

Major Statistical Series of the U.S. Department of Agriculture, Vol. 1, Agricultural Prices, Expenditures, Farm Employment, and Wages, Agricultural Handbook 671, USDA Economic Research Service, Washington, D.C., 1990.

Miller, Glenn H., Jr., "Employment Indicators of Economic Activity," *Economic Review of the Federal Reserve Bank of Kansas City* **72**, 42-52 (July/Aug. 1987).

Moore, Geoffrey Hoyt, *Improving the Presentation of Employment and Unemployment Statistics*, National Commission on Employment and Unemployment Statistics Background Paper No. 22, USGPO, Washington, D.C., 1978.

Farm Income

A measure of the farming sector's value-added product and the income of farmer operators and operator landlords.

A national gross farm income is derived by estimating the total cash marketing receipts, the value of physical changes in inventories of crops and livestock, direct government payments, other cash income, the value of farm products consumed in the farm households, and imputed rental value of farm dwellings. These estimates are based on market channel information, producer surveys, government records of payments, (including those for commodity price support loans), special surveys benchmarked to the most recent quinquennial Census of Agriculture data, and surveys of farmers. Production expenses are estimated from benchmark data from the Census of Agriculture and subtracted from the gross farm income to give the net farm income. This net farm income is then adjusted to account for nonmoney income, the value of inventory changes, net capital investments, and the value of perquisites to hired workers to give the net cash income. Most of these components are not seasonally adjusted, and the quarterly estimates involve considerable interpretation of annual data. Several of the publishers of this indicator also publish monthly values derived by extrapolating recent trends and applying seasonal adjustment factors.

Used by agriculture-related businesses and by governments as a general indicator of the economic activity of the farming sector of the U.S. economy.

Published annually by the U.S. Department of Agriculture, Economic Research Service, in *Economic Indicators of the Farm Sector*; quarterly in *Agricultural Income and Finance*, and monthly in *Agricultural Outlook*.

Source	Frequency	Extent	Form	Medium
Agricultural Income and Finance	q	h	t, g	p
Agricultural Outlook	m	h	t	p
Agricultural Statistics	a	h	t	p
Business Statistics	i	h	t	p
Economic Indicators	m	c, h	t, g	p, e
Economic Report of the President	a	h	t	p, e
Historical Statistics	i	h	t	p
S&P Basic Statistics - Agricultural Products	i	h	t	p
Statistical Abstract	a	h	t	p

Bibliography

Joint Economic Committee, *1980 Supplement to Economic Indicators, Historical and Descriptive Background*, USGPO, Washington, D.C., 1980, pp. 19-23.

Major Statistical Series of the U.S. Department of Agriculture, Vol. 3, Farm Income, Agricultural Handbook No. 671, USDA Economic Research Service, Washington, D.C., 1988.

Federal Budget Receipts by Source and Outlays by Function

Monthly reports, cumulated for the current fiscal year, of the receipts (from individual income taxes, corporate income taxes, and other sources) and the outlays (for national defense, international affairs, health and income security, interest paid, and other payments) of the Federal Government.

Data are derived from the accounts of the U.S. Treasury. These accounts tally the day-by-day inflows and outflows of the Treasury. Because of certain data difficulties, the reporting of the outlays by function is subject to a degree of error.

Used to monitor how much money the government will probably need to borrow, thereby affecting future credit markets and interest rates. Also used to classify budget outlays and related data, to establish budget authority and total-outlay targets, to present a budget based on national needs and agency mission structure, and to ensure that total outlay targets are not exceeded.

Published monthly by the U.S. Department of the Treasury and the Office of Management and Budget in *Monthly Treasury Statement of Receipts and Outlays of the United States Government.*

Source	Frequency	Extent	Form	Medium
Annual Statistical Digest (FRB)	a	h	t	p
Bank of Tokyo-Mitsubishi	a	c, h	t	e
Business Statistics	i	h	t	p
Economic Indicators	m	c, h	t, g	p, e
Federal Reserve Bulletin	m	c, h	t	p
Final Monthly Treasury Statement of Receipts and Outlays of the US Government	m	c	t	p
First Union	m	c, h	t	e
Government Finance Statistics Yearbook	a	h	t	p
Handbook of International Economic Statistics (CIA)	a	c	t	p, e
Historical Statistics	i		t	p
Statistical Abstract	a	h	t	p
Treasury Bulletin	q	c, h	t	p
US Budget	a	h	t	p

Bibliography

Joint Economic Committee, *1980 Supplement to Economic Indicators, Historical and Descriptive Background,* USGPO, Washington, D.C., 1980, pp. 119-121.

Slater, Courtenay M., Ed., Business Statistics of the United States, 1995 ed., Bernan Press, Lanham, Md., 1996, pp. 263-264.

U.S. Department of Commerce, Bureau of Economic Analysis, *Business Statistics, 1963-91,* USGPO, Washington, D.C., 1992, pp. 160-161.

Federal Budget Receipts, Outlays, and Debt
[See also Federal Sector, National Income Accounts Basis]

Commonly called the Federal Budget; provides monthly data on receipts, outlays, surpluses, deficits, and debt for the current fiscal year and the corresponding months of the previous fiscal year.

Data are derived from the records of the U.S. Treasury kept on a cash basis. Receipts include taxes, compulsory social insurance, collections similar and closely related to compulsory payments, fees, fines, deposits of earnings by the Federal Reserve System, and other sources. Outlays include all payments for budgeted programs, including offsetting collections. The Gross Federal Debt is the public debt of all federal agencies, some of which is in the form of investment instruments held by the government itself. The debt held by the public is the gross less that represented by federally held securities.

Used by the government and financial institutions to assess the state of the government's finances, to determine increases or decreases in the public debt, to guide executive and legislative fiscal policy, and to assess the need and appropriateness of tax and appropriation legislation.

Published monthly by the U.S. Department of the Treasury in *Monthly Treasury Statement of Receipts and Expenditures of the United States Government.*

Source	Frequency	Extent	Form	Medium
Annual Statistical Digest (FRB)	a	h	t	p
BEA	q	c, h	t	e
Business Statistics	i	h	t	p
Economic Indicators	m	c, h	t, g	p, e
Economic Report of the President	a	h	t	p, e
Federal Reserve Bulletin	m	c, h	t	p
Final Monthly Treasury Statement of Receipts and Outlays of the US Government	m	c	t, g	p
FRED	m	c, h	t	e
Government Finance Statistics Yearbook	a	h	t	p
Historical Statistics	i	h	t	p
International Financial Statistics	a	h	t	p
National Income and Product Accounts of the US	a	h	t	p
S&P Basic Statistics - Banking and Finance	i	h	t	p

Source	Frequency	Extent	Form	Medium
S&P Current Statistics	i	h	t	p
Statistical Abstract	a	h	t	p
Treasury Bulletin	q	c, h	t, g	p
US Budget	a	h	t	p

Bibliography:
Joint Economic Committee, *1980 Supplement to Economic Indicators, Historical and Descriptive Background*, USGPO, Washington, D.C., 1980, pp. 115-118.
Niemira, Michael P., and Gerald F. Zukowski, *Trading the Fundamentals: The Trader's Guide to Interpreting Economic Indicators and Monetary Policy*, McGraw-Hill, New York, 1998, pp. 109-113.
Slater, Courtenay M., Ed., Business Statistics of the United States, 1995 ed., Bernan Press, Lanham, Md., 1996, pp. 263-264.
U.S. Department of Commerce, Bureau of Economic Analysis, *Business Statistics, 1963-91*, USGPO, Washington, D.C., 1992, pp. 160-161.

Federal Funds Rate

The interest charged by one bank to another when the first bank "loans" excess funds they have on deposit at a regional Federal Reserve bank to the second so the second can maintain its legally required reserve with the Federal Reserve.

The rates charged for each of the day's overnight loans are weighted by the volume of transactions at each rate, and the results are averaged to give the daily effective rate. The Federal Reserve assesses the economy daily and controls these rates in general, but allows them to fluctuate within a range of values. Fluctuating daily, the federal funds rate is the most volatile of all interest rates because it is subject to the day-by-day volatility of a broad range of economic and technical factors. It acts, in essence, as a spot market for money.

Because these funds are banks' major source of funds to meet reserve requirements, this measure is closely watched as an indicator of future monetary policy. A leading indicator at peaks, but a lagging indicator at troughs. A depressed rate is considered a buy signal on the stock market; an elevated rate, a sell signal. Used as a benchmark by those who price short-term securities and set interest rates, such as the prime rate. Used to calculate the interset-rate spread, a component of the Leading Indicators Composite Index.

Published daily by the Board of Governors of the Federal Reserve System in a Federal Reserve System news release and monthly in Statistical Release G.13 (415), *Selected Interest Rates*.

Source	Frequency	Extent	Form	Source
Annual Statistical Digest (FRB)	a	c	t	p
Bank of America	q	f	t	e

– F –

Source	Frequency	Extent	Form	Source
Barron's	w	c	t	p
BCI	m	h	g	e
Business Week	w	c	t	p
Federal Reserve Board	d	c, h	t	e
Federal Reserve Bulletin	m	c, h	t	p
First Union	m	c, h	t	e
Forecast	a	c, f	t	p
FRB Dallas	m	c, h	t	e
FRB New York	d	c, h	t	e
FRED	d, w, m	c, h	t	e
International Financial Statistics	a	h	t	p
Investor's Business Daily	d	c, h	g, t	p
Moody's Bond Record	m	c	g	p
Mortgage Banking	m	c	t	p
New York Times	d	c	t	p
Northeast Louisiana University	w, m	c, h	t	e
Real Estate Outlook	m	c, h	t	p
Securities Industry Yearbook	a	h	t	p
Selected Interest Rates	m	c	t	p
S&P Basic Statistics - Banking and Finance	i	h	t	p
S&P Current Statistics	i	h	t	p
Statistical Abstract	a	h	t	p
Survey of Current Business	m	c	t	p, e
Treasury Bulletin	q	c	g	p
USA Today	d			p
US Financial Data	w	c	t, g	p
Value Line Investment Survey, Pt. 2: Selection and Opinion	w	c	t, g	p
Wall Street Journal	d	c	t, g	p

Bibliography

Fabozzi, Frank J., and Frank G. Zarb, Eds., *Handbook of Financial Markets: Securities, Options, and Futures*, 2nd ed., Dow Jones-Irwin, Homewood, Ill., 1986, pp. 189-190.

Heebner, A. Gilbert, "Detecting Changes in Federal Reserve Policy," *Business Economics* **26** (3), 33-37 (1991).

Hoel, Arline Alchian; Kenneth W. Clarkson; and Roger LeRoy Miller, *Economics Sourcebook of Government Statistics*, Lexington Books, Lexington, Mass., 1983, pp. 124-125.

Keleher, Robert E., "The Use of Market Price Data in the Formulation of Monetary Policy," *Business Economics* **25** (3), 36-40 (1990).

Publication Services, *The Federal Reserve System: Purposes and Functions*, Board of Governors of the Federal Reserve System, Washington, D.C., 1994, pp. 22, 33-34.

"The Federal Funds Market Revisited," *Economic Review*, Federal Reserve Bank of Cleveland, 3-13 (Feb. 1970).

"U.S. Dollar," *Euromoney* (Currencies Supplement), 19-21 (March 1994).

Willis, P. B., *The Federal Funds Market – Its Origin and Development*, 3rd ed., Federal Reserve Bank of Boston, Boston, 1968.

Zweig, Martin, "Four Key Indicators for Gauging Market Direction," *Investment Vision*, 65-67 (May/June 1990).

Federal Gross Debt

An accounting of the current national debt.

Each day, the U.S. Treasury totals up the outstanding debt of the U.S. Government, including investment transactions of the departments of Health and Human Services, Housing and Urban Development, Labor, Transportation, Treasury, and the Veterans Administration and adds to that sum the value of other government securities and obligations held by the public.

Used as a benchmark of the financial health of the U.S. Government.

Issued daily as a statement from the U.S. Treasury and posted on the Internet.

Source	Frequency	Extent	Form	Medium
Annual Statistical Digest (FRB)	a	c, h	t	p
Daily Treasury Statement	d	c	t	p
Federal Reserve Bulletin	m	c, h	t	p
Government Finance Statistics Yearbook	a	h	t	p
International Financial Statistics	a	h	t	p
Monthly Statement of the Public Debt of the US	m	c	t	p
Recession Recovery Watch	m	h	g	p
Statistical Abstract	a	h	t	p
Treasury Bulletin	q	c, h	t	p

Bibliography
Slater, Courtenay M., Ed., Business Statistics of the United States, 1995 ed., Bernan Press, Lanham, Md., 1996, pp. 263-264.
U.S. Department of Commerce, Bureau of Economic Analysis, *Business Statistics, 1963-91*, USGPO, Washington, D.C., 1992, pp. 160-161.

Federal Reserve Discount Rate

The charge made by Federal Reserve banks on loans to member commercial banks for short-term (usually less than 15 days) adjustments in their reserve holdings.

Under the authority of the Federal Reserve Act, the various Federal Reserve banks collectively set this rate every 14 days or more often, if needed. The discount rates proposed by the Federal Reserve banks are subject to review and approval by the Federal Reserve Board of Governors. Some of the factors that come into play in setting these rates are the labor markets, financial conditions, inflation, and values of monetary aggregates.

Used to estimate the basic cost of money; a determinant in the setting of many interest rates. With the discount rate, the Federal Reserve can influence the basic monetary aggregates and other lending rates, such as the prime rate, credit-card rates, equity loans, and adjustable-rate mortgages. A higher discount rate tightens the money supply leading to higher consumer prices and slower consumer demand; therefore, the discount rate can be used to counter inflationary pressures. A lower discount rate essentially makes money cheaper and enhances the status of equity investments, so a lower discount rate usually has a favorable effect on the stock market. Because it is the key bank lending rate, other rates often follow its lead, including mortgage rates, credit-card rates, prime rates, Treasury bond rates, and equity loans.

Published daily by the Board of Governors of the Federal Reserve System in a Federal Reserve Board press release and monthly in Statistical Release G.13 (415), *Selected Interest Rates*.

Source	Frequency	Extent	Form	Medium
Annual Statistical Digest (FRB)	a	c	t	p
Bank of Tokyo-Mitsubishi	w	c, h	t	e
Barron's	w	c	t	p
Business Statistics	i	h	t	p
Economic Indicators	m	c, h	t, g	p, e
Federal Reserve Board	d	c, h	t	e
Federal Reserve Bulletin	m	c, h	t	p
FRB Dallas	m	c, h	t	e
FRB Minneapolis	m	c, h	t	e

Source	Frequency	Extent	Form	Medium
FRB New York	d	c, h	t	e
International Financial Statistics	a	h	t	p
Investor's Business Daily	d	c, h	t, g	p
Moody's Bond Record	m	c	g	p
New York Times	d	c	t	p
Northeast Louisiana University	w, m	c, h	t	e
Real Estate Outlook	m	c, h	t	p
Securities Industry Yearbook	a	h	t	p
S&P Basic Statistics - Banking and Finance	i	h	t	p
S&P Current Statistics	i	h	t	p
Statistical Abstract	a	h	t	p
Treasury Bulletin	q	c	g	p
USA Today	d			p
US Financial Data	w	c	t, g	p
Value Line Investment Survey, Pt. 2. Selection and Opinion	w	c	t	p

Bibliography

Board of Governors of the Federal Reserve System, *Lending Functions of the Federal Reserve Banks: A History*, Federal Reserve Board, Washington, D.C., 1973.

Hoel, Arline Alchian; Kenneth W. Clarkson; and Roger LeRoy Miller, *Economics Sourcebook of Government Statistics*, Lexington Books, Lexington, Mass., 1983, pp. 120-121.

Joint Economic Committee, *1980 Supplement to Economic Indicators, Historical and Descriptive Background*, USGPO, Washington, D.C., 1980, p. 111.

McNeese, Stephen K., "The Discount Rate: The Other Tool of Monetary Policy," *New England Economic Review*, 3-22 (July/August 1993).

Pring, Martin J., *Technical Analysis Explained, An Illustrated Guide for the Investor*, McGraw-Hill, New York, 1980, pp. 196-198.

Publication Services, *The Federal Reserve System: Purposes and Functions*, Board of Governors of the Federal Reserve System, Washington, D.C., 1994, pp. 5, 20, and 43-45.

Zweig, Martin E., "The Fed Calls the Turn: Stock Prices Follow the Discount Rate," *Barron's* **64**, 66-67 (Dec. 3, 1984).

Federal Reserve Trade-Weighted Dollar
[See also FINEX U.S. Dollar Index and Morgan Guaranty Index]

A comparison of the value of the U.S. dollar to that of 10 foreign currencies.

The currencies of ten countries that are major trading partners with the United States were selected and assigned weights according to the dollar volume of their global trade each year. Those countries are: Germany, Japan, France, Great Britain, Canada, Italy, Netherlands, Belgium, Sweden, and Switzerland. The current value of the exchange rate for each country's currency (expressed in U.S. cents per unit of foreign currency) is raised to the power of the weighting factor for that country. These 10 values are multiplied together, and the result is multiplied by 100. The index has a base value of 100 for 1973.

Used as a measure of the strength of the dollar on global markets. A stronger dollar attracts foreign capital and lessens inflationary pressures by lowering the cost of imports. A weaker dollar dissuades foreign investors, enhancing inflationary pressures. A stronger dollar also causes overseas sales by American companies to decline because it makes their goods more expensive in foreign currencies.

Issued as a news release each business day by the Board of Governors of the Federal Reserve System.

Source	Frequency	Extent	Form	Medium
Annual Statistical Digest (FRB)	a	c	t	p
Barron's	w	c	g	p
BCI	m	h	g	e
Business Week	h	c	t	e
Chemical Week	w	c	t	p
Federal Reserve Board	w	c	t	e
Federal Reserve Bulletin	m	c, h	t	p
Foreign Exchange Rates	w	c	t	p
FRB Atlanta	m	c, h	t	e
FRB Dallas	m	c, h	t	e
FRED	d, w, m	c, h	t	e
New York Times	d	c	t	p
Selected Interest Rates: A Weekly Series of Charts	w	c	t, g	p
S&P Basic Statistics - Banking and Finance	i	h	t	p
US Financial Data	w	c	g	p

Bibliography
Berlin, Howard M. *The Handbook of Financial Market Indexes, Averages, and Indicators*, Dow Jones-Irwin, Homewood, Ill., 1990, pp. 110-112.
"Dollar Index Confusion," *World Financial Markets*, Oct./Nov. 1986, pp. 14-19.
"Index of the Weighted-Average Exchange Value of the U.S. Dollar: Revision," *Federal Reserve Bulletin* **64** (8), 700 (1978).
"Measuring the Foreign-Exchange Value of the Dollar," *Federal Reserve Bulletin* **73** (6), 411-422 (1987).
Publication Services, *The Federal Reserve System: Purposes and Functions*, Board of Governors of the Federal Reserve System, Washington, D.C., 1994, p. 31.
"U.S. Dollar," *Euromoney* (Currencies Supplement), 19-21 (March 1994).

Federal Sector, National Income Accounts Basis

Estimates of the receipts of the Federal Government (personal tax and nontax receipts, corporate profits tax accruals, indirect business tax and nontax accruals, and contributions for social insurance) and of expenditures of the Federal Government (purchases of goods and services, transfer payments, grants in aid to state and local governments, net interest paid, and subsidies less current surpluses of government enterprises, all less wages owed).

Data are based on the projections embodied in the federal budget and on the reports of federal agencies, particularly the Treasury Department. Quarterly data are presented in both seasonally adjusted and nonadjusted forms. Seasonal adjustment is accomplished by applying statistical factors to individual components of the receipts and expenditures; seasonal adjustment of the surplus or deficit results from the adjustments to the receipts and expenditures.

Used for the analysis of federal fiscal policy, specifically for determining the effect of federal purchasing on private capital and credit markets.

Published quarterly by the U.S. Department of Commerce, Bureau of Economic Analysis, in *Survey of Current Business*.

Source	Frequency	Extent	Form	Medium
BEA	q	c, h	t	e
Economic Indicators	m	c, h	t	p, e
National Income and Product Accounts of the US	a	h	t	p
Statistical Abstract	a	h	t	p
Survey of Current Business	q	c	t	p, e

Bibliography
"Federal Receipts," *Analytical Perspectives: Budget of the United States Government, Fiscal Year 1997*, USGPO, Washington, D.C., 1996, pp. 35-59.
Hoel, Arline Alchian; Kenneth W. Clarkson; and Roger LeRoy Miller, *Economics Sourcebook of Government Statistics*, Lexington Books, Lexington, Mass., 1983, pp. 222-223.

Joint Economic Committee, *1980 Supplement to Economic Indicators, Historical and Descriptive Background*, USGPO, Washington, D.C., 1980, pp. 122-124.

Special Analyses, The Budget of the United States Government Fiscal Year 1990, USGPO, Washington, D.C., 1989, pp. B1-B28.

"User's Guide to BEA Information," *Survey of Current Business*, 66-91 (Feb. 1994).

FINEX U.S. Dollar Index

[See also Federal Reserve Trade-Weighted Dollar and Morgan Guaranty Index]

A measure of the value of the U.S. dollar.

Since 1985, the Financial Instrument Exchange (FINEX), the financial division of the New York Cotton Exchange, has compiled its U.S. Dollar Index, which is a trade-weighted geometric average of the foreign exchange rates of 10 major world currencies (the German deutsche mark, Japanese yen, British pound, French franc, Canadian dollar, Italian lira, Netherlands' guilder, Belgian franc, Swedish krona, and Swiss franc) against the U.S. dollar. The U.S. Dollar Index is quoted relative to its base value of 100 and is calculated to two decimal places.

Used to judge the strength of the U.S. dollar on world currency markets and as the basis for futures and options contracts that are traded only at FINEX's facilities in New York and Dublin, Ireland.

Published daily by FINEX in the press release "NYCE Daily Closes" and posted on the World Wide Web at www.nyce.com/.

Source	Frequency	Extent	Form	Medium
Barron's	w	c	t	p

Bibliography

Johansen, Tom, "ECFI 541: Financial Institutions," www.fhsu.edu/ htmlpages/ finance/tom/Out541.html, visited July 17, 1999.

"U.S. Dollar Index Futures," www.nyce.com/finex/dx.html, visited July 17, 1999.

Finished Goods Price Index

[See also Index for Intermediate Materials and Producer Price Index]

A measure in the change of prices received by producers for goods purchased for personal consumption and for capital-investment equipment.

In deriving the Producer Price Index, the Bureau of Labor Statistics also constructs several commodity-based stage-of-processing indexes. The same surveys that are used to determine the Producer Price Index are used for these stage-of-processing indexes. That is to say, a market basket of items is identified, and producers are asked what prices they are receiving for each of those items. Each item's price (or that for a group of similar items) is weighted according to the magnitude of sales of the item, as determined from economic censuses taken every five years. The data are then seasonally adjusted, and the index is calculated according to a modified Lespeyres formula. One of the stage-of-processing indexes is for finished goods, commodities that are ready for sale to the end user, either an individual or a business. The index's commodities include unprocessed foods (e.g., eggs and fruit); processed foods (e.g., canned foods, bakery goods, and meat); energy goods (e.g., gasoline and residential electricity); durable goods (e.g., automobiles and household furniture); and nondurable goods (e.g., clothing and medicines).

Used as a leading indicator of inflation in retail markets and as a closely watched indicator of the nation's overall economic health.

Issued as a news release by the U.S. Department of Labor, Bureau of Labor Statistics.

Source	Frequency	Extent	Form	Medium
Business Statistics	i	h	t	p
Economic Indicators	m	c, h	t, g	p, e
Economic Report of the President	a	h	t	p, e
Federal Reserve Bulletin	a	c, h	t	p
International Financial Statistics	a	h	t	p
Monthly Labor Review	m	c, h	t	p
Producer Price Index Report	m	c	t	p
Statistical Abstract	a	h	t	p
Survey of Current Business	a	c	t, g	p, e

Bibliography
Gaddie, Robert, and Maureen Zoller, "New Stage-of-Process Price System Developed for the Producer Price Index," *Monthly Labor Review* 111 (4), 3-16 (April 1988).
U.S. Department of Labor, Bureau of Labor Statistics, *BLS Handbook of Methods*, Bull. 2490, USGPO, Washington, D.C., 1997, pp. 140-142.

First-of-the-Month Uptick
[See Appendix A. Nonquantitative Indicators]

Flow of Funds Accounts
An aggregate measure of the transactions that reflect the creation of income, capital, and products in the U.S. economy.

The Board of Governors conducts an input-output analysis of American corporate businesses by constructing a series of accounts that track capital that enters the economy and the end results of that capital induction. The input accounts include internal sources (e.g., undistributed profits; capital-consumption allowances; and the profits, dividends, and retained earnings of foreign branches of U.S. companies); credit-market funds (e.g., securities, mortgages, loans, and short-term paper); and other external sources (e.g., tax liabilities, trade debt, pension-fund liabilities, and direct foreign investment in U.S. companies). The output accounts include capital expenditures (e.g., for plant and equipment, residential structures, inventory investment, and mineral rights) and increases in financial assets. Although the inputs and outputs should be equal, measurements of this magnitude are inexact; so the discrepancy between the totals for the input and output accounts is also listed. The values for the input accounts are generally from the financial data gathered by the Federal Reserve System, and the values for the output accounts are generally subsets of the data gathered for the Gross National Product accounts.

Used to assess the needs and availability of money and to determine monetary policy that influences the money supply and credit. Used in the calculation of the Gross National Product and in estimating inflation.

Published quarterly since 1952 (annually before that) by the Board of Governors of the Federal Reserve System in a press release, *Flow of Funds*, Z.1 (780). Listed in *Economic Indicators* as Sources and Uses of Funds, Nonfarm Nonfinancial Corporate Business.

Source	Frequency	Extent	Form	Medium
Economic Indicators	m	c, h	t	p, e
Federal Reserve Board	q	c	t	e
Flow of Funds Accounts	q	c, h	t	p
Statistical Abstract	a	h	t	p

Bibliography
Board of Governors of the Federal Reserve System, *Introduction to Flow of Funds*, Publication Services, Board of Governors of the Federal Reserve System, Washington, D.C., 1980.

Frumkin, Norman, *Guide to Economic Indicators*, 2nd ed., M. E. Sharpe, Armonk, N.Y., 1994, pp. 132-135.

Hoel, Arline Alchian; Kenneth W. Clarkson; and Roger LeRoy Miller, *Economics Sourcebook of Government Statistics*, Lexington Books, Lexington, Mass., 1983, pp. 126-129.

Joint Economic Committee, *1980 Supplement to Economic Indicators, Historical and Descriptive Background*, USGPO, Washington, D.C., 1980, pp. 104-106.

Food Prices
[See Retail Food Prices]

Forbes Index

A broad measure of U.S. economic activity derived from various other economic indicators.

The current values for total industrial production, new claims for unemployment compensation, the cost of services relative to all consumer prices, manufacturers' new orders for durable goods compared with their inventories, total retail sales, new housing starts, personal income, and total consumer installment credit are normalized and totaled, with each normalized value being given equal weight. The resulting value is indexed to a value of 100 for 1967.

Presented as an assessment of the current performance of the U.S. economy Published biweekly by Forbes, Inc., in *Forbes*.

Source	Frequency	Extent	Form	Medium
Forbes	bw	c, h	t, g	p

Bibliography
"The Forbes Index," *Forbes* **131**, 50 (May 9, 1983).

Free Credit Balance
[See New York Stock Exchange Firms' Free Credit Balance]

Freight-Car Loadings
[See Car Loadings]

Freight-Car Orders

The monthly number of new orders placed for railroad freight cars.

Railroad equipment manufacturers, railroad shops, and private-line shops report each month the number of new freight cars ordered for domestic use by railroads, private-car lines, industries, and the government. The reported numbers are adjusted for cancellations by the reporting institutions. End-of-period backlog figures are not thus adjusted.

A leading indicator of future transportation and general economic activity.

Published monthly by the Association of American Railroads and American Railway Car Institute in *Rail News Update*.

Source	Frequency	Extent	Form	Medium
Business Statistics	i	h	t	p

Full Moon Theory
[See Appendix A. Nonquantitative Indicators]

G

Gasoline Prices

The average price per gallon of gasoline (all grades) in urban areas across the United States.

Each month, representatives of the Department of Labor's Bureau of Labor Statistics note the prices of three grades of gasoline (unleaded regular, unleaded midgrade, and unleaded premium) and a weighted average price for all grades in all the urban areas priced for the Consumer Price Index. Prices include all federal, state, and local taxes, and prices for regional blends of gasoline are included in the most appropriate of the three categories of gasoline. The averaged prices are weighted by the volume sold of each type of gasoline, and the national averages are weighted by the regional populations. Data are also presented by region, for region population size, and for selected metropolitan areas.

Used as a component of the Consumer Price Index and as a readily apparent indicator of inflation.

Published monthly by the Department of Labor's Bureau of Labor Statistics as a news release.

Source	Frequency	Extent	Form	Medium
Basic Petroleum Data Book	a	h	t	p
Business Statistics	a, m	h	t	p
Consumer Price Index Detailed Report	m	c	t	p
New York Times	m	c	t	p
S&P Basic Statistics - Energy, Electric Power, and Fuels	a, m	h	t	p
S&P Current Statistics	m	h	t	p

Source	Frequency	Extent	Form	Medium
Statistical Abstract	a	h	t	p

Bibliography
U.S. Department of Labor, Bureau of Labor Statistics, *CPI Detailed Report, Data for April 1994*, USGPO, Washington, D.C., 1994.

GM Indicator
[See Appendix A. Nonquantitative Indicators]

Gold and Silver Sector Index
An indicator of the aggregate price performance of the stocks of gold and silver companies.

The stock prices of nine widely held companies engaged in the mining of gold or silver (ASA Limited, Barrick Gold Corp., Battle Mountain Gold Company, Coeur D'Alene Mines Corporation, Echo Bay Mines Ltd., Hecla Mining Company, Homestake Mining Company, Newmont Mining Corporation, Pegasus Gold Inc., Placer Dome Inc., and TVX Gold Inc.) are each multiplied by the number of outstanding shares for that issue, the results are totaled, and the sum is divided by a base market divisor to give the index.

Used to gauge the current performance of the gold and silver sector on the stock market, as a secondary indicator of the value of gold and silver investments, and as the basis for cash-settled options on the Philadelphia Stock Exchange.

Announced each trading day in a news release by the Philadelphia Stock Exchange; current values are calculated throughout the trading day and posted on many sites on the Internet.

Source	Frequency	Extent	Form	Medium
Bloomberg	h	c	t	e
CBS	h	c	t	e
CheckFree	d	c	t	e
Philadelphia Exchange	h	c	t	e
StockMaster	d	c, h	g	e
USA Today	h	c	t	e

Bibliography
"Gold/Silver Sector (XAU)," www.phlx.com/products/xau.html#contract, visited July 17, 1999.
Zhou, Su, and Saeid Mahdavi, "Gold and Commodity Prices as Leading Indicators of Inflation," *Journal of Economics and Business* **49** (5), 475-490 (Sept.-Oct. 1997).

Gold Prices, International

The prices fixed for a troy ounce of gold on major gold markets, such as Zurich, London, and New York, under the influences of supply and demand.

The members of a gold market commonly meet twice a day, once in the morning and once in the afternoon. At those meetings, a suggested price is put forward by the chairman. The suggested price is determined by the previous fixing and intervening events. Members then announce whether they wish to buy or sell at the suggested price. The suggested price can be adjusted until there are both willing buyers and willing sellers. Quantities of gold to be sold at the suggested price are offered by the members. The suggested price is then adjusted again until the quantity desired for purchase equals the quantity desired to be sold. The official price is then fixed, the transactions are agreed to, and the price is announced to the customers of the members. Payment is made from one member to another within two days of the transaction agreement.

Used as a counter-indicator for inflationary trends and as an indicator of economic stability. Because gold is used as a store of value during economic crises, the price of gold tends to follow rather than lead other indicators. Short-term movements of the price of gold tend to be much more erratic than the movements in prices of other commodities. Recently, the price of gold has been highly sensitive to the value of the U.S. dollar and to crude oil prices.

Published twice daily by the major gold exchanges in news releases.

Source	Frequency	Extent	Form	Medium
Barron's	w	c	t	p
Business Statistics	a, m	h	t	p
Business Week	w	c	t	p
Commodity Yearbook	a, m	h	t	p
Gold: Mineral Industry Surveys, Annual Review	a	h	t	p
Minerals Yearbook	a	h	t	p
New York Times	d	c	t	p
Precious Metal: Mineral Industry Surveys, Monthly	m	c	t	p
Selected Interest Rates: A Weekly Series of Charts	w	c	t, g	p
S&P Basic Statistics - Metals	a, m	h	t	p
S&P Current Statistics	m	h	t	p
Statistical Abstract	a	h	t	p
Wall Street Journal	d	c	t	p

Bibliography

Boughton, James M., and William H. Branson, "Commodity Prices as a Leading Indicator of Inflation," pp. 305-338 in Kajal Lahiri and Moore, Geoffrey H. Moore, Eds., *Leading Economic Indicators: New Approaches and Forecasting Records,* Cambridge University Press, New York, 1991.

Gold, Merrill, Lynch, Pierce, Fenner, & Smith, New York, 1974.

Green, Timothy, *The New World of Gold: The Inside Story of the Mines, the Markets, the Politics, the Investors*, Walker, New York, 1984, pp. 138-150.

Laurent, Robert D., "Is There a Role for Gold in Monetary Policy?" *Economic Perspectives* **18** (2), 2-14 (1994).

Moore, Geoffrey H., "Gold Prices and a Leading Index of Inflation," *Challenge* **33** (4), 52-56 (1990).

Sarnoff, Paul, *Trading in Gold*, Simon and Schuster, New York, 1981, pp. 29-38.

Segars, Alan D., "Commodities an Inflation Indicator," *Pensions and Investments* **23** (1), 20 (Jan. 9, 1995).

Stein, Jon, "Gold, Silver: Economic Weather Vane or Tumbleweed?" *Futures: The Magazine of Commodities and Options* **17**, 57-65 (Nov. 1988).

Zhou, Su, and Saeid Mahdavi, "Gold and Commodity Prices as Leading Indicators of Inflation," *Journal of Economics and Business* **49** (5), 475-490 (Sept.-Oct. 1997).

Gold Prices, U.S.

The price for a troy ounce of 0.9995-pure gold.

Each day, Handy and Harman report the lowest price offered to them for a troy ounce of 0.9995-pure gold in commercial bar form, of acceptable brand and quality, in sufficient quantity to meet demand, and for delivery in or near New York City. Weekly and monthly prices are averages of daily quotations; annual prices are averages of the monthly values.

Used as a counter-indicator for inflationary trends and as an indicator of economic stability. Because gold is used as a store of value during economic crises, the price of gold tends to follow rather than lead other indicators. Short-term movements of the price of gold tend to be much more erratic than the movements in prices of other commodities. Recently, the price of gold has been highly sensitive to the value of the U.S. dollar and to crude oil prices.

Published each week in *Metals Week*.

Source	Frequency	Extent	Form	Medium
Barron's	w	c	t	p
Bridge	d	c	t	e
Business Statistics	a, m	h	t	p
Business Week	w	c	t	p
CNN	h	c	t	e

Source	Frequency	Extent	Form	Medium
Commodity Yearbook	a, m	h	t	p
Gold: Mineral Industry Surveys, Annual Review	a	h	t	p
Minerals Yearbook	a	h	t	p
New York Times	d	c	t	p
Northeast Louisiana University	w, m	c, h	t	e
Precious Metal: Mineral Industry Surveys, Monthly	m	c	t	p
Quote.com	h	c	t	e
Selected Interest Rates: A Weekly Series of Charts	w	c	t, g	p
S&P Basic Statistics - Metals	a, m	h	t	p
S&P Current Statistics	m	h	t	p
Statistical Abstract	a	h	t	p
USA Today	d	c	t	p
Wall Street Journal	d	c	t	p

Bibliography

Boughton, James M., and William H. Branson, "Commodity Prices as a Leading Indicator of Inflation," pp. 305-338 in Kajal Lahiri and Moore, Geoffrey H. Moore, Eds., *Leading Economic Indicators: New Approaches and Forecasting Records,* Cambridge University Press, New York, 1991.

Gold, Merrill, Lynch, Pierce, Fenner, & Smith, New York, 1974.

Green, Timothy, *The New World of Gold: The Inside Story of the Mines, the Markets, the Politics, the Investors*, Walker, New York, 1984, pp. 151-161.

Laurent, Robert D., "Is There a Role for Gold in Monetary Policy?" *Economic Perspectives* **18** (2), 2-14 (1994).

Moore, Geoffrey H., "Gold Prices and a Leading Index of Inflation," *Challenge* **33** (4), 52-56 (1990).

Sarnoff, Paul, *Trading in Gold*, Simon and Schuster, New York, 1981, pp. 29-38.

Segars, Alan D., "Commodities an Inflation Indicator," *Pensions and Investments* **23** (1), 20 (Jan. 9, 1995).

Stein, Jon, "Gold, Silver: Economic Weather Vane or Tumbleweed?" *Futures: The Magazine of Commodities and Options* **17**, 57-65 (Nov. 1988).

U.S. Department of Commerce, Bureau of Economic Analysis, *Business Statistics, 1963-91*, USGPO, Washington, D.C., 1992, p. 161.

Zhou, Su, and Saeid Mahdavi, "Gold and Commodity Prices as Leading Indicators of Inflation," *Journal of Economics and Business* **49** (5), 475-490 (Sept.-Oct. 1997).

Goldman Sachs Technology Indexes

A suite of indicators of the performance of the equity issues of companies engaged in technical enterprises.

The Goldman Sachs Technology Indexes (GSTI) include seven indexes, a composite index and six subindexes (hardware, Internet, multimedia, semi-conductor, software, and services), that are designed to track the performance of key components of the technological sector. For each subindex, Goldman, Sachs & Co. selects 9 to 45 companies. The composite index totals 175 to 200 high-capitalization technological companies. They are selected on the basis of industrial classification, capitalization, liquidity, float, and exchange membership. A company may be included in more than one index or only in the composite. The stock prices of those companies are capitalization weighted, summed, and indexed to a base value with a divisor. The selection of companies represented in each index is rebalanced semiannually. Adjustments for capitalization are made at the same time; the new values become effective after the close of business on expiration Friday, the third Friday of January and July.

The GSTI are used as equity benchmarks for U.S.-based technology securities and as the basis for options on the Chicago Board Options Exchange.

Daily, real-time index calculations are broadcast on several prominent electronic sources of securities data.

Source	Frequency	Extent	Form	Medium
Bloomberg	h	c	t	e

Bibliography
"CBOE Launches Options on Goldman Sachs Technology Indexes," www. fibv.com/focus904.htm, visited Nov. 16, 1997.
"Goldman Sachs Launches Comprehensive Technology Indexes, Represent New Composite and Single Sectors Technology Investment Benchmarks," www2.gs.com/about/media/press/gsti.html, visited July 17, 1999.

Government Consumption Expenditures (in Real Dollars and Chained 1992 Dollars)

[Formerly Government Purchases of Goods and Services in Current Dollars; see also Personal Consumption Expenditures]

An estimation of the value of the goods and services purchased by federal, state, and local governments.

The Bureau of Economic Analysis uses data from the Department of the Treasury's *Monthly Statement of Receipts and Outlays of the U.S. Government*; Bureau of Labor Statistics data on compensation of state- and local-government employees; values for new construction from the Construction Statistics Division of the Department of Commerce; and Department of Commerce's Governments Division data for state and local governments' other purchases of goods and services, other outlays, and self-insurance-fund payments. The process excludes transfer payments, interest paid, subsidies, current outlays by government enterprises, and sales and purchases of land and financial assets. The results are given in billions of current dollars and are deflated by a variety of means to produce a parallel series of data expressed in constant dollars. The data are also presented broken down into federal government purchases, national defense purchases, and state and local government purchases. In addition to being expressed in dollars, each of these is given as a percent of gross national product.

Used to calculated the Federal Government Current Expenditures and as a component of the Gross National Product.

Calculated quarterly by the Bureau of Economic Analysis and published each month in *Survey of Current Business*.

Source	Frequency	Extent	Form	Medium
BEA	q	c, h	t	e
Economic Indicators	q	c, h	t	p, e
Handbook of International Economic Statistics (CIA)	a	c	t	p, e
Survey of Current Business	q	c, h	t	p, e

Bibliography
Rogers, R. Mark, *Handbook of Key Economic Indicators*, Irwin Professional Pub., Burr Ridge, Ill., 1994, pp. 220-222.
U.S. Department of Commerce, Bureau of Economic Analysis, *Handbook of Cyclical Indicators*, USGPO, Washington, D.C., 1984, pp. 43-44.

Government Purchases of Goods and Services in Current Dollars
[See Government Consumption Expenditures (in Real Dollars and Chained 1992 Dollars)]

Gross Business Product Fixed Weighted Price Index
[See Gross Domestic Product]

Gross Domestic Product
[Also called Gross Business Product Fixed Weighted Price Index]
The prices of all goods and services that make up the gross domestic business product (the part of the gross national product held by the domestic business sector). Simply stated, Gross Domestic Product is the Gross National Product less payments to domestic owners for production that occurs outside the United States.

The prices of all goods and services produced by private enterprises, farms, independent professions, lessors of real property, mutual financial institutions, private noninsured pension funds, cooperatives, nonprofit organizations serving businesses, Federal Reserve banks, federally sponsored credit agencies, and government enterprises are weighted together with 1972 constant-value dollars as weights.

Used as a broad, general barometer of overall business activity or lack of activity.

Published quarterly by the U.S. Department of Commerce, Bureau of Economic Analysis, in *Survey of Current Business*.

Source	Frequency	Extent	Form	Medium
Agricultural Outlook	a, q	c	t	p
Bank of America	q	c, h, f	t	e
Bank of Tokyo-Mitsubishi	q	c, h	t	e
Barron's	q	c	t	p
BCI	m	h	g	e
BEA	q	c, h	t	e
Blue Chip Economic Indicators	a	c, f	t	p
Business Statistics	a, q	h	t	p
Confidence and Buying Plans	m	h	g	p
Economic Handbook of the Machine Tool Industry	a	h	g	p
Economic Indicators	a, q	h	t, g	p, e
Economic Report of the President	a	h	t	p, e
Federal Reserve Bulletin	a, q	c	t	p
Financial Digest	q	c	t	p
First Union	q	c, h	t	e
Forecast	q	c, f	t	p
FRB Chicago	q	c, h	t	e
FRB Dallas	q	c, h	t	e
FRB New York	m	c, h	g	e
FRED	m	c, h	t	e
Handbook of International Economic Statistics (CIA)	a	c	t	p, e
Industry Week	q	f	t	p
International Economic Scoreboard	a	f	t	p
International Financial Statistics	a, q	c, h	t	p
Mutual Fund Factbook	a	h	g	p
National Income and Product Accounts of the US	a	h	t	p

Source	Frequency	Extent	Form	Medium
Real Estate Outlook	a, q	c, h	t	p
Recession Recovery Watch	q	h	g	p
S&P Basic Statistics - Income and Trade	a, m	h	t	p
S&P Current Statistics	a, q	c	t	p
Statistical Abstract	a	h	t	p
Stat-USA	m	c	t	e
Survey of Current Business	a, q	c	t	p, e
Treasury Bulletin	a	h	g	p
US Foreign Trade Highlights	a	h	t	p
Value Line Investment Survey, Part 2: Selection and Opinion	a, q	c, h, f	t	p
World Financial Markets	a, q	c	t	p

Bibliography

Carson, Carol S., "Assuring Integrity for Federal Statistics: Focus on GDP," *Business Economics* **28** (3), 18-24 (1993).

Darnay, Arsen J., *Economic Indicators Handbook: Time Series, Conversions, Documentation*, Gale Research, Detroit, 1992, pp. 59-60.

Frumkin, Norman, *Guide to Economic Indicators*, 2nd ed., M. E. Sharpe, Armonk, N.Y., 1994, pp. 154-165.

Johnson, Bruce, and Lori Rectanus, "The Integrity of Federal Statistics: A Case Study from the GAO Perspective," *Business Economics* **28** (3), 12-17 (1993).

Niemira, Michael P., and Gerald F. Zukowski, *Trading the Fundamentals: The Trader's Guide to Interpreting Economic Indicators and Monetary Policy*, McGraw-Hill, New York, 1998, pp. 115-132.

Rogers, R. Mark, *Handbook of Key Economic Indicators*, Irwin Professional Pub., Burr Ridge, Ill., 1994, pp. 210-240.

Tainer, Evelina M., *Using Economic Indicators to Improve Investment Analysis*, John Wiley & Sons, New York, 1993, pp. 24-52.

"Updated Summary NIPA Methodologies," www.bea.doc.gov/bea/an/0997niw/maintext.htm, visited Feb. 5, 1998; also in *Survey of Current Business* **77** (9), 12-13 (Sept. 1997).

WEFA Group, *Guide to Economic Indicators: U.S. Macroeconomic Services*, WEFA Group, Bala Cynwyd, Pa., 1997, p. 14.

Gross National Product

The total national output of goods and services, expressed in both current and constant (1972) dollars.

Hundreds of series of economic statistics are collected and evaluated. These statistics include those on personal consumption expenditures, gross private domestic investment, net exports of goods and services, and government purchases of goods and services. Most of these statistics are concerned with money transactions in the market economy, although some, like the imputed rental value of owner-occupied buildings, are not. Each of these series is appropriately and separately adjusted to eliminate seasonal variations. The detailed components of the GNP are then divided by appropriate price indexes to express them in "deflated" terms or dollars of constant purchasing power. The adjusted and deflated component values are then summed to obtain the GNP.

The GNP is the most comprehensive measure of trends in the U.S. economy because movements in many sectors (including the sales of many industries and enterprises) are closely related to changes in the GNP. It is therefore a useful tool for assessing economic policy and for preparing economic projections.

Published quarterly by the U.S. Department of Commerce, Bureau of Economic Analysis, in the *Survey of Current Business*.

Source	Frequency	Extent	Form	Medium
Agricultural Outlook	a, q	c	t	p
Business Statistics	a, q	h	t	p
Commodity Yearbook	a, m	h	t	p
Economic Report of the President	a	h	t	p, e
FRB Dallas	q	c, h	t	e
FRED	m	c, h	t	e
National Income and Product Accounts of the US	a	h	t	p
Securities Industry Yearbook	a	h	t	p
Statistical Abstract	a	h	t	p
Survey of Current Business	a, q	c	t	p, e

Bibliography

Carlson, Keith M., "Do Price Indexes Tell Us about Inflation? A Review of the Issues," *Federal Reserve Bank of St. Louis Review* **71** (6), 12-30 (1989).

Carnes, W. Stansbury, and Stephen D. Slifer, *The Atlas of Economic Indicators: A Visual Guide to Market Forces and the Federal Reserve*, Harper Business, New York, 1991, pp. 27-44.

Carson, Carol S., "GNP: An Overview of Source Data and Estimating Methods," *Survey of Current Business* **67** (7), 103-127 (1987).

Carson, Carol S., *GNP: An Overview of Source Data and Estimating Methods*, Bureau of Economic Analysis Methodology Papers, U.S. National Income and Product Accounts No. 4, U.S. Department of Commerce, Bureau of Economic Analysis, USGPO, Washington, D.C., 1987.

Darnay, Arsen J., *Economic Indicators Handbook: Time Series, Conversions, Documentation*, Gale Research, Detroit, 1992, pp. 3-5.

Frumkin, Norman, *Tracking America's Economy*, 2nd ed., Sharpe, Armonk, N.Y., 1992, pp. 33-148.

Gross National Product Data Improvement Project Report, U.S. Department of Commerce, Office of Federal Statistical Policy and Standards, Washington, D.C., 1977.

Hoel, Arline Alchian; Kenneth W. Clarkson; and Roger LeRoy Miller, *Economics Sourcebook of Government Statistics*, Lexington Books, Lexington, Mass., 1983, pp. 42-54.

Joint Economic Committee, *1980 Supplement to Economic Indicators, Historical and Descriptive Background*, USGPO, Washington, D.C., 1980, pp. 1-8.

Lavin, Michael R., *Business Information: How to Find It, How to Use It*, Oryx Press, Phoenix, Ariz., 1992, p. 331.

Moore, Geoffrey Hoyt, and Melita H. Moore, *International Economic Indicators: A Sourcebook*, Greenwood Press, Westport, Conn., 1985, pp. 39-40.

Renshaw, Edward, Ed., *The Practical Forecasters' Almanac: 137 Reliable Indicators for Investors, Hedgers, and Speculators*, Business One Irwin, Homewood, Ill., 1992, pp. 33-35, 42, 60-62, 78-79.

"Updated Summary NIPA Methodologies," www.bea.doc.gov/bea/an/0997niw/maintext.htm, visited Feb. 5, 1998; also in *Survey of Current Business* **77** (9), 12-13 (Sept. 1997).

U.S. Department of Commerce, Bureau of Economic Analysis, *GNP: An Overview of Source Data and Estimating Methods*, Methodology Paper Series MP-4, USGPO, Washington, D.C., 1987, pp. 16-17.

WEFA Group, *Guide to Economic Indicators: U.S. Macroeconomic Services*, WEFA Group, Bala Cynwyd, Pa., 1997, p. 14.

Young, Allan H., "Evaluation of the GNP Estimates," *Survey of Current Business* **67** (8), 18-42 (1987).

Gross National Product Implicit Price Deflator
[See Implicit Price Deflators]

Gross Private Domestic Investment

The estimated total of (1) the net acquisitions of fixed capital goods by private business and nonprofit institutions; (2) the commissions arising in the sale and purchase of new and existing fixed assets, principally real estate; and (3) the value of the change in the volume of inventories held by businesses.

Estimates of nine types of private domestic investment are obtained from Bureau of the Census surveys of manufacturers, from trade source data, and from the Bureau of Economic Analysis survey of plant and equipment expenditures. These estimates are of (1 and 2) fixed investment in nonresidential farm and nonfarm structures, (3 and 4) producers' fixed investment in nonresidential farm and nonfarm durable equipment, (5 and 6) fixed investment in residential farm and nonfarm structures, (7) producers' fixed investment in residential durable equipment, and (8 and 9) changes in farm and nonfarm business inventories. Because inventory calculation by different businesses varies widely, numerous adjustments are made to the reported data to make these calculations comparable. The estimates are then totaled into three categories: change in business inventories, residential fixed investment, and nonresidential fixed investment. These three categories are then summed to produce the Gross Private Domestic Investment.

A major component of the Gross National Product; possibly the most important indicator of business conditions, past, present, and expected.

Published by the U.S. Department of Commerce, Bureau of Economic Analysis, in *Survey of Current Business*.

Source	Frequency	Extent	Form	Medium
Agricultural Outlook	a, q	c	t	p
Business Statistics	a, q	h	t	p
Economic Indicators	a, q	h	t, g	p, e
Federal Reserve Bulletin	a, q	c	t	p
Historical Statistics	a	h	t	p
S&P Current Statistics	a, q	c	t	p
Statistical Abstract	a	h	t	p
Survey of Current Business	a, q	c	t	p, e

Bibliography

Joint Economic Committee, *1980 Supplement to Economic Indicators, Historical and Descriptive Background*, USGPO, Washington, D.C., 1980, pp. 26-28.

Rogers, R. Mark, *Handbook of Key Economic Indicators*, Irwin Professional Pub., Burr Ridge, Ill., 1994, pp. 212-214.

U.S. Department of Commerce, Bureau of Economic Analysis, *Business Statistics, 1963-91*, USGPO, Washington, D.C., 1992, p. A-123.

U.S. Department of Commerce, Office of Federal Statistical Policy and Standards, *Gross National Product Data Improvement Project Report*, U.S. Department of Commerce, Washington, D.C., 1977.

GSTI Composite Index
[See Goldman Sachs Technology Indexes]

H

Hambrecht & Quist Internet Index

A measure of long-term trends and daily fluctuations among the stocks of companies that have some relationship to the Internet.

The Index includes the stocks of about 60 publicly traded companies that have some relationship to the Internet. The current stock prices are market-capitalization weighted, totaled, and indexed to the base value. The Index is based on a value of 100 for December 30, 1994. The component list is reviewed and, if needed, adjusted every six months; it includes access vendors, software houses, online services, and hardware manufacturers.

Used to measure performance of volatile securities tied to a dynamic sector of the technological economy.

Reported weekly by Hambrecht & Quist in *H&Q Weekly Review*. Current values are available on the H&Q Index Hotline at 415-576-3651.

Source	Frequency	Extent	Form	Medium
Business Week	h	c	t	e
H&Q Weekly Review	w	c	t	p
PCQuote	h	c	t	e

Bibliography
"The Hambrecht & Quist Indices," www.hambrect.com/research/stats/indices/ tech.html, visited Aug. 16, 1997.

Hambrecht & Quist Technology Index

A measure of long-term trends and daily fluctuations in the technology sector of the stock market.

The Index includes the stocks of about 275 publicly traded technology companies, broadly defined as computer hardware, computer software, communications, semiconductors, and information services. The composition of the index is changed as mergers, acquisitions, incorporations, changes in corporate direction, and failures occur. The Index is based on a value of 100 for December 1993. Before 1985, the Index was price weighted; in 1985, it was restructured as a market-capitalization-weighted index. In 1993, it was redefined to split off health-care related enterprises and was back-calculated to December 1980 so there would be a continuous, comparable statistical record.

Used to measure performance of volatile high-technology securities against other, broader market indicators.

Reported weekly by Hambrecht & Quist in *H&Q Weekly Review*. Current values are available on the H&Q Index Hotline at 415-576-3651.

Source	Frequency	Extent	Form	Medium
H&Q Weekly Review	w	c	t	p

Bibliography
"The Hambrecht & Quist Indices," www.hambrect.com/research/stats/indices/tech.html, visited Aug. 16, 1997.

Help-Wanted Advertising Index

A weighted counting of the help-wanted ads appearing in 51 newspapers across the United States.

The help-wanted advertisements (except display ads) in 51 newspapers in 51 cities across the United States are counted each month. These raw counts are adjusted to account for variations in the number of weekdays and Sundays in the month and to compensate for the seasonal variations normally exhibited in the data for each city. The adjusted data are divided by the adjusted number for 1967, and the resulting city indexes are then multiplied by a factor weighted to reflect the nonagricultural employment for that city. These weighted city indexes are summed to produce regional and national indexes.

This index provides a measure of the supply of jobs, of labor-market activity, and of the economic conditions in cities, regions, and the nation as a whole. It has been shown to exhibit very pronounced cyclical movements, the peaks of which generally lead other business-cycle reference peaks but the troughs of which usually coincide with those of other business-cycle indicators.

Published monthly by the Conference Board as a news release and on its World Wide Web site at www.conference-board.org.

Source	Frequency	Extent	Form	Medium
Bank of Tokyo-Mitsubishi	m	c, h	t, g	e
Barron's	m	c	t	p
BCI	m	h	g	e
Business Statistics	a, m	h	t	p

Source	Frequency	Extent	Form	Medium
Conference Board	m	c	t	e
FRED	m	c, h	t	e
S&P Basic Statistics - Production Indexes and Labor Statistics	a, m	h	t	p
S&P Current Statistics	m	h	t	p

Bibliography

Epstein, Gene, "Help-Wanted Index Needs Help," *Barron's* 73 (14), 58-60 (Apr. 5, 1993).

Friedmen, Susan Krug, "The Help-Wanted Advertising Index: A Leading Indicator of the Local Economy," *Business Economics* 17, 61-63 (May 1982).

Frumkin, Norman, *Guide to Economic Indicators*, 2nd ed., M. E. Sharpe, Armonk, N.Y., 1994, pp. 172-175.

Grant, John, *A Handbook of Economic Indicators*, University of Toronto Press, Toronto, 1992, pp. 163-164.

Preston, N. L., *The Help-Wanted Index: Technical Description and Behavioral Trends*, Report 7161, The Conference Board, New York, 1977.

Tainer, Evelina M., *Using Economic Indicators to Improve Investment Analysis*, John Wiley & Sons, New York, 1993, pp. 218-221.

U.S. Department of Commerce, Bureau of Economic Analysis, *Business Statistics, 1963-91*, USGPO, Washington, D.C., 1992, p. 157.

Hemline Index
[See Short Skirt Index in Appendix A. Nonquantitative Indicators]

High-Grade Municipal Bond Yields
[See Standard & Poor's High-Grade Municipal Bond Yields]

High Life Inflation Index
[See Moet Annual Market Basket in Appendix A. Nonquantitative Indicators]

High-Powered Money
[See Monetary Base]

Home Resales
[See Existing Home Sales]

Hourly Earnings Index
[See Employment Cost Index; see also Average Hourly and Weekly Earnings]

Hours per Unit Output
[See Change in Hours per Unit Output]

Housing Affordability Index
[See also Housing Opportunity Index]

A measure of the ability of a typical American family to buy a previously owned home.

Each quarter, the National Association of Realtors determines the median price of previously owned homes sold in the United States. It then considers five financial components of home ownership, the most important of which is median family income, for the average U.S. family and determines the maximum price for a home that that income would qualify a buyer to purchase with a conventional mortgage with a 20% down payment. The maximum purchase price the median family income would qualify for is divided by the median price of previously owned homes and multiplied by 100 to produce the index, which is expressed as a percentage. The index indicates that half of American families have that percentage of the income needed to purchase a median-priced home. The index is sensitive to both purchase price and mortgage rates. When the index is greater than 100, most American families can afford median-priced housing; when the index is less than 100, most American families cannot afford it.

Used as a gauge of the affordability of housing, as an indicator of the cost of living, and as a metric of inflation.

Issued quarterly by the National Association of Realtors as a news release.

Source	Frequency	Extent	Form	Medium
Real Estate Outlook	a, m	c	t	p

Bibliography

Kamath, Ravi, "The NAR's Housing Affordability Index," *Real Estate Review* 17, 100-103 (1988).

Housing Opportunity Index
[See also Housing Affordability Index]

A measure of the ability of a typical U.S. family to purchase a home in its own market.

The National Association of Home Builders determines the median prices of homes in local markets across the country. Prevailing mortgage rates are used to determine the value of a mortgage underwriting standard, a factor of annual income (typically 3.5 to 4.0) that indicates the financial burden from housing that a family can reasonably afford. The regional median family income is factored by the mortgage underwriting standard, and the result is compared with the median housing costs to determine the percentage of families that can currently afford housing in their own housing markets. When the index is greater than 100, most American families can afford median-priced housing in their local markets; when the index is less than 100, most American families cannot afford it. Local-market data are cumulated into regional and national data, all expressed as percentages.

Used as a gauge of the affordability of housing, as an indicator of the cost of living, as a metric of inflation, and as a measure of how well earnings are keeping pace with the cost of living.

Issued quarterly by the National Association of Home Builders as a news release.

Source	Frequency	Extent	Form	Medium
Real Estate Outlook	a, m	c	t	p

Housing Permits

The number and valuation of housing units authorized by local permit-issuing agencies.

A sample of 8,500 locations is taken from the roughly 19,000 places around the country that issue building permits. That sample includes practically all large cities and about 85% of all new residential construction in the United States. The sampled agencies report the number of building permits issued monthly. This sample is extended to represent the entire country by applying a ratio of reporting to nonreporting locations, and the data are seasonally adjusted. The methods of constructing this index and of sampling have varied over time, and the index values are not directly comparable over long periods of time. Publicly owned housing has not been included since 1986; hotels, motels, nursing homes, dormitories, and mobile homes are also excluded. The same data are used to estimate the actual number of new permits issued to authorize the construction of housing units; that value is reported as New Private Housing: Units Authorized by Permit Places.

Used as one of the components of the Leading Indicators Composite Index. A leading indicator for peaks, troughs, and overall. Housing construction is often the first industry to weaken at the onset of a new recession. Because so many sectors of the economy fluctuate with the housing market and because so many industries are dependent on housing construction, this indicator is a good general measure of overall economic growth. It is closely tied to and responsive to interest rates.

Published monthly by the U.S. Department of Commerce, Bureau of the Census, in *Housing Units Authorized by Building Permits*, Current Construction Reports C-40.

Source	Frequency	Extent	Form	Medium
Annual Statistical Digest (FRB)	m	c	t	p
Barron's	m	c	t	p
Business Statistics	a, m	h	t	p
Construction Review	a, m	c, h	t	p

Source	Frequency	Extent	Form	Medium
Economic Indicators	a, m	c, h	t	p, e
Economic Report of the President	a	h	t	p, e
Federal Reserve Bulletin	a, m	c	t	p
Forecast	a	c, f	t	p
Housing Starts	a, m	c, h	t	p
Housing Units Authorized by Building Permits	m	c	t	p
Mortgage Banking	m	c	t	p
S&P Basic Statistics - Income and Trade	a, m	h	t	p
Statistical Abstract	a	h	t	p

Bibliography

Carnes, W. Stansbury, and Stephen D. Slifer, *The Atlas of Economic Indicators: A Visual Guide to Market Forces and the Federal Reserve*, Harper Business, New York, 1991, pp. 103-110.

Hoel, Arline Alchian; Kenneth W. Clarkson; and Roger LeRoy Miller, *Economics Sourcebook of Government Statistics*, Lexington Books, Lexington, Mass., 1983, pp. 55-56.

Joint Economic Committee, *1980 Supplement to Economic Indicators, Historical and Descriptive Background*, USGPO, Washington, D.C., 1980, pp. 71-74.

Levinson, Marc, "Housing: No Longer the Cutting Edge," *Dun's Business Month* **126**, 58-60 (Dec. 1985).

Niemira, Michael P., and Gerald F. Zukowski, *Trading the Fundamentals: The Trader's Guide to Interpreting Economic Indicators and Monetary Policy*, McGraw-Hill, New York, 1998, pp. 139-144.

Plocek, Joseph E., *Economic Indicators: How America Reads Its Financial Health*, New York Institute of Finance, New York, 1991, pp. 213-216.

Renshaw, Edward, Ed., *The Practical Forecasters' Almanac: 137 Reliable Indicators for Investors, Hedgers, and Speculators*, Business One Irwin, Homewood, Ill., 1992, pp. 39, 137.

"Residential and Nonresidential Building Permit Authorization Data - Sources and Availability," *Construction Review*, 4-15 (Aug. 1979).

Rogers, R. Mark, *Handbook of Key Economic Indicators*, Irwin Professional Pub., Burr Ridge, Ill., 1994, pp. 192-195.

Slater, Courtenay M., Ed., Business Statistics of the United States, 1995 ed., Bernan Press, Lanham, Md., 1996, pp. 253-254.

Tainer, Evelina M., *Using Economic Indicators to Improve Investment Analysis*, John Wiley & Sons, New York, 1993, pp. 110-113.

U.S. Department of Commerce, Bureau of Economic Analysis, *Business Statistics, 1963-91*, USGPO, Washington, D.C., 1992, p. 151.

Housing Starts
[See also Housing Permits]

An estimate of the number of new homes for which construction began during a given month.

A sample of 8,500 locations is taken from the roughly 19,000 places around the country that issue building permits. That sample includes practically all large cities and about 85% of all new residential construction in the United States. On the first day of each month, the sampled agencies report the number of single-family homes and apartments on which construction started during the previous month. The results are then scaled up to estimate the number of such construction starts made nationwide in both permit-granting and non-permit-granting locations. The data include prefabricated and modular housing; mobile homes are also included, but are treated separately. Hotels, motels, nursing homes, dormitories, and conversions are excluded. For multiunit buildings (e.g., apartments and condominiums), construction on all units is considered to begin on the same day. The totals are adjusted to reflect the time lag between permit issuance and the actual start of construction and the number of projects that are canceled after permit issuance. The factors used to perform these scalings and adjustments are produced by surveys of sites, owners of sampled buildings, and local panels of persons knowledgeable about new construction.

Taken as a major indicator of the health and strength of the national economy. The number of housing starts reflects increased or continued employment, the purchase of building materials, and the adding of real property to tax rolls. Housing construction, moreover, is often the first industry to weaken at the onset of a new recession. Because so many sectors of the economy fluctuate with the housing market and because so many industries are dependent on housing construction, this indicator is a good general measure of overall economic growth. It is closely tied to and responsive to interest rates.

Published monthly by the U.S. Department of Commerce, Bureau of the Census, in *Housing Starts,* Current Construction Reports, Series C-20.

Source	Frequency	Extent	Form	Medium
Agricultural Outlook	a, q	c	t	p
Annual Statistical Digest (FRB)	m	c	t	p
Bank of Tokyo-Mitsubishi	m	c, h	t	e
Barron's	m	c	t	p
Builder	m	c, h	t, g	p
Business Statistics	a, m	c	t	p
Chemical Week	w	c	t	p
Commodity Yearbook	a, m	h	t	p
Construction Review	a, m	c, h	t	p

Source	Frequency	Extent	Form	Medium
Economic Indicators	a, m	c, h	t	p, e
Economic Report of the President	a	h	t	p, e
Federal Reserve Bulletin	a, m	c	t	p
Financial Digest	m	c	t	p
First Union	m	c, h	t	e
Forecast	q	c, f	t	p
FRB Chicago	m	c, h	t	e
FRB Dallas	m	c, h	t	e
FRB New York	m	c, h	g	e
Housing Starts	a, m	c, h	t, g	p
Mortgage Banking	m	c	t	p
Real Estate Outlook	a, m, q	c, h	t	p
Recession Recovery Watch	q	h	g	p
S&P Basic Statistics - Building and Building Materials	a, m	h	t	p
S&P Current Statistics	m	h	t	p
Statistical Abstract	a	h	t	p
Stat-USA	m	c	t	e
Survey of Current Business	a, m	c, h	t, g	p, e
US Census Bureau	m	c, h	t	e
Value Line Investment Survey, Part 2: Selection and Opinion	a, q	c, h, f	t	p

Bibliography

Carnes, W. Stansbury, and Stephen D. Slifer, *The Atlas of Economic Indicators: A Visual Guide to Market Forces and the Federal Reserve*, Harper Business, New York, 1991, pp. 103-110.

Frumkin, Norman, *Guide to Economic Indicators*, 2nd ed., M. E. Sharpe, Armonk, N.Y., 1994, pp. 182-185.

Grant, John, *A Handbook of Economic Indicators*, University of Toronto Press, Toronto, 1992, pp. 164-165.

Hoel, Arline Alchian; Kenneth W. Clarkson; and Roger LeRoy Miller, *Economics Sourcebook of Government Statistics*, Lexington Books, Lexington, Mass., 1983, pp. 57-58.

Holloway, Thomas M., "Economic Trends," *Mortgage Banking* **51** (12), 75-78 (Sept. 1991).

Levinson, Marc, "Housing: No Longer the Cutting Edge," *Dun's Business Month* **126**, 58-60 (Dec. 1985).

Nelson, C. R., *The Investor's Guide to Economic Indicators*, John Wiley & Sons, New York, 1987, p. 112.

Niemira, Michael P., and Gerald F. Zukowski, *Trading the Fundamentals: The Trader's Guide to Interpreting Economic Indicators and Monetary Policy*, McGraw-Hill, New York, 1998, pp. 139-144.

Plocek, Joseph E., *Economic Indicators: How America Reads Its Financial Health*, New York Institute of Finance, New York, 1991, pp. 213-216.

Renshaw, Edward, Ed., *The Practical Forecasters' Almanac: 137 Reliable Indicators for Investors, Hedgers, and Speculators*, Business One Irwin, Homewood, Ill., 1992, pp. 39-40, 137.

Rogers, R. Mark, *Handbook of Key Economic Indicators*, Irwin Professional Pub., Burr Ridge, Ill., 1994, pp. 195-197.

Siskind, David, "Housing Starts: Background and Derivation of Estimates, 1945-82," *Construction Review*, 4-7 (May-June 1982).

Slater, Courtenay M., Ed., Business Statistics of the United States, 1995 ed., Bernan Press, Lanham, Md., 1996, pp. 253-254.

Tainer, Evelina M., *Using Economic Indicators to Improve Investment Analysis*, John Wiley & Sons, New York, 1993, pp. 110-113.

U.S. Department of Commerce, Bureau of Economic Analysis, *Business Statistics, 1963-91*, USGPO, Washington, D.C., 1992, p. 150.

WEFA Group, *Guide to Economic Indicators: U.S. Macroeconomic Services*, WEFA Group, Bala Cynwyd, Pa., 1997, p. 15.

I

IBC's Money Fund Report All Taxable Average
[See Money Fund Average]

Implicit Price Deflators

A measure of the effects of inflation on the prices for goods and services.

An implicit price deflator is calculated by dividing the current-dollar value of a selection of goods and/or services by the constant-dollar value for that same selection. Implicit price deflators are calculated for the gross domestic product (which is usually referred to as *the* implicit price deflator) and for the components that make up the gross domestic product: personal consumption expenditures, gross private domestic investment, exports and imports of goods and services, and government purchases. Implicit price deflators are also calculated and published for subsections of each of these four components of the gross domestic product. The data are seasonally adjusted and indexed to a base value of 100 for 1992. In addition, implicit price deflators are calculated for subsections of the Consumer Price Index and for the Gross National Product.

Used as a quantitative indicator of inflation and as a factor for adjusting other values for the effects of inflation.

Published monthly by the U.S. Department of Commerce, Bureau of Economic Analysis, in the *Survey of Current Business*.

Source	Frequency	Extent	Form	Medium
Agricultural Outlook	a, q	c	t	p
Business Statistics	a, q	h	t	p
Economic Indicators	a, q	h	t	p, e
Forecast	a, q	f	t	p
FRB Dallas	q	c, h	t	e

Source	Frequency	Extent	Form	Medium
Statistical Abstract	a	h	t	p
Survey of Current Business	a, q	c	t	p, e
World Financial Markets	a, q	c	t	p
Value Line Investment Survey, Part 2: Selection and Opinion	a, q	c, h, f	t	p

Bibliography

Hoel, Arline Alchian; Kenneth W. Clarkson; and Roger LeRoy Miller, *Economics Sourcebook of Government Statistics*, Lexington Books, Lexington, Mass., 1983, pp. 8-11.

Joint Economic Committee, *1980 Supplement to Economic Indicators, Historical and Descriptive Background*, USGPO, Washington, D.C., 1980, pp. 5-8.

Plocek, Joseph E., *Economic Indicators: How America Reads Its Financial Health*, New York Institute of Finance, New York, 1991, pp. 288-291.

Renshaw, Edward, Ed., *The Practical Forecasters' Almanac: 137 Reliable Indicators for Investors, Hedgers, and Speculators*, Business One Irwin, Homewood, Ill., 1992, pp. 65-66, 69.

U.S. Department of Commerce, Bureau of Economic Analysis, *Handbook of Cyclical Indicators*, USGPO, Washington, D.C., 1984, pp. 38-39.

Imports
[More properly referred to as United States Merchandise Imports]

The dollar value of the goods imported into the United States, reported on a free-alongside-ship basis.

Import statistics are obtained from the Import Entry Form filed with U.S. Customs by the Bureau of the Census. The figures include both government and nongovernment imports of merchandise into the U.S. Customs territory, U.S. foreign trade zones, and the U.S. Virgin Islands regardless of whether the importation involves a commercial transaction. Excluded are goods being returned by the U.S. military and items of small statistical significance. Three classes of domestic imports of manufactured goods; crude materials and fuels; and food, beverages, and tobacco are reported separately. Statistics covering low-valued or small-volume imports are estimated on the basis of a sample. Sampling procedures have varied with time, value of import, and type of entry. The values reported are customs import values, which reflect the prices paid when sold for exportation to the United States, excluding U.S. import duties, freight, insurance, and other associated charges. A merchandise trade balance is calculated and presented. The data are adjusted for seasonal and working-day variation, where appropriate.

Used as an indicator of the movement of merchandise, a large portion of the international payments comprising the balance of payments.

Published monthly by the U.S. Department of Commerce, Bureau of the Census, in *United States Foreign Trade*.

Source	Frequency	Extent	Form	Medium
Annual Statistical Digest (FRB)	a, m	c	t	p
Bank of Tokyo-Mitsubishi	m	c, h	t	e
BCI	m	h	g	e
BEA	q	c, h	t	e
BLS	m	c, h	t	e
Barron's	q	c	t	p
Business Statistics	a, m	h	t	p
Economic Indicators	a, m, q	c, h	t	p, e
Economic Report of the President	a	h	t	p, e
Federal Reserve Bulletin	a, m	c	t	p
Forecast	a	c, f	t	p
FRB Dallas	q	c, h	t	e
FRED	m	c, h	t	e
Handbook of International Economic Statistics (CIA)	a	h (c)	t	p (e)
International Financial Statistics	a, q	c, h	t	p
International Trade Statistics Yearbook	a	h	t	p
National Income and Product Accounts of the US	a	h	t	p
S&P Basic Statistics - Income and Trade	a, m	h	t	p
S&P Current Statistics	m	h	t	p
Statistical Abstract	a	h	t	p
US Foreign Trade Highlights	a	h	t, g	p
Value Line Investment Survey, Part 2: Selection and Opinion	a	h	g	p

Bibliography

Joint Economic Committee, *1980 Supplement to Economic Indicators, Historical and Descriptive Background*, USGPO, Washington, D.C., 1980, pp. 130-132.

Niemira, Michael P., and Gerald F. Zukowski, *Trading the Fundamentals: The Trader's Guide to Interpreting Economic Indicators and Monetary Policy*, McGraw-Hill, New York, 1998, pp. 155-162.

Income Velocity of Money
[See Velocity of Money]

Incumbent President Theory
[See Appendix A. Nonquantitative Indicators]

Index for Intermediate Materials
[See also Finished Goods Price Index and Producer Price Index]

A measure in the change of prices received by producers for commodities that have been processed but still require further processing before they can be sold for personal consumption.

In deriving the Producer Price Index, the Bureau of Labor Statistics also constructs several commodity-based stage-of-processing indexes. The same surveys that are used to determine the Producer Price Index are used for these stage-of-processing indexes. That is to say, a market basket of items is identified, and producers are asked what prices they are receiving for each of those items. Each item's price (or that for a group of similar items) is weighted according to the magnitude of sales of the item, as determined from economic censuses taken every five years. The data are then seasonally adjusted, and the index is calculated according to a modified Lespeyres formula. One of the stage-of-processing indexes is for intermediate materials, supplies, and components. The index's 78 commodities include raw materials and nondurable, physically complete goods purchased by businesses as inputs for their operations, such as foods and feeds, leather, liquified petroleum gas, industrial electric power, fertilizers, paper, plumbing fixtures, ball bearings, glass, cement, and automotive parts.

Used as an indicator of materials-cost pressures that may influence the Finished Goods Price Index, the Producer Price Index, and the Consumer Price Index.

Issued as part of the Producer Price Index news release by the Bureau of Labor Statistics.

Source	Frequency	Extent	Form	Medium
Business Statistics	i	h	t	p
Economic Indicators	m	c, h	t, g	p, e
Economic Report of the President	a	h	t	p, e
Federal Reserve Bulletin	a	c, h	t	p
International Financial Statistics	a	h	t	p
Monthly Labor Review	m	c, h	t	p
Producer Price Index Report	m	c	t	p
Statistical Abstract	a	h	t	p
Survey of Current Business	a	c	t, g	p, e

Bibliography
Gaddie, Robert, and Maureen Zoller, "New Stage-of-Process Price System Developed for the Producer Price Index," *Monthly Labor Review* 111 (4), 3-16 (April 1988).

U.S. Department of Labor, Bureau of Labor Statistics, *BLS Handbook of Methods*, Bull. 2490, USGPO, Washington, D.C., 1997, p. 140.

Index of Consumer Expectations
[Also referred to as Index of Consumer Sentiment; see also Consumer Confidence Index]

A measure of how Americans perceive their economic lot as compared with that of the previous year.

Each month, the Survey Research Center of the University of Michigan conducts a multistage-area probability-sampling survey of 700 to 800 respondents. The same questions are asked each month, probing the personal financial situations of the respondents and their opinions about their economic futures. Essentially, they are asked whether they think that their economic conditions and outlook are better or worse than they were a year ago. For each of five basic questions, the responses are tabulated as better, no change, or worse. For each of the five questions, the proportion of "worse" responses is subtracted from the proportion of "better" responses; 100 is added to the difference; the five values are arithmetically averaged; and the resultant value is indexed to the value for the first quarter of 1966 (= 100).

Used as a near-term indicator of consumer spending and borrowing; such expectations drive consumption. Consumer expectations generally represent the inverse of inflation. When the economy is expanding and inflation is perceived as low, consumer expectations are high; but when inflation is setting in, consumer sentiment declines. A component of the Leading Indicators Composite Index.

Issued as a monthly report by the Survey Research Center of the University of Michigan.

Source	Frequency	Extent	Form	Medium
BCI	m	h	g	e
FRED	q	c, h	t	e

Bibliography

Lehmann, Michael B., *The Irwin Guide to Using the Wall Street Journal*, 5th ed., Irwin, Chicago, 1996, p. 80.

Niemira, Michael P., and Gerald F. Zukowski, *Trading the Fundamentals: The Trader's Guide to Interpreting Economic Indicators and Monetary Policy*, McGraw-Hill, New York, 1998, pp. 35-41.

Tainer, Evelina M., *Using Economic Indicators to Improve Investment Analysis*, John Wiley & Sons, New York, 1993, pp. 84-89.

U.S. Department of Commerce, Bureau of Economic Analysis, *Handbook of Cyclical Indicators*, USGPO, Washington, D.C., 1984, pp. 20-21.

WEFA Group, *Guide to Economic Indicators: U.S. Macroeconomic Services*, WEFA Group, Bala Cynwyd, Pa., 1997, p. 10.

Index of Industrial Materials Prices
[Also called the Industrial Materials Price Indices and the CRB (BLS-Formula) Spot Group Indices, Raw Materials; discontinued by BLS in 1981; see Bridge-CRB Index]

Index of Industrial Production
[See Industrial Production]

Index of Prices Paid by Farmers for Commodities and Services, Interest, Taxes, and Farm Wage Rates
[Also referred to as the Index of Prices Paid by Farmers]

A weighted indicator of the costs to farmers for items used in family living, for items used in farm production, for interest on indebtedness secured by farm real estate, and for wages paid to farm labor.

Produced by combining the Index of Commodities and Services with the indexes of interest, taxes, and wage rates. Data for these indexes are gathered from (1) reports by some 8500 firms and organizations providing roughly 135 specific items to agricultural producers, (2) surveys of farmers, (3) the Department of Agriculture Market News Service, (4) trade publications, (5) labor surveys, and (6) surveys of financial institutions. In the first index, the data are expressed state-by-state, and state weights based on the quantities of goods and services purchased by farmers are applied to the data. The weightings are updated periodically. National averages are then calculated for specified types of farm expenditures. These groups of expenditures are then summed, combined with a family living component, and indexed to a value of 100 for the period 1990 to 1992 to obtain the Index of Commodities and Services. Values of the indicator in terms of the other base period (1910 to 1914) are also calculated and published.

Used in market planning, negotiating marketing contracts, comparing changes in farming prices with those in nonfarm areas, establishing commodity parity prices for agricultural price-support programs, and calculating the federal grazing fee.

Published monthly by the U.S. Department of Agriculture, National Agricultural Statistics Service, in *Agricultural Prices*.

Source	Frequency	Extent	Form	Medium
Agricultural Prices Annual Summary	a, m	h	t	p
Agricultural Prices Monthly Report	m	c, h	t, g	p
Agricultural Statistics	a	h	t	p
Business Statistics	a, m	h	t	p
Economic Report of the President	a	h	t	p, e

Source	Frequency	Extent	Form	Medium
S&P Basic Statistics - Agricultural Products	a, q	h	t	p
Statistical Abstract	a	h	t	p

Bibliography

Joint Economic Committee, *1980 Supplement to Economic Indicators, Historical and Descriptive Background*, USGPO, Washington, D.C., 1980, pp. 91-93.

Major Statistical Series of the U.S. Department of Agriculture, Vol. 1, Agricultural Prices, Expenditures, Farm Employment, and Wages, Agricultural Handbook 671, USDA, Washington, D.C., 1987.

Scope and Method of the Statistical Reporting Service, Misc. Publ. 1308, USDA, Washington, D.C., 1975.

Tainer, Evelina M., *Using Economic Indicators to Improve Investment Analysis*, John Wiley & Sons, New York, 1993, pp. 231-233.

U.S. Department of Commerce, Bureau of Economic Analysis, *Business Statistics, 1963-91*, USGPO, Washington, D.C., 1992, p. 146.

Index of Prices Received by Farmers

A measure of the change from month to month in the average prices of all grades and qualities of farm products in sales to first buyers.

Prices for specified commodities are estimated from personal interviews with and mail and telephone surveys of buyers of farm products (e.g., grain elevators, stockyards, and meat packers), of producers that sell directly to consumers, and of interested institutions (e.g., the USDA's Agricultural Marketing Service, marketing organizations, state agencies, and universities). The data are collected monthly at the state level, and national averages are then calculated. Commodities are grouped into 11 subgroups, 5 of which are seasonally adjusted. These subgroup indexes are weighted according to average quantities of the respective commodities sold during the period 1990 to 1992 and combined. Values of the indicator in terms of the other base period (1910 to 1914) are also calculated and published.

Used to measure changes in average prices received for farm commodities, to approximate the price component of receipts by farmers for the sale of their products, and to calculate the commodity parity prices of agricultural products.

Published monthly by the U.S. Department of Agriculture, National Agricultural Statistics Service, in *Agricultural Prices* and as a news release that is available on the World Wide Web at mann77.mannlib.cornell.edu/reports/nassr/price/pap-bb/.

Source	Frequency	Extent	Form	Medium
Agricultural Prices Annual Summary	a, m	h	t	p

Source	Frequency	Extent	Form	Medium
Agricultural Prices Monthly Report	m	c, h	t, g	p
Agricultural Statistics	a	h	t	p
Business Statistics	a, m	h	t	p
Economic Report of the President	a	h	t	p, e
S&P Basic Statistics - Agricultural Products	a, q	h	t	p
Statistical Abstract	a	h	t	p

Bibliography

Joint Economic Committee, *1980 Supplement to Economic Indicators, Historical and Descriptive Background*, USGPO, Washington, D.C., 1980, pp. 89-91.

Slater, Courtenay M., Ed., Business Statistics of the United States, 1995 ed., Bernan Press, Lanham, Md., 1996, pp. 231-233.

Tainer, Evelina M., *Using Economic Indicators to Improve Investment Analysis*, John Wiley & Sons, New York, 1993, pp. 169-170.

U.S. Department of Agriculture, Economic Research Service, *Major Statistical Series of the U.S. Department of Agriculture, How They Are Constructed and Used, Vol. 1, Agricultural Prices, Expenditures, Farm Employment, and Wages*, U.S. Department of Agriculture, Economic Research Service, Washington, D.C., 1990.

U.S. Department of Commerce, Bureau of Economic Analysis, *Business Statistics, 1963-91*, USGPO, Washington, D.C., 1992, pp. 145-146.

Index of Productivity

[See also Change in Hours per Unit of Output; Industrial Production; Industrial Production, Major Industrial Countries; and Unit Labor Costs]

An estimate of the national average output, valued in dollars, per employee-hour worked.

The annual values of the National Income Product Accounts used to construct the Gross Domestic Product are adjusted to reflect income received by labor and property owners for services rendered in the current production of goods and services in the United States. Output from general government, nonprofit institutions, employees of private households, and the rental of owner-occupied real estate are excluded. Output is composed of employee compensation, profits, depreciation, indirect business taxes, and other income. It does not include intermediate purchases of goods and services, but the businesses that are included are responsible for three-fourths of U.S. economic activity. The labor input required to produce these goods and services is estimated from (1) BLS Current Employment Statistics' monthly survey data on employment and weekly hours of workers in nonagricultural establishments, (2) Current Population Survey data on farm employment, and (3) National Income and Product Accounts data for government-enterprise employment. Estimates of employment and hours paid are calculated for several subgroups (nonfarm business, nonfinancial corporations, durable-goods manufacturing, and nondurable-goods manufacturing) and then cumulated to arrive at the total business values. Labor productivity is then calculated as the constant-dollar output divided by the hours of labor input. The quarterly data are seasonally adjusted and indexed to a base of 100 for 1992, updated decennially.

Used to gauge the efficiency of American business; to investigate the relationships among productivity, wages, prices, profits, and costs of production; to forecast and analyze prices, wages, and technological change; and to assess the fundamental, underlying costs of production.

Quarterly and annual figures are published eight times a year by the Department of Labor, Bureau of Labor Statistics, in the news release *Productivity and Costs*.

Source	Frequency	Extent	Form	Medium
Business Statistics	a, q	h	t	p
Commodity Yearbook	a, q	h	t	p
Economic Handbook of the Machine Tool Industry	a	h	g	p
Economic Indicators	a, q	h	t	p, e
Monthly Labor Review	q	h	t	p
Productivity and Costs	a, q	c	t	p
Recession Recovery Watch	q	h	g	p
Statistical Abstract	a	h	t	p
Survey of Current Business	a, q	c	t	p
Value Line Investment Survey, Part 2: Selection and Opinion	a, q	c, h, f	t	p

Bibliography

Caves, D. W.; L. R. Christensen; and W. E. Diewert, "The Economic Theory of Index Numbers and the Measurement of Input, Output, and Productivity," *Econometrica* **50** (6), 1393-1414 (1983).

Dean, E.; M. Harper; and P. F. Otto, "Improvements to the Quarterly Productivity Measures," *Monthly Labor Review* **118**, 27-32 (1995).

Dovring, Folke, *Productivity and Value: The Political Economy of Measuring Progress*, Praeger Publishers, New York, 1987.

Hoel, Arline Alchian; Kenneth W. Clarkson; and Roger LeRoy Miller, *Economics Sourcebook of Government Statistics*, Lexington Books, Lexington, Mass., 1983, pp. 80-82.

Jorgenson, Dale Weldeau, *Productivity*, 2 vol., MIT Press, Cambridge, Mass. 1995.

Jorgenson, Dale W.; Frank M. Gollop; and Barbara M. Fraumeni, *Productivity and U.S. Economic Growth*, Harvard University Press, Cambridge, Mass., 1987.

Niemira, Michael P., and Gerald F. Zukowski, *Trading the Fundamentals: The Trader's Guide to Interpreting Economic Indicators and Monetary Policy*, McGraw-Hill, New York, 1998, pp. 205-209.

U.S. Department of Labor, Bureau of Labor Statistics, *BLS Handbook of Methods*, Bull. 2490, USGPO, Washington, D.C., 1997, pp. 89-109.

WEFA Group, *Guide to Economic Indicators: U.S. Macroeconomic Services*, WEFA Group, Bala Cynwyd, Pa., 1997, p. 24.

Index of Stock Prices
[See Standard and Poor's 500 Composite Stock Price Index]

Industrial and Commercial Failures
[See Business Failures]

Industrial Loans Outstanding
[See Commercial and Industrial Loans Outstanding]

Industrial Materials Price Index
[See Journal of Commerce Index and Change in Industrial Materials Price Index; also see Bridge-CRB Index]

Industrial Operating Rate
[See Capacity Utilization]

Industrial Production
[Also called Industrial Production Index; see also Index of Productivity and Industrial Production, Major Industrial Countries]

A measure of the change in nonagricultural-goods output of the nation, including mining, electric power, and natural-gas utilities, about 30% of the Gross National Product.

The Federal Reserve System derives two independent estimates of the monthly change in industrial production by tracking two sets of data, industry data and market data. The industry data track 235 products by means of such measures as physical-product data, production-worker hours, and kilowatt-hour data gathered from government agencies, trade organizations, and trade publications. The physical output of each product is weighted according to its percentage contribution to the index during the base period, and the resultant values are then summed and indexed to the base-period value, which is set at 100. These data are adjusted for undercoverage and seasonal change. The base period is updated approximately every ten years; the new base period predates the index in which it is first used by about seven years. Indexes for subgroupings (i.e., manufacturing, utilities, and mining) are also calculated. The market data track demand for consumer goods, business equipment, defense and space equipment, intermediate products (e.g., construction and business supplies), and materials (including parts, containers, and raw materials). The market-data version of the index is derived in much the same manner as the industry-data version, and the two values usually diverge by less than 0.1%. Indexes for major market groups and selected manufactures (i.e., consumer goods, equipment, intermediate products, and materials) are also calculated. The market-data version is used as the official value of the index.

A sensitive gauge of the robustness and direction of the national economy, the index tends to rise more than does the overall economy during expansions and to fall more during recessions. The index is used as a component of the Coincident Indicators Composite Index. Used with related data on employment, inventories, trade, prices, and other economic variables to analyze short- and long-term developments in the national economy. Used to determine the areas in which important changes have occurred and in analyses of the performance of individual businesses in comparison with the performance of the entire corresponding industry to which that business belongs.

Published monthly by the Board of Governors of the Federal Reserve System in *Industrial Production and Capacity Utilization*, Statistical Release G.17, and in the *Federal Reserve Bulletin*.

Source	Frequency	Extent	Form	Medium
Agricultural Statistics	a	h	t	p
Annual Statistical Digest (FRB)	a, m	c	t	p
Bank of Tokyo-Mitsubishi	m	c, h	t	e
Barron's	m	c	t	p
BCI	m	h	g	e
Blue Chip Economic Indicators	a	c, f	t	p
Commodity Yearbook	a, m	h	t	p
Economic Indicators	a, m	c, h	t, g	p, e
Economic Report of the President	a	h	t	p, e
Federal Reserve Board	m	c	t	e
Federal Reserve Bulletin	a, m, q	c	t	p
Financial Digest	m	c	t	p
First Union	m	c, h	t	e
Forecast	q	c, f	t	p
FRB Chicago	q	c, h	t	e
FRB Dallas	m	c, h	t	e

Source	Frequency	Extent	Form	Medium
FRB New York	m	c, h	g	e
FRED	m	c, h	t	e
Handbook of International Economic Statistics (CIA)	a	h (c)	t	p (e)
Industrial Production and Capacity Utilization	m	c	t, g	p
Industry Week	q	f	t	p
International Economic Review	a, m, q	c	t	p
International Financial Statistics	a, q	c, h	t	p
Recession Recovery Watch	q	h	t	p
S&P Basic Statistics - Production Indexes and Labor Statistics	a, m	h	t	p
S&P Current Statistics	m	h	t	p
Statistical Abstract	a	h	t	p
Stat-USA	m	c	t	e
Survey of Current Business	a, m	c, h	t, g	p, e
Value Line Investment Survey, Part 2: Selection and Opinion	a, q	c, h, f	t, g	p

Bibliography

Armitage, Kenneth, and Dixon A. Tranum, "Industrial Production: 1989 Developments and Historical Revision," *Federal Reserve Bulletin* 76, 187-204 (1990).

Carnes, W. Stansbury, and Stephen D. Slifer, *The Atlas of Economic Indicators: A Visual Guide to Market Forces and the Federal Reserve*, Harper Business, New York, 1991, pp. 93-101.

Frumkin, Norman, *Guide to Economic Indicators*, 2nd ed., M. E. Sharpe, Armonk, N.Y., 1994, pp. 190-194.

Frumkin, Norman, *Tracking America's Economy*, 2nd ed., Sharpe, Armonk, N.Y., 1992, pp. 149-150.

Grant, John, *A Handbook of Economic Indicators*, University of Toronto Press, Toronto, 1992, pp. 165-166.

Hoel, Arline Alchian; Kenneth W. Clarkson; and Roger LeRoy Miller, *Economics Sourcebook of Government Statistics*, Lexington Books, Lexington, Mass., 1983, pp. 66-68.

Joint Economic Committee, *1980 Supplement to Economic Indicators, Historical and Descriptive Background*, USGPO, Washington, D.C., 1980, pp. 55-61.

Keen, Howard, Jr., "Use of Weekly and Other Monthly Data as Predictors of the Industrial Production Index," *Business Economics* 23, 44-48 (Jan. 1988).

Kirk, John, "Economic Indicators: The How and the Why," *Banking*, 27-28 (Aug. 1964).

Moore, Geoffrey Hoyt, and Melita H. Moore, *International Economic Indicators: A Sourcebook*, Greenwood Press, Westport, Conn., 1985, pp. 40-41.

Moore, G. H., and J. Shiskin, "Why the Leading Indicators Really Do Lead," *Across the Board*, 71-75 (May 1978).

Nelson, C. R., *The Investor's Guide to Economic Indicators*, John Wiley & Sons, New York, 1987, pp. 62-64.

Niemira, Michael P., and Gerald F. Zukowski, *Trading the Fundamentals: The Trader's Guide to Interpreting Economic Indicators and Monetary Policy*, McGraw-Hill, New York, 1998, pp. 145-153.

Plocek, Joseph E., *Economic Indicators: How America Reads Its Financial Health*, New York Institute of Finance, New York, 1991, 159-162.

Raddock, Richard D., "Industrial Production, Capacity, and Capacity Utilization Since 1987," *Federal Reserve Bulletin* **79**, 590-605 (1993).

Renshaw, Edward, Ed., *The Practical Forecasters' Almanac: 137 Reliable Indicators for Investors, Hedgers, and Speculators*, Business One Irwin, Homewood, Ill., 1992, pp. 35-36.

Rogers, R. Mark, *Handbook of Key Economic Indicators*, Irwin Professional Pub., Burr Ridge, Ill., 1994, pp. 120-130.

Stratford, Jean S., and Juri Stratford, *Major U.S. Statistical Series: Definitions, Publications, Limitations*, American Library Association, Chicago, 1992, pp. 69-70.

Tainer, Evelina M., *Using Economic Indicators to Improve Investment Analysis*, John Wiley & Sons, New York, 1993, pp. 222-225.

U.S. Department of Commerce, Bureau of Economic Analysis, *Business Statistics, 1963-91*, USGPO, Washington, D.C., 1992, p. 143.

WEFA Group, *Guide to Economic Indicators: U.S. Macroeconomic Services*, WEFA Group, Bala Cynwyd, Pa., 1997, p. 17.

Industrial Production Index
[See Industrial Production; Industrial Production, Major Industrial Countries; and Index of Productivity]

Industrial Production, Major Industrial Countries
[See also Industrial Production and Index of Productivity]

The value of all goods produced by the industries of seven countries (United States, Canada, Japan, France, Germany, Italy, and United Kingdom), each indexed to the value of such output in 1987.

Each country calculates its industrial production differently, but generally the method is a base-weighted arithmetic average index. The base years vary considerably, but are normalized to 1987 by the Department of Commerce before publication. The weights used to combine products into group indexes are typically based on value-added market prices that have been appropriately adjusted (e.g., to eliminate duplications of values resulting from combining products). Indicators such as physical output, deflated values of output, deflated turnover, quantity of materials used, and man-hours are often used in calculating the production index.

Used to assess and indicate trends in the overall economic activity of the foreign nations surveyed and to compare them with economic activities in the United States.

Published monthly by the U.S. Department of Commerce, International Trade Administration, Office of Planning and Research, in *International Economic Indicators*.

Source	Frequency	Extent	Form	Medium
BCI	m	h	g	e
Conference Board/BCI	m	c	t	e
Economic Indicators	a, m	h	t	p, e
International Financial Statistics	a, q	h	t	p
Statistical Abstract	a	h	t	p

Bibliography

Joint Economic Committee, *1980 Supplement to Economic Indicators, Historical and Descriptive Background*, USGPO, Washington, D.C., 1980, pp. 125-127.

Moore, Geoffrey H., "What the Leading Indicators Indicate about Industrial Production in Certain Key Countries," *Across the Board*, 84-85 (Apr. 1980).

Raddock, Richard D., "Industrial Production, Capacity, and Capacity Utilization Since 1987," *Federal Reserve Bulletin* **79** (6), 590-605 (1993).

Industrial Raw Materials Price Index

[Also called Index of Industrial Materials Prices and the CRB (BLS-Formula) Spot Group Indices, Raw Materials; discontinued by BLS in 1981; see Bridge-CRB Index]

Initial Unemployment Claims

[See Unemployment Insurance Programs, Initial Claims]

Interest Rates

[See Average Prime Rate Charged by Banks, Bank Rate Monitor Index, Bankers' Acceptances, BanxQuote Index, Commercial Paper Interest Rates, Constant Maturities Treasury Securities, and Certificate of Deposit Interest Rates]

International Transactions

[See United States International Transactions]

Internet Index
[See Hambrecht and Quist Internet Index, TheStreet.com Internet Sector Index, and USA Today Internet 100 Index]

Inventory Change Index
[See also Manufacturers' Inventories and Manufacturing and Trade Inventories]

An indicator of the trend (up or down) in inventories held by manufacturing companies.

The National Association of Purchasing Management surveys a selected panel of 300 of its members. It asks the panel members if their companies' inventories have increased, decreased, or stayed the same during the past month. To calculate the index, the percentage of respondents that reply that their inventories have risen is added to one-half of the percentage that reply that their inventories have stayed the same.

Used as an indicator of the pace of the nation's economy and of future employment trends. If a recession is emerging, inventories will swell because of lack of sales; if excessive inventories caused by a recession start to decrease, this is taken as a sign that corrective measures are taking effect, that production and consumption are coming into balance, and that the recession may be ending. Increases in inventories cause production (and therefore employment) to be scaled back; decreases in inventories spur production, new hiring, and the use of overtime.

Issued monthly by the National Association of Purchasing Management in a report entitled *Report on Business*.

Source	Frequency	Extent	Form	Medium
First Union	q	c, h	t	e
Report on Business	m	c	t	p

Bibliography
Moore, Geoffrey H., *Leading Indicators for the 1990s*, Dow Jones-Irwin, Homewood, Ill., 1990, p. 137.
Tamm, Feliks, "An Agenda for Inventories Input to the Leading Composite Index," pp. 429-460 in Kajal Lahiri and Moore, Geoffrey H. Moore, Eds., *Leading Economic Indicators: New Approaches and Forecasting Records,* Cambridge University Press, New York, 1991.

Inventory-Sales Ratio
[See Manufacturers' Inventory-Sales Ratio]

Inventory-Shipments Ratio
[See Manufacturers' Inventory-Shipments Ratio]

Investment Expenditures, Plant and Equipment
[See Capital Expenditures]

Investment Portfolio Index
[See Betzold-Berg Investment Portfolio Index]

Investments
[See Loans and Investments]

J-K

January Indicator
[See Appendix A. Nonquantitative Indicators]

J. P. Morgan Index
[See Morgan Guaranty Index; see also Federal Reserve Trade-Weighted Dollar]

Journal of Commerce Index
[Also called the Industrial Materials Price Index; see also Bridge-CRB Index, Bridge-CRB Futures Price Index, Change in Industrial Materials Price Index, and Change in Sensitive Prices]

An indicator of the prices of industrial raw materials.

The spot (asking) prices are determined for specific quantities of particular grades of 17 industrial materials on specific markets. For materials for which such specific data are not available, the prices on multiple specific markets are determined and averaged. The 17 materials are crude oil, benzene, aluminum, copper scrap, lead, scrap steel, tin, zinc, burlap, cotton, polyester fiber, print cloth, plywood, hides, hardwood lumber red oak flooring, rubber, and tallow. These prices are weighted, arithmetically averaged, and indexed to the value at a base (currently 1990), which was assigned an index value of 100.

Used to track industry's costs for raw materials and to help foretell shifts in trends for the Consumer Price Index six or more months in advance (i.e., as a leading indicator of inflation).

Published weekly in the *Journal of Commerce*.

Source	Frequency	Extent	Form	Medium
Barron's	q	c	g	p

Source	Frequency	Extent	Form	Medium
Journal of Commerce	d	c	t, g	p
Recession Recovery Watch	q	h	g	p

KR-CRB Futures Price Index
[See Bridge-CRB Futures Price Index; also called the Knight-Ridder Commodity Research Bureau Futures Price Index, the KR-CRB Index, the KR-CRB Futures Index, and the CRB Futures Index; see also the Bridge-CRB Index]

KR-CRB Index
[See Bridge-CRB Index; also called the Tuesday Index of Spot Market Prices, the CRB Spot Price Index, the Knight-Ridder Commodity Research Bureau Index, the CRB Index, and the CRB-BLS Spot Market Index; see also the Change in Sensitive Prices, the Bridge-CRB Futures Index, the Journal of Commerce Index, and the Change in Industrial Materials Price Index]

L

L

[See also Bankers Acceptances, Commercial Paper Interest Rates, M1, M2, and M3]

A measure of the amount of money in the U.S. economy in the broadest sense, which includes long-term liquid funds; one of the four major money-stock measures of the Federal Reserve System.

The Federal Reserve adds to its M3 measure other liquid assets, such as the estimated amounts invested in Treasury bills, savings bonds, commercial paper, bankers acceptances, and nonbank Eurodollar holdings of U.S. citizens to compile this estimate of the amount of money in use in the U.S. economy. The resulting total is seasonally adjusted.

Used as one determinant of the reserves that banks are required to maintain and of the discount rate, both of which influence the availability of money in the economy. Also used to guide the Federal Open Market Operations, which injects money into the economy or withdraws it by trading in government securities. Too much money in the economy tends to increase prices and inflation and to force interest rates down; too little money tends to increase interest rates and unemployment and to decrease prices and output.

Published weekly by the Board of Governors of the Federal Reserve System in Statistical Release H.6: *Money Stock, Liquid Assets, and Debt Measures* and monthly in the *Federal Reserve Bulletin*.

Source	Frequency	Extent	Form	Medium
Annual Statistical Digest (FRB)	m, q	c, h	t	p
Business Statistics	a, m	c	t	p
Economic Indicators	a, m	c, h	t, g	p, e
Federal Reserve Board	m	c, h	t	e

Source	Frequency	Extent	Form	Medium
Federal Reserve Bulletin	m, q	c	t	p
FRED	d, w, m	c, h	t	e
International Financial Statistics	a, q	h	t	p
Statistical Abstract	a	h	t	p
Stat-USA	m	c, h	t	e

Bibliography

Board of Governors of the Federal Reserve System, *The Federal Reserve System: Purposes and Functions*, Publication Services, Board of Governors of the Federal Reserve System, Washington, D.C., 1994.

Downes, John, and Jordan Elliot Goodman, *Dictionary of Finance and Investment Terms*, Barron's Educational Series, Hauppage, N.Y., 1995.

Frumkin, Norman, *Guide to Economic Indicators*, 2nd ed., M. E. Sharpe, Armonk, N.Y., 1994, pp. 229-234.

Labor Productivity
[See Index of Productivity]

Lagging Indicators
[See Lagging Indicators Composite Index]

Lagging Indicators Composite Index

The average behavior of a group of economic indicators whose values have been noted to follow or lag behind business-cycle turns.

Seven economic indicators were selected because their values generally changed in a manner similar to changes in the business cycles but changed after those business-cycle changes were evident. Those indicators are:

▸ average duration of unemployment,
▸ changes in labor cost per unit of manufactured output,
▸ manufacturing and trade inventory-to-sales ratio,
▸ commercial and industrial loans outstanding,
▸ ratio of outstanding consumer installment credit to personal income,
▸ average prime rate charged by banks, and
▸ changes in consumer price index for services.

Month-to-month percent changes or differences are calculated for each component of the composite index. The percent changes (or differences) for each component are standardized to an absolute value of one by dividing each monthly change by the average of these changes. These standardized changes are then weighted according to the economic significance, statistical adequacy, cyclical timing, conformity to business cycles, smoothness, and currency of each component. A weighted average of the standardized changes is computed for all the components.

This average is then modified so its long-run average is equal to that of the coincident indicators composite's by deriving a ratio of the two long-term averages and then dividing the lagging indicators' monthly change by that ratio. Because many of its components are already seasonally adjusted, the composite index itself is not seasonally adjusted. The index is, however, periodically revised when a component is adjusted or revised.

Indicates changes in the direction of aggregate economic activity; viewed by many as an indicator of current and future levels of economic activity.

Issued monthly as a press release by The Conference Board and on their World Wide Web home page at www.conference-board.org.

Source	Frequency	Extent	Form	Medium
Barron's	m	c	t	p
BCI	m	h	g	e
Conference Board/BCI	m	c	t	e
FRB Dallas	m	c, h	t	e
Statistical Abstract	a	h	t	p
Stat-USA	m	c	t	e

Bibliography

Beckman, Barry A., and Tracy R. Tapscott, "Composite Indexes of Leading, Coincident, and Lagging Indicators," *Survey of Current Business* **67** (11), 24-28 (1987).

Burkholder, Alex A., "New Approaches to the Use of Lagging Indicators," *Business Economics* **15**, 20-24 (May 1980).

Frumkin, Norman, *Guide to Economic Indicators*, 2nd ed., M. E. Sharpe, Armonk, N.Y., 1994, pp. 217-223.

Frumkin, Norman, *Trucking America's Economy*, 2nd ed., Sharpe, Armonk, N.Y., 1992, pp. 283-302.

Hoel, Arline Alchian; Kenneth W. Clarkson; and Roger LeRoy Miller, *Economics Sourcebook of Government Statistics*, Lexington Books, Lexington, Mass., 1983, pp. 61-65.

"Indicators That Lag Economy's Ups and Downs Denote Strain That Often Leads to Recession," *Wall Street Journal*, 46 (Nov. 29, 1978).

Moore, Geoffrey H., "Leading and Confirming Indicators of general Business Changes," pp. 45-109 in Geoffrey H. Moore, Ed., *Business Cycle Indicators*, Vol. 1, Princeton University Press, Princeton, N.J., 1961.

Niemira, Michael P., and Gerald F. Zukowski, *Trading the Fundamentals: The Trader's Guide to Interpreting Economic Indicators and Monetary Policy*, McGraw-Hill, New York, 1998, pp. 61-66.

Renshaw, Edward, Ed., *The Practical Forecasters' Almanac: 137 Reliable Indicators for Investors, Hedgers, and Speculators*, Business One Irwin, Homewood, Ill., 1992, p. 24.

Rogers, R. Mark, *Handbook of Key Economic Indicators*, Irwin Professional Pub., Burr Ridge, Ill., 1994, pp. 245-251 and 260-261.

Samuelson, Paul, "Paradise Lost & Refound: The Harvard ABC Barometers," *Journal of Portfolio Management* **13** (3), 4-9 (1987).

Stratford, Jean S., and Juri Stratford, *Major U.S. Statistical Series: Definitions, Publications, Limitations*, American Library Association, Chicago, 1992, pp. 32-46.

Leading Indicators
[See Leading Indicators Composite Index]

Leading Indicators Composite Index

The average behavior of a group of economic indicators whose values have been noted to precede business cycle turns.

Ten economic indicators were selected because their values generally changed in a manner similar to changes in the business cycles but before those business-cycle changes were evident. The indicators in use since 1996 are:

▸ average weekly hours of manufacturing production workers,
▸ average weekly initial claims for unemployment insurance,
▸ vendor performance,
▸ manufacturers' new orders for consumer goods and materials in constant dollars,
▸ manufacturers' new orders of nondefense capital goods in constant dollars,
▸ interest rate spread,
▸ the index of consumer expectations,
▸ the index of stock prices (Standard & Poor's Composite Index),
▸ money supply M2 in constant dollars, and
▸ new private housing building permits.

Month-to-month percent changes or differences are calculated for each component of the composite index. The percent changes (or differences) for each component are standardized to an absolute value of one by dividing each monthly change by the average of these changes. These standardized changes are then weighted according to the economic significance, statistical adequacy, cyclical timing, conformity to business cycles, smoothness, and currency. A weighted average of the standardized changes is computed for all the components. This average is then modified so its long-run average is equal to that of the coincident indicators composite by deriving a ratio of the two long-term averages and then dividing the leading indicators' monthly change by that ratio. Because many components are already seasonally adjusted, the composite index itself is not seasonally adjusted.

Indicates changes in the direction of aggregate economic activity; viewed by many as an indicator of current and future levels of economic activity.

Issued monthly as a press release by The Conference Board and on their World Wide Web home page at www.conference-board.org.

Source	Frequency	Extent	Form	Medium
Bank of America	m	c, h	t	e
Bank of Tokyo-Mitsubishi	m	c, h	t	e
Barron's	m	c	t	p
BCI	m	h	g	e
Commodity Yearbook	a, m	c, h	t	p
Conference Board/BCI	m	c	t	e
Financial Digest	m	c	t	p
FRB Dallas	m	c, h	t	e
S&P Basic Statistics - Income and Trade	a, m	c, h	t	p
S&P Current Statistics	m	h	t	p
Statistical Abstract	a	h	t	p
Stat-USA	m	c	t	e

Bibliography

"Are They Wrong Even When They're Right," *Business Week*, 90 (May 4, 1983).

Beckman, Barry A., and Tracy R. Tapscott, "Composite Indexes of Leading, Coincident, and Lagging Indicators," *Survey of Current Business* **67** (11), 24-28 (1987).

Carnes, W. Stansbury, and Stephen D. Slifer, *The Atlas of Economic Indicators: A Visual Guide to Market Forces and the Federal Reserve*, Harper Business, New York, 1991, pp. 135-141.

de Leeuw, Frank, "Toward a Theory of Leading Indicators," pp. 15-56 in Kajal Lahiri and Moore, Geoffrey H. Moore, Eds., *Leading Economic Indicators: New Approaches and Forecasting Records,* Cambridge University Press, New York, 1991.

Diebold, Francis X., and Glenn D. Rudebusch, "Scoring the Leading Indicators," *Journal of Business* **62** (3), 369-391 (1989).

Frumkin, Norman, *Guide to Economic Indicators*, 2nd ed., M. E. Sharpe, Armonk, N.Y., 1994, pp. 217-223.

Frumkin, Norman, *Tracking America's Economy*, 2nd ed., Sharpe, Armonk, N.Y., 1992, pp. 283-302.

Garner, C. Alan, "How Useful Are Leading Indicators of Inflation?" *Economic Review of the Federal Reserve Bank of Kansas City* **80** (2), 5-18 (1995).

Grant, John, *A Handbook of Economic Indicators*, University of Toronto Press, Toronto, 1992, pp. 166-167.

Green, George R., and Barry A. Beckman, "Business Cycle Indicators: Upcoming Revision of the Composite Indexes," *Survey of Current Business* **73** (10), 44-51 (1993).

Harper, Lucinda, "U.S. to Tune Up an Inflation Measure and Farm Out Leading-Indicator Index," *Wall Street Journal*, May 5, 1995, p. A2.

Harris, Maury N., and Debrorah Jamroz, *Evaluating the Leading Indicators*, Federal Reserve Bank of New York, New York, 1976, pp. 165-171.

Hoel, Arline Alchian; Kenneth W. Clarkson; and Roger LeRoy Miller, *Economics Sourcebook of Government Statistics*, Lexington Books, Lexington, Mass., 1983, pp. 61-65.

Hymans, Saul H., "On the Use of Leading Indicators to Predict Cyclical Turning Points," *Brooking Papers on Economic Activity*, 339-375 (1973).

Jun, Duk Bin, and Young Jin Joo, "Predicting Turning Points in Business Cycles by Detection of Slope Changes in the Leading Composite Index," *Journal of Forecasting* 12 (3/4), 197-213 (1993).

Koenig, Evan F., and Kenneth M. Emery, "Why the Composite Index of Leading Indicators Does Not Lead," *Contemporary Economic Policy* 12 (1), 52-66 (1994).

Lahiri, Kajal, and Geoffrey H. Moore, Eds., *Leading Economic Indicators: New Approaches and Forecasting Records,* Cambridge University Press, New York, 1991.

Lavin, Michael R., *Business Information: How to Find It, How to Use It*, Oryx Press, Phoenix, Ariz., 1992, p. 328.

Lehmann, Michael B., *The Irwin Guide to Using the Wall Street Journal*, 5th ed., Irwin, Chicago, 1996, pp. 307-312.

Moore, Geoffrey H., "Leading and Confirming Indicators of general Business Changes," pp. 45-109 in Geoffrey H. Moore, Ed., *Business Cycle Indicators*, Vol. 1, Princeton University Press, Princeton, N.J., 1961.

Moore, Geoffrey H., "New Developments in Leading Indicators," pp. 141-147 in K. Lahiri and G. H. Moore, *Leading Economic Indicators: New Approaches and Forecasting Records,* Cambridge University Press, New York, 1991.

Moore, G. H., and J. Shiskin, "Why the Leading Indicators Really Do Lead," *Across the Board*, 71-75 (May 1978).

Nelson, C. R., *The Investor's Guide to Economic Indicators*, John Wiley & Sons, New York, 1987, pp. 95-118.

Niemira, Michael P., and Giela T. Fredman, "An Evaluation of the Composite Index of Leading Indicators for Signaling Turning Points in Business and Growth Cycles," *Business Economics* 26 (4), 49-55 (1991).

Niemira, Michael P., and Gerald F. Zukowski, *Trading the Fundamentals: The Trader's Guide to Interpreting Economic Indicators and Monetary Policy*, McGraw-Hill, New York, 1998, pp. 61-66.

"Official Indicators: What Are They? Can They Predict the Future?" *U.S. News and World Report*, 66-67 (Aug. 16, 1976).

Renshaw, Edward, Ed., *The Practical Forecasters' Almanac: 137 Reliable Indicators for Investors, Hedgers, and Speculators*, Business One Irwin, Homewood, Ill., 1992, pp. 22-23, 82-83.

Rogers, R. Mark, *Handbook of Key Economic Indicators*, Irwin Professional Pub.,
    Burr Ridge, Ill., 1994, pp. 241-264.
Samuelson, Paul, "Paradise Lost & Refound: The Harvard ABC Barometers,"
    Journal of Portfolio Management **13** (3), 4-9 (1987).
Tainer, Evelina M., *Using Economic Indicators to Improve Investment Analysis*,
    John Wiley & Sons, New York, 1993, pp. 238-241.
WEFA Group, *Guide to Economic Indicators: U.S. Macroeconomic Services*,
    WEFA Group, Bala Cynwyd, Pa., 1997, p. 19.

Lehman Brothers Long Treasury Bond Index

A total-return performance benchmark for long-term, U.S. Government, fixed-rate debt issues.

This index evaluates the performance of all outstanding U.S. Treasury notes and bonds with maturities of 10 years or more. The basis of performance is taken to be total return, which includes the price appreciation or depreciation plus the income, expressed as a percentage of the original investment. The index is market-value weighted; that is to say, each component is multiplied by a factor that is the product of the publicly held principal amount of the issue multiplied by its current market price. These factors are recalculated and the index rebalanced monthly. Finally, the calculation results are indexed to a value of 1000 for Dec. 31, 1980.

Used as a measure of the performance of long-term government securities in aggregate, as a benchmark for the performance of individual securities or portfolios, and (to a lesser degree) as a gauge of the performance of the U.S. bond market in general.

Issued daily as a news release by Lehman Brothers.

Source	Frequency	Extent	Form	Medium
Barron's	w	c	t	p
First Union	m	c, h	t	e
USA Today	d	c	t	p
Wall Street Journal	w	c	t	p

Bibliography
Berlin, Howard M. *The Handbook of Financial Market Indexes, Averages, and Indicators*, Dow Jones-Irwin, Homewood, Ill., 1990, pp. 83-84.

Lipper Growth and Income Fund Index

A measure of the performance of 30 of the largest mutual funds whose investment objectives are growth and income, funds that pursue both price and dividend growth. One of the more commonly cited of the approximately 60 mutual-fund-performance indexes compiled by Lipper Analytical Services.

Each day, Lipper Analytical Services notes the daily-close net asset values of the selected mutual funds; adjusts those net asset values to account for income, dividends, and capital-gains distributions that have occurred since the funds were declared ex dividend; sums the adjusted values; and indexes the result to the value for December 31, 1968, when the index was set at 100.

Used as a benchmark against which the performance of individual mutual funds with similar investment objectives are compared, as an indicator of the performance of the mutual-fund-investment industry, and as an indicator of the performance of the growth-and-income sector of the stock market.

Published daily as a news release by Lipper Analytical Services.

Source	Frequency	Extent	Form	Medium
Barron's	d, ytd	c	t	p
Lipper	d	c	t	e
USA Today	d	c	t	p
Wall Street Journal	d, ytd	c	t	p

Bibliography
Berlin, Howard M. *The Handbook of Financial Market Indexes, Averages, and Indicators*, Dow Jones-Irwin, Homewood, Ill., 1990, pp. 88-99.

Lipper Growth Fund Index

A measure of the performance of 30 of the largest mutual funds whose investment objective is growth; that is to say, of funds that invest in companies whose long-term earnings are expected to grow more rapidly than the norm. One of the more commonly cited of the approximately 60 mutual-fund-performance indexes compiled by Lipper Analytical Services.

Each day, Lipper Analytical Services notes the daily-close net asset values of the selected mutual funds; adjusts those net asset values to account for income, dividends, and capital-gains distributions that have occurred since the funds were declared ex dividend; sums the adjusted values; and indexes the result to the value for December 31, 1968, when the index was set at 100.

Used as a benchmark against which the performance of individual mutual funds with similar investment objectives are compared, as an indicator of the performance of the mutual-fund-investment industry, and as an indicator of the performance of the growth sector of the stock market.

Published daily as a news release by Lipper Analytical Services.

Source	Frequency	Extent	Form	Medium
Barron's	d, ytd	c	t	p
Lipper	d	c	t	e
USA Today	d	c	t	p
Wall Street Journal	d, ytd	c	t	p

Bibliography
Berlin, Howard M. *The Handbook of Financial Market Indexes, Averages, and Indicators*, Dow Jones-Irwin, Homewood, Ill., 1990, pp. 88-97.

Lipper International Fund Index

A measure of the performance of 30 of the largest mutual funds that specialize in the investment in non-U.S. stocks. One of the more commonly cited of the approximately 60 mutual-fund-performance indexes compiled by Lipper Analytical Services.

Each day, Lipper Analytical Services notes the daily-close net asset values of the selected mutual funds; adjusts those net asset values to account for income, dividends, and capital-gains distributions that have occurred since the funds were declared ex dividend; sums the adjusted values; and indexes the result to the value for December 31, 1984, when the index was set at 100.

Used as a benchmark against which the performance of individual mutual funds with similar investment objectives are compared, as an indicator of the performance of the mutual-fund-investment industry, and as an indicator of the performance of the non-U.S. stock market.

Published daily as a news release by Lipper Analytical Services.

Source	Frequency	Extent	Form	Medium
Barron's	d, ytd	c	t	p
Lipper	d	c	t	e
USA Today	d	c	t	p
Wall Street Journal	d, ytd	c	t	p

Bibliography
Berlin, Howard M. *The Handbook of Financial Market Indexes, Averages, and Indicators*, Dow Jones-Irwin, Homewood, Ill., 1990, pp. 88-97.

Lipper Small Cap Index

A measure of the performance of 30 of the largest mutual funds that specialize in the stocks of lesser-known, small companies whose long-term earnings are expected to grow more rapidly than the norm. One of the more commonly cited of the approximately 60 mutual-fund-performance indexes compiled by Lipper Analytical Services.

Each day, Lipper Analytical Services notes the daily-close net asset values of the selected mutual funds; adjusts those net asset values to account for income, dividends, and capital-gains distributions that have occurred since the funds were declared ex dividend; sums the adjusted values; and indexes the result to the value for Dec. 31, 1982, when the index was set at 100.

Used as a benchmark against which the performance of individual mutual funds with similar investment objectives are compared, as an indicator of the performance of the mutual-fund-investment industry, and as an indicator of the performance of the small-company growth sector of the stock market.

Published daily as a news release by Lipper Analytical Services.

Source	Frequency	Extent	Form	Medium
Barron's	d, ytd	c	t	p
Lipper	d	c	t	e
USA Today	d	c	t	p
Wall Street Journal	d, ytd	c	t	p

Liquid Assets
[See L]

Loan Demand
[See Commercial and Industrial Loans Outstanding, Weekly Reporting Large Commercial Banks]

Loans and Investments
[Also referred to as Bank Loans, Investments, and Reserves; see also Commercial and Industrial Loans Outstanding, Weekly Reporting Large Commercial Banks]

Estimates the total loans outstanding from (1) all commercial banks (which excludes mutual savings banks, savings and loan associations, and other institutions that do not accept demand deposits) and (2) member banks of the Federal Reserve System.

Prepared on the basis of selected weekly banking reports (the selection is stratified by size of reporting banks) and quarterly call report information. Heavy reliance is placed on the data from banks that are members of the Federal Reserve to estimate the activities of nonmember banks. To these data are added data from the monthly condition reports of foreign financial institutions operating in the United States. Data are normally for the last Wednesday of the month. A subset, total commercial and industrial loans (all business loans except those secured by real estate, loans for purchasing or carrying securities, and loans to financial institutions), is also compiled. It includes securities held by these institutions, broken down into U.S. Treasury securities and other securities (principally issues of states, municipalities, and federal agencies).

Used in current banking and monetary analysis, in discerning trends in bank credit and its components, and in evaluating the banking system's performance and response to change in monetary policy.

Published monthly by the Board of Governors of the Federal Reserve System in *Loans and Investments at All Commercial Banks*, Statistical Release G.7 (407).

Source	Frequency	Extent	Form	Medium
Annual Statistical Digest (FRB)	a	c	t	p
BCI	m	h	g	e
Business Statistics	i	h	t	p
Conference Board/BCI	m	c	t	e
Economic Indicators	m	c, h	t, g	p, e
Federal Reserve Bulletin	m	c	t	p
FRED	w	c, h	t	e
Statistical Abstract	a	h	t	p
Survey of Current Business	m	c, h	t	p, e

Bibliography

Joint Economic Committee, *1980 Supplement to Economic Indicators, Historical and Descriptive Background*, USGPO, Washington, D.C., 1980, pp. 101-104.

Long-Duration Unemployment

[See also Total Unemployment; Unemployment Insurance Programs, Initial Claims; and Unemployment Rate, Total]

The percentage of the civilian labor force that has been unemployed for 15 weeks or more.

Each month, the Bureau of the Census surveys about 60,000 households of workers in its Current Population Survey. The data collected and tabulated are then analyzed and published by the Department of Labor's Bureau of Labor Statistics. Workers report if they are unemployed or on layoff and, if so, the number of weeks since they have been employed for two consecutive weeks. The number of workers that have been out of work for 15 weeks or longer is totaled, divided by the number of workers (employed or unemployed) in the survey, and multiplied by 100. The values are seasonally adjusted.

Used as a measure of the availability of labor and of the health of the general economy.

Published monthly by the Bureau of Labor Statistics in *Employment Situation*.

Source	Frequency	Extent	Form	Medium
Business Statistics	a, m	h	t	p
Employment & Earnings	a, m	c	t	p

Bibliography

Moore, Geoffrey Hoyt, *Improving the Presentation of Employment and Unemployment Statistics*, National Commission on Employment and Unemployment Statistics Background Paper No. 22, USGPO, Washington, D.C., 1978.

Moore, Geoffrey Hoyt, and Melita H. Moore, *International Economic Indicators: A Sourcebook*, Greenwood Press, Westport, Conn., 1985, p. 43.

Ruggles, Richard, *Employment and Unemployment Statistics as Indexes of Economic Activity and Capacity Utilization*, National Commission on Employment and Unemployment Statistics Background Paper No. 28, USGPO, Washington, D.C., 1979.

U.S. Department of Labor, Bureau of Labor Statistics, *How the Government Measures Unemployment*, Report 864, USGPO, Washington, D.C., 1994.

U.S. Department of Labor, Bureau of Labor Statistics, *Major Programs of the Bureau of Labor Statistics*, USGPO, Washington, D.C., 1994, pp. 3-4.

Long-Term Corporate Bond Yields
[See Moody's Corporate Aaa Bond Yield Averages]

Long-Term Tax-Free Bond Yields
[See Bond Buyer Forty Municipal Bond Index]

Long Treasury Bond Index
[See Lehman Brothers Long Treasury Bond Index]

Lumber Production

An estimation of the amount of lumber in board feet that U.S. sawmills and planing mills have produced, have shipped, and have in stock during the given month.

About half of the sawmills and planing mills in the United States are surveyed monthly to determine the amount of rough, dressed, and worked (matched, shiplapped, or patterned) lumber that has been produced, has been shipped, or is in stock. The output of flooring mills and of plants producing structural panels is also included. The data are then adjusted against annual production figures published by the Bureau of the Census. Current data are revised as more-relevant figures become available.

Used as a leading indicator of future business activity, especially in the paper and housing segments of the economy.

Published monthly by the American Forest and Paper Association in *Statistical Roundup*.

Source	Frequency	Extent	Form	Medium
Barron's	m	c	t	p
Business Statistics	a, m	h	t	p
Business Week	w	c	t	p
Commodity Yearbook	a	h	t	p
Construction Review	m	c, h	t	p

Source	Frequency	Extent	Form	Medium
Lumber Production and Mill Stock	a	c	t	p
Statistical Abstract	a	h	t	p

Bibliography
U.S. Department of Commerce, Bureau of Economic Analysis, *Business Statistics 1963-1993*, USGPO, Washington, D.C., 1994, p. 177.

Lumber Production and Mill Stock

An estimate of the lumber produced by U.S. sawmills each year.

The Bureau of the Census annually surveys a sample of sawmills across the country. From the responses and historic data, it then estimates the output of all sawmills, expressed in millions or billions of board feet. The data are broken down by state or region of the country and by type of lumber (e.g., hardwoods and softwoods).

Used as a leading indicator of future business activity and of inflationary pressures in specific segments of the economy like construction.

Published annually by the Bureau of the Census in Current Industrial Reports, Series MA24T: *Lumber Production and Mill Stock.*

Source	Frequency	Extent	Form	Medium
Lumber Production and Mill Stocks	a	c	t	p

M

M1
[See also L, M2, and M3]

A measure of the amount of money in the U.S. economy; one of the four major money-stock measures of the Federal Reserve System.

From the required filings of its member banks and other sources, the Federal Reserve System estimates and totals the amounts of currency in circulation, commercial bank demand deposits, deposits in notice-of-withdrawal (NOW) and automatic-transfer-from-savings accounts, credit union share drafts, mutual savings bank demand deposits, and cash represented by nonbank travelers checks to compile this estimate of the amount of money in use in the U.S. economy. The totals are adjusted to avoid double counting and to account for float on checks. The resulting total is seasonally adjusted.

Used as one determinant of the reserves that banks are required to maintain and of the discount rate, both of which influence the availability of money in the economy. Also used to guide the Federal Open Market Operations, which injects money into the economy or withdraws it by trading in government securities. Too much money in the economy tends to increase prices and inflation and to force interest rates down; too little money tends to increase interest rates and unemployment and to decrease prices and output.

Published weekly by the Board of Governors of the Federal Reserve System in *Money Stock, Liquid Assets, and Debt Measures*, Statistical Release H.6 and monthly in the *Federal Reserve Bulletin*.

Source	Frequency	Extent	Form	Medium
Annual Statistical Digest (FRB)	q, m	c, h	t	p
Barron's	d	c	t	p
BCI	m	h	g	e

Source	Frequency	Extent	Form	Medium
Business Statistics	a, m	h	t	p
Commodity Yearbook	a, m	c, h	t	p
Federal Reserve Board	m	c, h	t	e
Federal Reserve Bulletin	q, m	c	t	p
Financial Digest	d	c	t	p
FRB Dallas	m	c, h	t	e
FRED	d, w, m	c, h	t	e
International Financial Statistics	a, q	c, h	t	p
S&P Basic Statistics - Banking and Finance	a, m	h	t	p
S&P Current Statistics	m	h	t	p
Statistical Abstract	a	h	t	p
Stat-USA	m	c, h	t	e
Survey of Current Business	a, m	c, h	t, g	p, e
US Financial Data	m, w	c	t, g	p
Value Line Investment Survey, Part 2: Selection and Opinion	w	c	t	p
Wall Street Journal	w	c	t	p

Bibliography

Berlin, Howard M. *The Handbook of Financial Market Indexes, Averages, and Indicators*, Dow Jones-Irwin, Homewood, Ill., 1990, pp. 115-116.

Board of Governors of the Federal Reserve System, *The Federal Reserve System: Purposes and Functions*, Publication Services, Board of Governors of the Federal Reserve System, Washington, D.C., 1994.

Colby, Robert W., and Thomas A. Meyers, *The Encyclopedia of Technical Market Indicators*, Dow Jones-Irwin, Homewood, Ill., 1988, p. 280.

Downes, John, and Jordan Elliot Goodman, *Dictionary of Finance and Investment Terms*, Barron's Educational Series, Hauppage, N.Y., 1995.

Dueker, Michael J., "Indicators of Monetary Policy: The View from Implicit Feedback Rules," *Federal Reserve Bank of St. Louis Review* **75** (5), 23-39 (1993).

Frumkin, Norman, *Guide to Economic Indicators*, 2nd ed., M. E. Sharpe, Armonk, N.Y., 1994, pp. 229-234.

Frumkin, Norman, *Tracking America's Economy*, 2nd ed., Sharpe, Armonk, N.Y., 1992, pp. 255-256.

Grant, John, *A Handbook of Economic Indicators*, University of Toronto Press, Toronto, 1992, pp. 170-173.

Hoel, Arline Alchian; Kenneth W. Clarkson; and Roger LeRoy Miller, *Economics Sourcebook of Government Statistics*, Lexington Books, Lexington, Mass., 1983, pp. 130-135.

Joint Economic Committee, *1980 Supplement to Economic Indicators, Historical and Descriptive Background*, USGPO, Washington, D.C., 1980, pp. 94-98.

Nelson, C. R., *The Investor's Guide to Economic Indicators*, John Wiley & Sons, New York, 1987, p. 32.

Niemira, Michael P., and Gerald F. Zukowski, *Trading the Fundamentals: The Trader's Guide to Interpreting Economic Indicators and Monetary Policy*, McGraw-Hill, New York, 1998, pp. 231-236.

Plocek, Joseph E., *Economic Indicators: How America Reads Its Financial Health*, New York Institute of Finance, New York, 1991, p. 272.

Publication Services, *The Federal Reserve System: Purposes and Functions*, Board of Governors of the Federal Reserve System, Washington, D.C., 1994, p. 28.

Renshaw, Edward, Ed., *The Practical Forecasters' Almanac: 137 Reliable Indicators for Investors, Hedgers, and Speculators*, Business One Irwin, Homewood, Ill., 1992, pp. 47-49.

Stern, Linda, "M1 Loses Status at the Fed," *Journal of Commerce*, pp. 1 and 14A, June 23, 1986.

M2

[Also called the Money Balance; see also M1]

A measure of real money supply; one of the four major money-stock measures of the Federal Reserve System.

The Federal Reserve adds to its M1 measure other forms of fund deposits, such as commercial banks' overnight repurchase agreements, overnight Eurodollars, savings accounts, time deposits of less than $100,000, and shares in money-market mutual funds to compile this estimate of the amount of money in use in the U.S. economy. The totals are adjusted to avoid double counting and to account for float on checks. The resulting total is seasonally adjusted.

Considered to be a leading indicator of all portions of the business cycle. Used as one determinant of the reserves that banks are required to maintain and of the discount rate, both of which influence the availability of money in the economy. Also used to guide the Federal Open Market Operations, which injects money into the economy or withdraws it by trading in government securities. Too much money in the economy tends to increase prices and inflation and to force interest rates down; too little money tends to increase interest rates and unemployment and to decrease prices and output. It is a component of the Leading Indicators Composite Index.

Published weekly by the Board of Governors of the Federal Reserve System in *Money Stock, Liquid Assets, and Debt Measures*, Statistical Release H.6 and monthly in the *Federal Reserve Bulletin*.

Source	Frequency	Extent	Form	Medium
Agricultural Outlook	a, q	c	t	p
Annual Statistical Digest (FRB)	q, m	c, h	t	p
Barron's	d	c	t	p
BCI	m	h	g	e
Business Statistics	a, m	h	t	p
Commodity Yearbook	a, m	c, h	t	p
Conference Board/BCI	m	c	t	e
Federal Reserve Board	m	c, h	t	e
Federal Reserve Bulletin	q, m	c	t	p
Financial Digest	d	c	t	p
FRB Dallas	m	c, h	t	e
FRB New York	m	c, h	g	e
FRED	d, w, m	c, h	t	e
International Financial Statistics	a, q	c, h	t	p
Recession Recovery Watch	q	h	g	p
S&P Basic Statistics - Banking and Finance	a, m	h	t	p
S&P Basic Statistics - Income and Trade	a, m	h	t	p
S&P Current Stats	m	h	t	p
Statistical Abstract	a	h	t	p
Stat-USA	m	c, h	t	e
Survey of Current Business	a, m	c	t, g	p, e
US Financial Data	m, w	c	t, g	p
Value Line Investment Survey, Part 2: Selection and Opinion	a, q, d	c, h, f	t, g	p
Wall Street Journal	w	c	t	p

Bibliography

Berlin, Howard M. *The Handbook of Financial Market Indexes, Averages, and Indicators*, Dow Jones-Irwin, Homewood, Ill., 1990, pp. 115-116.

Board of Governors of the Federal Reserve System, *The Federal Reserve System: Purposes and Functions*, Publication Services, Board of Governors of the Federal Reserve System, Washington, D.C., 1994.

Colby, Robert W., and Thomas A. Meyers, *The Encyclopedia of Technical Market Indicators*, Dow Jones-Irwin, Homewood, Ill., 1988, p. 280.

Downes, John, and Jordan Elliot Goodman, *Dictionary of Finance and Investment Terms*, Barron's Educational Series, Hauppage, N.Y., 1995.

Duca, John V., "The Case of the Missing M2," *Economic Review of the Federal Reserve Bank of Dallas* 1-24 (Second Quarter, 1992).

Dueker, Michael J., "Indicators of Monetary Policy: The View from Implicit Feedback Rules," *Federal Reserve Bank of St. Louis Review* **75** (5), 23-39 (1993).

Frumkin, Norman, *Guide to Economic Indicators*, 2nd ed., M. E. Sharpe, Armonk, N.Y., 1994, pp. 229-234.

Frumkin, Norman, *Tracking America's Economy*, 2nd ed., Sharpe, Armonk, N.Y., 1992, pp. 255-256.

Grant, John, *A Handbook of Economic Indicators*, University of Toronto Press, Toronto, 1992, pp. 170-173.

Hoel, Arline Alchian; Kenneth W. Clarkson; and Roger LeRoy Miller, *Economics Sourcebook of Government Statistics*, Lexington Books, Lexington, Mass., 1983, pp. 130-135.

Mishkin, Frederic S., "Commentary," *Federal Reserve Bank of St. Louis Review* **76** (2), 204-207 (1994).

Motley, Brian, "Should M2 Be Redefined?" *Federal Reserve Bank of San Francisco Economic Review* 33-51 (Winter 1988).

Nelson, C. R., *The Investor's Guide to Economic Indicators*, John Wiley & Sons, New York, 1987, 32-38, 99-103.

Niemira, Michael P., and Gerald F. Zukowski, *Trading the Fundamentals: The Trader's Guide to Interpreting Economic Indicators and Monetary Policy*, McGraw-Hill, New York, 1998, pp. 231-236.

Plocek, Joseph E., *Economic Indicators: How America Reads Its Financial Health*, New York Institute of Finance, New York, 1991, p. 272.

Publication Services, *The Federal Reserve System: Purposes and Functions*, Board of Governors of the Federal Reserve System, Washington, D.C., 1994, pp. 28-29.

Renshaw, Edward, Ed., *The Practical Forecasters' Almanac: 137 Reliable Indicators for Investors, Hedgers, and Speculators*, Business One Irwin, Homewood, Ill., 1992, pp. 49, 78.

M3

[See also L, M1, and M2]

A broad measure of the amount of money in the U.S. economy; one of the four major money-stock measures of the Federal Reserve System.

The Federal Reserve adds to its M2 measure other forms of fund deposits, such as time deposits of more than $100,000 and term repurchase agreements to compile this estimate of the amount of money in use in the U.S. economy. The totals are adjusted to avoid double counting and to account for float on checks. The resulting total is seasonally adjusted.

Used as one determinant of the reserves that banks are required to maintain and of the discount rate, both of which influence the availability of money in the economy. Also used to guide the Federal Open Market Operations, which injects money into the economy or withdraws it by trading in government securities. Too much money in the economy tends to increase prices and inflation and to force interest rates down; too little money tends to increase interest rates and unemployment and to decrease prices and output.

Published weekly by the Board of Governors of the Federal Reserve System in *Money Stock, Liquid Assets, and Debt Measures*, Statistical Release H.6 and monthly in the *Federal Reserve Bulletin*.

Source	Frequency	Extent	Form	Medium
Annual Statistical Digest (FRB)	q, m	c, h	t	p
Barron's	d	c	t	p
Business Statistics	a, m	h	t	p
Federal Reserve Board	m	c, h	t	e
Federal Reserve Bulletin	q, m	c	t	p
Financial Digest	d	c	t	p
FRED	d, w, m	c, h	t	e
International Financial Statistics	a, q	c, h	t	p
S&P Basic Statistics - Banking and Finance	a, m	h	t	p
S&P Current Stats	m	h	t	p
Statistical Abstract	a	h	t	p
Stat-USA	m	c, h	t	e
Value Line Investment Survey, Part 2: Selection and Opinion	d	c	t	p
Wall Street Journal	w	c	t	p

Bibliography

Berlin, Howard M. *The Handbook of Financial Market Indexes, Averages, and Indicators*, Dow Jones-Irwin, Homewood, Ill., 1990, pp. 115-116.

Board of Governors of the Federal Reserve System, *The Federal Reserve System: Purposes and Functions*, Publication Services, Board of Governors of the Federal Reserve System, Washington, D.C., 1994.

Colby, Robert W., and Thomas A. Meyers, *The Encyclopedia of Technical Market Indicators*, Dow Jones-Irwin, Homewood, Ill., 1988, p. 280.

Downes, John, and Jordan Elliot Goodman, *Dictionary of Finance and Investment Terms*, Barron's Educational Series, Hauppage, N.Y., 1995.

Frumkin, Norman, *Guide to Economic Indicators*, 2nd ed., M. E. Sharpe, Armonk, N.Y., 1994, pp. 229-234.

Frumkin, Norman, *Tracking America's Economy*, 2nd ed., Sharpe, Armonk, N.Y., 1992, pp. 255-256.

Grant, John, *A Handbook of Economic Indicators*, University of Toronto Press, Toronto, 1992, pp. 170-173.

Hoel, Arline Alchian; Kenneth W. Clarkson; and Roger LeRoy Miller, *Economics Sourcebook of Government Statistics*, Lexington Books, Lexington, Mass., 1983, pp. 130-135.

Joint Economic Committee, *1980 Supplement to Economic Indicators, Historical and Descriptive Background*, USGPO, Washington, D.C., 1980, pp. 94-98.

Niemira, Michael P., and Gerald F. Zukowski, *Trading the Fundamentals: The Trader's Guide to Interpreting Economic Indicators and Monetary Policy*, McGraw-Hill, New York, 1998, pp. 231-236.

Publication Services, *The Federal Reserve System: Purposes and Functions*, Board of Governors of the Federal Reserve System, Washington, D.C., 1994, p. 28.

Machine Tool Orders

A measure of the current sales level for metal-cutting and metal-forming machine tools.

Respondents to a monthly survey by the Association for Manufacturing Technology provide their gross new orders, cancellations, shipments, and backlog of unfilled orders. From these data, a value for net new orders is derived by subtracting cancellations from gross orders. The result is multiplied by an expansion factor to estimate all machine-tool-industry activity. That factor is periodically determined by comparing the shipment total reported in the surveys to that reported by the Census Bureau.

Used as a leading indicator of the activity in the industrial sector of the U.S. economy; analysts view machine-tool orders as an indicator of capital investment by the manufacturers of durable goods and large-ticket items like airplanes in preparation for increased production and/or greater efficiency and productivity. It is considered a leading indicator because these manufacturing tools can take up to 18 months to customize and install before they are used.

Published monthly by the Association for Manufacturing Technology in *AMT Industry Estimates: Machine Tool Orders and Shipments*.

Source	Frequency	Extent	Form	Medium
AMT Industry Estimates	m	c	t, g	p
Economic Handbook of the Machine Tool Industry	a, q, m	h	t, g	p
Handbook of International Economic Statistics (CIA)	a	h	t	p
S&P Basic Statistics - Transportation	a, m	h	t	p

Source	Frequency	Extent	Form	Medium
S&P Current Statistics	m	h	t	p

Magazine Cover Indicator
[See Appendix A. Nonquantitative Indicators]

Major Industrial Countries' Industrial Production
[See Industrial Production, Major Industrial Countries]

Major Market Groups and Selected Manufacturers' Industrial Production
[See Industrial Production]

Major Market Index
[See American Stock Exchange Major Market Index]

Manufacturers' Capacity Utilization
[See Capacity Utilization; also called Capacity Utilization Rate]

Manufacturers' Inventories
[See also Inventory Change Index and Manufacturing and Trade Inventories]

Estimates of manufacturers' book values (in constant dollars) of raw materials and supplies, work in progress, and finished goods on hand at the end of the period.

About 5000 companies or divisions of companies are surveyed monthly to determine what inventories of raw materials or goods they have on hand. The resulting data are broken down into about 80 industry categories. The estimate for the previous month for each category is adjusted by the ratio of change indicated by the survey data. The estimates are benchmarked annually, are seasonally adjusted, and (where appropriate) adjusted for the number of trading days in the month.

Used to discern trends in the difference between production and shipments of manufacturers, to predict the probable course of manufacturers' activity in selected industries in the near future, and to indicate future directions of the general business cycle. These data also allow the analysis of the impact of changes in demand in and on various sectors of the economy.

Published monthly by the U.S. Department of Commerce, Bureau of the Census, in *Manufacturers' Shipments, Inventories, and Orders*, Current Industrial Report M3-1.

Source	Frequency	Extent	Form	Medium
Business Statistics	a, m	h	t	p

Source	Frequency	Extent	Form	Medium
Economic Report of the President	a	h	t	p, e
FRED	m	c, h	t	e
Manufacturers' Shipments, Inventories, and Orders	m	c	t	p
S&P Basic Statistics - Income and Trade	a, m	h	t	p
S&P Current Statistics	m	h	t	p
Statistical Abstract	a	h	t	p
Stat-USA	m	c	t	e

Bibliography

Carnes, W. Stansbury, and Stephen D. Slifer, *The Atlas of Economic Indicators: A Visual Guide to Market Forces and the Federal Reserve*, Harper Business, New York, 1991, pp. 153-159.

Hoel, Arline Alchian; Kenneth W. Clarkson; and Roger LeRoy Miller, *Economics Sourcebook of Government Statistics*, Lexington Books, Lexington, Mass., 1983, pp. 69-72.

Joint Economic Committee, *1980 Supplement to Economic Indicators, Historical and Descriptive Background*, USGPO, Washington, D.C., 1980, pp. 79-81.

Moore, Geoffrey Hoyt, and Melita H. Moore, *International Economic Indicators: A Sourcebook*, Greenwood Press, Westport, Conn., 1985, pp. 44-45.

Niemira, Michael P., and Gerald F. Zukowski, *Trading the Fundamentals: The Trader's Guide to Interpreting Economic Indicators and Monetary Policy*, McGraw-Hill, New York, 1998, pp. 163-168.

Renshaw, Edward, Ed., *The Practical Forecasters' Almanac: 137 Reliable Indicators for Investors, Hedgers, and Speculators*, Business One Irwin, Homewood, Ill., 1992, pp. 41-42.

Rogers, R. Mark, *Handbook of Key Economic Indicators*, Irwin Professional Pub., Burr Ridge, Ill., 1994, pp. 143-156.

Slater, Courtenay M., Ed., Business Statistics of the United States, 1995 ed., Bernan Press, Lanham, Md., 1996, pp. 254-255.

Tainer, Evelina M., *Using Economic Indicators to Improve Investment Analysis*, John Wiley & Sons, New York, 1993, pp. 103-107.

Tamm, Feliks, "An Agenda for Inventories Input to the Leading Composite Index," pp. 429-460 in Kajal Lahiri and Moore, Geoffrey H. Moore, Eds., *Leading Economic Indicators: New Approaches and Forecasting Records*, Cambridge University Press, New York, 1991.

U.S. Department of Commerce, Bureau of Economic Analysis, *Business Statistics, 1963-91*, USGPO, Washington, D.C., 1992, p. 144.

Manufacturers' Inventory-Sales Ratio
[Also called Business Inventory-Sales Ratio]

The ratio of the value of inventory that retail and manufacturing establishments have on hand during a given period to the sales actually recorded by those establishments during that period.

Two ratios are actually calculated and reported, one for retail traders and one for manufacturers. The end-of-month book values of inventories held are divided by the total sales during the month for each of these classes. The data for this arithmetic operation are derived from the seasonally adjusted sales and inventory series for retailers (see Retail Sales and Retail Inventories) and for manufacturers (see Manufacturing and Trade Sales and Manufacturers' Inventories). The yearly data are calculated by dividing the weighted average of seasonally adjusted inventories by the monthly average of unadjusted sales for the year. No adjustments are made to bring inventory book values (which might be either actual cost or market value) up to selling prices.

Stock-sales ratios are inversely related to business activity. That is, the ratios tend to rise as sales decline and to fall as sales increase. They are therefore used to evaluate the current position of inventory holdings and to forecast production activity. If the ratio of stock to sales rises, future production may need to be curtailed; if the ratio declines, future production may need to be increased to meet consumer demand. The ratio is a component of the Lagging Indicators Composite Index.

Published monthly by the Bureau of the Census, in *Manufacturers' Shipments, Inventories, and Orders*, Current Industrial Report M3-1.

Source	Frequency	Extent	Form	Medium
Conference Board/BCI	m	c	t	e
First Union	m	c, h	t	e
FRED	m	c, h	t	e
S&P Current Statistics	m	h	t	p

Bibliography

Carnes, W. Stansbury, and Stephen D. Slifer, *The Atlas of Economic Indicators: A Visual Guide to Market Forces and the Federal Reserve*, Harper Business, New York, 1991, pp. 165-166.

Frumkin, Norman, *Guide to Economic Indicators*, 2nd ed., M. E. Sharpe, Armonk, N.Y., 1994, pp. 211-216.

Manufacturers' Inventory-Shipments Ratio

The ratio of the value of manufacturers' inventory on hand during a given period to the selling value of the goods shipped by them during that period.

For the monthly ratio, the end-of-month book value, seasonally adjusted, of the inventories that manufacturers of durable and nondurable goods have on hand (see Manufacturers' Inventories) is divided by the monthly average of shipments (sales) recorded by those manufacturers during that month. The data for this calculation are derived from the manufacturers' shipments and manufacturers' inventories series (see Manufacturers' Shipments, Manufacturers' Inventories, and Manufacturers' Orders). The yearly data are calculated by dividing the weighted average of seasonally adjusted inventories by the monthly average of shipments for the year.

Indicative of the match-up of production with demand. If the ratio rises, inventories (and therefore production) are getting ahead of demand for the goods produced, and perhaps future production should be reduced. If the ratio decreases, inventories and production are falling behind demand, and perhaps future production should be increased.

Published monthly by the U.S. Department of Commerce, Bureau of the Census, in *Manufacturers' Shipments, Inventories, and Orders*, Current Industrial Report M3-1.

Source	Frequency	Extent	Form	Medium
Manufacturers' Shipments, Inventories, and Orders	m	c	t, g	p
Statistical Abstract	a	h	t	p

Manufacturers' New Orders

[See also Durable Goods; Manufacturers' New Orders: Capital Goods Industries, Nondefense; and Manufacturers' Orders]

An estimate of the new orders for manufactured goods received during a given month less cancellations.

A subset of the Manufacturers' Orders data. Each month the Bureau of the Census surveys manufacturers to determine the sales value of orders for goods to be delivered at some future date, the sales value of orders filled immediately during the month, and the net sales value of contract changes that have resulted in increases or decreases in order values. New orders are defined as orders received during the reporting period that are supported by binding legal documents. The value of any cancellations is to be deducted from the totals. Because some companies report only backlogs of unfilled orders and in order to maintain the distinction between orders and shipments, orders remaining unfilled at the end of the monthly reporting period are estimated directly and separately and they are then combined with shipments data to produce the new-orders data. Although the new-orders data are not independently seasonally adjusted, they are derived from data that are seasonally adjusted. The totals are presented in current dollars.

Used as an indicator of future business activity.

Published monthly by the U.S. Department of Commerce, Bureau of the Census, in *Manufacturers' Shipments, Inventories, and Orders*, Current Industrial Report M3-1.

Source	Frequency	Extent	Form	Medium
Barron's	m	c	t	p
BCI	m	h	g	e
Business Statistics	a, m	h	t	p
Economic Report of the President	a	h	t	p, e
FRB Dallas	m	c, h	t	e
FRB New York	m	c, h	g	e
FRED	m	c, h	t	e
Manufacturers' Shipments, Inventories, and Orders	m	c	t	p
S&P Basic Statistics - Income and Trade	a, m	h	t	p
S&P Current Statistics	m	h	t	p
Statistical Abstract	a	h	t	p
Stat-USA	m	c	t	e

Bibliography

Moore, Geoffrey Hoyt, and Melita H. Moore, *International Economic Indicators. A Sourcebook*, Greenwood Press, Westport, Conn., 1985, pp. 29-30.

Nelson, Charles R., *The Investor's Guide to Economic Indicators*, John Wiley & Sons, New York, 1987, pp. 116-117.

Manufacturers' New Orders: Capital Goods Industries, Nondefense

[See also Durable Goods, Manufacturers' New Orders, and Manufacturers' Orders]

An estimate of the new orders (less cancellations) received during a given month less cancellations by manufacturers of durable goods that fall in the categories of nonelectrical machinery; electrical machinery; and the nondefense portions of communications equipment, ships, tanks, aircraft, and ordnance.

A subset of the Durable Goods data. Each month the Bureau of the Census surveys manufacturers to determine the sales value of orders for goods to be delivered at some future date, the sales value of orders filled immediately during the month, and the net sales value of contract changes that have resulted in increases or decreases in order values. New orders are defined as orders received during the reporting period that are supported by binding legal documents. The value of any cancellations is to be deducted from the totals. Because some companies report only backlogs of unfilled orders and in order to maintain the distinction between orders and shipments, orders remaining unfilled at the end of the monthly reporting period are estimated directly and separately and they are then combined with shipments data to produce the new-orders data. Although the new-orders data are not independently seasonally adjusted, they are derived from data that are seasonally adjusted. The totals are presented in current dollars.

Used as one of the components of the Leading Indicators Composite Index and as a gauge of future buying commitment (and hence of future business activity). This indicator is considered to reflect industry's plans to expand and modernize.

Published monthly by the U.S. Department of Commerce, Bureau of the Census, in *Manufacturers' Shipments, Inventories, and Orders*, Current Industrial Report M3-1.

Source	Frequency	Extent	Form	Medium
BCI	m	h	g	e
Conference Board/BCI	m	c	t	e
First Union	m	c, h	t	e
Manufacturers' Shipments, Inventories, and Orders	m	c	t, g	p
Statistical Abstract	a	h	t	p

Bibliography

Moore, Geoffrey Hoyt, and Melita H. Moore, *International Economic Indicators: A Sourcebook*, Greenwood Press, Westport, Conn., 1985, pp. 29-30.

Nelson, Charles R., *The Investor's Guide to Economic Indicators*, John Wiley & Sons, New York, 1987, pp. 116-117.

Manufacturers' Orders

[See also Durable Goods; Manufacturers' New Orders: Capital Goods Industries, Nondefense; and Manufacturers' New Orders]

Estimates of the net value of orders that manufacturers have in hand after cancellations and contract changes have been made.

Each month, the Bureau of the Census surveys about 5000 companies or divisions of companies to determine what new orders they have received that month and what orders remained unfilled at the end of the reporting period. These values are combined to determine the orders that manufacturers have in hand during the current month. The data are broken down into about 80 industry categories. The estimate for the previous month for each category is adjusted by the ratio of change indicated by the survey data. The estimates are benchmarked annually, are seasonally adjusted, and (where appropriate) adjusted for the number of trading days in the month. Data reflect both durable and nondurable goods and both military and nonmilitary purchases.

Used to discern trends in the difference between production and shipments of manufacturers, to predict the probable course of manufacturers' activity in selected industries in the near future, and to indicate future directions of the general business cycle. These data also allow the analysis of the impact of changes in demand in and on various sectors of the economy.

Published monthly by the U.S. Department of Commerce, Bureau of the Census, in *Manufacturers' Shipments, Inventories, and Orders*, Current Industrial Report M3-1.

Source	Frequency	Extent	Form	Medium
Bank of America	m	c, h	t	e
Bank of Tokyo-Mitsubishi	m	c, h	t	e
Manufacturers' Shipments, Inventories, and Orders	m	c	t	p
Quote.com	m	c	t	e
Statistical Abstract	a	h	t	p

Bibliography

Carnes, W. Stansbury, and Stephen D. Slifer, *The Atlas of Economic Indicators: A Visual Guide to Market Forces and the Federal Reserve*, HarperBusiness, New York, 1991, pp. 153-159.

Frumkin, Norman, *Guide to Economic Indicators*, 2nd ed., M. E. Sharpe, Armonk, N.Y., 1994, pp. 224-228.

Hoel, Arline Alchian; Kenneth W. Clarkson; and Roger LeRoy Miller, *Economics Sourcebook of Government Statistics*, Lexington Books, Lexington, Mass., 1983, pp. 69-72.

Joint Economic Committee, *1980 Supplement to Economic Indicators, Historical and Descriptive Background*, USGPO, Washington, D.C., 1980, pp. 79-81.

Niemira, Michael P., and Gerald F. Zukowski, *Trading the Fundamentals: The Trader's Guide to Interpreting Economic Indicators and Monetary Policy*, McGraw-Hill, New York, 1998, pp. 163-168.

Rogers, R. Mark, *Handbook of Key Economic Indicators*, Irwin Professional Pub., Burr Ridge, Ill., 1994, pp. 143-155.

Slater, Courtenay M., Ed., Business Statistics of the United States, 1995 ed., Bernan Press, Lanham, Md., 1996, pp. 254-255.

Tainer, Evelina M., *Using Economic Indicators to Improve Investment Analysis*, John Wiley & Sons, New York, 1993, pp. 103-104.

U.S. Department of Commerce, Bureau of Economic Analysis, *Business Statistics, 1963-91*, USGPO, Washington, D.C., 1992, p. 144.

Manufacturers' Sales
[See Manufacturers' Shipments]

Manufacturers' Shipments
Estimates of shipments (foreign and domestic), expressed in net selling values.

About 5000 companies or divisions of companies are surveyed monthly. Data are broken down into about 80 industry categories. The estimate for the previous month for each category is adjusted by the ratio of change indicated by the survey data. The estimates are benchmarked annually to the most recent level of the Average Monthly Shipments, are seasonally adjusted, and (where appropriate) adjusted for the number of trading days in the month.

Used to discern trends in the difference between production and shipments of manufacturers, to predict the probable course of manufacturers' activity in selected industries in the near future, and to indicate future directions of the general business cycle. These data also allow the analysis of the impact of changes in demand in and on various sectors of the economy.

Published monthly by the U.S. Department of Commerce, Bureau of the Census, in *Manufacturers' Shipments, Inventories, and Orders*, Current Industrial Report M3-1.

Source	Frequency	Extent	Form	Medium
Business Statistics	a, m	h	t	p
Economic Report of the President	a	h	t	p, e
Manufacturers' Shipments, Inventories, and Orders	m	c	t, g	p
S&P Basic Statistics - Income and Trade	a, m	h	t	p
Statistical Abstract	a	h	t	p
Stat-USA	m	c	t	e

Bibliography

Hoel, Arline Alchian; Kenneth W. Clarkson; and Roger LeRoy Miller, *Economics Sourcebook of Government Statistics*, Lexington Books, Lexington, Mass., 1983, pp. 69-72.

Joint Economic Committee, *1980 Supplement to Economic Indicators, Historical and Descriptive Background*, USGPO, Washington, D.C., 1980, pp. 79-81.

Niemira, Michael P., and Gerald F. Zukowski, *Trading the Fundamentals: The Trader's Guide to Interpreting Economic Indicators and Monetary Policy*, McGraw-Hill, New York, 1998, pp. 163-168.

Rogers, R. Mark, *Handbook of Key Economic Indicators*, Irwin Professional Pub., Burr Ridge, Ill., 1994, pp. 143-155.

Slater, Courtenay M., Ed., Business Statistics of the United States, 1995 ed., Bernan Press, Lanham, Md., 1996, pp. 254-255.

Tainer, Evelina M., *Using Economic Indicators to Improve Investment Analysis*, John Wiley & Sons, New York, 1993, pp. 103-107.

U.S. Department of Commerce, Bureau of Economic Analysis, *Business Statistics, 1963-91*, USGPO, Washington, D.C., 1992, p. 144.

Manufacturers' Unfilled Orders

An estimate of the orders placed with manufacturers of durable goods that remain unfilled at the end of a given month.

Manufacturers of durable goods (items with a normal life expectancy of three years or more) are surveyed monthly and asked to report the sales value of orders that have not been filled at the end of the month. Unfilled orders are defined as those that have not yet passed through the sales account. The value of any cancellations is deducted from the totals. Because some companies report only backlogs of unfilled orders, orders remaining unfilled at the end of the monthly reporting period are estimated directly and separately to maintain the distinction between orders and shipments. Monthly estimates are derived by multiplying the previous month's estimate by the percentage change from the previous month to the current month for companies reporting in the current month. Values are benchmarked to a modified ratio of unfilled orders to shipments (the latter being annually benchmarked to the most recent level of the *Annual Survey of Manufactures*). The unfilled-orders data are seasonally adjusted. The totals are presented in current dollars.

Used as a gauge of the present and near-future state of the producer and consumer durable-goods sectors of the economy.

Published monthly by the U.S. Department of Commerce, Bureau of the Census, in *Survey of Current Business*.

Source	Frequency	Extent	Form	Medium
Barron's	m	c	t	p
BCI	m	h	g	e
Economic Report of the President	a	h	t	p, e
FRB New York	m	c, h	g	e
S&P Basic Statistics - Income and Trade	a, m	h	t	p
S&P Current Statistics	m	h	t	p
Statistical Abstract	a	h	t	p
Survey of Current Business	m	c, h	t	p, e

Bibliography
Slater, Courtenay M., Ed., Business Statistics of the United States, 1995 ed., Bernan Press, Lanham, Md., 1996, pp. 254-255.
U.S. Department of Commerce, Bureau of Economic Analysis, *Business Statistics, 1963-91*, USGPO, Washington, D.C., 1992, pp. 144-145.

Manufacturing and Trade Inventories
[See also Inventory Change Index and Manufacturers' Inventories]

The dollar value (in current and constant dollars) of inventories held by manufacturers, wholesalers, and retailers.

Each month, the Bureau of the Census surveys manufacturers, merchant wholesalers, and retail traders to ascertain the book value of their end-of-month stocks on hand. Consignment goods are excluded. These book values are summed and adjusted to annual and quinquennial benchmarks derived from census data, the data are seasonally adjusted, and these current-dollar values are deflated with producer-price-index data. The resulting values are reported in terms of billions of dollars.

Used as an indicator of the pace of the nation's economy and of future employment. An emerging recession will swell inventories because of lack of sales; decreases in excessive inventories caused by a recession indicate that corrective measures are taking effect, production and consumption are coming into balance, and the recession may be ending. Excessive inventories cause production and employment to be scaled back; shortness in inventories spurs production, new hiring, and the use of overtime.

Issued monthly by the Bureau of the Census in the report *Manufacturing and Trade Inventories and Sales*.

Source	Frequency	Extent	Form	Medium
Bank of Tokyo-Mitsubishi	m	c, h	t	e
BCI	m	h	g	e
Business Statistics	a, m	h	t	p
Economic Report of the President	a	h	t	p, e
Financial Digest	m	c	t	p
First Union	m	c, h	t	e
FRB New York	m	c, h	g	e
S&P Basic Statistics - Income and Trade	a, m	h	t	p
Stat-USA	m	c	t	e
Survey of Current Business	a, q, m	c	t	p, e

Bibliography

Moore, Geoffrey Hoyt, and Melita H. Moore, *International Economic Indicators: A Sourcebook*, Greenwood Press, Westport, Conn., 1985, pp. 44-45.

Niemira, Michael P., and Gerald F. Zukowski, *Trading the Fundamentals: The Trader's Guide to Interpreting Economic Indicators and Monetary Policy*, McGraw-Hill, New York, 1998, pp. 19-23.

Slater, Courtenay M., Ed., Business Statistics of the United States, 1995 ed., Bernan Press, Lanham, Md., 1996, p. 227.

Tainer, Evelina M., *Using Economic Indicators to Improve Investment Analysis*, John Wiley & Sons, New York, 1993, pp. 107-108.

Tamm, Feliks, "An Agenda for Inventories Input to the Leading Composite Index," pp. 429-460 in Kajal Lahiri and Moore, Geoffrey H. Moore, Eds., *Leading*

Economic Indicators: New Approaches and Forecasting Records, Cambridge
   University Press, New York, 1991.
U.S. Department of Commerce, Bureau of Economic Analysis, *Business Statistics,*
   1963-91, USGPO, Washington, D.C., 1992, pp. 143-144.
U.S. Department of Commerce, Bureau of Economic Analysis, *Handbook of*
   Cyclical Indicators, USGPO, Washington, D.C., 1984, pp. 17-20.
WEFA Group, *Guide to Economic Indicators: U.S. Macroeconomic Services*,
   WEFA Group, Bala Cynwyd, Pa., 1997, p. 18.

Manufacturing and Trade Sales

**[See also Manufacturers' Shipments; also see Manufacturing and Trade
Inventories]**

The value (in current and constant dollars) of the sales of manufacturing,
merchant wholesalers, and retail establishments.

The Bureau of the Census surveys a sample of business establishments
monthly to determine their receipts, billings, value of products shipped, sales of
merchandise, or receipts from repairs or other services, depending on the type of
business surveyed. From these values are subtracted any discounts, returns,
allowances, or refunds. The totals are benchmarked to annual and quinquennial
census data and seasonally adjusted. The figures are deflated by the Bureau of
Economic Analysis with the appropriate Producer Price Index or Consumer Price
Index. The data are presented as both seasonally adjusted and unadjusted. The
seasonally adjusted figures are also broken down into separate categories for
manufacturing, retail trade, and merchant wholesalers, all of which are expressed
in values for durable goods, nondurable goods, and total. All of these values are in
current dollars; values expressed in constant dollars are also provided for total sale
of each of manufacturing, retail sales, and merchant wholesalers.

Used as a proof-positive of the current activity of the manufacturing sector
and of the robustness of the economy in general and as a component of the
Coincident Indicators Composite Index.

Issued monthly by the Bureau of the Census in the report *Manufacturing and
Trade Inventories and Sales.*

Source	Frequency	Extent	Form	Medium
BCI	m	h	g	e
Business Statistics	a, m	h	t	p
Conference Board/BCI	m	c	t	e
Economic Report of the President	a	h	t	p, e
Financial Digest	m	c	t	p
FRB New York	m	c, h	g	e

Source	Frequency	Extent	Form	Medium
S&P Basic Statistics - Income and Trade	a, m	h	t	p
Stat-USA	m	c	t	e
Survey of Current Business	a, q, m	c	t	p, e

Bibliography
Moore, Geoffrey Hoyt, and Melita H. Moore, *International Economic Indicators: A Sourcebook*, Greenwood Press, Westport, Conn., 1985, p. 42.
Slater, Courtenay M., Ed., Business Statistics of the United States, 1995 ed., Bernan Press, Lanham, Md., 1996, p. 227.
Tainer, Evelina M., *Using Economic Indicators to Improve Investment Analysis*, John Wiley & Sons, New York, 1993, pp. 107-108.
U.S. Department of Commerce, Bureau of Economic Analysis, *Business Statistics, 1963-91*, USGPO, Washington, D.C., 1992, pp. 143-144.
U.S. Department of Commerce, Bureau of Economic Analysis, *Handbook of Cyclical Indicators*, USGPO, Washington, D.C., 1984, pp. 17-20.

Margin Credit
[See Margin Debt]

Margin Debt

The total money borrowed from brokers and bankers by brokerage customers with securities as collateral.

The Federal Reserve Board and the Securities and Exchange Commission regulate the percentage of the total portfolio value that can be borrowed against securities to purchase other securities. Brokerage houses are required by law to report their total debt in dollars to the SEC and the FRB. The amounts reported are totaled to produce this indicator.

Used as a sentiment indicator and as a flow-of-funds indicator because, as prices rise on the stock market, the confidence of margin traders also grows. Thus, rising markets produce larger margin debts, pushing the market even higher. In a falling market, margin debtors must cover their losses by selling the securities that they had put up as collateral, thus causing the market to fall even faster.

Published monthly by the Board of Governors of the Federal Reserve System in the *Federal Reserve Bulletin*.

Source	Frequency	Extent	Form	Medium
Annual Statistical Digest (FRB)	a	c	t	p

Bibliography
Colby, Robert W., and Thomas A. Meyers, *The Encyclopedia of Technical Market Indicators*, Dow Jones-Irwin, Homewood, Ill., 1988, pp. 267-268.

Hayes, Michael, *The Dow Jones - Irwin Guide to Stock Market Cycles*, Dow Jones - Irwin, Homewood, Ill., 1977, pp. 158-160.

Pring, Martin J., *Technical Analysis Explained, An Illustrated Guide for the Investor*, McGraw Hill, New York, 1980, pp. 216-220.

Wilson, Sloan J., "The Customers' Free Credit Balances and Margin Debt," pp. 19-1 to 19-22 in *The Encyclopedia of Stock Market Techniques*, Investors Intelligence, Larchmont, N.Y., 1983.

Zarb, Frank G., and Gabriel T. Kerekes, Ed., *The Stock Market Handbook*, Dow Jones - Irwin, Homewood, Ill., 1970, pp. 316-324.

Market Value Index
[See American Stock Exchange Composite Index]

Materials Price Index
[See Change in Industrial Materials Price Index]

Measure of Business Confidence
[Also called Business Confidence Index and Business Executives' Expectations]

An assessment of the economic sentiment and expectations of business executives.

The chief executive officers of American business firms, both large and small, are surveyed each quarter. About 150 of them reply. They are asked three questions about the current prospects of the economy: How would you rate business conditions for the economy as a whole, as compared with six months ago? In looking ahead six months as compared to now, how do you think general business conditions will be? In appraising prospects for your own particular industry, how do you think business will be over the next six months, as compared to now? (A fourth question is also asked but not used in composing the Measure of Business Confidence: How would you rate business conditions for your own industry, as compared with those for six months ago?) Possible replies and their assigned scores are: Substantially Better (100), Moderately Better (75), Same (50), Moderately Worse (25), and Substantially Worse (0). The replies are averaged to produce the index and its subsets.

Used as a leading sentiment indicator; an informed, collective opinion of future movements in business activity.

Published quarterly by the Conference Board in *Business Executives' Expectations*, as a press release, and on the World Wide Web at www.conference-board.org/whoweare/frames.cfm?main=press.cfm.

Source	Frequency	Extent	Form	Medium
Business Executives Expectations	q	c	t	p

Media General Composite Index

A measure of the change in aggregate market value of the outstanding common shares of about 8000 stocks traded on the American Stock Exchange, on the New York Stock Exchange, and by NASDAQ.

The share price for common shares is multiplied by the number of shares outstanding for all corporations traded on the American Stock Exchange, New York Stock Exchange, and the NASDAQ System. Rights, preferred stocks, and when-issued stocks are not included. This calculation is then indexed to a base value, which was assigned an index value of 100.00 for Jan. 2, 1970. The effects on the index of new listings, delistings, splits, suspensions or halts of trading, or distributions of dividends are compensated for by recalculating the base market value. Proprietary subsidiary indexes for industry groups are also calculated.

Used as a measure of the overall market strength and of speculative activity.

Published daily on the Internet by Media General Financial Services, Inc., as part of the Daily Market Barometer at www.mgfs.com/barom/latest.htm.

Source	Frequency	Extent	Form	Medium
Media General	d	c	t	e

Merchandise Trade Balance
[See Balance of Trade]

Merrill Lynch 500 Municipal Bond Index

A representative yield for all general-obligation and revenue bonds issued by local governments of the United States.

From the thousands of municipal-bond issues that it trades, Merrill Lynch selects 500 major issuers of (mostly) investment-grade bonds. They then note the yields that these issuers are paying on long-term tax-exempt securities issued at par. General-obligation bonds are assumed to have a 20-year maturity, and revenue bonds a 30-year. The yields, expressed as percentages, are averaged. The data are presented for all 500 bonds, for all revenue bonds in the sample, and for subclasses of revenue bonds (e.g., airport, hospital, or transportation issues) and general-obligation bonds (e.g., city, county, or state issues).

Used as a measure of the overall strength of and trends in the long-term, tax-exempt bond market.

Issued weekly by Merrill Lynch as a report; data are reported as of close of business on Tuesday.

Source	Frequency	Extent	Form	Medium
Wall Street Journal	d	c	t	p

Merrill Lynch Corporate Master Bond Index

The average monthly total return of investments in the corporate bond market.

The 30-day total return (expressed as a percentage of the investment) is calculated for each investment-grade (rated BBB or better) corporate bond. This sample is made up of almost 4000 issues with maturities of 1 to more than 10 years. These 30-day total returns are then averaged to produce the Corporate Master index. The monthly values of the index are combined to produce the market's average, compounded total returns for the year to date and for the past 12 months. Also reported as a time-series index value.

Used as an indicator of the performance of the aggregate corporate-bond market and as a means of comparing that performance to the performance of other segments of the debt market (e.g., Treasury and mortgage securities).

Reported monthly by Merrill Lynch in *Merrill Lynch U.S. Domestic Bond Indices*.

Source	Frequency	Extent	Form	Medium
Wall Street Journal	d	c	t	p

Merrill Lynch Master Municipal Bond Index

The average monthly total return of investments in the municipal bond market.

The 30-day total return (expressed as a percentage of the investment) is calculated for each general-obligation, revenue, and pre-refunded municipal bond rated AAA to BBB (i.e., for the visible supply of such debt instruments on the market, roughly 1300 issues). These values are then averaged. The monthly values of the index are combined to produce the market's average, compounded total returns for the year to date and for the past 12 months.

Used as an indicator of the performance of the aggregate municipal-bond market and as a means of comparing that performance to the performance of other segments of the debt market (e.g., 10-year Treasury bonds).

Reported monthly by Merrill Lynch in *Fixed Income Digest, The Tax-Exempt Edition*.

Source	Frequency	Extent	Form	Medium
Wall Street Journal	w	c	t	p

Merrill Lynch Ready Assets 30-Day Average Yield

The average rate of return over 30 days from the investments that make up the current holdings of the Merrill Lynch Ready Assets Trust expressed as an annual percentage rate.

Merrill Lynch Ready Assets Trust is a mutual fund that invests in short-term money-market instruments (securities of the U.S. Government and its agencies, bank money instruments, commercial paper and other short-term obligations, foreign short-term debt instruments, corporate debt instruments, and repurchase and reverse-repurchase agreements). The 30-day yield of the fund's portfolio is calculated by dividing the fund's net investment income during the past 30 days by its maximum offering price (including loads) on the last of those 30 days, taking into account all fund expenses incurred during the period. The calculation of the net investment income is based on the assumption that long-term, interest-bearing investments will be held to their maturity dates. The 30-day yield can then be expressed either as an annualized yield or as a compounded annualized yield for the fund. The annualized yield is usually what is reported. The final 30-day yield is influenced by the purchase prices and interest rates on the money-market securities currently held by the fund, the average portfolio maturity, the types and quality of portfolio securities held, and the fund's operating expenses. The 30-day yield should not be assumed to be the same as the dividends paid by the fund; the dividends may be different from the 30-day yield.

Used as a benchmark of return on investment for managed money-market mutual funds and as a general indicator of current money rates.

Published daily by Merrill Lynch as a news release and reported on the Bridge Communications Telerate.

Source	Frequency	Extent	Form	Medium
Wall Street Journal	d	c	t	p

Bibliography
"Fidelity Investment Glossary," personal.fidelity.com/funds/glossary.html, visited
    Aug. 24, 1997.
"What Does 'SEC Yield' Mean?" www.mfmag.com/cgi-win/mfin002.exe/d:\
    internet\mfm\dec1994\q_and_a\also3, visited Aug. 24, 1997.

Misery Index
[Also called the Discomfort Index; see Appendix A. Nonquantitative Indicators]

Mitsubishi Bank Retail Chain Store Sales Index
[See Bank of Tokyo–Mitsubishi Chain Store Sales Index]

Mobile Home Sales
[Also called Mobile Home Shipments]
The number of mobile homes sold by manufacturers nationwide each month.

The number of residential units sold by manufacturers to dealers is collected from all mobile-home manufacturers in the continental United States monthly. The total is seasonally adjusted. Mobile homes are defined as single, expandable, or double-wide dwelling units with undercarriages and wheels; a double-wide unit consisting of two single units joined together at the site is counted as a single unit. Units must comply with Mobile Home Construction and Safety Standards Act of 1974. No mobile offices, classrooms, or other nonresidential units are included.

Data are presented for region of the country, by number of units placed for residential use, by average price, for number of dealer lots, and for thousands of shipments.

Used as a measure of the current state of the housing industry.

Published monthly by the National Conference of States on Building Codes and Standards and the U.S. Department of Commerce, Bureau of the Census, in *Housing Starts,* Current Construction Report.

Source	Frequency	Extent	Form	Medium
Annual Statistical Digest (FRB)	m	c	t	p
Business Statistics	a, m	h	t	p
Construction Review	a, m	c, h	t	p
Housing Starts	a, m	c, h	t	p
Real Estate Outlook	a, q	c, h	t	p
S&P Basic Statistics - Building and Building Materials	a, m	h	t	p
Statistical Abstract	a	h	t	p

Bibliography
"Mobile Homes - A Growing Force in the Housing Sector," *Construction Review*, 4-8 (Sept. 1972).

Slater, Courtenay M., Ed., Business Statistics of the United States, 1995 ed., Bernan Press, Lanham, Md., 1996, pp. 253-254.

U.S. Department of Commerce, Bureau of Economic Analysis, *Business Statistics, 1963-91*, USGPO, Washington, D.C., 1992, pp. 151.

Moet Annual Market Basket
[See Appendix A. Nonquantitative Indicators]

Monetary Aggregates
[See L, M1, M2, and M3]

Monetary Base
[Also called High-Powered Money]
The total liability of the Federal Reserve System: the currency in circulation and the money it holds in reserve for depository institutions.

Each week, financial institutions report to the Federal Reserve System the amounts of cash held in their vaults. To this is added the total amount these institutions have on deposit in Federal Reserve banks and the estimated amount of currency held by the public. The sum is called the nation's monetary base and is available in two forms: (1) adjusted for seasonal effects and current reserve requirements and (2) unadjusted.

Closely watched as the primary indicator of the available supply of spendable money and of the results of the Federal Reserve's monetary policy.

Calculated each week and distributed as a news release by the Banking Section of the Board of Governors of the Federal Reserve System; monthly values are published in the *Aggregate Reserves of Depository Institutions and the Monetary Base*, Statistical Release H.3 (502).

Source	Frequency	Extent	Form	Medium
Barron's	bw	c	t	p
Federal Reserve Bulletin	a, m	c	t	p
US Financial Data	m, w	c	t, g	p

Bibliography

Hoel, Arline Alchian; Kenneth W. Clarkson; and Roger LeRoy Miller, *Economics Sourcebook of Government Statistics*, Lexington Books, Lexington, Mass., 1983, pp. 136-137.

Niemira, Michael P., and Gerald F. Zukowski, *Trading the Fundamentals: The Trader's Guide to Interpreting Economic Indicators and Monetary Policy*, McGraw-Hill, New York, 1998, pp. 236-237.

Monetary Stock
[See L, M1, M2, and M3]

Money 30

A measure of the performance of the stocks of 30 companies that are judged to provide goods and services that will be in demand in the 21st century.

Thirty companies were chosen whose goods and services should be in high demand for the next 10 years, firms with established high performance, staying power, and growth potential. They were selected on the basis of current market capitalization, a strong showing in the Value Line Investment Survey, an above-average growth in market capitalization, and above-average projected growth in earnings for the succeeding five years. The total return (stock prices with all dividends reinvested) of the stocks of those companies is tracked, and the collective performance is indexed against a value of 1000 for January 1996.

Used as a comparative baseline of performance of the stock market.

Calculated continually and displayed on the World Wide Web at www.pathfinder.com/money/money30/; published monthly in *Money* magazine.

Source	Frequency	Extent	Form	Medium
Money	m (h)	c, h	t, g	p (e)

Bibliography

Keating, Peter, "How We Made the Money 30," www.pathfinder.com/money/money30/how.html, visited Dec. 9, 1998.

Money Balance
[See M2]

Money Fund Average

The average compounded yield of money-market mutual funds calculated for the past week.

The annualized total returns for the past seven days of all of the money-market mutual funds tracked by *Money Fund Reporter* are tallied and averaged. The data from more than 1300 funds are derived from information obtained from the funds themselves. The annualized total returns are net of management fees and expenses and are calculated as the taxable equivalent yield.

Used as an indicator of the current state of the capital markets and as a comparator for the performance of individual money-market mutual funds.

Published weekly in *IBC's Money Fund Report* and on its site on the World Wide Web at www.ibcdata.com/index.html.

Source	Frequency	Extent	Form	Medium
Bank Rate Monitor	w	c, h	t	e
Barron's	w	c	t	p
IBC Financial Data	w	c	t	e
USA Today	d	c	t	p

Bibliography

Donoghue, W. E., *William E. Donoghue's Complete Money Market Guide*, Harper and Row, New York, 1980.

Kantrow, Y. D., "Donoghue Sells Newsletters That Made His Image," *American Banker* **152**, 2 (1987).

Money-Market Assets

The amount of money invested in U.S. money-market mutual funds.

Each week, the Investment Company Institute, a mutual-funds trade group, notes the assets under management by each of the money-market mutual funds in the United States at close of business on Wednesday. These amounts are totaled up, and the value is expressed in billions of dollars. Week to week changes are also given, and the total value is broken down by type of management institution.

Used in calculating the Savings Rate, as a component of the money aggregates, and as an indicator of the disposable income existing in the noncorporate sector of the U.S. economy.

Issued weekly as a news release by the Investment Company Institute of Washington, D.C.

Source	Frequency	Extent	Form	Medium
Economic Indicators	a, m	c, h	t	p, e

Source	Frequency	Extent	Form	Medium
Wall Street Journal	w	c, h	t, g	p

Money Small Investor Index

A barometer of the value of the typical individual investor's portfolio.

Since the fall of 1988 (with data back-calculated to 1970), *Money* magazine has tracked the performance of a typical small investor's portfolio. That portfolio is assumed to be made up of investments in ten asset classes: gold, real estate, equity funds, small stocks, big stocks, bond funds, municipal bonds, taxable bonds, money funds, and certificates of deposit. Life insurance and residential real estate (including rental properties) are not included in the portfolio. An arbitrary initial investment amount was chosen, and that amount was allocated across the ten asset classes in proportion to the actual investments of individuals as indicated by data on actual investment practices from the Federal Reserve Board and other sources. Reallocations are made as new data become available. The value of the portfolio at the close of business at the end of the week (as judged from other indicator-surrogates, such as the S&P 500 for big stocks) is indexed to a base value of 100 (= Dec. 26, 1996). During the first half of each year, the index is rebenchmarked with data for the last trading day of the preceding year. Frequently, the indicator is also expressed as the change in value of a hypothetical investment during some period of time, such as the preceding month or year.

Used as a broad and somewhat amorphous indicator of the recent performance of the portions of the investment market most frequently participated in by individual investors.

Calculated weekly and published monthly by *Money* magazine.

Source	Frequency	Extent	Form	Medium
Money	m	c, h	t, g	p

Bibliography
Fitch, Malcolm, "So How Did You Do in 1995?" *Money* **25** (1), 116-117 (1996).
Goodman, Jordan E., "*Money*'s Small Investor Index," *Money* **17** (Fall Extra), 6-7 (Fall 1988).
Goodman, Jordan E., "Small Investor Index," *Money* **23** (1), 66 (1994).
Sivy, Michael, "How Are You Doing?" *Money* **18** (10), 78-83 (1989).

Money Stock
[See L, M1, M2, and M3]

Money Supply
[See L, M1, M2, and M3]

Moody's Corporate Aaa Bond Yield Averages

The currently prevailing maturity yield on seasoned, long-term corporate bonds of the highest quality.

A standard list of corporate-bond issues is selected, and the daily yield for each selected bond is computed on the basis of closing price, as reported in the dealer's asked quotation, adjusted occasionally for temporarily distorting factors (e.g., a bond's being called or selling too far above its call price). These yields are then arithmetically averaged.

Used to indicate the level and movement of average yields of selected seasoned bonds with sufficiently long maturities and other features to allow them to indicate long-term interest rates.

Published daily by Moody's Investors Service as a news release.

Source	Frequency	Extent	Form	Medium
Agricultural Outlook	a, q	c	t	p
Annual Statistical Digest (FRB)	a, m, w	c	t	p
Business Statistics	a, m	h	t	p
Federal Reserve Board	d	c, h	t	e
Federal Reserve Bulletin	a, m, w	c	t	p
Forecast	q	c, f	t	p
Moody's Bond Record	m	h	t, g	p
Moody's Credit Survey	m, d	c	t	p
Real Estate Outlook	a, q	c, h	t	p
Selected Interest Rates	m, w	c	t	p
Statistical Abstract	a	h	t	p
US Financial Data	m, w	c	t, g	p
Value Line Investment Survey, Part 2: Selection and Opinion	a, q, d	c, h, f	t	p

Bibliography

Berlin, Howard M. *The Handbook of Financial Market Indexes, Averages, and Indicators*, Dow Jones-Irwin, Homewood, Ill., 1990, pp. 81-82.

Hoel, Arline Alchian; Kenneth W. Clarkson; and Roger LeRoy Miller, *Economics Sourcebook of Government Statistics*, Lexington Books, Lexington, Mass., 1983, pp. 115-118.

Pring, Martin J., *Technical Analysis Explained, An Illustrated Guide for the Investor*, McGraw-Hill, New York, 1980, pp. 185-189.

Slater, Courtenay M., Ed., Business Statistics of the United States, 1995 ed., Bernan Press, Lanham, Md., 1996, pp. 245-246.

U.S. Department of Commerce, Bureau of Economic Analysis, *Business Statistics, 1963-91*, USGPO, Washington, D.C., 1992, pp. 163-164.

Moody's Corporate Bond Average

A measure of the yields of investment-grade corporate issues on the bond market.

A representative sample of 80 to 100 corporate bonds are selected from the different ratings (Aaa, Aa, A, and Baa) and from different sectors of the economy (industrial corporations and public utilities; the category of railroads has not been used for decades because of the lack of representative issues). All of these issues are nonconvertible, are taxable, have maturities that are less than five years, and have fixed coupons. A daily yield based on the closing price is computed for each issue. An unweighted arithmetic average yield is calculated for each rating classification within each sectorial group. Averages are then calculated for each rating class and for each group, providing two series of averages, which are published separately (see, for example, the entry for Moody's Corporate Aaa Bond Yield Averages). The overall corporate yield average is the arithmetic average of the averages for the groups (public utilities etc.).

Used as an indicator of the performance of the corporate bond market as a whole and of the future movement of credit markets.

Published daily as a news release by Moody's Investors Service.

Source	Frequency	Extent	Form	Medium
Business Statistics	a, m	h	t	p
Federal Reserve Bulletin	a, m, w	c	t	p
FRB Chicago	d, w	c, h	t	e
Moody's Bond Record	m	h	t	p
Moody's Credit Survey	m, d	c	t	p

Bibliography

Berlin, Howard M. *The Handbook of Financial Market Indexes, Averages, and Indicators*, Dow Jones-Irwin, Homewood, Ill., 1990, pp. 81-82.

Slater, Courtenay M., Ed., Business Statistics of the United States, 1995 ed., Bernan Press, Lanham, Md., 1996, pp. 245-246.

U.S. Department of Commerce, Bureau of Economic Analysis, *Business Statistics, 1963-91*, USGPO, Washington, D.C., 1992, pp. 163-164.

Moody's Corporate Bond Index

A comparator of the corporate bond market to indicate trends in the performance of that market.

Each afternoon, Moody's polls a sample of bond dealers and brokers to determine the total return based on current prices on each of about 80 corporate bond issues having ratings of Aaa, Aa, A, or Baa. All of these issues are nonconvertible, are taxable, have maturities that are less than five years, and have fixed coupons. The derived values are averaged and indexed to a value of 100 for Dec. 31, 1978.

Used as an indicator of the performance of the corporate bond market as a whole.

Published daily as a news release by Moody's Investors Service.

Source	Frequency	Extent	Form	Medium
Moody's Bond Record	m	h	t	p
Statistical Abstract	a	h	t	p

Bibliography

Berlin, Howard M. *The Handbook of Financial Market Indexes, Averages, and Indicators*, Dow Jones-Irwin, Homewood, Ill., 1990, pp. 81-82.

Morgan Guaranty Index

[Also called the J. P. Morgan Index; see also Federal Reserve Trade-Weighted Dollar and FINEX U.S. Dollar Index]

A comparison of the value of the U.S. dollar to that of 18 other foreign currencies.

The currencies of 18 other countries that are major trading partners with the United States were selected and assigned weights according to the dollar volume of their trade with the United States each year. Those countries are (in order of greatest weight): Canada, Japan, Germany, France, Italy, Great Britain, Australia, Belgium, Denmark, Finland, Netherlands, Norway, Spain, Sweden, Switzerland, Greece, Austria, and Portugal. The current value of the exchange rate for each country's currency (expressed in U.S. cents per unit of foreign currency) is raised to the power of the weighting factor for that country. These 18 values are multiplied together, and the result is multiplied by 100. The index has a base value of 100 for 1990.

Used as a measure of the strength of the dollar on global markets. A stronger dollar attracts foreign capital and lessens inflationary pressures by lowering the cost of imports. A weaker dollar dissuades foreign investors, enhancing inflationary pressures. A stronger dollar also causes overseas sales by American companies to decline because it makes their goods more expensive in foreign currencies.

Issued as a news release each business day by the Morgan Guaranty Trust Co. of New York City; also posted daily on the World Wide Web at www.jpmorgan.com/cgi-bin/Indices.

Source	Frequency	Extent	Form	Medium
Business Week	w	c	t	p
International Economic Review	a, q, m	c	t	p
JP Morgan	d	c, h	t	e
USA Today	d	c, h	t	p
Wall Street Journal	m	c	g	p

Source	Frequency	Extent	Form	Medium
World Financial Markets	a, q	c	t	p

Bibliography
Berlin, Howard M. *The Handbook of Financial Market Indexes, Averages, and Indicators*, Dow Jones-Irwin, Homewood, Ill., 1990, pp. 113-114.
"Dollar Index Confusion," *World Financial Markets*, Oct./Nov. 1986, pp. 14-19.
"Index of the Weighted-Average Exchange Value of the U.S. Dollar: Revision," *Federal Reserve Bulletin* **64** (8), 700 (1978).
"Measuring the Foreign-Exchange Value of the Dollar," *Federal Reserve Bulletin* **73** (6), 411-422 (1987).
"U.S. Dollar," *Euromoney* (Currencies Supplement), 19-21 (March 1994).

Mortgage Delinquencies
[See also Delinquency Rate on Consumer Loans and Mortgage Delinquency Rate]
A measure of the ability of the business community to meet its financial obligations.

The American Council of Life Insurance surveys about 85% of its members each quarter to determine what percentage of their mortgage loans, which are mostly commercial, are at least 30 days past due and how many are in the process of foreclosure. The values are expressed as percentages to two decimal places and are compared with the percentages of previous quarters.

Used as a general indicator of the robustness of the economy and of the current profitability of American business.

Published by the American Council of Life Insurance as a news story in *National Underwriter*.

Source	Frequency	Extent	Form	Medium
National Delinquency Survey	q	c	t	p

Mortgage Delinquency Rate
[See also Delinquency Rate on Consumer Loans and Mortgage Delinquencies]
A measure of the ability of the borrowing public to meet its financial obligations.

The Mortgage Bankers Association surveys its members each quarter to determine what percentage of one- to four-unit residential mortgage loans are at least 30 days past due. This percentage is called the mortgage delinquency rate. The data are then broken down into categories of seriousness: 30 to 59 days late, 60 to 89 days late, and 90 days or more late. The values are expressed as percentages to two decimal places and are compared with the percentages of previous quarters.

Used as an indicator of unemployment, the affordability of housing, and the availability of disposable income.

Published in the Mortgage Bankers Association's quarterly report, *National Delinquency Survey*.

Source	Frequency	Extent	Form	Medium
National Delinquency Survey	q	c	t	p

Mortgage Interest Rates, FHFB

The average interest rate charged on lower fixed-rate home mortgages.

Each month, the Federal Housing Finance Board surveys about 200 major lenders from among their affiliated institutions (which include commercial banks, savings and loan associations, mutual savings banks, and mortgage bankers) to determine the number, terms, and purposes of fully amortized, first-mortgage loans closed for the purchase of single-family nonfarm residences during the previous five days. This information is collected as part of the Board's Monthly Interest Rate Survey. Among the data collected and calculated are the average contract interest rate (the rate stated on a loan) and the effective rate (the interest rate plus the loan-initiation fees and other charges amortized over ten years). In calculating the effective interest rate, the data are weighted to reflect the shares of mortgage lending by type of lender. These rates are expressed as percentages.

Used as an indicator of the affordability of housing and of the availability of money for housing and other uses.

Published monthly in the *Federal Housing Finance Board News* and in the Federal Housing Finance Board's report *Conventional Home Mortgage Rates*; it is also announced as a Federal Housing Finance Board press release, which is posted on the World Wide Web at www.fhfb.gov.

Source	Frequency	Extent	Form	Medium
Annual Statistical Digest (FRB)	a, m	c	t	p
Business Week	w	c	t	p
Construction Review	a, m	c, h	t	p
Conventional Home Mortgage Rates	m	c	t	p
Federal Reserve Bulletin	a, m	c	t	p
Rates and Terms on Conventional Home Mortgages	a, m	h	t	p
Statistical Abstract	a	h	t	p

Bibliography

Hoel, Arline Alchian; Kenneth W. Clarkson; and Roger LeRoy Miller, *Economics Sourcebook of Government Statistics*, Lexington Books, Lexington, Mass., 1983, p. 139 and 141-145.

"Monthly Interest Rate Survey Information," www.fhfb.gov, visited July 17, 1999.

Mortgage Interest Rates, FHLM

The average interest rates charged on fixed-rate and adjustable-rate home mortgages.

Since April 1971, the Federal Home Loan Mortgage Corp. (usually referred to as Freddie Mac) has surveyed lenders across the nation each week to determine the average rate on 30-year fixed-rate mortgages; in 1984, the 1-year adjustable-rate mortgage (ARM) was added to the survey; in 1991, the 15-year fixed-rate mortgage rate was included. About 125 lenders are surveyed each week; the lender types in the sample (thrifts, commercial banks and mortgage lending companies) are represented roughly proportionally to the level of mortgage business that each type conducts nationwide. The average contract rate and average number of points are calculated and reported for each of the three types of loans. The average margin for one-year Treasury-indexed ARMs is also calculated and reported. The data are given for the five Freddie Mac regions and as a national average.

Used as an indicator of the affordability of housing and of the availability of money for housing and other uses; it is also used as the measure of conventional 30-year mortgage rates by the Federal Reserve Board in its list of *Selected Interest Rates* (Statistical Release H.15).

Published weekly by the Federal Home Loan Mortgage Corp. as a press release, which is also posted on the agency's home page on the World Wide Web at www.freddiemac.com.

Source	Frequency	Extent	Form	Medium
American Banker	d	c	t	e
Builder	m	c	g	p
Business Statistics	a, m	h	t	p
First Union	m	c, h	t	e
Mortgage Banking	m	c	t	p
Mortgage Market Trends	a, m	h	t	p
Primary Mortgage Market Survey Results	d	c	t	p
Real Estate Outlook	a, q	c, h	t	p
Selected Interest Rates	m, w	c	t	p
S&P Basic Statistics - Building and Building Materials	a, m	h	t	p
S&P Current Statistics	m	h	t	p
Wall Street Journal	d	c	t	p

Bibliography

"About the Primary Mortgage Market Survey," www.freddiemac.com/pmms/abtpmms.htm, visited July 17, 1999.

Motor Vehicle Production
[See Auto and Light Truck Production]

Motor Vehicle Sales
[See Auto and Light Truck Sales]

Municipal Bond Yields
[See Standard & Poor's High-Grade Municipal Bond Yields]

N

NAPM Survey
[See Purchasing Managers' Index]

NASDAQ 100-Stock Index

A descriptor of the ups and downs of the aggregate prices of the largest nonfinancial stocks issues not listed on the major exchanges.

The National Association of Securities Dealers (NASD) determines the current median bid prices of the securities of the 100 largest nonfinancial issues among the stocks traded on the NASDAQ (NASD Automated Quotation system) National Market System. Each of these securities is weighted based on the company's capitalization. These weights are adjusted daily to reflect capitalization changes, stock splits, stock dividends, new listings, and delistings. These weighted values are cumulated and indexed to a value of 250 for Jan. 31, 1985. It was later reset by dividing the Jan. 1, 1994, value by 2. Listings include restaurant chains, food outlets, furniture manufacturers, computer companies, software houses, publishers, and educational services, among other types of corporations.

This indicator reflects the trends in the prices of securities not listed on the major exchanges. It also provides a general comparison of the aggregate performance of those stocks with those that are listed on the major exchanges.

Published daily by the National Association of Securities Dealers in a news release.

Source	Frequency	Extent	Form	Medium
Barron's	d	c	t	p
Bloomberg	h	c	t	e
CBS	h	c	t	e
NASD	d	c	t	e

Source	Frequency	Extent	Form	Medium
NASDAQ Factbook	m	h	t	p
StockMaster	d	c, h	g, t	e

Bibliography
"Nasdaq Index Overview," beta.nasdaq.com/asp/offsite_about.asp?content= http://www.nasd.com/ar_section5.html, visited Feb. 3, 1998.

NASDAQ Bank Index

A descriptor of the ups and downs of the aggregate prices of the stocks of banks and companies related to the banking industry that are not listed on the major exchanges.

The National Association of Securities Dealers determines the current median bid prices of the securities of about 350 banking-related companies that participate in the Association's National Market System or are traded regularly over the counter as part of the NASDAQ market. Each of these securities is weighted based on the company's capitalization. These weights are adjusted daily to reflect capitalization changes, stock splits, stock dividends, new listings, and delistings. These weighted values are cumulated and indexed to a value of 100 for Feb. 5, 1971. Listings include savings banks, a very few commercial banks, some trust companies, check-cashing businesses, and currency exchanges, among other types of corporations.

This indicator reflects the trends in the prices of banking-industry securities not listed on the major exchanges. It provides a general comparison of the aggregate performance of those stocks with that of stocks in other sectors of the economy and of those that are listed on the major exchanges.

Published daily by the National Association of Securities Dealers in a news release.

Source	Frequency	Extent	Form	Medium
Barron's	d	c	t	p
Bloomberg	h	c	t	e
Business Statistics	a	h	t	p
NASD	d	c	t	e
NASDAQ Factbook	a, m	h	t	p
New York Times	d	c	t	p
Statistical Abstract	a	h	t	p
Wall Street Journal	t	c	t	p

Bibliography
Berlin, Howard M. *The Handbook of Financial Market Indexes, Averages, and Indicators*, Dow Jones-Irwin, Homewood, Ill., 1990, pp. 39-40.

"Nasdaq Index Overview," beta.nasdaq.com/asp/offsite_about.asp?content=http://
www.nasd.com/ar_section5.html, visited Feb. 3, 1998.

NASDAQ Biotechnology Index

A descriptor of the ups and downs of the aggregate prices of the stocks of companies related to the biotechnology industry that are not listed on the major exchanges.

The National Association of Securities Dealers determines the current median bid prices of the securities of about 100 computer-related companies that participate in the Association's National Market System or are traded regularly over the counter as part of the NASDAQ market. Each of these securities is weighted based on the company's capitalization. These weights are adjusted daily to reflect capitalization changes, stock splits, stock dividends, new listings, and delistings. These weighted values are cumulated and indexed to a value of 200 for Nov. 1, 1993. Listings include companies that perform research and develop new treatments and cures for diseases. Listed companies are limited to those having a market capitalization of at least $50 million.

This indicator reflects the trends in the prices of biotechnology-industry securities not listed on the major exchanges; it provides a general comparison of the aggregate performance of those stocks with that of stocks in other sectors of the economy and of those that are listed on the major exchanges.

Published daily by the National Association of Securities Dealers in a news release.

Source	Frequency	Extent	Form	Medium
NASD	d	c	t	e
NASDAQ Factbook	a, m	c	t	p
StockMaster	d	c, h	g, t	e

Bibliography
"Nasdaq Index Overview," beta.nasdaq.com/asp/offsite_about.asp?content=http://
www.nasd.com/ar_section5.html, visited Feb. 3, 1998.

NASDAQ Composite Index

A descriptor of the ups and downs of the aggregate prices of stocks that are not listed on the major exchanges.

The National Association of Securities Dealers determines the current median bid prices of the securities of more than 5000 companies that are traded regularly over the counter as part of the NASDAQ market. Each of these securities is weighted based on the company's capitalization. These weights are adjusted daily to reflect capitalization changes, stock splits, stock dividends, new listings, and delistings. These weighted values are cumulated and indexed to a value of 100 for Feb. 5, 1971.

This indicator and its derivative indexes for subsets of the issues are the only indicators of the trends of prices of securities not listed on the major exchanges. It provides a general comparison of the performances of stocks that are listed on the major exchanges with those of stocks that are not.

Published daily by the National Association of Securities Dealers in a news release.

Source	Frequency	Extent	Form	Medium
Barron's	d	c	t	p
Bloomberg	h	c	t	e
Bridge	d	c	t	e
Business Statistics	a	h	t	p
Business Week	w (h)	c	t	p (c)
CBS	h	c	t	e
CNN	h	c	t	e
First Union	m	c, h	t	e
Investor's Business Daily	d	c, h	g, t	p
Media General	d	c	t	e
Mutual Funds Update	m	c	t	p
NASD	d	c	t	e
NASDAQ Factbook	a, m, d	c, h	t, g	p
New York Times	d (h)	c	t	p (e)
Outlook	w	c	t	p
PCQuote	h	c	t	e
Philadelphia Exchange	h	c	t	e
Quote.com	h	c	t	e
Securities Industry Trends	a, m	c, h	t	p
Securities Industry Yearbook	a	h	t	p
Statistical Abstract	a	h	t	p
StockMaster	d	c, h	g, t	e
USA Today	d (h)	c	t	p (e)
Value Line Investment Survey, Part 2: Selection and Opinion	w	c	t	p
Wall Street Journal	d	c	t	p

Bibliography

Berlin, Howard M. *The Handbook of Financial Market Indexes, Averages, and Indicators*, Dow Jones-Irwin, Homewood, Ill., 1990, pp. 37-39.

Darnay, Arsen J., *Economic Indicators Handbook: Time Series, Conversions, Documentation*, Gale Research, Detroit, 1992, p. 1032.

Frumkin, Norman, *Guide to Economic Indicators*, 2nd ed., M. E. Sharpe, Armonk, N.Y., 1994, pp. 276-277, 279-280, and 284-285.

"Nasdaq Index Overview," beta.nasdaq.com/asp/offsite_about.asp?content=http://www.nasd.com/ar_section5.html, visited Feb. 3, 1998.

"What's in an Index?" *Barron's*, Nov. 11, 1965, pp. 5+.

NASDAQ Computer Index

A descriptor of the ups and downs of the aggregate prices of the stocks of companies related to the computer industry that are not listed on the major exchanges.

The National Association of Securities Dealers determines the current median bid prices of the securities of about 560 computer-related companies that participate in the Association's National Market System or are traded regularly over the counter as part of the NASDAQ market. Each of these securities is weighted based on the company's capitalization. These weights are adjusted daily to reflect capitalization changes, stock splits, stock dividends, new listings, and delistings. These weighted values are cumulated and indexed to a value of 200 for Nov. 1, 1993. Listings include computer hardware and software companies that supply computer-programming and/or data-processing services as well as companies that manufacture and/or sell computers, office equipment, or electronic components.

This indicator reflects the trends in the prices of computer-industry securities not listed on the major exchanges; it provides a general comparison of the aggregate performance of those stocks with that of stocks in other sectors of the economy and of those that are listed on the major exchanges.

Published daily by the National Association of Securities Dealers in a news release.

Source	Frequency	Extent	Form	Medium
Business Week	h	c	t	e
NASD	d	c	t	e
NASDAQ Factbook	a, m	c	t	p
StockMaster	d	c, h	g, t	e

Bibliography

"Nasdaq Index Overview," beta.nasdaq.com/asp/offsite_about.asp?content=http://www.nasd.com/ar_section5.html, visited Feb. 3, 1998.

NASDAQ Financial-100 Index

A descriptor of the ups and downs of the aggregate prices of the stocks of large financial companies that are not listed on the major exchanges.

The National Association of Securities Dealers determines the current median bid prices of the securities of the 100 largest financial companies that participate in the Association's National Market System. Each of these securities is weighted based on the company's capitalization. These weights are adjusted daily to reflect capitalization changes, stock splits, stock dividends, new listings, and delistings. These weighted values are cumulated and indexed to a value of 250 for Jan. 31, 1985.

This indicator reflects the trends in the prices of finance-industry securities not listed on the major exchanges; it provides a general comparison of the aggregate performance of those stocks with that of stocks in other sectors of the economy and of those that are listed on the major exchanges.

Published daily by the National Association of Securities Dealers in a news release.

Source	Frequency	Extent	Form	Medium
Bloomberg	h	c	t	e
NASD	d	c	t	e
NASDAQ Factbook	m	h	t	p
New York Times	d	c	t	p

Bibliography
"Nasdaq Index Overview," beta.nasdaq.com/asp/offsite_about.asp?content=http:// www.nasd.com/ar_section5.html, visited Feb. 3, 1998.

NASDAQ Industrial Index

A descriptor of the ups and downs of the aggregate prices of the stocks of agricultural, mining, construction, manufacturing, and public-administration companies that are not listed on the major exchanges and that are not included in the other NASDAQ subgroup indexes.

The National Association of Securities Dealers determines the current median bid prices of the securities of more than 3000 companies that are traded regularly over the counter as part of the NASDAQ market but that are not included in any of the other NASDAQ subsets of the NASDAQ Composite Index. Each of these securities is weighted based on the company's capitalization. These weights are adjusted daily to reflect capitalization changes, stock splits, stock dividends, new listings, and delistings. These weighted values are cumulated and indexed to a value of 100 for Feb. 5, 1971. Listings include grocery chains, computer companies, manufacturing industries, and oil companies, among other types of corporations.

This indicator reflects the trends in the prices of industrial securities not listed on the major exchanges; it provides a general comparison of the aggregate performance of those stocks with that of stocks in other sectors of the economy and of those that are listed on the major exchanges.

Published daily by the National Association of Securities Dealers in a news release.

Source	Frequency	Extent	Form	Medium
Barron's	d	c	t	p
Bloomberg	h	c	t	e
Business Statistics	a	h	t	p
NASD	d	c	t	e
NASDAQ Factbook	a, m	h	t	p
New York Times	d	c	t	p
Statistical Abstract	a	h	t	p
Wall Street Journal	d	c	t	p

Bibliography

Berlin, Howard M. *The Handbook of Financial Market Indexes, Averages, and Indicators*, Dow Jones-Irwin, Homewood, Ill., 1990, pp. 45-46.

"Nasdaq Index Overview," beta.nasdaq.com/asp/offsite_about.asp?content=http://www.nasd.com/ar_section5.html, visited Feb. 3, 1998.

NASDAQ Insurance Index

A descriptor of the ups and downs of the aggregate prices of the stocks of insurance companies and businesses related to the insurance industry that are not listed on the major exchanges.

The National Association of Securities Dealers determines the current median bid prices of the securities of about 150 insurance-related companies that participate in the Association's National Market System or are traded regularly over the counter as part of the NASDAQ market. Each of these securities is weighted based on the company's capitalization. These weights are adjusted daily to reflect capitalization changes, stock splits, stock dividends, new listings, and delistings. These weighted values are cumulated and indexed to a value of 100 for Feb. 5, 1971. Listings include insurance companies, brokers, insurance agents, and corporations that provide related services.

This indicator reflects the trends in the prices of insurance-industry securities not listed on the major exchanges; it provides a general comparison of the aggregate performance of those stocks with that of stocks in other sectors of the economy and of those that are listed on the major exchanges.

Published daily by the National Association of Securities Dealers in a news release.

Source	Frequency	Extent	Form	Medium
Barron's	d	c	t	p
Bloomberg	h	c	t	e

Source	Frequency	Extent	Form	Medium
Business Statistics	a	h	t	p
NASD	d	c	t	e
NASDAQ Factbook	a, m	h	t	p
New York Times	d	c	t	p
Statistical Abstract	a	h	t	p
StockMaster	d	c, h	g, t	e
Wall Street Journal	d	c	t	p

Bibliography
Berlin, Howard M. *The Handbook of Financial Market Indexes, Averages, and Indicators*, Dow Jones-Irwin, Homewood, Ill., 1990, pp.40-41.
"Nasdaq Index Overview," beta.nasdaq.com/asp/offsite_about.asp?content=http://www.nasd.com/ar_scction5.html, visited Feb. 3, 1998.

NASDAQ National Market Composite Index

A descriptor of the ups and downs of the aggregate prices of stocks that are listed on the NASDAQ National Market tier of the NASDAQ Stock Market.

The National Association of Securities Dealers determines the current median bid prices of the securities of more than 3000 companies that are traded regularly over the counter as part of the National Market tier of the NASDAQ market. Each of these securities is weighted based on the company's capitalization. These weights are adjusted daily to reflect capitalization changes, stock splits, stock dividends, new listings, and delistings. These weighted values are cumulated and indexed to a value of 100 for July 10, 1984.

An indicator of the trends of prices of the most actively traded securities that are not listed on the major exchanges.

Published daily by the NASD in a news release.

Source	Frequency	Extent	Form	Medium
Bloomberg	h	c	t	e
Business Statistics	a	h	t	p
NASD	d	c	t	e
NASDAQ Factbook	m	h	t	p
New York Times	d	c	t	p
StockMaster	d	c, h	g, t	e
Wall Street Journal	d	c	t	p

Bibliography
"Nasdaq Index Overview," beta.nasdaq.com/asp/offsite_about.asp?content=http://www.nasd.com/ar_section5.html, visited Feb. 3, 1998.

NASDAQ/NMS Composite Index
[See NASDAQ National Market Composite Index]

NASDAQ Other Finance Index

A descriptor of the ups and downs of the aggregate prices of the stocks of financial firms that are not listed on the major exchanges.

The National Association of Securities Dealers determines the current median bid prices of the securities of about 620 nonbank financial firms that participate in the Association's National Market System or are traded regularly over the counter as part of the NASDAQ market. Each of these securities is weighted based on the company's capitalization. These weights are adjusted daily to reflect capitalization changes, stock splits, stock dividends, new listings, and delistings. These weighted values are cumulated and indexed to a value of 100 for Feb. 5, 1971. Listings include savings and loan associations, brokers and brokerage houses, and investment firms, among other types of corporations.

This indicator reflects the trends in the prices of finance-industry securities not listed on the major exchanges; it provides a general comparison of the aggregate performance of those stocks with that of stocks in other sectors of the economy and of those that are listed on the major exchanges.

Published daily by the National Association of Securities Dealers in a news release.

Source	Frequency	Extent	Form	Medium
NASD	d	c	t	e
NASDAQ Factbook	a, m	h	t	p
StockMaster	d	c, h	g, t	e

Bibliography
Berlin, Howard M. *The Handbook of Financial Market Indexes, Averages, and Indicators*, Dow Jones-Irwin, Homewood, Ill., 1990, pp. 41-42.
"Nasdaq Index Overview," beta.nasdaq.com/asp/offsite_about.asp?content=http://www.nasd.com/ar_section5.html, visited Feb. 3, 1998.

NASDAQ Telecommunications Index
[Formerly the NASDAQ Utilities Index]

A descriptor of the ups and downs of the aggregate prices of the stocks of telecommunication firms and companies related to the communications industry that are not listed on the major exchanges.

The National Association of Securities Dealers determines the current median bid prices of the securities of about 150 telecommunication-related companies that participate in the Association's National Market System or are traded regularly over the counter as part of the NASDAQ market. Each of these securities is weighted based on the company's capitalization. These weights are adjusted daily to reflect capitalization changes, stock splits, stock dividends, new listings, and delistings. For the original NASDAQ Utilities Index, these weighted values were cumulated and indexed to a value of 100 for Feb. 5, 1971. The index was renamed the NASDAQ Telecommunications Index on Nov. 1 1993, and rebased to a value of 200 with a factor of 5.74805. Listings include cable-television firms, radio and television broadcasters, Internet providers, software houses, long-distance and local telephone companies, and cellular services, among other types of corporations.

This indicator reflects the trends in the prices of telecommunication-industry securities not listed on the major exchanges; it provides a general comparison of the aggregate performance of those stocks with that of stocks in other sectors of the economy and of those that are listed on the major exchanges.

Published daily by the National Association of Securities Dealers in a news release.

Source	Frequency	Extent	Form	Medium
Barron's	d	c	t	p
Bloomberg	h	c	t	e
NASD	d	c	t	e
NASDAQ Factbook	a, m	h	t	p
StockMaster	d	c, h	g, t	e

Bibliography
"Nasdaq Index Overview," beta.nasdaq.com/asp/offsite_about.asp?content=http://www.nasd.com/ar_section5.html, visited Feb. 3, 1998.

NASDAQ Transportation Index

A descriptor of the ups and downs of the aggregate prices of the stocks of companies that provide transportation services or are related to the transportation industry that are not listed on the major exchanges.

The National Association of Securities Dealers determines the current median bid prices of the securities of fewer than 100 transportation-related companies that participate in the Association's National Market System or are traded regularly over the counter as part of the NASDAQ market. Each of these securities is weighted based on the company's capitalization. These weights are adjusted daily to reflect capitalization changes, stock splits, stock dividends, new listings, and delistings. These weighted values are cumulated and indexed to a value of 100 for Feb. 5, 1971. Listings include not only railroads, bus, and airline companies, but also pipeline companies, travel agents, and warehousers, among other types of corporations.

This indicator reflects the trends in the prices of transportation-industry securities not listed on the major exchanges; it provides a general comparison of the aggregate performance of those stocks with that of stocks in other sectors of the economy and of those that are listed on the major exchanges.

Published daily by the National Association of Securities Dealers in a news release.

Source	Frequency	Extent	Form	Medium
Bloomberg	h	c	t	e
NASD	d	c	t	e
NASDAQ Factbook	a, m	h	t	p

Bibliography
Berlin, Howard M. *The Handbook of Financial Market Indexes, Averages, and Indicators*, Dow Jones-Irwin, Homewood, Ill., 1990, pp. 43-44.
"Nasdaq Index Overview," beta.nasdaq.com/asp/offsite_about.asp?content=http:// www.nasd.com/ar_section5.html, visited Feb. 3, 1998.

NASDAQ Utilities Index
[See NASDAQ Telecommunications Index]

NASDAQ Volume
The number of shares traded on the NASDAQ market on a given day.

The number of shares traded in each transaction conducted with NASDAQ are tallied and then totaled.

Used to judge market breadth and, in concert with other indicators, the attitudes of investors.

Published daily by NASDAQ in a news release.

Source	Frequency	Extent	Form	Medium
Business Statistics	a	h	t	p
NASDAQ Factbook	a, m	c, h	t, g	p
New York Times	d	c	t	p
Securities Industry Trends	a, m	c, h	t	p
Securities Industry Yearbook	a	h	t	p
Value Line Investment Survey, Part 2: Selection and Opinion	w	c	t	p

National Association of Purchasing Management Survey
[See Purchasing Managers' Index]

National Income
The aggregate earnings by labor and property that arise from the production of goods and services in the U.S. economy, consisting of compensation of employees, proprietors' income, rental income of individuals, net interest, and corporate profits.

The Bureau of Labor Statistics estimates compensation on employment and earnings from monthly reports by employers; these estimates are benchmarked to annual data from the unemployment insurance system. Other income is estimated from Internal Revenue Service data, which is supplemented with information from surveys and data from the Census Bureau and the Federal Reserve System. Seasonal adjustments are not available for these data, and quarterly data for proprietors' income and net interest are not available and must be interpolated.

Because this index measures the rate of flow of earnings from current output, its movements correspond with movements in production and show the relative contribution of wages and profits to those movements. It is also used as an indicator of the future availability of disposable income and, therefore, of near-term growth or decline of consumer purchases.

Published quarterly by the U.S. Department of Commerce, Bureau of Economic Analysis, in *Survey of Current Business*.

Source	Frequency	Extent	Form	Medium
Agricultural Statistics	a	h	t	p
Business Statistics	a, q	h	t	p
CRB Commodity Yearbook	m	h	t	p
Economic Report of the President	a	h	t	p, e
Federal Reserve Bulletin	a, q	c	t	p
FRED	m	c, h	t	e
International Financial Statistics	a, q	h	t	p
National Income and Product Accounts of the US	a	h	t	p
S&P Basic Statistics - Income and Trade	a	h	t	p
S&P Current Statistics	a, q	c	t	p
Statistical Abstract	a	h	t	p
Survey of Current Business	a, q	c	t	p (e)

Bibliography

Hoel, Arline Alchian; Kenneth W. Clarkson; and Roger LeRoy Miller, *Economics Sourcebook of Government Statistics*, Lexington Books, Lexington, Mass., 1983, pp. 42-53.

Joint Economic Committee, *1980 Supplement to Economic Indicators, Historical and Descriptive Background*, USGPO, Washington, D.C., 1980, pp. 10-13.

Kirk, John, "Economic Indicators: The How and the Why," *Banking*, 27-28 (Aug. 1964).

Office of Federal Statistical Policy and Standards, *Gross National Product Data Improvement Project Report*, Department of Commerce, Washington, D.C., 1977.

Tainer, Evelina M., *Using Economic Indicators to Improve Investment Analysis*, John Wiley & Sons, New York, 1993, pp. 44-52.

"Updated Summary NIPA Methodologies," *Survey of Current Business* **77** (9), 12-13 (Sept. 1997).

National Income Accounts
[See Federal Sector, National Income Accounts Basis]

National Income and Product Accounts
[See Federal Sector, National Income Accounts Basis; Gross Domestic Product; Gross National Product; National Income; and Net National Product]

National Market Industrial Index
[See NASDAQ Industrial Index]

National Product
[See Net National Product]

Negotiable Certificate of Deposit Interest Rates
[See Certificate of Deposit Interest Rates]

Net Generation
[See Electric Power Production]

Net National Product
[See also Gross Domestic Product, Gross National Product, and National Income]

An estimate of the total value of all of the country's goods and services produced and provided during the year after the costs of production have been deducted.

Two forms of the Net National Product are calculated, that at market prices and that at factor cost. The Net National Product at Market Prices is derived from the Gross National Product by deducting the depreciation on capital plant and equipment expenditures. This deduction is an effort to account for the capital that has been used in producing the gross output. Total depreciation allowances (both actual and imputed) are used. That is to say, the total financial allowances calculated by producers is counted along with imputed depreciation allowances for those sectors of the economy where no data exist (e.g., for farmers' tools and for the houses of homeowners). The Net National Product at Factor Cost goes beyond that for market cost by deducting additional costs introduced by the factors of production (indirect taxes, such as excise and property taxes; business transfer payments; the current surpluses of government enterprises; and the statistical discrepancy) and by adding any subsidies received by producers.

The Net National Product at Factor Cost is used to estimate the total factor income of the nation in the same manner that the Gross National Product is used to estimate the Gross National Income. The total factor income is referred to as the National Income.

Published quarterly by the U.S. Department of Commerce, Bureau of Economic Analysis, in *Survey of Current Business*.

Source	Frequency	Extent	Form	Medium
Business Statistics	a, q	h	t	p
Economic Report of the President	a	h	t	p, e
International Financial Statistics	a, q	c, h	t	p
Statistical Abstract	a	h	t	p
Survey of Current Business	a, q	c	t	p (e)

Bibliography
Collins, Lora S., "What NNP - not GNP - Tells Us," *Across the Board*, 25-29 (June 1981).
Ruggles, Richard, and Nancy D. Ruggles, *National Income Accounts and Income Analysis*, 2nd ed., McGraw-Hill, New York, 1956.
Snyder, Richard M., *Measuring Business Changes*, Wiley, New York, 1955, p. 16 ff.
"Updated Summary NIPA Methodologies," *Survey of Current Business* 77 (9), 12-13 (Sept. 1997).

New Business Incorporations
[Also called New Business Starts]
The number of stock corporations issued charters under the general business incorporation laws of the 50 states and the District of Columbia for a given month.

Dun & Bradstreet, Inc., gathers data for each state from the secretaries of state at the end of each month and totals those values. New incorporations are defined as completely new businesses that are incorporated, existing businesses that change from unincorporated to incorporated businesses, existing corporations that have been given certificates of authority to operate in an additional state, and existing corporations that have transferred to a new state. The data are seasonally adjusted with census data by the Bureau of Economic Analysis. Data are presented in aggregate and broken down by geographic area and by industry.

Considered to be a leading indicator at peaks, troughs, and the entirety of the business cycle; considered to be an indicator of economic opportunity.

Published monthly by Dun & Bradstreet, Inc., in *Monthly New Incorporations*; also published as a news release that is posted on the World Wide Web at www.dnb.com/newsview/economic.htm.

Source	Frequency	Extent	Form	Medium
Barron's	w	c	t	p
BCI	m	h	g	e
Business Statistics	a, m	h	t	p
Economic Report of the President	a	h	t	p, e
New Business Incorporations	m	c	t	p
Statistical Abstract	a	h	t	p

Bibliography

Hirschberg, David A., "On the Formation of Business Firms," *Monthly Labor Review* **117** (10), 55-58 (1994).

U.S. Department of Commerce, Bureau of Economic Analysis, *Business Statistics, 1963-91*, USGPO, Washington, D.C., 1992, pp. 144-145.

New Capital Expenditures
[See Capital Expenditures]

New Construction
[See Value of New Construction Put in Place]

New Construction Planning

An estimation of the dollar value of new construction plans for public and private projects in the United States.

Field reporters in all 50 states review the results of competitive bids for construction projects and report the dollar value of federal, state, municipal, and private-sector construction projects involving nonindustrial buildings costing more than $500,000 or other items costing more than $100,000. The values reported from the first of the month to the last Thursday of the month are totaled. Thus monthly totals are not strictly comparable. Data are broken down by type of construction and by geographic area.

Used as a leading indicator of construction activity.

Published monthly by McGraw-Hill Information Systems Co. in *Engineering News-Record*.

Source	Frequency	Extent	Form	Medium
Business Statistics	a	h	t	p
ENR	m	c	t	p
Survey of Current Business	m	c	t	p (e)

Bibliography

"Construction Costs Tracked for U.S.," *Engineering News-Record* 210 (12), 114-121 (Mar. 24, 1983).

New Home Mortgage Yield
[See Mortgage Interest Rates, FHFB and Mortgage Interest Rates, FHLM]

New Home Sales
[See also Existing Home Sales and Housing Starts]

The number of new, single-family homes sold during a given month, expressed as an annual rate.

Each month, the Bureau of the Census surveys a sample of developers to determine how many sales contracts have been signed or buyers' deposits accepted by the developers for new, single-family homes (unattached houses, townhouses, and townhouse condominiums) during the survey month.

Reported in thousands of units sold. The numbers are seasonally adjusted and annualized; that is to say, the numbers represent how many homes would be sold in the course of the year if all monthly sales were equal to those observed for the current month. The data are presented in the aggregate and broken down by region of the country.

Used as a general indicator of the strength of the economy; new home sales often reflect consumer purchasing power (resulting from current business activity) and the general demand for consumer goods and services. Houses (and the materials and labor that go into building them) represent a major portion of the consumer purchases that dominate and drive the national economy. These values are very sensitive to interest rates, particularly mortgage rates, and are also sensitive to the prices of new homes, which in turn reflect inflation.

Published monthly in a press release and as the report *New One-Family Houses Sold*, issued jointly by the U.S. Department of Commerce, Bureau of the Census, and the U.S. Department of Housing and Urban Development.

Source	Frequency	Extent	Form	Medium
Annual Statistical Digest (FRB)*	m	c	t	p
Bank of America	m	c, h	t	e
Bank of Tokyo-Mitsubishi	m	c, h	t	e
Barron's	m	c	t	p
Builder	m	c	t	p
Construction Review*	a, m	c, h	t	p
Federal Reserve Bulletin*	a, m	c, h	t	p
FRB Chicago	q	c, h	t	e
Mortgage Banking	m	c	t	p
New One Family Houses Sold (CCR C25)*	a, m	c, h	t, g	p
Real Estate Outlook*	a, m, q	c, h	t	p

Source	Frequency	Extent	Form	Medium
S&P Basic Statistics - Building and Building Materials*	m	h	t	p
Statistical Abstract*	a	h	t	p
Stat-USA	m	c	t	e
Survey of Current Business	a, m	c, h	t, g	p (e)
US Census Bureau	m	c, h	t	e

*Includes mean and median sales prices.

Bibliography

Carnes, W. Stansbury, and Stephen D. Slifer, *The Atlas of Economic Indicators: A Visual Guide to Market Forces and the Federal Reserve*, Harper Business, New York, 1991, pp. 143-146.

Niemira, Michael P., and Gerald F. Zukowski, *Trading the Fundamentals: The Trader's Guide to Interpreting Economic Indicators and Monetary Policy*, McGraw-Hill, New York, 1998, pp. 133-138.

Plocek, Joseph E., *Economic Indicators: How America Reads Its Financial Health*, New York Institute of Finance, New York, 1991, p. 217.

Tainer, Evelina M., *Using Economic Indicators to Improve Investment Analysis*, John Wiley & Sons, New York, 1993, pp. 113-117.

New Incorporations
[See New Business Incorporations]

New One-Family Houses Sold
[See Price Index of New One-Family Houses Sold]

New Orders, Aircraft
[See Aerospace Vehicles, New Orders]

New Orders, Consumer Goods and Materials
[See Manufacturers' New Orders: Capital Goods Industries, Nondefense; see also Durable Goods, Manufacturers' New Orders, and Manufacturers' Orders]

New Orders, Nondefense Capital Goods
[See Manufacturers' New Orders: Capital Goods Industries, Nondefense; see also Durable Goods, Manufacturers' New Orders, and Manufacturers' Orders]

New Plant and Equipment Expenditures
[See Capital Expenditures]

New Private Housing: Units Authorized by Permit Places
[See Housing Permits]

New Year's Celebration Index
[See Dom Perignon Champagne New Year's Celebration Index, Appendix A. Nonquantitative Indicators]

New York Stock Exchange Average Daily Volume
[See New York Stock Exchange Volume]

New York Stock Exchange Big-Block Activity
The number of transactions during a month on the New York Stock Exchange that exceed 10,000 shares.

New York Stock Exchange members report all large-block (10,000 shares or more) buy and sell orders electronically via the Block Automation System. The orders are transmitted to the Exchange floor where they are matched and executed. These big-block orders account for more than 50% of the volume. A tally of these trades is made daily.

Because such large transactions are almost always the actions of institutions, these statistics are taken to indicate the gross market activity of traders with large financial and sophisticated analytical resources. This statistic is a coincident indicator that generally confirms movements in other stock-market indicators.

Published daily by the New York Stock Exchange in a news release.

Source	Frequency	Extent	Form	Medium
Barron's	d	c	t	p
New York Times	d	c	t	p
NYSE Fact Book	a, m	c, h	t	p

Bibliography
Bohlen, Dudley R., "Large Block Transactions: A Premier Contrary Indicator," pp. 42-1 to 42-5 in *The Encyclopedia of Stock Market Techniques*, Investors Intelligence, Larchmont, N.Y., 1983.

Colby, Robert W., and Thomas A. Meyers, *The Encyclopedia of Technical Market Indicators*, Dow Jones-Irwin, Homewood, Ill., 1988, p. 252.

Müller, Thomas, and Harold Nietzer, *Das Grosse Buch der Technischen Indikatoren: Alles über Oszillatoren, Trendfolger, Zyklentechnik*, Thomas Müller, Börsenverlag, Rosenheim, Germany, 1995, p. 447.

Pring, Martin J., *Technical Analysis Explained, An Illustrated Guide for the Investor*, McGraw-Hill, New York, 1980, pp. 158-159.

Zweig, Martin E., "Trusty Market Indicator, Bring the Record of the Big-Block Index up to Date," *Barron's*, 11-12 (Jan. 24, 1983).

New York Stock Exchange Composite Index

A measure of the change in aggregate market value of common shares of all stocks listed on the New York Stock Exchange adjusted to eliminate the nonprice effects of changes in firm capitalization and exchange listings and delistings. Indexes are also prepared for four subgroups of stocks: industrial, transportation, utility, and financial. The data are compiled at least hourly and reported daily.

The price per share of each listed stock is multiplied by its number of shares listed to give its market value. The market values of all listed stocks are summed, and the total is divided by the market value on a base date (Dec. 31, 1965). This quotient is multiplied by 50.00 (the base value of the index). Nonprice effects are eliminated by adjustments to the base-date market value.

Used as an indicator of general market conditions.

Published daily by the New York Stock Exchange in a news release and on the World Wide Web at www.nyse.com/public/market/2b/2bix.htm.

Source	Frequency	Extent	Form	Medium
Annual Statistical Digest (FRB)	a, m	c	t	p
Barron's	d	c	t	p
Bridge	d	c	t	e
Business Statistics	a	h	t	p
CBS	h	c	t	e
CNN	h	c	t	e
Federal Reserve Bulletin	a, m	c, h	t	p
Financial Digest	d	c	t	p
Investor's Business Daily	d	c	t	p
Media General	d	c	t	e
Moody's Handbook of Common Stocks	m	h	g	p
Mutual Funds Update	m	c	t	p
New York Times	d (h)	c	t	p (e)
NYSE	d	c	t	e
NYSE Fact Book	a, d	c, h	t	p
PCQuote	h	c	t	e
Securities Industry Trends	a, m	c, h	t	p
Securities Industry Yearbook	a	h	t	p
Statistical Abstract	a	h	t	p
StockMaster	d	c, h	g, t	e
USA Today	d (h)	c	t	p (e)

Source	Frequency	Extent	Form	Medium
Value Line Investment Survey, Part 2: Selection and Opinion	w, q	c	t, g	p
Wall Street Journal	d	c	t	p

Bibliography

Berlin, Howard M. *The Handbook of Financial Market Indexes, Averages, and Indicators*, Dow Jones-Irwin, Homewood, Ill., 1990, pp. 46-50.

Fisher, Lawrence, "Some New Stock-Market Indexes," *The Journal of Business*, 191-225 (Jan. 1966).

Frumkin, Norman, *Guide to Economic Indicators*, 2nd ed., M. E. Sharpe, Armonk, N.Y., 1994, pp. 276, 279, 284-285.

Hoel, Arline Alchian; Kenneth W. Clarkson; and Roger LeRoy Miller, *Economics Sourcebook of Government Statistics*, Lexington Books, Lexington, Mass., 1983, pp. 155-159.

Joint Economic Committee, *1980 Supplement to Economic Indicators, Historical and Descriptive Background*, USGPO, Washington, D.C., 1980, pp. 112-113.

Kirk, John, "N.Y. Stock Exchange Launches Its Market Indicator," *Banking*, 4-5 (Aug. 1966).

Laderman, Jeff, "How's the Market? It Depends on the Yardstick," *Business Week*, p. 124 (Sept. 21, 1987).

"Market Guides," *Barron's*, 9+ (Sept. 26, 1966).

Pearce, Douglas K., "Stock Prices and the Economy," *Economic Review of the Federal Reserve Bank of Kansas City*, 7-22 (Nov. 1983).

Smith, Keith V., "Stock Price and Economic Indexes for Generating Efficient Portfolios," *Journal of Business*, 326-336 (July 1969).

New York Stock Exchange Firms' Free Credit Balance

The proceeds of sales going to individual brokers and left by them in their accounts rather than being immediately reinvested or withdrawn as cash; the aggregate total of the account balances of NYSE members.

The amount of cash held in individual accounts of NYSE firms is totaled.

Used to forecast market trends. The theory has it that investors will tend to use this excess cash during a rising market and not during a falling one. Therefore credit balances are expected to decline at the beginning of bull markets and to rise in bear markets.

Published monthly by the New York Stock Exchange in a press release.

Source	Frequency	Extent	Form	Medium
Barron's	m	c	t	p
Federal Reserve Bulletin	a, m	h	t	p
NYSE Fact Book	q	h	t	p

Bibliography
Cohen, J.; A. Zinbarg; and A. Zeikel, *Investment Analysis and Portfolio Management*, 3rd ed., Irwin, Homewood, Ill., 1977, p.77.
Gordon, William, *The Stock Market Indicators as a Guide to Market Timing*, Investors Press, Palisades Park, N. J., 1968, p. 113.
Hayes, Michael, *The Dow Jones - Irwin Guide to Stock Market Cycles*, Dow Jones - Irwin, Homewood, Ill., 1977, pp. 161-167.
Wilson, Sloan J., "The Customers' Free Credit Balances and Margin Debt," pp. 19-1 to 19-22 in *The Encyclopedia of Stock Market Techniques*, Investors Intelligence, Larchmont, N.Y., 1983.
Zweig, M., "New Sell Signal," *Barron's*, Oct. 13, 1975, pp. 5, 14.

New York Stock Exchange Firms' Margin Accounts

The amount of cash owed to NYSE brokerage houses; also known as their debit balances.

All of the funds owed to NYSE brokerage houses by their clients are totaled each month by each brokerage house. These totals are reported to the Exchange, and it totals all of the reported figures for the month. All debt is included.

To predict short-term highs and lows in stock-market activity. A market decline is expected when there is a low use of margin purchases. During an expansion of the market, margin purchases increase because investors expect to recoup the cost of the loans through the increases of the market value of their purchases.

Published monthly by the New York Stock Exchange in a press release.

Source	Frequency	Extent	Form	Medium
Federal Reserve Bulletin	a, m	h	t	p
NYSE Fact Book	q	h	t	p

Bibliography
Hayes, Michael, *The Dow Jones - Irwin Guide to Stock Market Cycles*, Dow Jones - Irwin, Homewood, Ill., 1977, pp. 158-160.

New York Stock Exchange Members' Short Sales

The total shares sold short for the accounts of NYSE members during a given week.

A short sale is the selling of shares that are not owned by the seller but rather are borrowed from another account. The borrowed shares are sold at the current share price in anticipation of the seller's being able to purchase replacement shares at a lower price in the future and returning them to the account from which the original shares were borrowed. The practice is followed when a declining market is expected. The Exchange's specialists total up the number of shares sold short each day by different classes of traders, and those totals are reported each week by the Exchange.

Used to predict peaks and troughs in stock-market activity. The theory is that when the members of the Exchange, who are regarded as knowledgeable and insightful about the workings of the market, are selling short, they are anticipating a decline in the market. When few of the trades of the members are short sales, they are collectively anticipating an upturn in the market in the near term.

Published weekly by the New York Stock Exchange in a news release.

Source	Frequency	Extent	Form	Medium
Barron's	w	c	t	p
NYSE Fact Book	a	h	t	p
Wall Street Journal	w	c	t	p

Bibliography

Berlin, Howard M. *The Handbook of Financial Market Indexes, Averages, and Indicators*, Dow Jones-Irwin, Homewood, Ill., 1990, pp. 226-227.

Colby, Robert W., and Thomas A. Meyers, *The Encyclopedia of Technical Market Indicators*, Dow Jones-Irwin, Homewood, Ill., 1988, pp. 450-451.

Müller, Thomas, and Harold Nietzer, *Das Grosse Buch der Technischen Indikatoren: Alles über Oszillatoren, Trendfolger, Zyklentechnik*, Thomas Müller, Börsenverlag, Rosenheim, Germany, 1995, p. 447.

Pring, Martin J., *Technical Analysis Explained, An Illustrated Guide for the Investor*, McGraw-Hill, New York, 1980, pp. 210-212.

New York Stock Exchange Nonmembers' Short Sales

The total shares sold short during a given week for the accounts of traders who are not members of the Exchange.

A short sale is the selling of shares that are not owned by the seller but rather are borrowed from another account. The borrowed shares are sold at the current share price in anticipation of the seller's being able to purchase replacement shares at a lower price in the future and returning them to the account from which the original shares were borrowed. The practice is followed when a declining market is expected. The Exchange's specialists total up the number of shares sold short each day by different classes of traders, and those totals are reported each week by the Exchange.

Used to predict peaks and troughs in stock-market activity. The theory is that when shares are being sold short, the sellers are anticipating a decline in the market. When few of the trades are short sales, the traders are collectively anticipating an upturn in the market in the near term.

Published weekly by the New York Stock Exchange in a news release.

Source	Frequency	Extent	Form	Medium
Barron's	w	c	t	p
NYSE Fact Book	a	h	t	p

Bibliography

Berlin, Howard M. *The Handbook of Financial Market Indexes, Averages, and Indicators*, Dow Jones-Irwin, Homewood, Ill., 1990, pp. 226-227.

Colby, Robert W., and Thomas A. Meyers, *The Encyclopedia of Technical Market Indicators*, Dow Jones-Irwin, Homewood, Ill., 1988, pp. 450-451.

Müller, Thomas, and Harold Nietzer, *Das Grosse Buch der Technischen Indikatoren: Alles über Oszillatoren, Trendfolger, Zyklentechnik*, Thomas Müller, Börsenverlag, Rosenheim, Germany, 1995, p. 447.

Pring, Martin J., *Technical Analysis Explained, An Illustrated Guide for the Investor*, McGraw-Hill, New York, 1980, pp. 210-212.

New York Stock Exchange Odd-Lot Sales

A measure of the daily or weekly sales on the New York Stock Exchange that are made up of 100 shares or less.

The total number of shares transferred as odd-lot sales (transactions involving 100 or fewer shares) on the Exchange are summed up and reported by the Exchange's specialists.

Used to predict future movements in stock market activity; a contrary indicator of market activity because purchasers of small lots are considered to be small, unsophisticated, inexperienced investors who are likely to be wrong in their reading of the market.

Published daily (supplemented by weekly summaries) by the New York Stock Exchange in a news release.

Source	Frequency	Extent	Form	Medium
Barron's	w	c	t	p
NYSE Fact Book	a, m	h	t	p
Wall Street Journal	d. w	c	t	p

Bibliography

Gordon, William, *The Stock Market Indicators as a Guide to Market Timing*, Investors Press, Palisades Park, N. J., 1968, pp. 61-71.

Hayes, Michael, *The Dow Jones - Irwin Guide to Stock Market Cycles*, Dow Jones - Irwin, Homewood, Ill., 1977, pp. 168-172.

New York Stock Exchange Seat Sales

The price paid in dollars for one seat on or membership in the New York Stock Exchange; such membership is required to actively trade on the exchange, and the number of seats is limited. Prices paid are determined by supply and demand, and the sales are private ones between individuals.

Seats can be transferred by an auction system. The price paid for a seat is determined by prevailing stock-market conditions and by supply and demand. Brokers involved in these sales report them and the prices to the Exchange.

Used as an indicator of expected future profitability of the exchange; used mostly for historical comparisons of stock-market activity and current strength of the market.

Published monthly by the New York Stock Exchange in a news release.

Source	Frequency	Extent	Form	Medium
Barron's	m	c	t	p
NYSE Fact Book	m	c	t	p

Bibliography

Eaton, Leslie, "No Hot Seat: Value of Exchange Memberships Plunges," *Barron's* **70** (4), 36 (Jan. 22, 1990).

Müller, Thomas, and Harold Nietzer, *Das Grosse Buch der Technischen Indikatoren: Alles über Oszillatoren, Trendfolger, Zyklentechnik*, Thomas Müller, Börsenverlag, Rosenheim, Germany, 1995, p. 447.

Reilly, Frank K., "Secondary Markets," pp. 135-164 in Frank J. Fabozzi and Frank G. Zarb, Handbook of Financial Markets, Dow Jones - Irwin, Homewood, Ill, 1981.

New York Stock Exchange Short Interest Ratio

The number of trading days it would take to cover the total short position of the market given the recent average trading volume.

The monthly uncovered short positions on the New York Stock Exchange expressed in shares are divided by the average daily volume for each day of the preceding month.

Used as a buy or sell signal; a measure of the demand for future trading. Short sellers eventually have to cover their positions. In a rising market, this necessity increases the demand for the shorted stocks, increasing their prices. In a declining market, no such immediate demand for the stocks exists, and their values are likely to decline. A rise in short sales has traditionally been considered bullish for the market.

Published monthly by the New York Stock Exchange in a midmonth news release.

Source	Frequency	Extent	Form	Medium
Barron's	m	c	t	p
Investor's Business Daily	d	c, h	t	p
NYSE Fact Book*	m	c	t	p
S&P Basic Statistics - Banking and Finance*	a, m	h	t	p
Value Line Investment Survey, Part 2: Selection and Opinion	w	c	t	p

*Reports volume.

Bibliography

Berlin, Howard M. *The Handbook of Financial Market Indexes, Averages, and Indicators*, Dow Jones-Irwin, Homewood, Ill., 1990, pp. 227-228.

Cohen, J. B.; E. D. Zinbarg: and Arthur Zeikel, *Investment Analysis and Portfolio Management*, Irwin, Homewood, Ill., 1977, pp. 311-313.

Gordon, William, *The Stock Market Indicators as a Guide to Market Timing*, Investors Press, Palisades Park, N. J., 1968, pp. 93-110.

Hayes, Michael, *The Dow Jones - Irwin Guide to Stock Market Cycles*, Dow Jones - Irwin, Homewood, Ill., 1977, pp. 147-150.

Kerrigan, Thomas J., "The Short Interest Ratio and Its Component Parts," *Financial Analysts Journal*, 45-49 (Nov./Dec. 1974).

Müller, Thomas, and Harold Nietzer, *Das Grosse Buch der Technischen Indikatoren: Alles über Oszillatoren, Trendfolger, Zyklentechnik*, Thomas Müller, Börsenverlag, Rosenheim, Germany, 1995, p. 450.

Savitz, Eric J., "Street Full of Bears," *Barron's* **70** (22), 20 and 22 (May 28, 1990).

Schulz, John W., "Thank You, Short Sellers," *Barron's* **72** (41), 22-24 (Oct. 12, 1992).

Smith, Randall O., "Short Interest and Stock Market Prices," *Financial Analysts Journal*, 151-154 (Nov./Dec, 1968).

New York Stock Exchange TICK
[See TICK]

New York Stock Exchange Volume

The number of shares traded on the New York Stock Exchange on a given day.

The number of shares traded in each transaction are tallied and then totaled.

Used to judge market breadth and, in concert with other indicators, the attitudes of investors.

Published daily by the New York Stock Exchange in a news release and posted on the World Wide Web at www.nyse.com/public/market/2b/2bix.htm.

Source	Frequency	Extent	Form	Medium
Annual Statistical Digest (FRB)	a, m	c	t	p
Barron's	m	c	g	p
Business Statistics	a	h	t	p
Federal Reserve Bulletin	a, m	c	t	p
Financial Digest	d	c	t	p
Investor's Business Daily	d	c	t	p
Moody's Handbook of Common Stocks	m	h	g	p

Source	Frequency	Extent	Form	Medium
New York Times	d	c	t	p
NYSE	d	c	t	e
NYSE Fact Book	a, m	c, h	t	p
SEC Annual Report	a	c	t	p
Securities Industry Trends	a, m	c, h	t	p
Securities Industry Yearbook	a	h	t	p
S&P Basic Statistics - Banking and Finance	a, m	h	t	p
S&P Current Statistics	d, m	c, h	t	p
Statistical Abstract	a	h	t	p
Value Line Investment Survey, Part 2: Selection and Opinion	w	c	t	p
Wall Street Journal	m	c	g	p

Bibliography

Colby, Robert W., and Thomas A. Meyers, *The Encyclopedia of Technical Market Indicators*, Dow Jones-Irwin, Homewood, Ill., 1988, p. 515.

NNM Industrial Index
[See NASDAQ Industrial Index]

Nonagricultural Employment

Estimates of the total number of persons employed in nonagricultural establishments in the United States during a specified payroll period; includes all those who worked during, received wages for, or were sick or on strike during any part of the payroll period as full-time, part-time, or temporary employees. Those that work more than one job are counted by each reporting establishment that employs them. Proprietors, the self employed, unpaid family workers, and domestic workers in households are not included.

Data are collected each month as part of the Establishment Survey from a sample of nonagricultural establishments in the private sector and in state and local governments by cooperating state agencies that mail questionnaires to those establishments and edit the responses before passing the information on to the Bureau of Labor Statistics. These data are supplemented with monthly data on federal civilian employment obtained from the Office of Personnel Management. The sampling is proportionate to the average size of the establishment; all large establishments are included in the sample, but coverage is much lower for small establishments. Data are broken down by type of employer according to Standard Industrial Classification code with about 500 such categories. The data are benchmarked to a reasonably complete count prepared annually from a number of sources and adjusted with a ratio of the current month's employment to the previous month's employment computed from the sample establishments reporting for both months. The data are then seasonally adjusted.

Widely used as a timely indicator of changes in economic activity in the manufacturing, transportation, public utilities, wholesale and retail trade, finance, insurance, real estate, and governmental sectors of the U.S. economy. It is used to follow business trends in nearly 260 labor markets across the country. It is frequently factored into other economic indicators dealing with production, productivity, and national income. It is also a component of the Coincident Indicators Composite Index.

Published monthly by the U.S. Department of Labor, Bureau of Labor Statistics, in a press release entitled "The Employment Situation" and in *Employment and Earnings*.

Source	Frequency	Extent	Form	Medium
Annual Statistical Digest (FRB)	a, m	c	t	p
Bank of Tokyo-Mitsubishi	m	c, h	t	e
Barron's	m	c	t	p
BLS	m	c, h	t	e
Business Statistics	a, m	h	t	p
Conference Board/BCI	m	c	t	e
Employment & Earnings	a, m	c, h	t	p
The Employment Situation	a, m	c	t, g	p
Federal Reserve Bulletin	a, m	c	t	p
Forecast	a, q	c, f	t	p
FRB Dallas	m	c, h	t	e
Handbook of International Economic Statistics (CIA)	a	h	t	p
International Financial Statistics	a, q	h	t	p
Recession Recovery Watch	q	h	g	p
S&P Basic Statistics - Production Indexes and Labor Statistics	a, m	h	t	p
S&P Current Statistics	m	c	t	p
Statistical Abstract	a	h	t	p
Stat-USA	m	c	t	e
Survey of Current Business	a, m	c	t	p (e)

Bibliography

Carnes, W. Stansbury, and Stephen D. Slifer, *The Atlas of Economic Indicators: A Visual Guide to Market Forces and the Federal Reserve*, Harper Business, New York, 1991, pp. 59-72.

Forsyth, Randall W., "It Doesn't Work: The Monthly Employment Data Can Mislead," *Barron's* **77** (39), 47 (Sept. 29, 1997).

Frumkin, Norman, *Guide to Economic Indicators*, 2nd ed., M. E. Sharpe, Armonk, N.Y., 1994, pp. 109-115.

Frumkin, Norman, *Tracking America's Economy*, 2nd ed., Sharpe, Armonk, N.Y., 1992, pp. 198-204.

Hoel, Arline Alchian; Kenneth W. Clarkson; and Roger LeRoy Miller, *Economics Sourcebook of Government Statistics*, Lexington Books, Lexington, Mass., 1983, pp. 198-200.

Joint Economic Committee, *1980 Supplement to Economic Indicators, Historical and Descriptive Background*, USGPO, Washington, D.C., 1980, pp. 43-47.

Kirk, John, "Economic Indicators: The How and the Why," *Banking*, 27-28 (Aug. 1964).

Koretz, Gene, "State Employment Gains Are Outpacing the Official Tally," *Business Week*, No. 3303, p. 20 (Feb. 1, 1993).

Lavin, Vance, and James Heitman, "Employment and Unemployment Data: Dramatic Changes of Key Indicators," *Government Finance Review* **10**, 35 (1994).

Miller, Glenn H., Jr., "Employment Indicators of Economic Activity," *Economic Review of the Federal Reserve Bank of Kansas City* **72** (7), 42-62 (July/Aug. 1987).

Moore, Geoffrey Hoyt, and Melita H. Moore, *International Economic Indicators: A Sourcebook*, Greenwood Press, Westport, Conn., 1985, pp. 37-38.

Moore, G. H., and J. Shiskin, "Why the Leading Indicators Really Do Lead," *Across the Board*, 71-75 (May 1978).

Moore, Geoffrey, "Employment: The Neglected Indicator," *Wall Street Journal*, 10 (Feb. 3, 1972).

Moore, Geoffrey Hoyt, *Improving the Presentation of Employment and Unemployment Statistics*, National Commission on Employment and Unemployment Statistics Background Paper No. 22, USGPO, Washington, D.C., 1978.

Niemira, Michael P., and Gerald F. Zukowski, *Trading the Fundamentals: The Trader's Guide to Interpreting Economic Indicators and Monetary Policy*, McGraw-Hill, New York, 1998, pp. 73-102.

Plocek, Joseph E., *Economic Indicators: How America Reads Its Financial Health*, New York Institute of Finance, New York, 1991, pp. 53-54.

Renshaw, Edward, Ed., *The Practical Forecasters' Almanac: 137 Reliable Indicators for Investors, Hedgers, and Speculators*, Business One Irwin, Homewood, Ill., 1992, pp. 29-30.

Rogers, R. Mark, *Handbook of Key Economic Indicators*, Irwin Professional Pub., Burr Ridge, Ill., 1994, pp. 20-40.

Ruggles, Richard, *Employment and Unemployment Statistics as Indexes of Economic Activity and Capacity Utilization*, National Commission on

Employment and Unemployment Statistics Background Paper No. 28, USGPO, Washington, D.C., 1979.

Shiskin, Julius, "Employment and Unemployment: The Doughnut or the Hole," *Monthly Labor Review*, 3-10 (Feb. 1976).

Slater, Courtenay M., Ed., Business Statistics of the United States, 1995 ed., Bernan Press, Lanham, Md., 1996, pp. 239-240.

U.S. Department of Commerce, Bureau of Economic Analysis, *Business Statistics, 1963-91*, USGPO, Washington, D.C., 1992, pp. 154-155.

U.S. Department of Labor, Bureau of Labor Statistics, *A Guide to Seasonal Adjustment of Labor Force Data*, Bull. 2114, U.S. Department of Labor, Washington, D.C., 1982.

U.S. Department of Labor, Bureau of Labor Statistics, *BLS Handbook of Methods*, Bull. 2490, USGPO, Washington, D.C., 1997, pp. 15-31.

U.S. Department of Labor, Bureau of Labor Statistics, *Major Programs of the Bureau of Labor Statistics*, USGPO, Washington, D.C., 1994, pp. 3-4.

U.S. Department of Labor, Bureau of Labor Statistics, *Workers, Jobs, and Statistics*, Rept. 698, U.S. Department of Labor, Washington, D.C., 1983.

U.S. Department of Labor, Bureau of Labor Statistics and Bureau of the Census, *Concepts and Methods Used in Labor Force Statistics Derived from the Current Population Survey*, BLS Rept. 463 and Current Population Report (Ser. P-23) 62, U.S. Department of Labor and U.S. Department of Commerce, Washington, D.C., 1976.

Nondefense Orders

[See Manufacturers' New Orders: Capital Goods Industries, Nondefense]

Nonfarm Business Productivity

[See Index of Productivity]

Number of Business Failures

[See Business Failures]

O

Odd-Lot Index
[See American Stock Exchange Odd-Lot Index and New York Stock Exchange Odd-Lot Sales]

Odd-Lot Sales and Purchase Index
[See New York Stock Exchange Odd-Lot Sales]

Oil and Gas Index
[See American Stock Exchange Oil Index]

Oil Prices

Daily closing prices for contracts for the delivery of a variety of crude petroleum and of petroleum products.

Each day at the close of trading on the New York Mercantile Exchange, the prevailing prices for crude petroleum from a variety locations and for several primary petroleum products (like heating oil and unleaded gasoline), both for immediate and future delivery, are recorded. Among the petroleum commodities traded, West Texas intermediate for immediate delivery and East Texas light, sweet crude stand out as the bellwethers of U.S. crude oil. Light sweets are especially preferred by refiners because they produce yield high levels of high-value products like gasoline, jet fuel, diesel fuel, and heating oil. Intermediate and light, sweet crudes are widely used as overall gauges in trends of oil prices on both domestic and international markets. Contractual oil prices are tracked and reported to subscribers by several specialized information services, such as Platt's, Petroleum Argus, London Oil Reports, Telerate, and Reuters. The values reported by these services (and often averages or other combinations of these values) form the basis for pricing on the international oil market that result in the spot and futures prices that are reported in the business and financial literature.

Because petroleum constitutes a major cost for industry (as a raw material, energy source, and transportation fuel) and for consumers (in the form of gasoline and heating oil) its spot and futures prices are key indicators of future manufacturing, transportation, and living costs. Oil prices also play a large role in fueling or controlling inflation. In addition, crude oil is the world's most actively traded commodity, making its price changes a major indicator of movements on the commodities market.

Reported daily as a news release by the New York Mercantile Exchange; the closing price for West Texas intermediate for immediate delivery is reported daily by the *Wall Street Journal*, and that for light sweet crude is reported daily by *USA Today* and weekly by *Barron's*.

Source	Frequency	Extent	Form	Medium
Basic Petroleum Data Book	a	h	t	p
Bridge	d	c	t	e
CNN	h	c	t	e
FRED	m	c, h	t	e
Handbook of International Economic Statistics (CIA)	a	h	t	p
Monthly Energy Review	a, m	h	t, g	p
New York Times	d	c	t	p
Northeast Louisiana University	w, m	c, h	t	e
S&P Basic Statistics - Energy, Electric Power, and Fuels	h	h	t	p
Statistical Abstract	a	h	t	p
USA Today	d	c	t	p
Value Line Investment Survey, Part 2: Selection and Opinion	a, q	c, h, f	t	p
Wall Street Journal	d	c	t	p

Bibliography

Burley, Robin, and Ian Bourne, "Price Reporting: Too Many Reports Spoil the Price," *Petroleum Economist* **58**, 18-19 (May 1991).

Tainer, Evelina M., *Using Economic Indicators to Improve Investment Analysis*, Wiley & Sons, New York, 1993, pp. 163-164.

Operating Rate
[See Capacity Utilization]

Orders for Durable Goods
[See Durable Goods]

Output per Employee Hour
[See Index of Productivity; see also Change in Hours per Unit of Output, Implicit Price Deflators, and Unit Labor Costs]

Over-the-Counter Average
[See NASDAQ Composite Index]

Over-the-Counter Index
[See NASDAQ Composite Index]

P

Paperboard Production

Estimated national total of new and unfilled orders for and production of paperboard.

Approximately 90% of the paperboard mills are surveyed by the American Forest and Paper Association. These reports are supplemented with and extrapolated with estimates for the other ~10% based on annual reports on the entire industry. For new orders and production, the data are averaged to produce monthly and yearly data. Because of the manner in which new orders are received, new-order data and production data are not for the same periods. For unfilled orders, the data are those for the end of the month.

A reliable leading indicator of overall industrial activity. Its reliability is commonly attributed to the need of manufacturers for paperboard to ship their products in. When business is slow, less paperboard is needed. When an upturn in business is anticipated, orders for paperboard are increased.

Published by the American Forest and Paper Association in *Paper, Paperboard, and Wood Pulp Monthly Statistical Summary.*

Source	Frequency	Extent	Form	Medium
Business Statistics	a	h	t	p
Paper, Paperboard, and Wood Pulp	a, m	c	t, g	p
S&P Basic Statistics - Textiles, Chemicals, and Paper	a	h	t	p
S&P Current Statistics	m	h	t	p
Statistical Abstract	a	h	t	p
Statistics of Paper, Paperboard, and Wood Pulp	a	h	t, g	p

Bibliography
"The Rage for Faster Forecasts," *Business Week*, 135-136 (Oct. 18, 1982).
U.S. Department of Commerce, Bureau of Economic Analysis, *Business Statistics, 1963-91*, USGPO, Washington, D.C., 1992, p. 186.

Parity Index

The Index of Prices Paid by Farmers for Commodities and Services, Interest, Taxes, and Farm Wage Rates expressed on a 1910-1914 base. A weighted indicator of the costs to farmers for items used in family living, for items used in farm production, for interest on indebtedness secured by farm real estate, and for wages paid to farm labor.

Produced by combining the Index of Commodities and Services with the indexes of interest, taxes, and wage rates, all indexed to 1910-1914 as the base and all for the costs to farmers. The data are gathered from reports by firms and organizations providing production inputs to agricultural producers, surveys of farmers, the Department of Agriculture, trade publications, labor surveys, and surveys of financial institutions. Compilation of the first index is the most complicated. In the compilation of this index, the data are expressed state-by-state, and state weights (based on the quantities of goods and services purchased by farmers) are applied to the data. National averages are then calculated for specified types of farm expenditures. These groups of expenditures are then summed and combined with a family living component to obtain the Index of Commodities and Services.

Used in market planning, negotiating marketing contracts, comparing changes in farming prices with those in nonfarm areas, and establishing commodity parity prices for agricultural price-support programs.

Published monthly by the U.S. Department of Agriculture, National Agricultural Statistics Service, in *Agricultural Prices*.

Source	Frequency	Extent	Form	Medium
Agricultural Prices Monthly Report	m	c	t	p
Statistical Abstract	a	h	t	p

Bibliography
Joint Economic Committee, *1980 Supplement to Economic Indicators, Historical and Descriptive Background*, USGPO, Washington, D.C., 1980, p. 92.
Major Statistical Series of the U.S. Department of Agriculture, Vol. 1, Agricultural Prices, USDA, Economic Research Service, Agricultural Handbook No. 671, Washington, D.C., 1990.
Scope and Method of the Statistical Reporting Service, Misc. Publ. 1308, USDA, Washington, D.C., 1975.

Parity Ratio

A measure of the purchasing power of the products sold by farmers in terms of the goods and services they buy compared with the comparable purchasing power in a base period. The ratio of the income of farmers to the costs of operation paid by farmers indexed to a particular base time.

The Index of Prices Received by Farmers and the Index of Prices Paid by Farmers are both expressed on a base of 1910-1914. The Index of Prices received by Farmers is then divided by the Index of Prices Paid by Farmers and multiplied by 100. When this Parity Ratio is less than 100, prices paid have increased at a faster rate than the prices the farmers received for their goods since the 1910-1914 base period. Conversely, when the Ratio is more than 100, prices paid have increased at a slower rate than the prices farmers received for their goods since the base period.

Actuates Department of Agriculture price-support programs to farmers, which guard against sharp fluctuations in price. These actions, in turn, affect food prices and farm purchasing power.

Published by the U.S. Department of Agriculture, National Agricultural Statistics Service, Agricultural Statistics Board, in *Agricultural Prices*.

Source	Frequency	Extent	Form	Medium
Agricultural Prices Monthly Report	m	c	t	p
Statistical Abstract	a	h	t	p

Bibliography

Frumkin, Norman, *Guide to Economic Indicators*, 2nd ed., M. E. Sharpe, Armonk, N.Y., 1994, pp. 127-131.

Joint Economic Committee, *1980 Supplement to Economic Indicators, Historical and Descriptive Background*, USGPO, Washington, D.C., 1980, p. 93.

Major Statistical Series of the U.S. Department of Agriculture, Vol. 1, Agricultural Prices, USDA, Economic Research Service, Agricultural Handbook No. 671, Washington, D.C., 1990.

Pentafilia Paradigm

[See Appendix A. Nonquantitative Indicators]

Personal Consumption Expenditures

[See also Government Consumption Expenditures, Disposition of Personal Income, and Retail Sales]

An estimate of the total expenditures made by individuals, nonprofit institutions, etc. for services and new goods.

Estimates for benchmark years are made from census data and expressed in billions of dollars. Estimates for years between benchmarks and for quarters are derived chiefly from trends shown by the Census Bureau's retail sales figures by kind of store and other source data. The data are seasonally adjusted and include virtually all expenditures except interest payments on debt.

Used in the calculation of Disposition of Personal Income. Data trends will closely follow the trends of total retail sales. Personal consumption drives about two-thirds of the economy, so this measure is a strong indicator of the overall economy.

Quarterly data are published monthly by the U.S. Department of Commerce, Bureau of Economic Analysis, in *Survey of Current Business*.

Source	Frequency	Extent	Form	Medium
Agricultural Outlook	a, q	c	t	p
Bank of America	q	c, h	t	e
Bank of Tokyo-Mitsubishi	m	c, h	t	e
Barron's	q	c	t	p
BEA	q	c, h	t	e
Blue Chip Economic Indicators	a	c, f	t	p
Business Statistics	a	h	t	p
Economic Report of the President	a	h	t	p, e
Federal Reserve Bulletin	a, q	c	t	p
First Union	m	c, h	t	c
FRB Dallas	q	c, h	t	e
FRED	m	c, h	t	e
International Financial Statistics	a, q	c, h	t	p
Statistical Abstract	a	h	t	p
Survey of Current Business	a, q, m	c	t	p, e

Bibliography

Carnes, W. Stansbury, and Stephen D. Slifer, *The Atlas of Economic Indicators: A Visual Guide to Market Forces and the Federal Reserve*, Harper Business, New York, 1991, pp. 127-134.

Harris, Ethan S., and Clara Vega, *What Do Chain Store Sales Tell Us about Consumer Spending?*, Research Paper 9614, Federal Reserve Bank of New York, New York, 1996.

Joint Economic Committee, *1980 Supplement to Economic Indicators, Historical and Descriptive Background*, USGPO, Washington, D.C., 1980, pp. 15-17.

Kirk, John, "Economic Indicators: The How and the Why," *Banking*, 25-26 (July 1964).

Niemira, Michael P., and Gerald F. Zukowski, *Trading the Fundamentals: The Trader's Guide to Interpreting Economic Indicators and Monetary Policy*, McGraw-Hill, New York, 1998, pp. 187-195.

Plocek, Joseph E., *Economic Indicators: How America Reads Its Financial Health*, New York Institute of Finance, New York, 1991, pp. 103-106.

Rogers, R. Mark, *Handbook of Key Economic Indicators*, Irwin Professional Pub., Burr Ridge, Ill., 1994, pp. 47-49, 69-70, 212.

Tainer, Evelina M., *Using Economic Indicators to Improve Investment Analysis*, John Wiley & Sons, New York, 1993, pp. 70-74.

U.S. Department of Commerce, Bureau of Economic Analysis, *Personal Consumption Expenditures*, Methodology Papers: U.S. National Income and Product Accounts, BEA-MP-6, USGPO, Washington, D.C., 1990.

WEFA Group, *Guide to Economic Indicators: U.S. Macroeconomic Services*, WEFA Group, Bala Cynwyd, Pa., 1997, p. 21.

Personal Income
[See Disposable Personal Income and Sources of Personal Income; see also Disposition of Personal Income]

Personal Outlays
[See also Disposition of Personal Income]

Expenditures of individuals exclusive of tax and other payments to government; a subset of Disposition of Personal Income.

The cost of goods and services purchased by individuals, the operating expenses of nonprofit organizations, the values of goods or services received in kind by individuals, interest payments by individuals to businesses, and personal transfer payments made to foreigners are obtained from the the Bureau of Labor Statistics, the Bureau of the Census, and the Internal Revenue Service and summed.

Used as a gauge of the health of the consumer section of the economy.

Published monthly by the U.S. Department of Commerce, Bureau of Economic Analysis, in *Personal Income and Outlays* and in *Survey of Current Business*.

Source	Frequency	Extent	Form	Medium
Business Statistics	a	h	t	p
Statistical Abstract	a	h	t	p
Stat-USA	m	c	t	e
Survey of Current Business	a, q, m	c	t	p, e

Bibliography

Hoel, Arline Alchian; Kenneth W. Clarkson; and Roger LeRoy Miller, *Economics Sourcebook of Government Statistics*, Lexington Books, Lexington, Mass., 1983, pp. 73-79.

Niemira, Michael P., and Gerald F. Zukowski, *Trading the Fundamentals: The Trader's Guide to Interpreting Economic Indicators and Monetary Policy*, McGraw-Hill, New York, 1998, p. 189.

Plocek, Joseph E., *Economic Indicators: How America Reads Its Financial Health*, New York Institute of Finance, New York, 1991, pp. 103-106.
Rogers, R. Mark, *Handbook of Key Economic Indicators*, Irwin Professional Pub., Burr Ridge, Ill., 1994, pp. 47-49.

Personal Prosperity Index

An assessment of the state of prosperity of the typical American family.

This index defines prosperity as the market value of all goods and services purchased by households in the course of a year plus the value of the goods already owned by the household. To calculate the index, national figures for personal-consumption expenditures are adjusted to reflect the retained value of the durable goods purchased during the year. Household net worth is extracted from Federal Reserve Board and other data, including the value of corporate equities, pension-fund reserves, consumer debt, and mortgage obligations. Accrued Social Security benefits are derived from Social Security Administration data. These values are summed, and the total is divided by the Bureau of the Census's number of households in the nation to yield a per household figure that is expressed in thousands of dollars.

Used to compare the prosperity of American families over time.

Published annually by *Changing Times* magazine.

Source	Frequency	Extent	Form	Medium
Changing Times	a	h	g	p

Bibliography

Miller, Theodore J., "Are You Better Off than You Think?" *Changing Times*, 50-53 (January 1988).

Personal Saving

[See also Savings Rate]

An estimation of the current saving of individuals (including the owners of unincorporated businesses); nonprofit institutions; and private health, welfare, and trust funds.

A number of available statistical series are used to estimate personal savings. Disposable personal income is the starting point. From it is subtracted personal consumption expenditures, interest paid by consumers, and net personal transfer payments to foreigners (cash, goods, or services sent or donated abroad less any remittances from abroad). The remainder is assumed to be what is saved.

Used to judge long-term trends in income, expenditures, and economic growth. It is a measure of consumer behavior and the availability of discretionary income.

Published quarterly by the U.S. Department of Commerce, Bureau of Economic Analysis, in *Survey of Current Business*.

Source	Frequency	Extent	Form	Medium
Business Statistics	a	h	t	p
Federal Reserve Bulletin	a, q	c	t	p
S&P Current Statistics	a, q	c	t	p
Statistical Abstract	a	h	t	p
Survey of Current Business	a, q, m	c	t	p, e

Bibliography
Frumkin, Norman, *Guide to Economic Indicators*, 2nd ed., M. E. Sharpe, Armonk, N.Y., 1994, pp. 235-239.

Schor, Stanley, "Who Saves," *Review of Economics and Statistics* **41** (2), 213-248 (1959).

Snyder, Richard M., *Measuring Business Changes*, John Wiley, New York, 1955, p. 21 ff.

Webb, Roy H., "Personal Saving Behavior and Real Economic Activity," *Economic Quarterly of the Federal Reserve Bank of Richmond* **79** (2), 68-94 (1993).

Personal Savings Rate
[See Savings Rate]

Personal Spending
[See Personal Consumption Expenditures and Retail Sales]

Petroleum Production

The net petroleum produced and intended for refineries in the United States (after adjustment for imports and exports), expressed in thousands of barrels per day.

Petroleum producers in the United States report production to the Energy Information Administration (EIA) of the U.S. Department of Energy (DOE) weekly on EIA forms 800 to 804 (reports on refineries, bulk terminals, product pipelines, crude-oil stocks, and imports). The reports are made by a sample of the largest petroleum companies (representing 90% of the market). Monthly estimates are derived from these weekly submissions. Foreign crude oil and petroleum-product imports are estimated from Census Bureau foreign-trade reports. Monthly exports data are derived from data published in the *Weekly Petroleum Status Report*. Field production of natural gas liquids (including finished petroleum products) is reported monthly to DOE by all operators of such facilities. Nonrespondents are contacted by telephone, and imputed values are calculated for nonresponding companies that submitted reports the previous month. Values obtained through all of these collection methods are summed.

Indicates the near-term availability of oil and therefore presages the costs of petroleum-derived fuels. Those prices are important contributors to the costs of industrial production and to the cost of living. Moreover, shortages of these fuels could severely impair industrial production on a national scale.

Published monthly by the U.S. Department of Energy, Energy Information Administration, in *Petroleum Supply Monthly* two months after the data are reported to the EIA; the data also appear in the *Monthly Energy Review*.

Source	Frequency	Extent	Form	Medium
Annual Energy Review	a	h	g	p
Barron's	m	c	t	p
Basic Petroleum Data Book	a, m	h	t	p
Business Statistics	a	h	t	p
EIA	w	c, h	t	e
Handbook of International Economic Statistics (CIA)	a	h	t	p
International Financial Statistics	a, q	h	t	p
International Petroleum Statistics Report	m	h	g	p
Monthly Energy Review	a, m	h	t, g	p
Monthly Statistical Report (API)	m	c	g	p
Petroleum Supply Annual	a, m	h	t, g	p
Petroleum Supply Monthly	a, m	c, h	t	p
S&P Basic Statistics - Energy, Electric Power, and Fuels	a	h	t	p
S&P Current Statistics	m	h	t	p
Statistical Abstract	a	h	t	p
Weekly Statistical Bulletin (API)	w	c	t	p

Bibliography

Boughton, James M., and William H. Branson, "Commodity Prices as a Leading Indicator of Inflation," pp. 305-338 in Kajal Lahiri and Moore, Geoffrey H. Moore, Eds., *Leading Economic Indicators: New Approaches and Forecasting Records,* Cambridge University Press, New York, 1991.

Energy Information Administration, "Explanatory Notes," *Petroleum Supply Monthly*, USGPO, Washington, D.C., monthly.

Segars, Alan D., "Commodities an Inflation Indicator," *Pensions and Investments* **23** (1), 20 (Jan. 9, 1995).

Planned Expenditures for New Plant and Equipment
[Ceased publication; see Capital Expenditures]

Plant and Equipment Contracts and Orders
[See Business Investment and Plans]

Plant and Equipment Expenditures
[See Capital Expenditures]

Poverty Rate

The percentage of Americans with incomes less than a level determined to be the minimum required to provide the necessities of life for family members.

The Bureau of the Census surveys a sample of American families to determine family income. At the same time, the minimum incomes required to maintain families of various sizes are calculated; these poverty levels are adjusted annually to reflect inflation. The number of households with incomes below the poverty level for their family sizes is determined and expressed as a percentage of all American families. This percentage is referred to as the Poverty Rate. The data are also expressed as a percentages of individuals, children, elderly, and ethnicities.

Used to assess the economic well-being of American society and as an indicator of the need for social, political, and economic actions. Also used as the determinant for eligibility for benefits from government social programs.

Published annually by the Bureau of the Census in *Income, Poverty, and the Valuation of Noncash Benefits.*

Source	Frequency	Extent	Form	Medium
Statistical Abstract	a	h	t	p
US Census Bureau	a	c, h	t	e

Price-Dividend Ratio
[See Standard & Poor's 500 Price-Earnings Ratio]

Price-Earnings Ratio
[See Standard & Poor's 500 Price-Earnings Ratio]

Price Index of New One-Family Houses Sold

A measure of change in the cost for new housing.

The Bureau of the Census conducts its Housing Sales Survey monthly, interviewing a national sample of builders or owners of new one-family houses. The houses so identified are divided into attached and detached models, and the detached models are subdivided into those in the Northeast, Midwest, South, and West. Five initial indexes are calculated: one for attached, and four for detached models (one for each geographic area). Each house sold is characterized by sale price, floor area, number of bedrooms, number of fireplaces, size of garage, and other traits. These data are related to comparable 1992 data, and the current-period index number is calculated for each of the five initial indexes. The final price index for the United States is a weighted average (reflecting the distribution of house sales in 1992) of the five initial indexes. Because the index is derived from the total sales price of a house, it reflects both supply (e.g., wage rates, material costs, and productivity) and demand (e.g., demographics, income, and availability of mortgage money) factors.

Used as a measure of inflation in the cost of housing.

Published quarterly by the U.S. Department of Commerce, Bureau of the Census, in Current Construction Report C25, *New One-Family Houses Sold*.

Source	Frequency	Extent	Form	Medium
Characteristics of New Housing	a	h	t	p
New One-Family Houses Sold (CCR C25)	q	c	t	p

Bibliography

Hoel, Arline Alchian; Kenneth W. Clarkson; and Roger LeRoy Miller, *Economics Sourcebook of Government Statistics*, Lexington Books, Lexington, Mass., 1983, pp. 59-60.

Price of New Houses
[See Price Index of New One-Family Houses Sold]

Prices Paid by Farmers Index
[See Index of Prices Paid by Farmers for Commodities and Services, Interest, Taxes, and Farm Wage Rates]

Prices Received by Farmers Index
[See Index of Prices Received by Farmers]

Prime Commercial Paper
[See also Commercial Paper Interest Rates]

The prevailing rate on 7- to 180-day credit granted to businesses with high credit standings.

Daily, the Federal Reserve Bank of New York determines the prevailing interest rates on commercial paper from information provided by seven direct issuers and five major dealers in such debt in New York City. These interest rates are for short-term unsecured debt issued in the form of promissory notes by industrial firms with Aa bond ratings. After being rounded to two decimal places, daily offering rates are averaged to produce weekly and monthly figures for a variety of maturities.

Used to measure the cost of open-market short-term credit available to large business borrowers.

Published weekly by the Board of Governors of the Federal Reserve System in *Selected Interest Rates*, Statistical Release H.15 (519).

Source	Frequency	Extent	Form	Medium
Economic Indicators	m	c, h	t	p
Federal Reserve Bulletin	w, m, a	c, h	t	p
S&P Current Statistics	m	c, h	t	p
Wall Street Journal	d	c	t	p

Bibliography
Cocheo, Steve, "Commercial Paper: Friend or Foe?" *ABA Banking Journal* **84**, 53+ (1992).
"Fedpoint 29: Commercial Paper," www.ny.frb.org/pihome/fedpoint/fed29.html, visited July 17, 1999.
Hahn, Thomas K., "Commercial Paper," *Federal Reserve Bank of Richmond Economic Quarterly* **79**, 45-67 (Spring 1993).
Kanatos, George, "Commercial Paper, Bank Reserve Requirements, and the Informational Role of Loan Commitments," *Journal of Banking and Finance* **11**, 425-448 (1987).
Post, Mitchell A., "The Evolution of the U.S. Commercial Paper Market Since 1980," *Federal Reserve Bulletin* **78**, 879-891 (1992).
Selden, Richard T., *Trends and Cycles in the Commercial Paper Market*, Occasional Paper 85, National Bureau of Economic Research, New York, 1963.

Prime Rate
[See Average Prime Rate Charged by Banks]

Producer Price Index
[Formerly called Wholesale Price Index]

Measures of the average changes in prices received in primary markets of the United States by producers of commodities in all stages of processing. The indexes are designed to measure real price changes, not changes in quality, quantity, or terms of sale; moreover, they do not measure changes in manufacturers' average realized prices. Producer Price Indexes can be organized by stage of processing (degree of fabrication: from crude materials to finished goods) or by commodity (similarity in end use or material composition).

Each month, the Bureau of Labor Statistics surveys a sample of approximately 2,800 commodities, receiving about 10,000 quotations from producers in the manufacturing, agriculture, forestry, fishing, mining, gas, electricity, and public utility sectors about the prices received for their goods. The responses provide the average net prices (with all applicable discounts) received by the producers for their products on a given day. Each reporter usually has equal weight with all the other reporters. List or book prices are used if transaction prices are not available. Some prices are taken from trade publications or received from other government agencies. Insofar as possible, identical qualities of the commodities are priced from period to period. For each commodity, the ratio of the current month's average price to the previous month's average price is then multiplied with the previous month's index to derive the current month's index. To derive indexes for commodity groupings, the sequential months' price ratio for each commodity in the group is first weighted, and then they are summed and divided by the corresponding weighted value for the index base period. Most producer price indexes are computed on a reference base of 1967 = 100. Price changes for the various commodities are weighted to represent their importance in the total net selling value of all commodities and then averaged. Weights are revised periodically with data from the industrial census.

An indicator of underlying inflationary pressures in the economy before they affect the consumer. Frequently used in escalation clauses of long-term sales contracts, to determine pricing policies that are congruous with the prices charged for similar products in national trade, to measure inflation at the primary market level, to analyze the sources and transmission of price changes through the American economy, to formulate and evaluate the fiscal and monetary policies and activities of the government and specific industries, to make or review corporate and government budgets, to deflate time series so they can be reported in constant dollars, to establish replacement cost estimates, to appraise the value of inventories, and to research and predict business cycles.

Published monthly by the U.S. Department of Labor, Bureau of Labor Statistics, in a news release.

Source	Frequency	Extent	Form	Medium
Agricultural Outlook	a, m	c	t	p
Agricultural Statistics	a	h	t	p
Annual Statistical Digest (FRB)	a, m	c	t	p
Bank of Tokyo-Mitsubishi	m	c, h	t	e
Barron's	m	c	t	p
BCI	m	h	g	e
BLS	m	c, h	t	e
Business Statistics*	a	h	t	p
Economic Indicators*	a, m	c, h	t, g	p, e
Economic Report of the President*	a	h	t	p, e
Federal Reserve Bulletin*	a, q, m	c	t	p
Federal Reserve Bulletin	a, q	c	t	p
Financial Digest	m	c	t	p

Source	Frequency	Extent	Form	Medium
First Union	m	c, h	t	e
FRB Chicago	q	c, h	t	e
FRB Dallas	m	c, h	t	e
FRED	m	c, h	t	e
International Financial Statistics*	a, q	h	t	p
Monthly Labor Review*	a, m	c, h	t	p
Producer Price Index Report*	m	c	t	p
S&P Basic Statistics - Price Indexes	a, m	h	t	p
S&P Current Statistics	m	h	t	p
Statistical Abstract*	a	h	t	p
Statistical Yearbook of the Electric Utility Industry	a	h	t	p
Stat-USA	m	c	t	e
Survey of Current Business*	a, m	c	t, g	p, e
Treasury Bulletin	a	h	g	p
Value Line Investment Survey, Part 2: Selection and Opinion	a, q	c, h, f	t	p
World Financial Markets	a, q	c	t	p

*With stages-of-processing indexes; others, finished goods only.

Bibliography

Carlson, Keith M., "Do Price Indexes Tell Us about Inflation? A Review of the Issues," *Federal Reserve Bank of St. Louis Review* **71** (6), 12-30 (1989).

Carnes, W. Stansbury, and Stephen D. Slifer, *The Atlas of Economic Indicators: A Visual Guide to Market Forces and the Federal Reserve*, Harper Business, New York, 1991, pp. 73-83.

Darnay, Arsen J., *Economic Indicators Handbook: Time Series, Conversions, Documentation*, Gale Research, Detroit, 1992, pp. 831-833.

Grant, John, *A Handbook of Economic Indicators*, University of Toronto Press, Toronto, 1992, pp. 175-177.

Hoel, Arline Alchian; Kenneth W. Clarkson; and Roger LeRoy Miller, *Economics Sourcebook of Government Statistics*, Lexington Books, Lexington, Mass., 1983, pp. 12-15.

Joint Economic Committee, *1980 Supplement to Economic Indicators, Historical and Descriptive Background*, USGPO, Washington, D.C., 1980, pp. 82-85.

Lavin, Michael R., *Business Information: How to Find It, How to Use It*, Oryx Press, Phoenix, Ariz., 1992, p. 333.

Nelson, C. R., *The Investor's Guide to Economic Indicators*, John Wiley & Sons, New York, 1987, pp. 24-26, 134-137.

Niemira, Michael P., and Gerald F. Zukowski, *Trading the Fundamentals: The Trader's Guide to Interpreting Economic Indicators and Monetary Policy*, McGraw-Hill, New York, 1998, pp. 197-204.

Plocek, Joseph E., *Economic Indicators: How America Reads Its Financial Health*, New York Institute of Finance, New York, 1991, pp. 276-282.

Renshaw, Edward, Ed., *The Practical Forecasters' Almanac: 137 Reliable Indicators for Investors, Hedgers, and Speculators*, Business One Irwin, Homewood, Ill., 1992, pp. 59-60.

Rogers, R. Mark, *Handbook of Key Economic Indicators*, Irwin Professional Pub., Burr Ridge, Ill., 1994, pp. 106-119.

Slater, Courtenay M., Ed., Business Statistics of the United States, 1995 ed., Bernan Press, Lanham, Md., 1996, pp. 229-231.

Tainer, Evelina M., *Using Economic Indicators to Improve Investment Analysis*, John Wiley & Sons, New York, 1993, pp. 170-174.

U.S. Department of Commerce, Bureau of Economic Analysis, *Business Statistics, 1963-91*, USGPO, Washington, D.C., 1992, pp. 148-149.

U.S. Department of Labor, Bureau of Labor Statistics, *BLS Handbook of Methods*, Bull. 2490, USGPO, Washington, D.C., 1997, pp. 130-153.

U.S. Department of Labor, Bureau of Labor Statistics, *Major Programs of the Bureau of Labor Statistics*, USGPO, Washington, D.C., 1994, pp. 11-12.

WEFA Group, *Guide to Economic Indicators: U.S. Macroeconomic Services*, WEFA Group, Bala Cynwyd, Pa., 1997, p. 23.

Productivity
[See Index of Productivity]

Productivity and Related Data, Private Business Sector
[See Index of Productivity, Unit Labor Costs, and Implicit Price Deflators]

Public Short Ratio
[See New York Stock Exchange Nonmembers Short Sales]

Purchasing Managers' Index
An assessment of the contemporary trend in manufacturing activity.

Each month, the National Association of Purchasing Management surveys 300 purchasing managers at more than 20 major manufacturing companies. The selection of companies is weighted to reflect each industry's contribution to the national income and represents a wide geographic diversity. The purchasing managers are asked a series of questions that bear on business activity (e.g., whether orders increased over the previous month, if prices for materials went down, and if inventories declined). To each question, respondents indicate whether conditions improved, deteriorated, or stayed the same during the current month as compared with the previous month. Each response to each question is considered separately. From these data, nine diffusion indexes are constructed, reflecting new orders, backlog of orders, new export orders, imports, production, employment, inventories, prices, and supplier deliveries (vendor performance). In each of these categories, half of the responses indicating no change are added to the number of positive responses, and the sum is divided by the total number of responses and multiplied by 100 to produce the index value. Five of these nine diffusion indexes are used to calculate the Purchasing Managers' Index: new orders, production, employment, inventories, and supplier deliveries. Each of these is assigned a weighting factor, and the weighted average of the index values is calculated and reported as the Purchasing Managers' Index.

Used to predict activity in the industrial sector of the economy and on short-run cyclical relationships with the entire national economy. Portions of these data are used to calculate a component of the Leading Indicators Composite Index.

Issued as a monthly report, *NAPM Report on Business*, by the National Association of Purchasing Management.

Source	Frequency	Extent	Form	Medium
Bank of America	m	c, h	t	e
Bank of Tokyo-Mitsubishi	m	c, h	t	e
Barron's	m	c	t	p
BCI*	m	h	g	e
Conference Board/BCI*	m	c	t	e
Economic Handbook of the Machine Tool Industry	a	h	t	p
Financial Digest	m	c	t	p
First Union	m	c, h	t	e
FRB Chicago	m	c, h	t	e
FRED	m	c, h	t	e
Stat-USA	m	c	t	e

*Vendor performance only.

Bibliography

Bahrenburg, Kristi, "When It Comes to Inflation Indicators, Purchasing Managers May Know Best," *Wall Street Journal*, Oct. 2, 1997, p. B15.

Bretz, Robert J., "Behind the Economic Indicators of the NAPM Report on Business," *Business Economics* **25** (3), 42-48 (1990).

Carnes, W. Stansbury, and Stephen D. Slifer, *The Atlas of Economic Indicators: A Visual Guide to Market Forces and the Federal Reserve*, Harper Business, New York, 1991, pp. 51-57.

Dasgupta, Susmita, and Kajal Lahiri, "On the Use of Dispersion Measures from NAPM Surveys in Business Cycle Forecasting," *Journal of Forecasting* **12** (3, 4), 239-253 (1993).

Frumkin, Norman, *Guide to Economic Indicators*, 2nd ed., M. E. Sharpe, Armonk, N.Y., 1994, pp. 265-270.

Grant, John, *A Handbook of Economic Indicators*, University of Toronto Press, Toronto, 1992, pp. 177-178.

Harris, Ethan S., "Tracking the Economy with the Purchasing Managers' Index," *Federal Reserve bank of New York Quarterly Review* **16** (3), 61-69 (1991).

Klein, Philip A., and Geoffrey H. Moore, "N.A.P.M. Business Survey Data: Their Value as Leading Indicators," *Journal of Purchasing and Materials Management* **24** (4), 32-40 (1988).

Klein, Philip A., and Geoffrey H. Moore, "Purchasing Management Survey Data: Their Value as Leading Indicators," pp. 403-428 in Kajal Lahiri and Moore, Geoffrey H. Moore, Eds., *Leading Economic Indicators: New Approaches and Forecasting Records,* Cambridge University Press, New York, 1991.

Niemira, Michael P., and Gerald F. Zukowski, *Trading the Fundamentals: The Trader's Guide to Interpreting Economic Indicators and Monetary Policy*, McGraw-Hill, New York, 1998, pp. 169-185.

Plocek, Joseph E., *Economic Indicators: How America Reads Its Financial Health*, New York Institute of Finance, New York, 1991, pp. 170-172.

Raedels, Alan, "Forecasting the NAPM Purchasing Managers' Index," *Journal of Forecasting and Materials Management* **26** (4), 34-39 (1990).

Rogers, R. Mark, *Handbook of Key Economic Indicators*, Irwin Professional Pub., Burr Ridge, Ill., 1994, pp. 162-171.

Tainer, Evelina M., *Using Economic Indicators to Improve Investment Analysis*, John Wiley & Sons, New York, 1993, pp. 227-231.

Tamm, Feliks, "An Agenda for Inventories Input to the Leading Composite Index," pp. 429-460 in Kajal Lahiri and Moore, Geoffrey H. Moore, Eds., *Leading Economic Indicators: New Approaches and Forecasting Records,* Cambridge University Press, New York, 1991.

"The Purchasing Managers' Index (PMI) Overview," www.napm.org/public/rob/index2.html, visited Aug. 25, 1997.

Torda, Theodore S., "Purchasing Manager Index Provides Early Clue on Turning Points," *Business America* **8** (13), 11-13 (June 24, 1985).

WEFA Group, *Guide to Economic Indicators: U.S. Macroeconomic Services*, WEFA Group, Bala Cynwyd, Pa., 1997, p. 25.

Q-R

Quasimodo Principle
[See Appendix A. Nonquantitative Indicators]

Rail Freight Index
[See BLS Railroad Freight Price Index]

Raw Materials Price Index
[See Industrial Raw Materials Price Index]

Real Earnings
[Also called Average Hourly and Weekly Earnings in Constant 1982 Dollars; see also Average Hourly and Weekly Earnings]

The average hourly and weekly earnings by the American workforce expressed in constant dollars to reflect the influence of inflation and the current purchasing power of those earnings.

The average hourly and weekly earnings of nonfarm workers (including government employees) determined each month by the Current Employment Statistics survey (the Establishment Survey) of the Bureau of Labor Statistics are adjusted by means of the Consumer Price Index for Urban Wage Earners and Clerical Workers for the month under consideration. The resulting deflated values indicate the changes in purchasing power of American workers' wages over time, changes that are brought about by increases and decreases in the prices for consumer goods and services. To a certain degree, these changes are also influenced by the mix of full-time and part-time participants in the workforce, the distribution of high-pay and low-pay workers, and other factors. The values are seasonally adjusted and expressed in constant 1982 dollars; they are broken down by private and industry groups and reported for total private, goods-providing, and service-providing subcategories.

Used as a meaningful measure of the payment received by workers for their labor and, as such, in the formulation of government fiscal and economic policy, in business planning, and in labor-management negotiations.

Published monthly by the U.S. Department of Labor, Bureau of Labor Statistics, in *Real Earnings*.

Source	Frequency	Extent	Form	Medium
BLS	m	c, h	t	e
Business Statistics	a, m	h	t	p
Economic Indicators	a, m	c, h	t	p, e
Employment & Earnings	m	c, h	t	p
Monthly Labor Review	a	c, h	t	p
Real Earnings	m	c	t	p
Statistical Abstract	a	h	t	p

Bibliography

Hoel, Arline Alchian; Kenneth W. Clarkson; and Roger LeRoy Miller, *Economics Sourcebook of Government Statistics*, Lexington Books, Lexington, Mass., 1983 pp. 183-190.

Niemira, Michael P., and Gerald F. Zukowski, *Trading the Fundamentals: The Trader's Guide to Interpreting Economic Indicators and Monetary Policy*, McGraw-Hill, New York, 1998, p. 190.

U.S. Department of Labor, Bureau of Labor Statistics, *BLS Handbook of Methods*, Bull. 2490, USGPO, Washington, D.C., 1997, pp. 15-31.

Realtors' Index
[See Housing Affordability Index]

Reserves and Borrowings
[A portion of and also referred to as Bank Loans, Investments, and Reserves]

The total assets and liabilities of the nationally chartered and state-chartered banks that are members of the Federal Reserve System.

Each week, each member bank reports its assets and liabilities to the Federal Reserve System. From these reports, the minimum reserve balance for that bank is computed. The total reserves are the sum of reserve balances of member banks (each is required to maintain a specific minimum balance determined by the type, maturity, and size of its deposit liabilities) held at Federal Reserve Banks in the current week, the average of member-bank vault cash held two weeks earlier, and a minor amount of waivers of penalties for reserve deficiencies. The total borrowings include all member-bank seasonal and regular borrowings on Federal Reserve credit. Reserves are reported as required, nonborrowed, and total; borrowings are reported as seasonal and total. The required reserves are tabulated weekly by the Federal Reserve System and seasonally adjusted. To this aggregate reserve are added excess reserves (deposits with the Federal Reserve above and beyond the minimum required); these excess reserves are not seasonally adjusted. The borrowings by member banks are totaled and (without being seasonally adjusted) are subtracted from the seasonally adjusted total reserves to give the seasonally adjusted nonborrowed reserves. Monthly data are derived as prorations of the weekly data.

The rates of growth of reserve aggregates are used by some analysts as indicators of monetary policy.

Published each Thursday by the Board of Governors of the Federal Reserve System in *Aggregate Reserves of Depository Institutions and the Monetary Base*, Statistical Release H.3 (502).

Source	Frequency	Extent	Form	Medium
BCI	m	h	g	e
Business Statistics	m	c, h	t	p
Economic Indicators	m, a	c, h	t	p, e
Federal Reserve Board	w	c	t	e
Federal Reserve Bulletin	m	c	t	p
FRED	d, w, m	c, h	t	e
New York Times	w	c	t	p
Wall Street Journal	w	c	t	p

Bibliography

Colby, Robert W., and Thomas A. Meyers, *The Encyclopedia of Technical Market Indicators*, Dow Jones-Irwin, Homewood, Ill., 1988, p. 446.

Hoel, Arline Alchian; Kenneth W. Clarkson; and Roger LeRoy Miller, *Economics Sourcebook of Government Statistics*, Lexington Books, Lexington, Mass., 1983, pp. 151-154.

Joint Economic Committee, *1980 Supplement to Economic Indicators, Historical and Descriptive Background*, USGPO, Washington, D.C., 1980, pp. 101-104.

Plocek, Joseph E., *Economic Indicators: How America Reads Its Financial Health*, New York Institute of Finance, New York, 1991, pp. 266-271.

Publication Services, *The Federal Reserve System: Purposes and Functions*, Board of Governors of the Federal Reserve System, Washington, D.C., 1994, pp. 18-22.

Slater, Courtenay M., Ed., Business Statistics of the United States, 1995 ed., Bernan Press, Lanham, Md., 1996, p. 257.

U.S. Department of Commerce, Bureau of Economic Analysis, *Business Statistics, 1963-91*, USGPO, Washington, D.C., 1992, p. 159.

Retail Chain Store Sales

[See Bank of Tokyo–Mitsubishi/Chain Store Age Weekly Leading Indicator of Chain Store Sales, Bank of Tokyo–Mitsubishi Chain Store Sales Index, and

Bank of Tokyo–Mitsubishi/Schroders Weekly U.S. Retail Chain Store Sales Index]

Retail Food Prices
[Also called Average Retail Food Prices; See also Consumer Price Index]

The average prices for foods and beverages paid by American consumers.

As part of calculating the Consumer Price Indexes, the U.S. Department of Labor's Bureau of Labor Statistics determines or estimates the current prices for a variety of foods and beverages (both raw and processed) in cities across the United States. These prices for each of about 100 specific (in quantity and quality) foodstuffs are averaged. Values are reported as aggregates for food and beverages totaled, for food and beverages separately, for classes of foods and beverages, and for the individual foods and beverages selected and specified. Values are presented for average prices for the specified foodstuffs in each of the four Census geographic regions and in the United States as a whole; in the report, the food and beverage index is reported separately from the prices and is not broken down in such detail.

Used to calculate a component of the Consumer Price Index and as a comparator for the prices of commodities that effect each consumer directly.

Published monthly in the *CPI Detailed Report* by the U.S. Department of Labor's Bureau of Labor Statistics.

Source	Frequency	Extent	Form	Medium
Consumer Price Index Detailed Report	m	c	t	p

Bibliography
Fixler, Dennis, "The Consumer Price Index: Underlying Concepts and Caveats," *Monthly Labor Review* 116 (12), 3-12 (1993).

Moulton, Brent P., "Basic Components of the CPI: Estimation of Price Changes," *Monthly Labor Review* 116 (12), 13-24 (1993).

U.S. Department of Labor, Bureau of Labor Statistics, *BLS Handbook of Methods*, Bull. 2490, USGPO, Washington, D.C., 1997, p. 192.

U.S. Department of Labor, Bureau of Labor Statistics, *CPI Detailed Report*, USGPO, Washington, D.C., monthly.

Retail Inventories

Estimates of the cost of end-of-month inventories of establishments primarily engaged in retail trade to individuals, industrial users, and other retailers.

A sample representing all sizes of firms and types of businesses in retail trade throughout the nation are surveyed by mail monthly by the Bureau of the Census. The data received are periodically benchmarked to the results of censuses of retail trade and the Annual Retail Trade Survey. The data are adjusted for seasonal variations and reported in durable- and nondurable-goods categories.

Used to discern relative trends between demand and supply of goods. The relative balance can indicate probable future economic activity at the manufacturing and other, earlier stages of production and distribution. Also used in determining the Gross National Product.

Published monthly by the U.S. Department of Commerce, Bureau of the Census, in *Monthly Retail Sales and Inventories* (part of the Current Business Reports series).

Source	Frequency	Extent	Form	Medium
Barron's	m	c	t	p
Business Statistics	a	h	t	p
Economic Report of the President	a	h	t	p, e
Monthly Retail Trade Sales and Inventories	a, m	c, h	t, g	p
S&P Current Statistics	m	h	t	p
Statistical Abstract	a	h	t	p

Bibliography
Joint Economic Committee, *1980 Supplement to Economic Indicators, Historical and Descriptive Background*, USGPO, Washington, D.C., 1980, pp. 77-79.

Retail Price Index
[See Consumer Price Index]

Retail Sales
[Also called Retail Trade Sales; see also Bank of Tokyo–Mitsubishi/Chain Store Age Weekly Leading Indicator of Chain Store Sales, Bank of Tokyo–Mitsubishi Chain Store Sales Index, and Bank of Tokyo–Mitsubishi/ Schroders Weekly U.S. Retail Chain Store Sales Index]

Estimates of the monthly sales by establishments primarily engaged in retail trade to individuals, industrial users, and other retailers; the values include merchandise and services sold for cash or credit after deductions for refunds and allowances and before carrying charges, taxes, commissions, and nonoperating income are factored in.

A sample representing all sizes of firms and types of businesses in retail trade throughout the nation are surveyed by mail monthly by the Bureau of the Census to determine the dollar value of their sales during the preceding month. The data received are periodically benchmarked to the results of censuses of retail trade and the Annual Retail Trade Survey. The data are adjusted for seasonal variations and for holiday and trading-day differences before being reported in durable- and nondurable-goods categories and within those categories by type of store.

Used to indicate probable future economic activity at the manufacturing and other, earlier stages of production and distribution. Also used in determining the gross national product.

Published monthly by the U.S. Department of Commerce, Bureau of the Census, in *Monthly Retail Trade and Sales Inventories* (part of the Current Business Reports series).

Source	Frequency	Extent	Form	Medium
Agricultural Outlook	a, q	c	t	p
Bank of Tokyo-Mitsubishi	m	c, h	t	e
Barron's	m	c	t	p
BCI	m	h	g	e
Business Statistics	a	h	t	p
Chemical Week	w	c	t	p
Economic Report of the President	a	h	t	p, e
Federal Reserve Bulletin	a, m	c	t	p
First Union	m	c, h	t	e
FRB Dallas	m	c, h	t	e
FRB New York	m	c, h	g	e
FRED	m	c, h	t	e
ICSC	m	c, h	g	e
Monthly Retail Trade Sales and Inventories	a, m	c, h	t, g	p
Recession Recovery Watch	q	h	g	p
S&P Basic Statistics - Income and Trade	a	h	t	p
S&P Current Statistics	m	h	t	p
Statistical Abstract	a	h	t	p
Stat-USA	m	c	t	e
US Census Bureau	m	c	t	e

Bibliography

Carnes, W. Stansbury, and Stephen D. Slifer, *The Atlas of Economic Indicators: A Visual Guide to Market Forces and the Federal Reserve*, Harper Business, New York, 1991, pp. 85-92.

Grant, John, *A Handbook of Economic Indicators*, University of Toronto Press, Toronto, 1992, pp. 178-182.

Harris, Ethan S., and Clara Vega, *What Do Chain Store Sales Tell Us about Consumer Spending?*, Research Paper 9614, Federal Reserve Bank of New York, New York, 1996.

Joint Economic Committee, *1980 Supplement to Economic Indicators, Historical and Descriptive Background*, USGPO, Washington, D.C., 1980, pp. 77-79.

Niemira, Michael P., and Gerald F. Zukowski, *Trading the Fundamentals: The Trader's Guide to Interpreting Economic Indicators and Monetary Policy*, McGraw-Hill, New York, 1998, pp. 211-219.

Plocek, Joseph E., *Economic Indicators: How America Reads Its Financial Health*, New York Institute of Finance, New York, 1991, pp. 122-125.

Rogers, R. Mark, *Handbook of Key Economic Indicators*, Irwin Professional Pub., Burr Ridge, Ill., 1994, pp. 62-74.

Slater, Courtenay M., Ed., Business Statistics of the United States, 1995 ed., Bernan Press, Lanham, Md., 1996, pp. 274-275.

Tainer, Evelina M., *Using Economic Indicators to Improve Investment Analysis*, John Wiley & Sons, New York, 1993, pp. 63-67.

U.S. Department of Commerce, Bureau of Economic Analysis, *Business Statistics, 1963-91*, USGPO, Washington, D.C., 1992, p. 153.

U.S. Department of Commerce, Bureau of the Census, *Revised Monthly Retail Sales and Inventories: January 1981 Through December 1990*, BR90-R, Current Business Reports, U.S. Department of Commerce, Washington, D.C., 1991.

WEFA Group, *Guide to Economic Indicators: U.S. Macroeconomic Services*, WEFA Group, Bala Cynwyd, Pa., 1997, p. 26.

Retail Trade Sales
[See Retail Sales]

Revenue Passenger Miles

The number of miles flown by paying passengers on flights within the United States.

Airlines calculate the number of miles flown on their aircraft by each ticketed customer, total these "revenue passenger miles" each month, and report that total each month to the U.S. Department of Transportation, Bureau of Transportation Statistics, which sums the revenue passenger miles of all U.S. scheduled airlines. Also calculated and presented are the number of revenue passengers, and the distance of the average trip.

Besides being an obvious indicator of the health of the airline industry, the number of passenger miles flown is also an indicator of the current intensity of business activity because most air travel is made by businessmen.

Published monthly by the Department of Transportation, Bureau of Transportation Statistics, in *Air Carrier Traffic Statistics*.

Source	Frequency	Extent	Form	Medium
Air Carrier Industry Scheduled Service Traffic Statistics Quarterly	a, q	c	t	p
Air Carrier Traffic Statistics Monthly	m, q	c	t	p

Source	Frequency	Extent	Form	Medium
Air Transport	a	h	t	p
Business Statistics	a	h	t	p
FAA Statistical Handbook	a	h	t	p
National Transportation Statistics	a	h	t	p
Preliminary Scheduled Passenger Traffic Statistics	m	c	t, g	p
S&P Basic Statistics - Transportation	a	h	t	p
S&P Current Statistics	m	h	t	p
Statistical Abstract	a	h	t	p

Bibliography

Donlan, Thomas G., "Canaries in the Mine: Airlines Offer a Leading Economic Indicator," *Barron's* **77** (10), 51 (July 28, 1997).

U.S. Department of Commerce, Bureau of Economic Analysis, *Business Statistics, 1963-91*, USGPO, Washington, D.C., 1992, p. 167.

Russell 2000 Index

A measure of the advances and declines of prices for the small-capitalization segment of the stock market.

One of the series of indexes prepared by the Frank Russell Company, the Russell 2000 Index includes the stocks of 2000 U.S. corporations that are capitalized in the small range, with market values between $15 and 350 million with a median of about $85 million. These equities account for less than 10% of the total market. The index is a subindex of the Russell 3000 Index. The index is capitalization weighted, and adjustments are made to the calculations to exclude the effects of overlapping ownerships. (That is to say, if Company A owns 25% of Company B and both are included in the index, then the capitalization weight of Company B is reduced to 75% of its total to exclude the interest of Company A that is already accounted for elsewhere in the index.) It is indexed to a base value of 100.0 in June of 1979.

Used as an indicator of the price trends among small-capitalized equities, which otherwise suffer from a lack of liquidity, a lack of coverage by Wall Street, and an inefficient market for trading.

Issued daily as a news release by the Frank Russell Company.

Source	Frequency	Extent	Form	Medium
Barron's	d	c	t	p
Bloomberg	h	c	t	e
Business Week	h	c	t	e

Source	Frequency	Extent	Form	Medium
CBS	h	c	t	e
CNN	h	c	t	e
First Union	m	c, h	t	e
Investor's Business Daily	d	c, h	t	p
Mutual Funds Update	d	c	t	p
New York Times	d (h)	c (h)	t (g)	p (e)
PCQuote	h	c	t	e
StockMaster	d	c, h	g, t	e
USA Today	d (h)	c	t	p (e)
Wall Street Journal	d	c	t	p

Bibliography

Berlin, Howard M. *The Handbook of Financial Market Indexes, Averages, and Indicators*, Dow Jones-Irwin, Homewood, Ill., 1990, pp. 56-57.

Pierog, Karen, "Will Russell Indexes Become Institutional Benchmarks?" *Futures: Magazine of Commodities & Options* **16**, 60-61 (Sept. 1987).

Via, Michael M., "Small Cap Stocks: A Long-Term View from the Trenches," *CPA Journal* **62** (1), 72-73 (1992).

Ryan Index

[Also called the Ryan Labs Treasury Index]

A measure of the total return associated with recently issued notes and bonds of the U.S. Treasury.

Seven categories of Treasury issues (2-, 3-, 4-, 5-, 7-, 10-, and 30-year notes and bonds) are tracked. For each category, the price and income return of recent issues are calculated from market price changes and actual accrued interest. These total returns are indexed to values that were current on Dec. 31, 1979. The seven values are then averaged to produce the composite Ryan Index.

Used as a tool to judge the performance of recent non-T-bill Treasury issues. Issued daily as a news release by the Ryan Financial Strategies Group.

Source	Frequency	Extent	Form	Medium
Barron's	w	c	t	p

Bibliography

Berlin, Howard M. *The Handbook of Financial Market Indexes, Averages, and Indicators*, Dow Jones-Irwin, Homewood, Ill., 1990, pp. 82-83.

Reilly, Frank K.; G. Wenchi Kao; and David J. Wright, "Alternative Bond Market Indexes," *Financial Analysis Journal* **48** (3), 44-58 (1992).

S

Sales-Inventory Ratio
[See Manufacturers' Inventory-Sales Ratio]

Sales of Existing Homes
[See Existing Home Sales]

Salomon Brothers Broad Investment-Grade Bond Index
A measure of the performance of all Treasury, U.S.-government-agency, corporate, and mortgage securities.

The performance of all Treasury, U.S.-government-agency, corporate, and mortgage-backed investment-grade bonds with a maturity of at least one year and with at least $25 million outstanding is judged in terms of each bond's total return, which is calculated by cumulating the bond's price changes, principal payments, interest payments, accrued interest, and reinvestment income and dividing by the portfolio's value at the beginning of the analysis period. About 4000 issues are included. Prices (and price changes) are determined at the end of each month from the reports of traders. Each bond is weighted to reflect relative size, age to maturity, rating, and other features; the weights are adjusted monthly. The weighted total returns are added together and indexed to a base value of 100 as of Dec. 31, 1977.

Used as an indicator of the overall performance of the bond market.

Published monthly as a news release by Salomon Brothers.

Source	Frequency	Extent	Form	Medium
Mutual Fund Factbook	a	h	g	p

Bibliography
Berlin, Howard M. *The Handbook of Financial Market Indexes, Averages, and Indicators*, Dow Jones-Irwin, Homewood, Ill., 1990, p. 84.

Fabozzi, Frank J., *Bond Markets, Analysis, and Strategies*, 2nd ed., Prentice Hall, New York, 1993, pp. 517-519.

Salomon Brothers Mortgage Index

A measure of the performance of all mortgage securities.

The performance of all investment-grade mortgage-backed bonds with a maturity of at least one year and with at least $25 million outstanding is judged in terms of each bond's total return, which is calculated by cumulating the bond's price changes, principal payments, interest payments, accrued interest, and reinvestment income. Prices (and price changes) are determined at the end of each month from the reports of traders. Each bond is weighted to reflect relative size, age to maturity, rating, and other features; the weights are adjusted monthly. The weighted total returns are added together and indexed to a base value of 100 as of Dec. 31, 1977. The Mortgage Index is a subindex of the Salomon Brothers Broad Investment-Grade Bond Index.

Used as an indicator of the overall performance of the mortgage-backed bond market.

Published monthly as a news release by Salomon Brothers.

Source	Frequency	Extent	Form	Medium
Mutual Funds Update	m	c	t	p
Wall Street Journal	d	c	t	p

Bibliography
Berlin, Howard M. *The Handbook of Financial Market Indexes, Averages, and Indicators*, Dow Jones-Irwin, Homewood, Ill., 1990, p. 84.

Santa Claus Rally

[See Appendix A. Nonquantitative Indicators]

Savings Rate

[Also called Savings Ratio and Personal Savings Rate]

The percentage of current disposable personal income that is made up of current personal savings.

The total Personal Saving is divided by Disposable Personal Income, and the resulting ratio is converted into a percentage.

Used to judge long-term trends in income, expenditures, and economic growth; savings are a major source of money for investment, development, and technological progress.

Published monthly by the U.S. Department of Commerce, Bureau of Economic Analysis, in *Survey of Current Business*.

Source	Frequency	Extent	Form	Medium
BEA	q	c, h	t	e
FRED	m	c, h	t	e
Handbook of International Economic Statistics (CIA)	a	h	t	p
Securities Industry Yearbook	a	h	t	p
Statistical Abstract	a	h	t	p
Survey of Current Business	m	c, h	t	p, e

Bibliography

Alm, Richard, and David M. Gould, "The Saving Grace," *Economic Review of the Federal Reserve Bank of Dallas*, Third Quarter, 43-52 (1994).

Frumkin, Norman, *Guide to Economic Indicators*, 2nd ed., M. E. Sharpe, Armonk, N.Y., 1994, pp. 235-239.

Niemira, Michael P., and Gerald F. Zukowski, *Trading the Fundamentals: The Trader's Guide to Interpreting Economic Indicators and Monetary Policy*, McGraw-Hill, New York, 1998, pp. 189, 194.

Tainer, Evelina M., *Using Economic Indicators to Improve Investment Analysis*, John Wiley & Sons, New York, 1993, pp. 78-79.

U.S. Department of Commerce, Bureau of Economic Analysis, *Handbook of Cyclical Indicators*, USGPO, Washington, D.C., 1984, p. 48.

Savings Ratio
[See Savings Rate]

Seat Sales
[See American Stock Exchange Seat Sales and New York Stock Exchange Seat Sales]

Selected Measures of Unemployment and Unemployment Insurance Programs, Initial Claims
[See Unemployment Insurance Programs, Initial Claims]

Selected Measures of Unemployment and Unemployment Insurance, Total Unemployment
[See Total Unemployment]

Sensitive Prices
[See Change in Sensitive Prices]

Sentiment Index of the Leading Services
[See Advisory Sentiment Index]

Shearson Lehman
[See Lehman Brothers]

Shipments-Inventory Ratio
[See Manufacturers' Inventory-Shipments Ratio]

Short Interest Ratio
[See American Stock Exchange Short Interest Ratio and New York Stock Exchange Short Interest Ratio]

Short Sells Ratio
[See New York Stock Exchange Members' Short Sales and New York Stock Exchange Nonmembers' Short Sales]

Short-Skirt Index
[See Appendix A. Nonquantitative Indicators]

Short-Term Trading Index
[Also called the Arms Index and TRIN]

An hour-by-hour measure of the activity on the New York Stock Exchange.

Each hour, the Advance-Decline Ratio is calculated for the day's trading. The ratio of up volume (the total volume of all stocks that have risen during the day) to down volume is also calculated. The Advance-Decline Ratio is then divided by the ratio of up volume to down volume to give the Short-Term Trading Index.

Used as an indicator of what the market is currently doing and of what it might do in the very short, near, and intermediate terms. The Index will be below one on days when the market rises a lot and above one on days when it falls a lot. These values indicate bullish and bearish markets, respectively, on the very short and near terms. Some analysts use values of the Index smoothed with a moving average in an attempt to gain insight into intermediate and major trends.

Announced hourly by the New York Stock Exchange on Quotron.

Source	Frequency	Extent	Form	Medium
Wall Street Journal	d	c	t	p

Bibliography
Arms, Richard W., Jr., *The Arms Index (TRIN)*, Dow Jones-Irwin, Homewood, Ill., 1989.

Colby, Robert W., and Thomas A. Meyers, *The Encyclopedia of Technical Market Indicators*, Dow Jones-Irwin, Homewood, Ill., 1988, pp. 98-101.

McGinley, John R., Jr., "The Short Term Trading Index," pp. 38-1 to 38-6 in *The Encyclopedia of Stock Market Techniques*, Investors Intelligence, Larchmont, N.Y., 1983.

Müller, Thomas, and Harold Nietzer, *Das Grosse Buch der Technischen Indikatoren: Alles über Oszillatoren, Trendfolger, Zyklentechnik*, Thomas Müller, Börsenverlag, Rosenheim, Germany, 1995, pp. 431, 436, 450.

Stein, Jon, "Richard Arms: Keeping Markets Within Arms' Reach," *Futures: The Magazine of Commodities and Options* **21** (12), 98 (Oct. 1992).

Zweig, Martin E., "Handy Trader's Tool, A Long Look at a Short-Term Indicator," *Barron's*, 34+ (May 24, 1982).

Sindlinger Positive Household Liquidity Percentage

[Also called the Sindlinger Household Money Supply]

A barometer of consumer sentiment about the general economy.

About 900 households are surveyed each week and asked four questions:

▸ Is your household income higher than it was six months ago?

▸ Do you expect it to be higher, the same, or lower six months from now?

▸ Do you feel that the job held by the major wage earner in your family is secure?

▸ What are the business expectations in your geographic area?

The number of respondents that give a positive or at least neutral answer to all four questions is divided by the total number of respondents and multiplied by 100 to give a percentage of families with a positive household liquidity. That term reflects a belief that the future is economically secure enough for them that they can spend without fear. The data are broken down by gender of the respondent and by geographic region as well as being presented in the aggregate.

Used as a leading indicator to consumers' responses to employment levels and inflation, specifically consumer spending (as reflected in automobile sales, retail sales, sales of new houses, and sales of existing homes) and the savings rate.

Published weekly in *The Sindlinger Report*, the printed form of which is distributed by fax; monthly aggregates of data are posted on the World Wide Web by The Lincoln Institute at www.lincolninstitute.org/SINDCOMP/Sindcomp.htm.

Source	Frequency	Extent	Form	Medium
Lincoln Institute	m	c, h	t	e
The Sindlinger Report	w	c, h	t	p

Bibliography

Mahar, Maggie, "Women: A Nose for Bad News," *Working Woman* **18** (9), 21 (1993).

Shilling, A. Gary, "Money & Investments: A Bum Steer?" *Forbes* **147** (9), 346 (1991).

Six-Month Treasury Bills

An average interest rate expressed on a bank discount basis computed for issuances of short-term U.S. Government securities auctioned weekly.

Bids are accepted by the Treasury, and securities are auctioned weekly, usually on Mondays. Payment for the securities must accompany the bids; the securities are discounted (i.e., the interest for the full term is paid immediately; the principal is repaid at maturity). At the auction, all noncompetitive bids are accepted, and then competitive bids are accepted (starting with the lowest bids) until the target amount of borrowing is reached. The computed average interest rate is the weighted average of accepted competitive bids; noncompetitive bidders receive this average interest rate. Monthly cumulations are simple averages of the auction average rates for the issues sold during the month. Week-to-week variations in the yield are often expressed in terms of basis points; a basis point is one-hundredth of a percentage point. The yield (rate) is the annualized return on the investment.

Used as a measure of the availability of money and of short-term rates for default-free borrowing; several rates for borrowing are pegged to this rate.

Announced weekly by the U.S. Treasury and published weekly by the Board of Governors of the Federal Reserve System in *Selected Interest Rates*, Statistical Release G.13 (415).

Source	Frequency	Extent	Form	Medium
Bank Rate Monitor	w	c, h	t	e
Barron's	d	c	t	p
CNN*	h	c	t	e
Federal Reserve Board**	d	c, h	t	e
Federal Reserve Bulletin	a, m, w	c	t	p
Financial Digest	d	c	t	p
First Union	m	c, h	t	e
FRB Chicago*	d, w	c, h	t	e
FRB Dallas	m	c, h	t	e
FRED	w, m	c, h	t	e
Mortgage Banking	m	c	t	p
New York Times	d	c	t	p
Securities Industry Yearbook	a	h	t	p
Selected Interest Rates	m, w	c	t	p
S&P Basic Statistics - Banking and Finance	a, m	h	t	p
Statistical Abstract	a	h	t	p

Source	Frequency	Extent	Form	Medium
USA Today	d	c	t	p

*Secondary-market values. **Both auction results and secondary-market values.

Bibliography

A Guide to Buying Treasury Securities, Federal Reserve Bank of San Francisco, San Francisco, Sept. 1996.

Bureau of the Public Debt, *Buying Treasury Securities*, Department of the Treasury, Washington, D.C., 1995.

Bureau of the Public Debt, *Information about Marketable Treasury Securities (Bills, Notes, and Bonds)*, Department of the Treasury, Washington, D.C., 1991.

Bureau of the Public Debt, T-Bills, Notes, & Bonds Online, www.publicdebt. treas.gov/sec/sec.htm, visited July 17, 1999.

Handbook of Securities of the United States Government and Federal Agencies and Related Money Market Instruments, First Boston Corp., Boston, 1982.

Hoel, Arline Alchian; Kenneth W. Clarkson; and Roger LeRoy Miller, *Economics Sourcebook of Government Statistics*, Lexington Books, Lexington, Mass., 1983.

Nelson, C. R., *The Investor's Guide to Economic Indicators*, John Wiley & Sons, New York, 1987.

Publication Services, *The Federal Reserve System: Purposes and Functions*, Board of Governors of the Federal Reserve System, Washington, D.C., 1994, pp. 35-39.

Ray, Christina I., *The Bond Market: Trading and Risk Management*, Business One Irwin, Homewood, Ill., 1993, pp. 13-17.

Small Investor Index
[See Money Small Investor Index]

Sotheby Index
[See Appendix A. Nonquantitative Indicators]

Sources and Uses of Funds, Nonfarm Nonfinancial Corporate Business

A comprehensive picture of the financial lending and borrowing transactions of the U.S. economy. The sources of funds are apportioned into internal sources (undistributed profits, capital consumption allowances, and foreign branch profits) and external (long- and short-term credit-market funds and other sources). The uses are apportioned into the purchase of physical assets (plant and equipment, residential structures, inventory investment, and mineral rights from the U.S. Government) and the increase in financial assets.

Data for the internal sources and for the purchase of physical assets come from National Income and Products Accounts of the Department of Commerce (see the entries under National Income and Gross National Product). Data for the external sources and financial assets are compiled from the Federal Trade Commission's *Quarterly Report for Manufacturing, Mining, and Trade Corporations*, the quarterly U.S. International Transactions in the *Survey of Current Business*, New Security Issues of Corporations published monthly in the *Federal Reserve Bulletin*, and the Federal Reserve.

Used for developing projections of capital financing that are both realistic and consistent with projections of gross national product, in establishing targets for monetary policy associated with employment and inflation, and for projecting the probable trend of interest rates.

Published monthly by the Board of Governors of the Federal Reserve System in *Flow of Funds Accounts*.

Source	Frequency	Extent	Form	Medium
Economic Indicators	a, q	c, h	t	p, e
Statistical Abstract	a	h	t	p

Bibliography
Board of Governors of the Federal Reserve System, *Introduction to Flow of Funds*, Federal Reserve System, Washington, D.C., 1975.
Joint Economic Committee, *1980 Supplement to Economic Indicators, Historical and Descriptive Background*, USGPO, Washington, D.C., 1980, pp. 104-106.

Sources of Personal Income
[See also Disposable Personal Income and Disposition of Personal Income]
An analysis and tabulation of the different ways that individuals in the United States gain their earnings.

Monthly, the Bureau of Economic Analysis totals the following types of income, which it estimates from the results of surveys: wage and salary disbursements, other labor income, farm and nonfarm proprietors' income, rental income of individuals, dividend and interest income of individuals, and transfer payments (e.g., Social Security benefits, direct-relief payments, and veterans' benefits). From this total are subtracted contributions to social insurance programs. What results is an estimate of the current income received before taxes by individuals, nonprofit institutions, private trust funds, and private health and welfare funds from all sources except transfers among themselves that is broken down into labor income, farm and nonfarm proprietors' income, rental income, dividends, personal interest income, and transfer payments (such as social security benefits and military pensions).

Used to measure trends in the spending power of individuals and to predict future consumer spending.

Published monthly by the U.S. Department of Commerce, Bureau of Economic Analysis, in *Personal Income and Outlays*.

Source	Frequency	Extent	Form	Medium
Statistical Abstract	a	h	t	p

Bibliography

Carnes, W. Stansbury, and Stephen D. Slifer, *The Atlas of Economic Indicators: A Visual Guide to Market Forces and the Federal Reserve*, Harper Business, New York, 1991, pp. 127-134.

Creamer, D., *Personal Income During Business Cycles*, Princeton University Press, Princeton, N.J., 1956.

Frumkin, Norman, *Guide to Economic Indicators*, 2nd ed., M. E. Sharpe, Armonk, N.Y., 1994, pp. 235-239.

Grant, John, *A Handbook of Economic Indicators*, University of Toronto Press, Toronto, 1992, pp. 173-175.

Hoel, Arline Alchian; Kenneth W. Clarkson; and Roger LeRoy Miller, *Economics Sourcebook of Government Statistics*, Lexington Books, Lexington, Mass., 1983, pp. 73-79.

Joint Economic Committee, *1980 Supplement to Economic Indicators, Historical and Descriptive Background*, USGPO, Washington, D.C., 1980, pp. 14-15.

Kirk, John, "Economic Indicators: The How and the Why," *Banking*, 27-28 (Aug. 1964).

Moore, Geoffrey Hoyt, and Melita H. Moore, *International Economic Indicators: A Sourcebook*, Greenwood Press, Westport, Conn., 1985, p. 41.

Rogers, R. Mark, *Handbook of Key Economic Indicators*, Irwin Professional Pub., Burr Ridge, Ill., 1994, pp. 41-46.

Slater, Courtenay M., Ed., Business Statistics of the United States, 1995 ed., Bernan Press, Lanham, Md., 1996, pp. 236-240.

Snyder, Richard M., *Measuring Business Changes*, Wiley, 1955, p. 18 ff.

Tainer, Evelina M., *Using Economic Indicators to Improve Investment Analysis*, John Wiley & Sons, New York, 1993, pp. 74-77.

U.S. Department of Commerce, Bureau of Economic Analysis, *Business Statistics, 1963-91*, USGPO, Washington, D.C., 1992, pp. 141-142.

Specialist Short Ratio
[See New York Stock Exchange Members' Short Sales]

Spot Market Price Index
[See Bridge-CRB Index]

Stage of Processing Indexes
[See Finished Goods Price Index and Index for Intermediate Materials]

Standard & Poor's 100 Stocks Index
[Also called the S&P 100 OEX]

A measure of the change in aggregate market value of 100 highly capitalized stocks that have index option contracts being traded on the Chicago Board Options Exchange (CBOE).

The Standard & Poor's Index Committee selects 100 stocks from among those for which index-option contracts are traded on the CBOE, and their aggregate market value is calculated hourly. The aggregate market value is calculated by multiplying the price per share of each selected stock by the number of shares listed for that stock; these values are then totaled for all of the selected stocks, and the sum is expressed relative to the value for a 1983 base period. The trading volume of each company's stock is analyzed daily, monthly, and annually to ensure liquidity and efficiency of pricing. Appropriate adjustments are made for stock dividends, splits, consolidations, and similar events to ensure that the index will reflect only price movements.

Used to track the performance of index-option contracts en masse and as the basis for a tradable stock index itself.

Published daily by Standard & Poor's Corporation as a press release and posted on the Internet at www.spglobal.com/currentindexstat.html.

Source	Frequency	Extent	Form	Medium
Barron's	d	c	t	p
Bloomberg	h	c	t	e
Business Week	h	c	t	e
CBS	h	c	t	e
New York Times	d (h)	c	t	p (e)
PCQuote	h	c	t	e
Quote.com	h	c	t	e
S&P Security Price Index Record	m, w, d	h	t	p
StockMaster	d	c, h	g, t	e
USA Today	h	c	t	e

Bibliography
"About the S&P Indices" www.spglobal.com/ssindexmain.html, visited July 17, 1999.

Berlin, Howard M. *The Handbook of Financial Market Indexes, Averages, and Indicators*, Dow Jones-Irwin, Homewood, Ill., 1990, pp. 64-65.

Simmonds, Henry T., "The Irresistible Lure of the S&P 100," *Financial World* **154**, 98-103 (Feb. 6, 1985).

Standard & Poor's 400
[See Standard & Poor's Midcap 400 Index]

Standard & Poor's 500 Composite Stock Price Index
[Frequently referred to as the S&P 500]

A measure of the change in aggregate market value of 500 common stocks, primarily (but not entirely) stocks traded on the New York Stock Exchange.

The Standard & Poor's Corporation selects 500 stocks (almost 400 industrials, 40 utilities, nearly 70 financials, and more than 10 transportations. The great majority are stocks of U.S. firms, and about a dozen are those of foreign companies. Standard and Poor's then calculates the aggregate market value of these equities hourly. The aggregate market value is calculated by multiplying the price per share of each selected stock by the number of shares listed for that stock; these values are then totaled for all of the selected stocks, and the sum is expressed relative to the value for a particular base period (1941 to 1943). Appropriate adjustments are made for stock dividends, splits, consolidations, and similar events to ensure that the index will reflect only price movements. Companies are selected to represent a broad range of industry segments within the U.S. economy, and their financial and operating conditions are analyzed to ensure that the selected corporations are relatively stable. Their market values range from about $300 million to more than $150 billion with a mean market value of about $10 billion. More than 90% of the issues are listed on the New York Stock Exchange, and most of the rest of them are listed on the American Exchange. Closely held companies are excluded from the index. A company is removed from the index if it is the subject of merger, acquisition, restructuring, lack of representation, leveraged buyout, or bankruptcy proceedings. The index focuses on liquidity and ignores stocks that do not trade every day or that have unusually large spreads between the bid and asked prices. Listing on the Index is controlled and determined by S&P's Index Committee.

Used as a broad-based benchmark of price movement in the stock market, and is widely used as a benchmark of U.S. equity performance. It is also used as one of the components of the Leading Indicators Composite Index and as a leading indicator in general because it anticipates business cycle rises and declines. The S&P 500 is considered highly representative of the stock market in general because the market value of the 500 stocks is about 75% of the value of all stocks traded on the New York Stock Exchange, the American Stock Exchange, and the over-the-counter U.S. market. It is also used as the basis for index futures trading to give investors a hedge against price swings.

Published daily by Standard & Poor's Corporation as a press release and posted on the Internet at www.spglobal.com/currentindexstat.html; released hourly as a recording at 1-800-592-6051. Daily closing values are reported by the major television networks as part of the evening news. Current values (delayed by 20 minutes) are posted on many sites on the Internet and displayed on several cable news services.

– S –

Source	Frequency	Extent	Form	Medium
Annual Statistical Digest (FRB)	a, m	c	t	p
Barron's	d	c	t	p
BCI	m	h	g	e
Bloomberg	h	c	t	e
Bridge	d	c	t	e
Business Statistics	a	h	t	p
Business Week	h	c	t	e
CBS	h	c	t	e
CNN	h	c	t	e
Conference Board/BCI	m	c	t	e
Economic Indicators	a, m, w	c, h	t	p, e
Federal Reserve Bulletin	a, m	c	t	p
First Union	m	c, h	t	e
FRB New York	m	c, h	g	e
Investor's Business Daily	d	c, h	t, g	p
Mutual Fund Factbook	a	h	g	p
Mutual Funds Update	m	c	t	p
NASDAQ Factbook	a	h	g	p
New York Times	d (h)	c	t	p (e)
Outlook	d	c	t	p
PCQuote	h	c	t	e
Pensions and Investments	a, m	c	t	p
Quote.com	h	c	t	e
Recession Recovery Watch	q	c	g	p
Securities Industry Trends	a, m	c, h	t	p
Securities Industry Yearbook	a	h	t	p
S&P Basic Statistics - Income and Trade	a	h	t	p
S&P Current Statistics	d	c	t	p
S&P Security Price Index Record	m, w, d	h	t	p
Statistical Abstract	a	h	t	p
StockMaster	d	c, h	g, t	e
Survey of Current Business	a, m	c	t	p, e
USA Today	d (h)	c	t	p (e)

Source	Frequency	Extent	Form	Medium
Wall Street Journal	d	c	t	p
Value Line Investment Survey, Part 2: Selection and Opinion	d	c	t	p

Bibliography

"About the S&P Indices" www.spglobal.com/ssindexmain.html, visited July 17, 1999.

Berlin, Howard M. *The Handbook of Financial Market Indexes, Averages, and Indicators*, Dow Jones-Irwin, Homewood, Ill., 1990, pp. 57-64.

Harris, Lawrence, and Eitan Gurel, "Price and Volume Effects Associated with Changes in the S&P 500 List: New Evidence for the Existence of Price Pressures," *Journal of Finance* 41, 815-830 (Sept. 1986).

Hoel, Arline Alchian; Kenneth W. Clarkson; and Roger LeRoy Miller, *Economics Sourcebook of Government Statistics*, Lexington Books, Lexington, Mass., 1983, p. 157.

Lamoureux, Christopher G., and James W. Wansley, "Market Effects of Changes in the Standard & Poor's 500 Index," *The Financial Review* 22, 53-70 (1987).

Levine, S. N. (Ed.), *Financial Analyst's Handbook,* 2nd ed., Dow Jones - Irwin, Homewood, Ill., 1988, pp. 88-89.

"Market Guides," *Barron's*, 9+ (Sept. 26, 1966).

Mills, Leonard, "Can Stock Prices reliably Predict Recessions?" *Business Review of the Federal Reserve Bank of Philadelphia*, 3-14 (Sept./Oct. 1988).

Moore, Geoffrey Hoyt, and Melita H. Moore, *International Economic Indicators: A Sourcebook*, Greenwood Press, Westport, Conn., 1985, pp. 34-35.

Moore, G. H., and J. Shiskin, "Why the Leading Indicators Really Do Lead," *Across the Board*, 71-75 (May 1978).

Nelson, C. R., *The Investor's Guide to Economic Indicators*, John Wiley & Sons, New York, 1987, pp. 106-109.

"Official Indicators: What Are They? Can They Predict the Future?" *U.S. News and World Report*, 66-67 (Aug. 16, 1976).

Pring, Martin J., *Technical Analysis Explained, An Illustrated Guide for the Investor*, McGraw-Hill, New York, 1980, p. 112.

Renshaw, Edward, Ed., *The Practical Forecasters' Almanac: 137 Reliable Indicators for Investors, Hedgers, and Speculators*, Business One Irwin, Homewood, Ill., 1992, pp. 43-44, 64-65, 92-95.

"S&P Realigns 500-Stock Index," *Wall Street Journal*, Nov. 9, 1989, pp. C6 and C14.

Smith, Keith V., "Stock Price and Economic Indexes for Generating Efficient Portfolios," *Journal of Business*, 326-336 (July 1969).

Zweig, Martin, "Four Key Indicators for Gauging Market Direction," *Investment Vision*, 65-67 (May/June 1990).

Standard & Poor's 500 Dividend-Price Ratio

A comparison of the cash dividends earned by 500 selected stocks with their market value at the end of a quarter.

The cash dividends paid by the companies included in the Standard and Poor's 500 Composite Stock Price Index are totaled at the end of a quarter, and this sum is divided by the aggregate market value of those stocks at the end of the same quarter. Annual data are averages of the four calculated quarterly ratios.

Used to forecast future movements of the market. Higher ratios are taken as an indication that the market is at or near a peak; lower ratios are taken to indicate that the market is due for an upswing.

Published quarterly by Standard & Poor's Corporation in *Standard & Poor's Outlook*.

Source	Frequency	Extent	Form	Medium
Annual Statistical Digest (FRB)	a, m, w	c	t	p
Federal Reserve Bulletin	a, m, w	c	t	p
S&P Current Statistics	q	h	t	p

Bibliography

Hayes, Michael, *The Dow Jones - Irwin Guide to Stock Market Cycles*, Dow Jones - Irwin, Homewood, Ill., 1977, pp. 56-57.

Standard & Poor's 500 Price-Earnings Ratio

A measure of the value of the stocks listed in the Standard & Poor's 500 Composite Stock Price Index; more accurately, a measure of the speculative nature of the purchases of those stocks.

Five hundred companies are selected by Standard & Poor. The earnings of those companies each quarter are summed and divided by the total market value of all outstanding shares of their common stocks at the end of that quarter. The result is referred to as the Standard & Poor Price-Earnings Ratio. Annual values are derived by averaging the four quarterly values for each year.

Used as a gauge of speculative activity in the market and to assess turning points of the market in the near term. The higher the ratio, the more speculative the market is considered to be because increased investment is not being reflected in increased returns (earnings) from the corporations' performances. Conversely, a lower ratio indicates better value of purchases in the market.

Published quarterly by Standard & Poor's Corporation in *Standard & Poor's Outlook*.

Source	Frequency	Extent	Form	Medium
Barron's	w	c	t	p
Economic Indicators	a, m, w	c, h	t, g	p, e
Outlook	w	c	t	p

Source	Frequency	Extent	Form	Medium
S&P Current Statistics	q	c	t	p

Bibliography
Nelson, C. R., *The Investor's Guide to Economic Indicators*, John Wiley & Sons, New York, 1987, pp. 90-91.
Zweig, Martin, "Four Key Indicators for Gauging Market Direction," *Investment Vision*, 65-67 (May/June 1990).

Standard & Poor's 600 Index
[See Standard & Poor's SmallCap 600 Index]

Standard & Poor's 1500 Supercomposite

A measure of the change in aggregate market value of 1500 common stocks, primarily (but not entirely) stocks traded on the New York Stock Exchange and the American Stock Exchange.

The stocks used to derive the Standard & Poor's 500 Composite Stock Price Index, SmallCap 600 Index, and MidCap 400 Index are used to calculate the Standard & Poor's 1500 Supercomposite. Their aggregate market value is computed hourly by multiplying the price per share of each stock by the number of shares listed for that stock; these values are then totaled for all of the stocks, and the sum is expressed relative to the value for the 1941-1943 base period. The trading volume of each company's stock is analyzed daily, monthly, and annually to ensure liquidity and efficiency of pricing. Appropriate adjustments are made for stock dividends, splits, consolidations, and similar events to ensure that the index will reflect only price movements.

Used as a measure of the performance of the stock market as a whole and as a benchmark of performance for managers of stock portfolios (e.g., mutual-fund managers or institutional investors).

Published daily by Standard & Poor's Corporation as a press release and posted on the Internet at www.spglobal.com/currentindexstat.html.

Source	Frequency	Extent	Form	Medium
Business Week	d	c	t	p
Outlook	d	c	t	p
Wall Street Journal	d	c	t	p

Bibliography
"About the S&P Indices" www.spglobal.com/ssindexmain.html, visited July 17, 1999.
Norris, Floyd, "S&P, Responding to Its Rival, Introduces a New Stock Index," *New York Times*, Oct. 18, 1994, p. D10.

Standard & Poor's Financials

A measure of the change in aggregate market value of 40 common stocks of financial institutions, primarily (but not entirely) stocks traded on the New York Stock Exchange.

The Standard & Poor's Corporation selects 40 stocks of financial institutions and calculates their aggregate market value hourly. The aggregate market value is calculated by multiplying the price per share of each selected stock by the number of shares listed for that stock; these values are then totaled for all of the selected stocks, and the sum divided by the market value for a base period (1941-1943). Appropriate adjustments are made for stock dividends, splits, consolidations, and similar events to ensure that the index will reflect only price movements.

Used as a leading indicator because it anticipates business-cycle rises and declines.

Published daily by Standard & Poor's Corporation on the Internet at www.spglobal.com/currentindexstat.html and in *Standard & Poor's Outlook*.

Source	Frequency	Extent	Form	Medium
Barron's	d	c	t	p
Business Statistics	a	h	t	p
Business Week	d	c	t	p
New York Times	d	c	t	p
Outlook	d	c	t	p
S&P Current Statistics	d	c	t	p
S&P Security Price Index Record	m, w, d	h	t	p

Bibliography

Berlin, Howard M. *The Handbook of Financial Market Indexes, Averages, and Indicators*, Dow Jones-Irwin, Homewood, Ill., 1990, p. 59.

Hoel, Arline Alchian; Kenneth W. Clarkson; and Roger LeRoy Miller, *Economics Sourcebook of Government Statistics*, Lexington Books, Lexington, Mass., 1983, p. 157.

"Market Guides," *Barron's*, 9+ (Sept. 26, 1966).

Standard & Poor's High-Grade Municipal Bond Yields

A general measure of the performance in the market of the best tax-exempt municipal bonds.

Fifteen high-grade, tax-exempt, general-obligation, domestic municipal bonds with about 20 years to maturity are selected on the basis of quality, trading activity, and geographic representation, and their yields to maturity based on their closing bid quotations on Wednesday are arithmetically averaged. As selected bonds move away from 20 years to maturity, new selections are substituted. Monthly values are the averages of the weekly figures for each month.

Used as an inverse indicator of securities prices. These yields are highly sensitive to harbingers of inflation: lower unemployment, growth in the number of jobs, higher interest rates, and decreases in the value of the dollar on foreign-exchange markets. Therefore, they are taken as an indicator of emerging changes in inflation.

Published weekly by Standard & Poor's Corp. in *Standard & Poor's Outlook*.

Source	Frequency	Extent	Form	Medium
Business Statistics	a	h	t	p
Economic Indicators	a, m, w	c, h	t	p, e
S&P Current Statistics	w, m	c, h	t	p
S&P Security Price Index Record	m, w	h	t	p

Bibliography

Berlin, Howard M. *The Handbook of Financial Market Indexes, Averages, and Indicators*, Dow Jones-Irwin, Homewood, Ill., 1990, p. 85.

Darst, David M., *The Complete Bond Book, A Guide to All Types of Fixed Income Securities*, McGraw-Hill, New York, 1975.

Hoel, Arline Alchian; Kenneth W. Clarkson; and Roger LeRoy Miller, *Economics Sourcebook of Government Statistics*, Lexington Books, Lexington, Mass., 1983, pp. 144-145.

Standard & Poor's Industrials

A measure of the change in aggregate market value of 400 common stocks of industrial corporations, primarily (but not entirely) stocks traded on the New York Stock Exchange.

The Standard & Poor's Corporation selects 400 stocks of industrial companies and calculates their aggregate market value. The aggregate market value is calculated by multiplying the price per share of each selected stock by the number of shares listed for that stock; these values are then totaled for all of the selected stocks, and the sum divided by the market value for a base period (1941-1943). Appropriate adjustments are made for stock dividends, splits, consolidations, and similar events to ensure that the index will reflect only price movements.

Used as a leading indicator because it anticipates business-cycle rises and declines.

Published daily by Standard & Poor's Corporation on the Internet at www.spglobal.com/currentindexstat.html and in *Standard & Poor's Outlook*.

Source	Frequency	Extent	Form	Medium
Barron's	d	c	t	p
Bloomberg	h	c	t	e
Business Statistics	a	h	t	p

Source	Frequency	Extent	Form	Medium
New York Times	d	c	t	p
Outlook	d	c	t	p
S&P Current Statistics	d	c	t	p
S&P Security Price Index Record	m, w, d	h	t	p
Statistical Abstract	a	h	t	p
Wall Street Journal	d	c	t	p

Bibliography

Berlin, Howard M. *The Handbook of Financial Market Indexes, Averages, and Indicators*, Dow Jones-Irwin, Homewood, Ill., 1990, p. 59.

Hoel, Arline Alchian; Kenneth W. Clarkson; and Roger LeRoy Miller, *Economics Sourcebook of Government Statistics*, Lexington Books, Lexington, Mass., 1983, p. 157.

"Market Guides," *Barron's*, 9+ (Sept. 26, 1966).

Standard & Poor's Long-Term Government Bond Price Index

A measure of the demand for long-term government bonds.

From the variety of U.S. Government bonds traded on the market, Standard & Poor selects four issues with maturities of 15 years. The bid prices of these four issues are determined from the yields published in the *Wall Street Journal*; the yields top maturity are converted into a price by assuming a 3% coupon and 15 years to maturity and expressed in dollars per $100 of par value. These four bid prices are then arithmetically averaged. The index has been calculated and published monthly since 1942 and weekly since 1971.

Used to judge the current prices of long-term government bonds, trends in those prices, and demand for those issues and to estimate their performance.

Issued as a news release by Standard & Poor.

Source	Frequency	Extent	Form	Medium
S&P Security Price Index Record	m, w	h	t	p

Bibliography

Berlin, Howard M. *The Handbook of Financial Market Indexes, Averages, and Indicators*, Dow Jones-Irwin, Homewood, Ill., 1990, pp. 85-86.

Levine, Sumner N., *The Financial Analyst's Handbook*, 2nd ed., Dow Jones-Irwin, Homewood, Ill., 1988, pp. 137-189.

Standard & Poor's MidCap 400 Index

A benchmark of price movement within midcapitalized stocks.

The S&P MidCap 400 Index consists of 400 domestic stocks chosen for market size, liquidity (the trading volume of each company's stock is analyzed daily, monthly, and annually to ensure liquidity and efficiency of pricing), and industry group representation (about 300 industrials, about 50 utilities, nearly 35 financials, and more than 10 transportations). Companies are selected to represent a broad range of industry segments within the U.S. economy. The financial and operating conditions of the companies are analyzed to ensure that the selected corporations are relatively stable. Their market values range from about $175 million to $6.5 billion with a mean market value of about $1.5 billion. Almost three-quarters of the issues are listed on the New York Stock Exchange, and most of the rest of them are listed on the American Exchange. Closely held companies are excluded from the index. A company is removed from the index if it is the subject of merger, acquisition, leveraged buyout, or bankruptcy proceedings. The index is market-value weighted, with each stock's weight in the Index proportionate to its market value (i.e., its price multiplied by the number of shares that are outstanding). The index focuses on liquidity and ignores stocks that do not trade every day or that have unusually large spreads between the bid and asked prices. Listing on the Index is controlled and determined by S&P's Index Committee.

Used as a gauge of the performance of this segment of the stock market. Also used by many investment institutions to define "midrange capitalization" for the purpose of constructing mutual funds that concentrate on this portion of the equities market and that will, therefore, track the performance of this indicator.

Published daily by Standard & Poor's Corporation as a press release and posted on the Internet at www.spglobal.com/currentindexstat.html.

Source	Frequency	Extent	Form	Medium
Barron's	d	c	t	p
Bloomberg	h	c	t	e
Business Week	d (h)	c	t	p (e)
CBS	h	c	t	e
Investor's Business Daily	d	c	t	p
New York Times	d	c	t	p
Outlook	d	c	t	p
USA Today	d (h)	c	t	p (e)
Wall Street Journal	d	c	t	p

Bibliography
"About the S&P Indices" www.spglobal.com/ssindexmain.html, visited July 17, 1999.

Standard & Poor's Municipal Bond Yields
[See Standard & Poor's High-Grade Municipal Bond Yields]

Standard & Poor's Price-Earnings Ratio
[See Standard & Poor's 500 Price-Earnings Ratio]

Standard & Poor's SmallCap 600 Index

A benchmark of price movement within small-capitalized stocks.

The S&P SmallCap 600 Index consists of 600 domestic stocks chosen for market size, liquidity (bid-asked spread, ownership, share turnover, and number of no-trade days are periodically analyzed to ensure liquidity and efficiency of pricing), and industry group representation (almost 500 industrials, about 30 utilities, nearly 70 financials, and almost 20 transportations). Companies are selected to represent a broad range of industry segments within the U.S. economy. The financial and operating conditions of the companies are analyzed to ensure that the selected corporations are relatively stable. Their market values range from about $35 million to more than $2.5 billion with a mean market value of about $450 million. More than 50% of the issues are listed on the New York Stock Exchange, and most of the rest of them are listed on the American Exchange. Closely held companies are excluded from the index. A company is removed from the index if it is the subject of merger, acquisition, leveraged buyout, or bankruptcy proceedings. The index is market-value weighted, with each stock's weight in the Index proportionate to its market value (i.e., its price multiplied by the number of shares that are outstanding). The index focuses on liquidity and ignores stocks that do not trade every day or that have unusually large spreads between the bid and asked prices. Listing on the Index is controlled and determined by S&P's Index Committee.

Used as a gauge of the performance of this segment of the stock market. Also used by many investment institutions to define "small capitalization" for the purpose of constructing mutual funds that concentrate on this portion of the equities market and that will, therefore, track the performance of this indicator.

Published daily by Standard & Poor's Corporation as a press release and posted on the Internet at www.spglobal.com/currentindexstat.html.

Source	Frequency	Extent	Form	Medium
Barron's	d	c	t	p
Bloomberg	h	c	t	e
Business Week	d	c	t	p
New York Times	d	c	t	p
Outlook	d	c	t	p
Wall Street Journal	d	c	t	p

Bibliography
"About the S&P Indices" www.spglobal.com/ssindexmain.html, visited July 17, 1999.

Norris, Floyd, "S&P, Responding to Its Rival, Introduces a New Stock Index," *New York Times*, Oct. 18, 1994, p. D10.

Standard & Poor's Stock Yields
[See Standard & Poor's 500 Price-Earnings Ratio]

Standard & Poor's Transportations

A measure of the change in aggregate market value of 20 common stocks of corporations in the transportation industry, primarily (but not entirely) stocks traded on the New York Stock Exchange.

The Standard & Poor's Corporation selects 20 stocks of transportation companies and calculates their aggregate market value hourly. The aggregate market value is calculated by multiplying the price per share of each selected stock by the number of shares listed for that stock; these values are then totaled for all of the selected stocks, and the sum divided by the market value on a base period (1941-1943). Appropriate adjustments are made for stock dividends, splits, consolidations, and similar events to ensure that the index will reflect only price movements.

Used as a leading indicator because it anticipates business-cycle rises and declines.

Published daily by Standard & Poor's Corporation on the Internet at www.spglobal.com/currentindexstat.html and in *Standard & Poor's Outlook*.

Source	Frequency	Extent	Form	Medium
Barron's	d	c	t	p
Bloomberg	h	c	t	e
Business Statistics	a	h	t	p
New York Times	d	c	t	p
Outlook	d	c	t	p
S&P Current Statistics	d	c	t	p
S&P Security Price Index Record	m, w, d	h	t	p

Bibliography
Berlin, Howard M. *The Handbook of Financial Market Indexes, Averages, and Indicators*, Dow Jones-Irwin, Homewood, Ill., 1990, p. 61.
Hoel, Arline Alchian; Kenneth W. Clarkson; and Roger LeRoy Miller, *Economics Sourcebook of Government Statistics*, Lexington Books, Lexington, Mass., 1983, p. 157.
"Market Guides," *Barron's*, 9+ (Sept. 26, 1966).

Standard & Poor's Utilities

A measure of the change in aggregate market value of 40 common stocks of private utilities, primarily (but not entirely) stocks traded on the New York Stock Exchange.

The Standard & Poor's Corporation selects 40 stocks of private utilities and calculates their aggregate market value hourly. The aggregate market value is calculated by multiplying the price per share of each selected stock by the number of shares listed for that stock; these values are then totaled for all of the selected stocks, and the sum divided by the market value for a base period (1941-1943). Appropriate adjustments are made for stock dividends, splits, consolidations, and similar events to ensure that the index will reflect only price movements.

Used as a leading indicator because it anticipates business-cycle rises and declines.

Published daily by the Standard & Poor's Corporation on the Internet at www.spglobal.com/currentindexstat.html and in *Standard & Poor's Outlook*.

Source	Frequency	Extent	Form	Medium
Barron's	d	c	t	p
Bloomberg	h	c	t	e
Business Statistics	a	h	t	p
Business Week	d	c	t	p
New York Times	d	c	t	p
Outlook	d	c	t	p
S&P Current Statistics	d	c	t	p
S&P Security Price Index Record	m, w, d	h	t	p
Wall Street Journal	d	c	t	p

Bibliography

Berlin, Howard M. *The Handbook of Financial Market Indexes, Averages, and Indicators*, Dow Jones-Irwin, Homewood, Ill., 1990, p. 60-61.

Hoel, Arline Alchian; Kenneth W. Clarkson; and Roger LeRoy Miller, *Economics Sourcebook of Government Statistics*, Lexington Books, Lexington, Mass., 1983, p. 157.

"Market Guides," *Barron's*, 9+ (Sept. 26, 1966).

Status of the Labor Force

[See Nonagricultural Employment; Total Unemployment; Unemployment Rate, Total; and Unemployment Insurance Programs, Initial Claims]

Steel Production

Total number of tons of raw steel produced in the U.S. each week.

The American Iron and Steel Institute receives production data from virtually all makers of ingots and steel for castings in the nation. Raw steel is defined as steel in the first solid state after melting, suitable for further processing or sale. In addition to ingots and castings, it includes strand or pressure-cast blooms, billets, slabs, and other product forms. The reported tonnages are totaled.

Used as a gauge of future activity of the heavy-industry and construction sectors of the economy.

Published weekly by the American Iron and Steel Institute in *Weekly Raw Steel Production.*

Source	Frequency	Extent	Form	Medium
Annual Statistical Report (AISI)	a, m, q	h	t, g	p
Barron's	m	c	t	p
Business Statistics	a	h	t	p
Business Week	w	c	t	p
Handbook of International Economic Statistics (CIA)	a	h	t	p
Industry, Trade, and Technology Review	m	c	t	p
S&P Basic Statistics	a	h	t	p
S&P Current Statistics	m	h	t	p
Statistical Abstract	a	h	t	p

Bibliography

Boughton, James M., and William H. Branson, "Commodity Prices as a Leading Indicator of Inflation," pp. 305-338 in Kajal Lahiri and Moore, Geoffrey H. Moore, Eds., *Leading Economic Indicators: New Approaches and Forecasting Records,* Cambridge University Press, New York, 1991.

Segars, Alan D., "Commodities an Inflation Indicator," *Pensions and Investments* **23** (1), 20 (Jan. 9, 1995).

Snyder, Richard M., *Measuring Business Changes*, Wiley, New York, 1955, pp. 193-194.

"The Rage for Faster Forecasts," *Business Week*, Oct. 18, 1982, pp. 135-138.

U.S. Department of Commerce, Bureau of Economic Analysis, *Business Statistics 1963-1993*, USGPO, Washington, D.C., 1994.

Superbowl Predictor
[See Appendix A. Nonquantitative Indicators]

Surly Waiter Index
[See Appendix A. Nonquantitative Indicators]

T

Technical Market Index
[Formerly the Wall $treet Week Technical Market Index]

A composite of stock market indicators that is used to forecast aggregate stock-market performance in the medium to long term.

Ten indicators are considered:

▸ The Dow Jones Momentum Ratio (the difference between the current Dow Jones Industrial Average and its 30-day average expressed as a percentage)

▸ The ten-day High-Low Differential for the New York Stock Exchange

▸ The ten-day moving average of the New York Stock Exchange Advance-Decline Line

▸ The ten-day moving average of the Short-Term Trading Index

▸ The prices of equities listed on the New York Stock Exchange versus their 10-week and 30-week moving averages

▸ The average premium on all put options listed during a week divided by the average premium on all call options listed during that week

▸ The Advisory Service Index

▸ The trading volume of low-priced equities on the New York Stock Exchange divided by the trading volume in equities included in the Dow Jones Industrial Average, expressed as a percentage

▸ The number of insider sell transactions during a week divided by the number of insider buy transactions during that week

▸ The four-day average of the ratio of the Federal Funds rate to the Discount Rate

Each of these is assigned a +1, 0, or -1, depending on the current value of the indicator and the location of that value (high, intermediate, or low) in the range of values possible for that specific indicator. These assigned values are then summed to produce the Index; index values greater than 5 are taken to portend an extremely bullish market 3 to 6 months hence, and index values less than -5 are taken to portend an extremely bearish market, with intermediate values taken to forecast proportionally less-extreme courses for the stock market.

Used to forecast aggregate stock-market performance in the medium to long term.

Published semiweekly in *Bob Nurock's Advisory*, the printed form of which is distributed by fax.

Source	Frequency	Extent	Form	Medium
Bob Nurock's Advisory	sw	c	t	p

Bibliography

Berlin, Howard M. *The Handbook of Financial Market Indexes, Averages, and Indicators*, Dow Jones-Irwin, Homewood, Ill., 1990.

Colby, Robert W., and Thomas A. Meyers, *The Encyclopedia of Technical Market Indicators*, Dow Jones-Irwin, Homewood, Ill., 1988.

Technology Stock Index
[See Hambrecht and Quist Technology Index]

Ten-Day Auto Sales
[Discontinued; see Auto and Light Truck Sales]

TheStreet.com E-Commerce Index

A measure of the price performance of the stocks of companies that provide consumers goods or services over the Internet.

The staff of TheStreet.com selected the stocks of 15 online retail sales, brokerage, travel, and auction and other companies that produce all or a significant portion of their revenues from commerce conducted over the Internet. The prices of these stocks are summed and indexed to a value of 75.00 on Dec. 1, 1998. The list of companies is reviewed quarterly, and substitutions are made to compensate for mergers and acquisitions and to adequately reflect the nature of the electronic-commerce sector. Although some companies appear in both indexes, TheStreet.com E-Commerce Index is not a subset of TheStreet.com Internet Sector Index.

Used as a benchmark for the performance of the electronic-commerce sector of the stock market; options based on this index are traded on the American Stock Exchange under the symbol ICX.X.

Published throughout the trading day on the Internet as ICX.X at quote.thestreet.com/cgi-bin/texis/StockQuotes?tkr=icx.x&SearchBy=Ticker& DataChoice=StockQuotes.

Source	Frequency	Extent	Form	Medium
TheStreet.com	h	c	t	e

Bibliography
TSC Staff, "Frequently Asked Questions about the TSC E-Commerce Index," www.thestreet.com/markets/marketfeatures/762173.html, accessed Sept. 13, 1999.

TheStreet.com E-Finance Index

A measure of the price performance of the stocks of financial companies that do business on the Internet.

The staff of TheStreet.com selected the stocks of 11 online banking, brokerage, and transaction companies. The prices of these stocks are summed and indexed to a value of 100 for May 21, 1999. The list of companies is reviewed periodically, and substitutions are made to compensate for mergers and acquisitions and to adequately reflect the nature of the online-finance sector. Although some companies appear in both indexes, TheStreet.com E-Finance Index is not a subset of TheStreet.com Internet Sector Index.

Used as a benchmark for the performance of the electronic-finance sector of the stock market; options based on this index are traded on the American Stock Exchange under the symbol XEF.X.

Published throughout the trading day on the Internet as XEF.X at quote.thestreet.com/cgi-bin/texis/StockQuotes?tkr=XEF.X.

Source	Frequency	Extent	Form	Medium
TheStreet.com	h	c	t	e

Bibliography
TSC Staff, "What Is TheStreet.com E-Finance Index?," www.thestreet.com/markets/marketfeatures/762090.html, accessed Aug. 17, 1999.

TheStreet.com Internet Sector Index

A measure of the price performance of the stocks of companies that do business on or for the Internet.

The staff of TheStreet.com selected the stocks of 20 companies engaged in e-commerce, online trading, online auctions, Internet service provision, software and hardware development, and search services. The prices of these stocks are summed and indexed to a value of "around 100 in February 1997." The list of companies is reviewed quarterly, and substitutions are made to compensate for mergers and acquisitions and to adequately reflect the nature of the Internet sector.

Used as a benchmark for the performance of the broad Internet sector of the stock market; options based on this index are traded on the Philadelphia Stock Exchange under the symbol DOT.

Published throughout the trading day on the Internet as DOT at www.thestreet.com.

Source	Frequency	Extent	Form	Medium
TheStreet.com	h	c	t	e

Bibliography
TSC Staff, "Frequently Asked Questions about the TSC Internet Sector Index," www.thestreet.com/markets/marketfeatures/90219.html, accessed Aug. 17, 1999.

Thirteen-Week Treasury Bills
[See Three-Month Treasury Bills]

Thirty-Year Treasury Bonds
[See also Lehman Brothers Long Treasury Bond Index]

Long-term government issues whose yield and price together constitute an important barometer of interest-rate trends.

Initially sold by Federal Reserve banks and member banks, Treasury bonds are resold and traded by brokers and banks that handle securities. This secondary market for bonds is quite active, but the Federal Reserve Bank will not accept bonds before 10 business days prior to maturity. Minimum denominations (usually $1000) are set with each issue. The bonds are sold at auction by the Federal Reserve several times a year (at least quarterly). Interest is paid semiannually and is exempt from state and local (but not federal) taxes. Although the quarterly Treasury auctions produce a settled price upon issuance, the yields and prices most frequently quoted are for those bonds that are resold by traders. Because those bond sales are not reported (being largely one-on-one telephone trades between brokers and buyers), the quotations published are usually index values (e.g., the Lehman Brothers Long-Term Treasury Bond Index) or the bid/asked values that appear on trading systems. These values are the current prices paid for the securities, which allow the yields to be calculated and reported along with the prices.

Used as a bellwether for a goodly portion of the credit market and as a benchmark for setting the interest rates on many types of loans. Higher yields on these instruments portend higher corporate borrowing costs, slower consumer spending, and stiffer competition for investment funds among the various markets. Trading for these bonds and the resulting prices are affected by a number of economic conditions and indicators: the employment outlook and current levels, the Producer Price Index, the Consumer Price Index, orders for durable goods, industry's current capacity utilization, levels of industrial production, construction spending, the economic outlook projected by the Purchasing Managers Index, and the federal budget.

Published daily by Smith-Barney (Lehman Brothers indexes) and Bridge Communications Telerate/Cantor Fitzgerald.

Source	Frequency	Extent	Form	Medium
Bank of America	q	f	t	e
BCI	m	h	g	e
Bridge	d	c	t	e
Business Week	w	c	t	p
CBS	h	c	t	e
CNN	h	c	t	e
Construction Review	a, m	c, h	t	p
Economic Indicators	a, m, w	c, h	t	p, e
Federal Reserve Board	d	c, h	t	e
Federal Reserve Bulletin	a, m, w	c	t	p
Financial Digest	d	c	t	p
First Union	m	c, h	t	e
Forecast	q	c, f	t	p
FRB Dallas	m	c, h	t	e
FRED	d, w, m	c, h	t	e
Investors Business Daily	d	c, h	g	p
Moody's Bond Record	m	c	g	p
New York Times	d	c	t	p
Quote.com	h	c	t	e
Real Estate Outlook	a, q	c, h	t	p
Securities Industry Yearbook	a	h	t	p
Selected Interest Rates	a, w	c	t	p
S&P Creditweek	m	h	g	p
Statistical Abstract	a	h	t	p
Survey of Current Business	a, m	c, h	t, g	p, e
Treasury Bulletin	m	c, h	t, g	p
USA Today	d (h)	c	t	p (e)
Value Line Investment Survey, Part 2: Selection and Opinion	a, q	c, h, f	t	p

Bibliography

A Guide to Buying Treasury Securities, Federal Reserve Bank of San Francisco, San Francisco, Sept. 1996.

Bureau of the Public Debt, *Buying Treasury Securities*, Department of the Treasury, Washington, D.C., 1995.

Bureau of the Public Debt, *Information about Marketable Treasury Securities (Bills, Notes, and Bonds)*, Department of the Treasury, Washington, D.C., 1991.

Bureau of the Public Debt, T-Bills, Notes, & Bonds Online, www.publicdebt.treas.gov/sec/sec.htm, visited July 17, 1999.

Ederington, Louis H., and Jae Ha Lee, "How Markets Process Information: New Releases and Volatility," *Journal of Finance* 48 (4), 1161-1191 (1993).

Federal Reserve Bank, *United States Treasury Securities: Basic Information*, no date or location of publication.

Fleming, Michael J., and Eli M. Remolona, *What Moves the Bond Market?*, Research Paper 9706, Federal Reserve Bank of New York, New York, 1997.

Larson, James Alan, *Treasury Auction Results as Interest Rate Predictors*, Garland, New York, 1994.

Publication Services, *The Federal Reserve System: Purposes and Functions*, Board of Governors of the Federal Reserve System, Washington, D.C., 1994, pp. 35-39.

Wann, Peter, *Inside the U.S. Treasury Market*, Greenwood Press/Quorum Books, Westport, Conn., 1989.

Three-Month Treasury Bills

An average interest rate expressed on a bank discount basis computed for issuances of short-term U.S. Government securities auctioned weekly.

Bids are accepted by the Treasury, and securities are auctioned weekly, usually on Mondays. Payment for the securities must accompany the bids; the securities are discounted (i.e., the interest for the full term is paid immediately; the principal is repaid at maturity). At the auction, all noncompetitive bids are accepted, and then competitive bids are accepted (starting with the lowest bids) until the target amount of borrowing is reached. The computed average interest rate is the weighted average of accepted competitive bids; noncompetitive bidders receive this average interest rate. Monthly cumulations are simple averages of the auction average rates for the issues sold during the month. Week-to-week variations in the yield are often expressed in terms of basis points; a basis point is one-hundredth of a percentage point. The yield (rate) is the annualized return on the investment.

Used to set the current interest rate for many money-market and other financial instruments.

Announced weekly as a news release by the U.S. Treasury and published weekly by the Board of Governors of the Federal Reserve System in *Selected Interest Rates*, Statistical Release G.13 (415).

Source	Frequency	Extent	Form	Medium
Agricultural Outlook	a, q	c	t	p
Bank Rate Monitor	w	c, h	t	e

Source	Frequency	Extent	Form	Medium
Barrons	d	c	t	p
BCI	m	h	g	e
Business Statistics	a	h	t	p
Business Week	d	c	t	p
CNN*	h	c	t	e
Construction Review	a, m	c, h	t	p
Economic Indicators	a, m	c, h	t, g	p, e
Federal Reserve Board**	d	c, h	t	e
Federal Reserve Bulletin	a, m, w	c	t	p
Financial Digest	d	c	t	p
First Union	m	c, h	t	e
Forecast	q	c, f	t	p
FRB Chicago*	d, w	c, h	t	e
FRB Dallas	m	c, h	t	e
FRED	w, m	c, h	t	e
International Economic Scoreboard	a	f	t	p
International Financial Statistics	a	q	t	p
Investor's Business Daily	d	c, h	g	p
Moody's Bond Record	m	c	g	p
Mutual Funds Update	m	c	t	p
New York Times	d	c	t	p
Real Estate Outlook	a, q	c, h	t	p
Recession Recovery Watch	q	c	g	p
Selected Interest Rates	m, w	c	t	p
S&P Basic Statistics - Banking and Finance	a, m	h	t	p
S&P Creditweek	m	h	g	p
S&P Current Statistics	m	h	t	p
Statistical Abstract	a	h	t	p
Survey of Current Business	a, m	c, h	t, g	p, e
Treasury Bulletin	m	c	g	p
USA Today	d	c	t	p
Value Line Investment Survey, Part 2: Selection and Opinion	a, q	c, h, f	t	p

Source	Frequency	Extent	Form	Medium
Wall Street Journal	d	c	t	p

*Secondary market; **Both initial sale and secondary market.

Bibliography

A Guide to Buying Treasury Securities, Federal Reserve Bank of San Francisco, San Francisco, Sept. 1996.

Bureau of the Public Debt, *Buying Treasury Securities*, Department of the Treasury, Washington, D.C., 1995.

Bureau of the Public Debt, *Information about Marketable Treasury Securities (Bills, Notes, and Bonds)*, Department of the Treasury, Washington, D.C., 1991.

Bureau of the Public Debt, T-Bills, Notes, & Bonds Online, www.publicdebt. treas.gov/sec/sec.htm, visited July 17, 1999.

Hoel, Arline Alchian; Kenneth W. Clarkson; and Roger LeRoy Miller, *Economics Sourcebook of Government Statistics*, Lexington Books, Lexington, Mass., 1983, pp. 160-162.

Joint Economic Committee, *1980 Supplement to Economic Indicators, Historical and Descriptive Background*, USGPO, Washington, D.C., 1980, p. 108.

Munn, Glenn G.; F. L. Garcia; and Charles J. Woelfel, *Encyclopedia of Banking and Finance*, 9th ed., Bankers Publishing, Rolling Meadows, Ill., 1991.

Nelson, C. R., *The Investor's Guide to Economic Indicators*, John Wiley & Sons, New York, 1987, pp. 42-43.

Publication Services, *The Federal Reserve System: Purposes and Functions*, Board of Governors of the Federal Reserve System, Washington, D.C., 1994, pp. 35-39.

Ray, Christina I., *The Bond Market: Trading and Risk Management*, Business One Irwin, Homewood, Ill., 1993, pp. 13-17.

TICK

A measure of the robustness of the stock market.

Periodically on a stock exchange, the most recent change in price of each stock is considered. The number of changes that reflect a decrease in price is deducted from the number of changes that reflect an increase in price to produce the TICK. Closing TICKs are calculated for all the stocks listed on the New York Stock Exchange, all the stocks listed on the American Stock Exchange, and for the stocks in the Dow Jones Industrial Average. A high positive value for a closing TICK is generally assumed to indicate a strong market near the close, and a negative value to indicate a weak market. The TICK is calculated for the stocks on the New York Stock Exchange throughout the day and is included among the other quotation data from the exchange.

Used as an indicator of the stock markets direction in the near-term future. Issued at least daily as a news release by each of the stock markets.

Source	Frequency	Extent	Form	Medium
Wall Street Journal	d	c	t	p

Bibliography

Berlin, Howard M. *The Handbook of Financial Market Indexes, Averages, and Indicators*, Dow Jones-Irwin, Homewood, Ill., 1990, pp. 228-229.

Colby, Robert W., and Thomas A. Meyers, *The Encyclopedia of Technical Market Indicators*, Dow Jones-Irwin, Homewood, Ill., 1988, p. 493.

Total Private Investment
[See Gross Private Domestic Investment]

Total Unemployment
[See also Long-Duration Unemployment, Unemployment Insurance Programs, Initial Claims, and Unemployment Rate, Total]

An estimate of the number of unemployed persons in the United States during a given month.

The total civilian labor force is estimated from decennial census figures and more-frequent benchmarks. Unemployment among this population is estimated from the Current Population Survey, a monthly survey of a sample that includes about 47,000 households nationwide. Employment of the members of the households is determined for the week that includes the twelfth day of the month. To be counted as unemployed, a person has to be 16 years of age or older and actively seeking work or awaiting recall to a position from which he or she had been laid off. The surveyed population includes the military and inmates of penal, welfare, and health institutions. All data are seasonally adjusted. The estimated total unemployment is then calculated from the perceived unemployment rate and the size of the labor force; it is expressed as a percentage of the civilian labor force. Since 1994, total unemployment has been one (U-3) of six measures of unemployment derived from the Current Population Survey:

U-1 Persons unemployed 15 weeks or longer

U-2 Job losers and persons who completed temporary jobs

U-3 Total unemployed persons

U-4 Total unemployed persons plus discouraged workers

U-5 Total unemployed persons plus discouraged workers plus all other "marginally attached" workers

U-6 Total unemployed persons plus all "marginally attached" workers plus all persons employed part time for economic reasons

Used as a major and highly current indicator of the general state of the U.S. economy, of the present activity in the manufacturing and commercial sectors of the economy, and as a predictor of the near-term to midterm sales of consumer goods and availability of money for saving. Inversely related to general business fluctua-tions, it is a leading indicator at peaks and a lagging indicator at troughs.

Published monthly by the U.S. Department of Labor, Bureau of Labor Statistics, in *The Employment Situation.*

Source	Frequency	Extent	Form	Medium
Agricultural Outlook	a, q	c	t	p
Annual Statistical Digest (FRB)	a, m	c	t	p
Barrons	m	c	t	p
BCI	m	h	g	e
BLS	m	c, h	t	e
Business Statistics	a	h	t	p
Economic Indicators	a, m	c, h	t, g	p, e
Economic Report of the President	a	h	t	p, e
Employment & Earnings	a, m	c, h	t	p
The Employment Situation	m	c	t	p
Federal Reserve Bulletin	a, m	c	t	p
Monthly Labor Review	a, m	c, h	t	p
S&P Basic Statistics - Production Indexes and Labor Statistics	a, m	h	t	p
S&P Current Statistics	m	h	t	p
Statistical Abstract	a	h	t	p
Stat-USA	m	c	t	e
Survey of Current Business	a, m	c	t	p, e

Bibliography

Bregger, John E., "BLS Introduces New Range of Alternative Unemployment Measures," *Monthly Labor Review* **118** (10) 19-26 (1995).

Bregger, John E., "Unemployment Statistics and What They Mean," *Monthly Labor Review* **94** (11), 22-29 (1971).

Bregger, John E., and Cathryn Dippo, "Why Is It Necessary to Change?" *Monthly Labor Review* **116** (9) 3-9 (1993).

Frumkin, Norman, *Guide to Economic Indicators*, 2nd ed., M. E. Sharpe, Armonk, N.Y., 1994, pp. 287-294.

Frumkin, Norman, *Tracking America's Economy*, 2nd ed., Sharpe, Armonk, N.Y., 1992, pp. 177-197.

Green, Gloria P., "Measuring Total and State Insured Unemployment," *Monthly Labor Review* **94** (6), 37-48 (1971).

Moore, Geoffrey Hoyt, *Improving the Presentation of Employment and Unemployment Statistics*, National Commission on Employment and Unemployment Statistics Background Paper No. 22, USGPO, Washington, D.C., 1978.

National Bureau of Economic Research, *The Measurement and Behavior of Unemployment*, Princeton Univ. Press, Princeton, N.J., 1957.1983.

National Commission on Employment and Unemployment Statistics, Counting the Labor Force, National Commission on Employment and Unemployment Statistics, Washington, D.C., 1978.

Norwood, Janet L., "The Statistics Corner: Interpreting the Unemployment Statistics," *Business Economics* **28** (1), 56-60 (1993).

Ruggles, Richard, *Employment and Unemployment Statistics as Indexes of Economic Activity and Capacity Utilization*, National Commission on Employment and Unemployment Statistics Background Paper No. 28, USGPO, Washington, D.C., 1979.

Shiskin, Julius, "Employment and Unemployment: The Doughnut or the Hole," *Monthly Labor Review*, 3-10 (Feb. 1976).

Shiskin, Julius, *Labor Force and Unemployment*, BLS Rept. 486, U.S. Department of Labor, Washington, D.C., 1976.

U.S. Department of Labor, Bureau of Labor Statistics, *How the Government Measures Unemployment*, Rept. 505, U.S. Department of Labor, Washington, D.C., 1977.

U.S. Department of Labor, Bureau of Labor Statistics, *State and Local Area Estimates of Employment and Unemployment*, Lecture Notes in Statistics, No. 108, Springer-Verlag, New York (1996).

U.S. Department of Labor, Bureau of Labor Statistics, *Workers, Jobs, and Statistics*, Rept. 698, U.S. Department of Labor, Washington, D.C.

U.S. Department of Labor, Bureau of Labor Statistics, *Major Programs of the Bureau of Labor Statistics*, USGPO, Washington, D.C., 1994, pp. 4-5.

Wolfbein, Seymour L., *Employment and Unemployment in the United States*, Science Research Assoc., Chicago, 1964.

Trade in Goods and Services
[See Balance of Payments, Current Account; Exports; and Imports]

Trade-Weighted Dollar
[See Federal Reserve Trade-Weighted Dollar]

Treasury Bills
[See Three-Month Treasury Bills and Six-Month Treasury Bills]

Treasury Bonds
[See Lehman Brothers Long Treasury Bond Index and Thirty-Year Treasury Bonds]

Treasury Yield Curve
The interest rates of all outstanding debt instruments of the U.S. Treasury plotted against the maturities of each of those instruments.

Each day, the yields for each type of Treasury debt instrument is calculated from its price on the primary or secondary market. Those yields are then plotted against the maturities of their respective bills, notes, or bonds.

Used to visualize the relationship between maturity and interest rate. Normally, longer maturities carry more uncertainty and thus higher rates. However, a flat yield curve indicates a period of unchanging interest rates, and a negative yield curve indicates a period of lower interest rates ahead and (often) a period of lower inflation and increased economic activity.

Published daily by Technical Data in *Bond Data*.

Source	Frequency	Extent	Form	Medium
Barrons	w	c	g	p
Bloomberg	h	c	t, g	e
First Union	m	c, h	t	e
Investor's Business Daily	d	c	g	p
Stat-USA	d	c, h	t	e
Value Line Investment Survey, Part 2: Selection and Opinion	w	c	g	p
Wall Street Journal	d	c	g	p

Bibliography

Dueler, Michael K., "Strengthening the Case for the Yield Curve as a Predictor of U.S. Recessions," *Federal Reserve Bank of St. Louis Review* **79** (2) 41-50 (Mar.-Apr. 1997).

Dziwura, Joseph R., and Eric M. Green, *Interest Rate Expectations and the Shape of the Yield Curve*, Research Paper 9631, Federal Reserve Bank of New York, New York, 1996.

Estrella, Arturo, and Frederic S. Mishkin, "Predicting U.S. Recessions: Financial Variables as Leading Indicators," *Review of Economics and Statistics* **80** (1), 45-61 (Feb. 1998).

Fleming, Michael J., and Eli M. Remolona, *What Moves the Bond Market?*, Research Paper 9706, Federal Reserve Bank of New York, New York, 1997.

Lehmann, Michael B., *The Business One Irwin Guide to Using the Wall Street Journal*, 5th ed., Irwin, Chicago, 1996, pp. 270, 301-302.

Publication Services, *The Federal Reserve System: Purposes and Functions*, Board of Governors of the Federal Reserve System, Washington, D.C., 1994, pp. 30-31.

Ray, Christina I., *The Bond Market: Trading and Risk Management*, Business One Irwin, Homewood, Ill., 1993, pp. 255-287.

TRIN

[See Short-Term Trading Index]

Truck Sales
[See also Auto and Light Truck Sales]
Monthly sales of trucks by manufacturers in the United States.

The American Automobile Manufacturers Association surveys the industry monthly. Some small producers are not included in the survey. The numbers of factory and retail sales that month of trucks, buses, diesel trucks, and light trucks are reported. Data include sales, production, and exports. Sales data are grouped by gross vehicle weight. Data are subsequently seasonally adjusted by the U.S. Department of Commerce, Bureau of Economic Analysis.

Used as an indicator of capital-goods investment and of the strength of the transportation sector of the economy.

Published quarterly in the AAMA's *Economic Indicators*.

Source	Frequency	Extent	Form	Medium
AAMA	q, a	c, h	t	e
Business Statistics	a	h	t	p
Commercial Carrier Journal	a	h	t	p
Motor Vehicle Facts and Figures	a	h	t	p
S&P Basic Statistics - Transportation*	a	h	t	p
Statistical Abstract	a	h	t	p
World Motor Vehicle Data	a	h	t	p

*Truck production only.

Bibliography
Niemira, Michael P., and Gerald F. Zukowski, *Trading the Fundamentals: The Trader's Guide to Interpreting Economic Indicators and Monetary Policy*, McGraw-Hill, New York, 1998, pp. 25-30.

Rogers, R. Mark, *Handbook of Key Economic Indicators*, Irwin Professional Pub., Burr Ridge, Ill., 1994, p. 78.

Slater, Courtenay M., Ed., Business Statistics of the United States, 1995 ed., Bernan Press, Lanham, Md., 1996, p. 271.

U.S. Department of Commerce, Bureau of Economic Analysis, *Business Statistics, 1963-91*, USGPO, Washington, D.C., 1992, pp. 191-192.

Tuesday Index of Spot Market Prices
[See Bridge-CRB Index]

Twenty-Six-Week Treasury Bills
[See Six-Month Treasury Bills]

U

Unemployment
[See Long-Duration Unemployment; Total Unemployment; Unemployment Insurance Programs, Initial Claims; and Unemployment Rate, Total]

Unemployment Insurance Programs, Initial Claims
[See also Long-Duration Unemployment; Total Unemployment; and Unemployment Rate, Total]

A measure of unemployment among workers covered by the employment-security programs of the Employment and Training Administration (ETA) of the Department of Labor. The figures give the number of certified workers filing claims for having been totally or partially unemployed during the previous week and those requesting a determination of eligibility. These data cover beneficiaries of state programs, the program of federal-state extended-unemployment compensation, the program for federal employees, the ex-servicemen's unemployment-compensation program, veteran's benefit programs, and temporary unemployment programs. Reported as the insured unemployment under state programs, initial claims under state programs, insured unemployment under all regular programs, and special unemployment benefit claims.

Completed weeks of unemployment for which benefits are claimed are reported by the state employment security agencies and the Railroad Retirement Board to the ETA weekly. These figures are summed and seasonally adjusted. Initial claims (requests for a determination of eligibility) are also reported to and listed by the ETA, but they are not added into the tally of unemployed because they do not represent certified unemployed to whom benefits are paid. Monthly data are averages of the weekly data.

Used as a major and highly current indicator of the general state of the U.S. economy, of the present activity in the manufacturing and commercial sectors of the economy, and as a predictor of the near-term to midterm sales of consumer goods and the availability of money for saving; a component of the Leading Indicators Composite Index.

Published weekly by the U.S. Department of Labor, Employment and Training Administration, in *Unemployment Insurance Claims*.

Source	Frequency	Extent	Form	Medium
Bank of America	m	c, h	t	e
Bank of Tokyo-Mitsubishi	w	c, h	t	e
Barron's	w	c	t	p
BCI	m	h	g	e
Business Statistics	a	h	t	p
Economic Indicators	a, m	c, h	t	p, e
Economic Report of the President	a	h	t	p, e
First Union	m	c, h	t	e
Quote.com	m	c	t	e
S&P Basic Statistics - Income and Trade	a	h	t	p
Statistical Abstract	a	h	t	p
Stat-USA	m	c	t	e
Unemployment Insurance Claims	a, w	c, h	t, g	p
Unemployment Insurance Weekly Claims Report	w	c	t	p
Value Line Investment Survey, Part 2: Selection and Opinion	a	h	g	p

Bibliography

Frumkin, Norman, *Tracking America's Economy*, 2nd ed., Sharpe, Armonk, N.Y., 1992, pp. 182-186.

Grant, John, *A Handbook of Economic Indicators*, University of Toronto Press, Toronto, 1992, pp. 147-148.

Green, Gloria P., "Comparing Total and State Insured Unemployment," *Monthly Labor Review* **94** (6), 37-48 (June 1971).

Joint Economic Committee, *1980 Supplement to Economic Indicators, Historical and Descriptive Background*, USGPO, Washington, D.C., 1980.

Moore, Geoffrey Hoyt, *Improving the Presentation of Employment and Unemployment Statistics*, National Commission on Employment and Unemployment Statistics Background Paper No. 22, USGPO, Washington, D.C., 1978.

Moore, Geoffrey Hoyt, and Melita H. Moore, *International Economic Indicators: A Sourcebook*, Greenwood Press, Westport, Conn., 1985.

National Bureau of Economic Research, *The Measurement and Behavior of Unemployment*, Princeton Univ. Press, Princeton, N.J., 1957.

Nelson, C. R., *The Investor's Guide to Economic Indicators*, John Wiley & Sons, New York, 1987, pp. 112, 114-115.

Niemira, Michael P., and Gerald F. Zukowski, *Trading the Fundamentals: The Trader's Guide to Interpreting Economic Indicators and Monetary Policy*, McGraw-Hill, New York, 1998, pp. 221-226.

Renshaw, Edward, Ed., *The Practical Forecasters' Almanac: 137 Reliable Indicators for Investors, Hedgers, and Speculators*, Business One Irwin, Homewood, Ill., 1992, p. 32.

Ruggles, Richard, *Employment and Unemployment Statistics as Indexes of Economic Activity and Capacity Utilization*, National Commission on Employment and Unemployment Statistics Background Paper No. 28, USGPO, Washington, D.C., 1979.

Shiskin, Julius, *Labor Force and Unemployment*, BLS Rept. 486, U.S. Department of Labor, Washington, D.C., 1976.

Tainer, Evelina M., *Using Economic Indicators to Improve Investment Analysis*, John Wiley & Sons, New York, 1993, pp. 200-203.

U.S. Department of Commerce, Bureau of Economic Analysis, *Business Statistics 1963-1993*, USGPO, Washington, D.C., 1994.

WEFA Group, *Guide to Economic Indicators: U.S. Macroeconomic Services*, WEFA Group, Bala Cynwyd, Pa., 1997, p. 27.

Unemployment Rate
[See Unemployment Rate, Total]

Unemployment Rate, 15 Weeks and Over
[See Long-Duration Unemployment]

Unemployment Rate, Total
[See also **Long-Duration Unemployment; Total Unemployment; and Unemployment Insurance Programs, Initial Claims**]

An estimate of the percentage of the U.S. workforce that is unemployed during a given month.

The total civilian labor force is estimated from decennial census figures and more-frequent benchmarks. Unemployment among this population is estimated from monthly surveys of a sample that includes 47,000 households nationwide. Employment of the members of the households is determined for the week that includes the twelfth day of the month. To be counted as unemployed, a person has to be 16 years of age or older and actively seeking work or awaiting recall to a position from which he or she has been laid off. The surveyed population includes the military and inmates of penal, welfare, and health institutions. All data are seasonally adjusted. The percentage of unemployment is then calculated from the survey results for the total population and for groups of the population according to sex, age, and race.

Used as a major and highly current indicator of the general state of the U.S. economy, as an indicator of the present activity in the manufacturing and commercial sectors of the economy, and as a predictor of the near-term to midterm sales of consumer goods and availability of money for saving. The unemployment rate is inversely related to general business fluctuations.

Published monthly by the U.S. Department of Labor, Bureau of Labor Statistics, in *The Employment Situation.*

Source	Frequency	Extent	Form	Medium
Agricultural Outlook	a, q	c	t	p
Annual Statistical Digest (FRB)	a, m	c	t	p
Bank of America	q	f	t	e
Barron's	m	c	t	p
BLS	m	c, h	t	e
Business Statistics	a	h	t	p
Confidence and Buying Plans	m	h	g	p
Economic Handbook of the Machine Tool Industry	a	h	g	p
Economic Indicators	a, m	c, h	t	p, e
Economic Report of the President	a	h	t	p, e
Employment & Earnings	a, m	c, h	t	p
The Employment Situation	a, m	c	t, g	p
Federal Reserve Bulletin	a, m	c	t	p
Financial Digest	m	c	t	p
First Union	m	c, h	t	e
Forecast	q	c, f	t	p
FRB Dallas	m	c, h	t	e
FRED	m	c, h	t	e
Handbook of International Economic Statistics (CIA)	a	h (c)	t	p (e)
International Economic Review	a, q, m	c	t	p
International Economic Scoreboard	a	f	t	p
International Financial Statistics	a, q	c, h	t	p
Monthly Labor Review	a, q, m	c, h	t	p
Mortgage Banking	m	c	t	p

Source	Frequency	Extent	Form	Medium
Quote.com	m	c	t	e
Real Estate Outlook	a, q, m	c, h	t	p
Recession Recovery Watch	q	h	g	p
Securities Industry Yearbook	a	h	t	p
S&P Basic Statistics - Production Indexes and Labor Statistics	a, m	h	t	p
S&P Current Statistics	m	h	t	p
Statistical Abstract	a	h	t	p
Survey of Current Business	a, m	c, h	t, g	p, e
Treasury Bulletin	m	c	g	p
Value Line Investment Survey, Part 2: Selection and Opinion	a, q	c, h, f	t	p
World Financial Markets	a, q	c	t	p

Bibliography

Cain, Glen G., "The Unemployment Rate as an Economic Indicator," *Monthly Labor Review* **102** (3), 24-35 (March 1979).

Counting the Labor Force, National Commission on Employment and Unemployment Statistics, Washington, D.C., 1978.

Frumkin, Norman, *Guide to Economic Indicators*, 2nd ed., M. E. Sharpe, Armonk, N.Y., 1994, pp. 287-294.

Frumkin, Norman, *Tracking America's Economy*, 2nd ed., Sharpe, Armonk, N.Y., 1992, pp. 178-197.

Green, Gloria P., "Measuring Total and State Insured Unemployment," *Monthly Labor Review* 94 (6), 37-48 (June 1971).

Moore, Geoffrey Hoyt, *Improving the Presentation of Employment and Unemployment Statistics*, National Commission on Employment and Unemployment Statistics Background Paper No. 22, USGPO, Washington, D.C., 1978.

Moore, Geoffrey Hoyt, and Melita H. Moore, *International Economic Indicators: A Sourcebook*, Greenwood Press, Westport, Conn., 1985, pp. 38-39.

Niemira, Michael P., and Gerald F. Zukowski, *Trading the Fundamentals: The Trader's Guide to Interpreting Economic Indicators and Monetary Policy*, McGraw-Hill, New York, 1998, pp. 79-80.

Renshaw, Edward, Ed., *The Practical Forecasters' Almanac: 137 Reliable Indicators for Investors, Hedgers, and Speculators*, Business One Irwin, Homewood, Ill., 1992, pp. 31-32, 83-84.

Ruggles, Richard, *Employment and Unemployment Statistics as Indexes of Economic Activity and Capacity Utilization*, National Commission on

Employment and Unemployment Statistics Background Paper No. 28, USGPO, Washington, D.C., 1979.

Shiskin, Julius, "Employment and Unemployment: The Doughnut or the Hole," *Monthly Labor Review*, **99** (2), 3-10 (Feb. 1976).

Shiskin, Julius, *Labor Force and Unemployment*, BLS Rept. 486, U.S. Department of Labor, Washington, D.C., 1976.

Tainer, Evelina M., *Using Economic Indicators to Improve Investment Analysis*, John Wiley & Sons, New York, 1993, pp. 204-210.

U.S. Department of Labor, Bureau of Labor Statistics, *BLS Handbook of Methods*, Bull. 2490, USGPO, Washington, D.C., 1997, pp. 4-14, 36-41.

U.S. Department of Labor, Bureau of Labor Statistics, *How the Government Measures Unemployment*, Rept. 864, U.S. Department of Labor, Washington, D.C., 1994.

U.S. Department of Labor, Bureau of Labor Statistics, *Major Programs of the Bureau of Labor Statistics*, USGPO, Washington, D.C., 1994, pp. 3-4.

U.S. Department of Labor, Bureau of Labor Statistics, *Workers, Jobs, and Statistics*, Rept. 698, U.S. Department of Labor, Washington, D.C., 1983.

Unfilled Orders
[See Manufacturers' Unfilled Orders]

Unit Labor Costs

An estimate of the wages and salaries expended in producing an average unit in the private business sector.

Compensation-per-hour data are taken from the national accounts of the Bureau of Economic Analysis and are adjusted by the Bureau of Labor Statistics to include an estimate of the wages, salaries, and supplements of proprietors. An index of this measure (compensation per hour) is then divided by an index of the output per hour (output per hour of all persons) to calculate the unit labor cost. The estimates are divided into contributions from the nonfarm business sector and the total private business sector and expressed as indexes to a base year.

Used as a gauge of inflation and of the contribution of wages to the costs of production and in the calculation of productivity of industry and its workforce.

Published annually by the Bureau of Labor Statistics as a news release and in the *Monthly Labor Review*.

Source	Frequency	Extent	Form	Medium
BCI	m	h	g	e
BLS	q	c, h	t	e
Economic Indicators	a, q	h	t	p, e
FRED	m	c, h	t	e
Productivity and Costs	a, q	c	t	p

Source	Frequency	Extent	Form	Medium
Recession Recovery Watch	q	h	g	p
Statistical Abstract	a	h	t	p
Survey of Current Business	a, m	c	t	p, e

Bibliography

Caves, Douglas W.; Laurits R. Christensen; and W. Erwin Diewert, "The Economic Theory of Index Numbers and the Measurement of Input, Output, and Productivity," *Econometrica* 50 (6), 1393-1414 (1983).

Frumkin, Norman, *Guide to Economic Indicators*, 2nd ed., M. E. Sharpe, Armonk, N.Y., 1994, pp. 231-235.

Joint Economic Committee, *1980 Supplement to Economic Indicators, Historical and Descriptive Background*, USGPO, Washington, D.C., 1980, pp. 51-54.

Lehmann, Michael B., *The Irwin Guide to Using the Wall Street Journal*, 5th ed., Irwin, Chicago, 1996, p. 113.

Niemira, Michael P., and Gerald F. Zukowski, *Trading the Fundamentals: The Trader's Guide to Interpreting Economic Indicators and Monetary Policy*, McGraw-Hill, New York, 1998, pp. 205-229.

U.S. Department of Labor, Bureau of Labor Statistics, *BLS Handbook of Methods*, Bull. 2490, USGPO, Washington, D.C., 1997, pp. 89-109.

U.S. Department of Labor, Bureau of Labor Statistics, *Major Programs of the Bureau of Labor Statistics*, USGPO, Washington, D.C., 1994, pp. 29-30.

United States Balance of Payments
[See Balance of Payments, Current Account]

United States Commerce Department Composite Construction Cost Index
[See Composite Construction Price Index]

United States Dollar
[See Federal Reserve Trade-Weighted Dollar and Morgan Guaranty Index]

United States Dollar Index
[See FINEX U.S. Dollar Index]

United States International Trade in Goods and Services
[See Balance of Trade; Balance of Payments, Current Account; Exports; and Imports]

United States International Transactions

A summary of economic transactions between the residents of the United States and the residents of the rest of the world.

International transactions are divided into current accounts and capital accounts. The current accounts include tabulations of merchandise imports and exports, investment receipts and payments, net military transactions, net travel and transportation receipts, the net of other services, and unilateral transfers (such as transfers, government grants, remittances, and pensions). The capital accounts are divided into the broad categories of U.S. assets abroad and foreign assets in the United States. The U.S. assets abroad are subdivided into official reserves (gold, special drawing rights, convertible currencies, and the U.S. reserve position in the International Monetary Fund), other U.S. Government assets, and private assets. Foreign assets in the United States are subdivided into the assets of foreign official agencies and other foreign assets. Data on allocations of special drawing rights, the statistical discrepancy, and the value of the stock of U.S. official reserve assets at the end of the period are also included. Data for this indicator come from a broad range of sources. Data on merchandise imports and exports are received from the Bureau of the Census and are adjusted for coverage, valuation, and timing. U.S. companies with branches abroad provide quarterly reports of international transactions. Investments abroad and foreign investments in the United States are determined from benchmark surveys. The foreign transactions of U.S. Government agencies including grants, loans, purchases, and sales are directly reported. Reports are received from U.S. and foreign shipping lines and financial data from the Maritime Administration. U.S. travelers are surveyed about their expenditures abroad, and these data are compared with and supplemented by travel statistics from the Immigration and Naturalization Service. Reports on international claims and liabilities are received from the Treasury Department. All of these data are supplemented with data from questionnaires and government administrative data. The components of the data are expressed in billions of current dollars and seasonally adjusted if they display significant seasonal variation.

Used to assess the international financial position of the United States and to compare that position with the economic strengths and weaknesses of other countries.

Published quarterly by the U.S. Department of Commerce, Bureau of Economic Analysis, in *Survey of Current Business*.

Source	Frequency	Extent	Form	Medium
Annual Statistical Digest (FRB)	a, q	c	t	p
BEA	q	c, h	t	e
Economic Indicators	a, q	c, h	t, g	p, e
Economic Report of the President	a	h	t	p, e
Statistical Abstract	a	h	t	p

Source	Frequency	Extent	Form	Medium
Survey of Current Business	q	c, h	t	p, e

Bibliography

Hoel, Arline Alchian; Kenneth W. Clarkson; and Roger LeRoy Miller, *Economics Sourcebook of Government Statistics*, Lexington Books, Lexington, Mass., 1983, pp. 207-209.

Joint Economic Committee, *1980 Supplement to Economic Indicators, Historical and Descriptive Background*, USGPO, Washington, D.C., 1980.

Plocek, Joseph E., *Economic Indicators: How America Reads Its Financial Health*, New York Institute of Finance, New York, 1991.

Rogers, R. Mark, *Handbook of Key Economic Indicators*, Irwin Professional Pub., Burr Ridge, Ill., 1994, pp. 172-190.

United States Merchandise Exports
[See Exports]

United States Merchandise Imports
[See Imports]

United States Trade in Goods and Services
[See Balance of Payments, Exports, and Imports]

United States Treasury Bills and Bonds
[See Six-Month Treasury Bills, Thirty-Year Treasury Bonds, and Three-Month Treasury Bills]

USA Today Internet 100 Index

A measurement of the aggregate movement in the stock prices of Internet-related companies.

Editors and reporters from *USA Today* selected 100 U.S. companies that (1) derived at least half their revenues from Internet-related business; (2) conducted the majority of their business in the United States; and (3) in June 1999, had a share price of at least $12 and a market capitalization of at least $200 million. A capitalization-weighted index of these companies' share prices is calculated by multiplying each company's share price by its number of shares outstanding. The results are totaled, and the sum is divided by that value for June 30, 1999, and multiplied by 100. As a result, variations in the share prices of larger-capitalized companies will have a disproportionate influence on the index. The companies in the index include online retailers, online financial services, Internet-content developers, telecommunication companies, Web hosts, Internet-hardware suppliers, consultants, software developers, and online marketers. The list of companies is reviewed quarterly to ensure that limits on share price and capitalization have not been broached and to replace companies that no longer operate because of bankruptcy or merger. The index has two subindexes: the e-Consumer 50, which is made up of 50 companies that serve consumers directly, and the e-Business 50, which is made up of another 50 companies that support in some way the Internet's commercial development.

Used to judge market trends in the online-business sector, to compare the performance of individual companies' stocks to that of their peers, and to assess how much of an individual stock's price performance stems from broad market movements.

Calculated daily by Media General Financial Services and published in *USA Today*.

Source	Frequency	Extent	Form	Medium
USA Today	d	c	t	p, e

Bibliography

Smith, Elliot Blair, "New Index Measures Wide Range of Net Stocks," *USA Today*, p. 3B (Aug. 9, 1999).

V-Z

Value Line Arithmetic Composite Average

An equally weighted average of the prices of the stocks regularly reviewed in *The Value Line Investment Survey*, indexed to a base value.

Each market day, the closing prices of roughly 1700 stocks are surveyed. Of those stocks, about 75% are traded on the New York Stock Exchange, 20% on NASDAQ, and 5% on the American Stock Exchange. Each stock's closing price is divided by its preceding-day's close, with the preceding-day value indexed to a base value of 100 for June 30, 1961. Those resulting indices of daily change are then arithmetically averaged. The preceding-day's prices are adjusted to reflect any stock splits or dividends, and the present-day's average is then multiplied by the value of the average for the preceding day to get the latest value. As stocks are added to or dropped from the survey, the average is enlarged or decreased accordingly.

Used to estimate (1) the price strength of a particular stock relative to the overall performance of the market and (2) the relative price strength of an industry and as an overall gauge of the small-capitalization stock sector. Also used as the basis for stock-index futures contracts traded on the Kansas City Board of Trade.

Published weekly by Value Line, Inc., in the *Value Line Investment Survey* and issued daily as a press release.

Source	Frequency	Extent	Form	Medium
Barron's	d	c	t	p
CBS	h	c	t	e
New York Times	d	c	t	p
Securities Industry Yearbook	a	h	t	p
StockMaster	d	c, h	g, t	e
USA Today	h	c	t	e

Source	Frequency	Extent	Form	Medium
Value Line Investment Survey, Part 2: Selection and Opinion	d	c	t	p

Bibliography
Berlin, Howard M. *The Handbook of Financial Market Indexes, Averages, and Indicators*, Dow Jones-Irwin, Homewood, Ill., 1990, pp. 65-66.
How to Invest in Common Stocks, Value Line Publishing, New York, 1996, p. 49.
"ValueLine," www.valueline.com, visited July 17, 1999.

Value Line Geometric Composite Average

An equally weighted geometric average of the prices of the stocks regularly reviewed in *The Value Line Investment Survey*, indexed to a base value.

Each market day, the closing prices of roughly 1700 stocks are surveyed. Of those stocks, about 75% are traded on the New York Stock Exchange, 20% on the NASDAQ system, and 5% on the American Stock Exchange. Each stock's closing price is divided by its preceding-day's close, with the preceding-day value indexed to a base value of 100 for June 30, 1961. Those resulting indices of daily change are then geometrically averaged; that is to say, the n indices of change are multiplied together, and the nth root of the product is taken. The preceding-day's prices are adjusted to reflect any stock splits or dividends, and the present-day's geometric average is then multiplied by the value of the average for the preceding day to get the latest value. As stocks are added to or dropped from the survey, the average is enlarged or decreased accordingly. The composite average is broken down into major categories (industrials, utilities, and rails), which are reported separately, and into about 150 subgroups.

Used to estimate (1) the price strength of a particular stock relative to the overall performance of the market and (2) the relative price strength of an industry and as an overall gauge of the small-capitalization stock sector.

Published weekly by Value Line, Inc., in the *Value Line Investment Survey* and issued daily as a press release.

Source	Frequency	Extent	Form	Medium
CBS	h	c	t	e
USA Today	h	c	t	e
Value Line Investment Survey, Part 2: Selection and Opinion	w, d	c	t, g	p
Wall Street Journal	d	c	t	p

Bibliography
Berlin, Howard M. *The Handbook of Financial Market Indexes, Averages, and Indicators*, Dow Jones-Irwin, Homewood, Ill., 1990, pp. 65-66.

Bernhard, Arnold, *Value Line Methods of Evaluating Common Stocks, Building and Maintaining a Portfolio*, Arnold Bernhard & Co., New York, 1979.
Hoel, Arline Alchian; Kenneth W. Clarkson; and Roger LeRoy Miller, *Economics Sourcebook of Government Statistics*, Lexington Books, Lexington, Mass., 1983, p. 158.
How to Invest in Common Stocks, Value Line Publishing, New York, 1996, p. 49.
"Market Guides," *Barron's*, 9+ (Sept. 26, 1966).
"ValueLine," www.valueline.com, visited July 17, 1999.

Value of Exports
[See Exports]

Value of Imports
[See Imports]

Value of New Construction Put in Place

An estimate of the dollar value of the construction work done on residential and nonresidential new buildings and of renovations to existing structures.

The construction cost of new one-unit houses is estimated each month by taking the data from the Census Bureau's surveys of housing authorized by building permits and of housing units started, adjusting it to compensate for construction not covered by permits, adjusting for undervaluation and fees not covered in permit valuations, and distributing the computed values over the coming months by applying fixed patterns of monthly construction progress. The value of new multiple-unit private residential buildings is directly measured from monthly progress reports from a sample of such projects started each month. Includes erection of new structures; additions and alterations to existing buildings; mechanical installations to upgrade existing structures; outside improvements; installation of specific major components of industrial buildings; certain appliances, when installed as part of the construction; all fixed, mainly site-fabricated equipment; land development; and structural changes made to a building to accommodate new equipment. The value of additions and alterations is obtained from quarterly surveys of owners of residences and of rental properties; monthly values are interpolated from the quarterly data. Nonresidential, nonfarm building values are estimated from data gathered by the Bureau of the Census from a sample of project contractors who are asked to report the value of work done each month until the project is completed. Nonresidential farm construction expenditures are obtained annually by the U.S. Department of Agriculture through its Farm Production Expenditures Survey; monthly values are imputed by smoothing the data over the years and linking it with seasonal factors. Values for the construction by public utilities are derived by interpolating annual data gathered by the Census Bureau for communications utilities and by regulatory agencies (such as the Interstate Commerce Commission) for electric, gas, railroad, and pipeline utilities.

All other private construction is estimated by adjusting the data reported by the F. W. Dodge Division of the McGraw-Hill Information Systems Company for additional costs not covered by the Dodge estimates, projects not covered by the survey, and geographical areas not covered. Federal construction expenditures are estimated from data reported to the Bureau of the Census by each federal agency for the fiscal year; these are prorated for each month. State and local governments' expenditures are estimated from progress reports solicited from a sample of such projects. The monthly values derived are converted to constant dollars by applying different cost indexes that have been derived for each category of construction.

Used in short-term cyclical and long-term growth analyses; used to estimate the current volume of the economic activity in this segment of the U.S. economy, which represents about 7% of the Gross Domestic Product and has an important impact on employment in the construction and building-materials industries and on additions to capital stocks of structures in the private and public sectors.

Published monthly by the U.S. Department of Commerce, Bureau of the Census, in a press release and (two weeks later) in *Value of New Construction Put in Place*, Current Construction Report C30.

Source	Frequency	Extent	Form	Medium
Annual Statistical Digest (FRB)	m	c	t	p
Bank of America	m	c, h	t	e
Bank of Tokyo-Mitsubishi	m	c, h	t	e
Business Statistics	a	h	t	p
Construction Review	a, m	c, h	t, g	p
Economic Indicators	a, m	c, h	t	p, e
ENR [4th issue of month]	m	c	t	p
Federal Reserve Bulletin	a, m	c	t	p
Financial Digest	m	c	t	p
Mortgage Banking	m	c	t	p
S&P Basic Statistics - Building and Building Materials	a	h	t	p
S&P Current Statistics	m	h	t	p
Statistical Abstract	a	h	t	p
Survey of Current Business	a, m	c	t	p, e
US Census Bureau	m	c, h	t	e
Value of New Construction Put in Place (CCR C30)	a, m	c, h	t, g	p

Bibliography

Carnes, W. Stansbury, and Stephen D. Slifer, *The Atlas of Economic Indicators: A Visual Guide to Market Forces and the Federal Reserve*, HarperBusiness, New York, 1991, pp. 147-152.

Hoel, Arline Alchian; Kenneth W. Clarkson; and Roger LeRoy Miller, *Economics Sourcebook of Government Statistics*, Lexington Books, Lexington, Mass., 1983, p. 31.

Joint Economic Committee, *1980 Supplement to Economic Indicators, Historical and Descriptive Background*, USGPO, Washington, D.C., 1980, pp. 66-71.

"New Construction, Housing and Mobile Homes - A Look Ahead," *Construction Review*, 4 (Sept. 1971).

Niemira, Michael P., and Gerald F. Zukowski, *Trading the Fundamentals: The Trader's Guide to Interpreting Economic Indicators and Monetary Policy*, McGraw-Hill, New York, 1998, pp. 31-33.

Rogers, R. Mark, *Handbook of Key Economic Indicators*, Irwin Professional Pub., Burr Ridge, Ill., 1994, pp. 196-202.

Slater, Courtenay M., Ed., *Business Statistics of the United States*, 1995 ed., Bernan Press, Lanham, Md., 1996, p. 266.

Tainer, Evelina M., *Using Economic Indicators to Improve Investment Analysis*, John Wiley & Sons, New York, 1993, pp. 198-110.

U.S. Department of Commerce, Bureau of Economic Analysis, *Business Statistics, 1963-91*, USGPO, Washington, D.C., 1992, pp. 149-150.

"Value of New Construction Put in Place," www.census.gov/econ/www/co0300.html, visited July 17, 1999.

WEFA Group, *Guide to Economic Indicators: U.S. Macroeconomic Services*, WEFA Group, Bala Cynwyd, Pa., 1997, p. 7.

Value of the Dollar

[See Federal Reserve Trade-Weighted Dollar, FINEX U.S. Dollar Index, and Morgan Guaranty Index]

Velocity of Money

[Also called Income Velocity of Money; see also Flow of Funds Accounts]

The ratio of the income of the economy to the money supply; from another perspective, the number of times each dollar is spent in a unit of time.

The total income of the economy is taken from the Flow of Funds Accounts and divided by the total money supply. Different measures of income (e.g., Gross Domestic Product and Personal Income) and money supply (e.g., M1 and M2) are often used to assess the conditions and effects of different components of the monetary system. Economic growth is likely to increase in a year that follows one in which the velocity of money decreases from its value the year before but is likely to decrease when the velocity of money increases over its value the previous year.

Used as leading indicator of the pace of economic activity (as measured by the Gross National Product), as a leading indicator of changes in inflation (as measured by the Consumer Price Index), and in the formulation of monetary policy. Stability (or at least predictability) in the velocity of money is frequently considered necessary if monetary policy is to be effective.

No agency is specifically responsible for publishing this indicator. The data necessary to calculate the values of this indicator are published monthly in *Economic Indicators*. Current values of the indicator appear monthly in the *Survey of Current Business*. Historical values are available at www.globalexposure.com/index.html.

Source	Frequency	Extent	Form	Medium
BCI	m, q	h	g	e
Survey of Current Business	m	c, h	g	p, e

Bibliography

Darnay, Arsen J., *Economic Indicators Handbook: Time Series, Conversions, Documentation*, Gale Research, Detroit, 1992, p. 174.

Humphrey, Thomas M., "The Origins of Velocity Functions," *Federal Reserve Board of Richmond Economics Quarterly* **79**, 1-17 (1993).

Judd, John P., and Brian Motley, "The 'Great Velocity Decline' of 1982-83: A Comparative Analysis of M1 and M2," *Federal reserve Bank of San Francisco Economic Review*, 56-74 (Summer 1984).

Lorrado, Carol, and Paul A. Spindt, "The Measurement and Analysis of Monetary Transactions," *Journal of Economics and Business* **45**, 193-211 (1993).

Palivos, T., and P. Wang, "Money, Output, and Income Velocity," *Applied Economics* **27**, 1113-1125 (1995).

Publication Services, *The Federal Reserve System: Purposes and Functions*, Board of Governors of the Federal Reserve System, Washington, D.C., 1994, pp. 27-29.

Serletis, Apostolos, "Random Walks, Breaking Trend Functions, and the Chaotic Structure of the Velocity of Money," *Journal of Business and Economic Statistics* **13**, 453-458 (1995).

Wrightsman, Dwayne, "A New Leading Indicator of Booms and Busts and in Between," *Journal of Business Forecasting* **6** (3), 27-29 (1987).

Wrightsman, Dwayne, "Three Leading Indicators of Changes in Inflation," *Journal of Business Forecasting* **9** (3), 11-14 (1990).

Wrightsman, Dwayne, "Using Velocity to Forecast Changes in Resource Utilization," *Journal of Business Forecasting* **9** (1), 16-19 (1990).

Vendor Performance
[See Purchasing Managers' Index]

Volume Momentum
[See American Stock Exchange Volume Momentum]

Wages and Salaries in Mining, Manufacturing, and Construction
[See Average Hourly and Weekly Earnings]

Wall $treet Week Technical Market Index
[See Technical Market Index]

Weekly Chain Store Sales
[See Bank of Tokyo–Mitsubishi/Chain Store Age Weekly Leading Indicator of Chain Store Sales, Bank of Tokyo–Mitsubishi Chain Store Sales Index, and Bank of Tokyo–Mitsubishi/Schroders Weekly U.S. Retail Chain Store Sales Index]

Weekly Index of Chemical Prices
[See Chemical Week Price Index]

Wholesale Price Index
[See Producer Price Index]

Wholesale Trade
Estimates of wholesale sales (after deducting returns, allowances, discounts, and services to customers) by and inventories (at cost) owned by and available for sale from merchant wholesalers.

A sample of merchant wholesalers representing all kinds of wholesale-trade businesses is surveyed each month. The respondents provide dollar estimates of their sales and inventories. The sales and inventory data are adjusted for seasonal variation, and the sales data are also adjusted for trading-day variation.

Used by business, industry, and government to assess the aggregate performance of American business because the data reflect the level of economic activity at an intermediate stage of the distributive process. The data are also used in determining the Gross National Product.

Published monthly by the U.S. Department of Commerce, Bureau of the Census, in *Monthly Wholesale Trade Sales and Inventories*, Current Business Reports, BW.

Source	Frequency	Extent	Form	Medium
Barron's	m	c	t	p
Business Statistics	a	h	t	p
Monthly Wholesale Trade Sales and Inventories	a, m	c, h	t, g	p

Source	Frequency	Extent	Form	Medium
S&P Basic Statistics - Income and Trade	a	h	t	p
S&P Current Statistics	m	h	t	p
Statistical Abstract	a	h	t	p
US Census Bureau	m	c	t	e

Bibliography

Bureau of the Census, *Revised Monthly Retail Sales and Inventories: January 1967-December 1979*, Department of Commerce, Washington, D.C., 1980.

Hoel, Arline Alchian; Kenneth W. Clarkson; and Roger LeRoy Miller, *Economics Sourcebook of Government Statistics*, Lexington Books, Lexington, Mass., 1983, pp. 87-89.

Joint Economic Committee, *1980 Supplement to Economic Indicators, Historical and Descriptive Background*, USGPO, Washington, D.C., 1980, pp. 74-76.

Rogers, R. Mark, *Handbook of Key Economic Indicators*, Irwin Professional Pub., Burr Ridge, Ill., 1994, pp. 156-157.

U.S. Department of Commerce, Bureau of Economic Analysis, *Business Statistics 1963-1993*, USGPO, Washington, D.C., 1994.

WEFA Group, *Guide to Economic Indicators: U.S. Macroeconomic Services*, WEFA Group, Bala Cynwyd, Pa., 1997, p. 28.

Wilshire 4500 Equity Index

The total dollar value in billions of dollars of all actively traded common stocks in the United States less the equities included in the Standard and Poor 500.

The price per share of each stock actively traded on the New York Stock Exchange (about 58%), the American Stock Exchange (about 3%), and the NASDAQ system (about 40%) except for those listed on the Standard and Poor 500 is multiplied by the number of shares listed to give the market value of that stock. The market values of all (roughly) 6500 stocks are then summed, and the total is divided by the market value on the base date of Dec. 31, 1983. This quotient is then multiplied by the base value of the index. The resulting value is in billions of dollars rounded to two decimal places. Nonprice effects are eliminated by adjustments to the base-date market value. Monthly values are averages of daily values. The index is more volatile than other averages, such as the Dow Jones, because it includes smaller companies that are more susceptible to changes in valuation.

Used to measure portfolio performance, and to calculate the net increase or decrease in the value of the smaller end of the marketplace; also used as the basic portfolio of a large number of mutual funds.

Published daily by Wilshire Associates as a news release.

Bibliography

"Wilshire 4500 Fundamental Characteristics, June 1997" wilshire.com/home/products/w5stats.htm, visited Aug. 15, 1997.

"Wilshire Indexes" www.wilshire.com/indexes/all_descriptions.htm, visited
    Oct. 18, 1999.

Wilshire 5000 Equity Index
[Also called the Wilshire Total Market Value]
    The total dollar value in billions of dollars of all actively traded common
stocks in the United States.
    The price per share of each stock actively traded on the New York Stock
Exchange (about 80%), the American Stock Exchange (about 2%), and the
NASDAQ system (about 15%) is multiplied by the number of shares listed to give
the market value of that stock. The market values of all stocks are then summed,
and the total is divided by the market value on the base date of Dec. 31, 1980,
which was $1,404,596 billion. This quotient is then multiplied by the base value
of the index. The resulting value is in billions of dollars rounded to two decimal
places. Nonprice effects are eliminated by adjustments to the base-date market
value. Monthly values are averages of daily values. The index is more volatile than
other averages, such as the Dow Jones, because it includes smaller companies that
are more susceptible to changes in valuation. Four other indexes are also derived
from the Wilshire database: their Capital Weighted Price Index, Equal Weighted
Price Index, Capital Weighted Total Return Index, and Equal Weighted Total
Return Index.
    Used as a measure of the value of the U.S. equity marketplace, to measure
portfolio performance, and to calculate the net increase or decrease in the value of
the marketplace.
    Published daily by Wilshire Associates in a news release and on the World
Wide Web at wilshire.com/home/products/w5today.htm.

Source	Frequency	Extent	Form	Medium
Barron's	d	c	t	p
Bloomberg	h	c	t	e
First Union	m	c, h	t	e
Mutual Funds Update	d	c	t	p
New York Times	d	c	t	p
Statistical Abstract	a	h	t	p
USA Today	d	c	t	p
Wall Street Journal	d	c	t	p

Bibliography
Berlin, Howard M. *The Handbook of Financial Market Indexes, Averages, and
    Indicators*, Dow Jones-Irwin, Homewood, Ill., 1990.
Hoel, Arline Alchian; Kenneth W. Clarkson; and Roger LeRoy Miller, *Economics
    Sourcebook of Government Statistics*, Lexington Books, Lexington, Mass.,
    1983, pp. 158-159.

Pierce, Phyllis S. (Ed.), *The Irwin Investor's Handbook*, Irwin Professional Publishing, Burr Ridge, Ill, 1995, p. 70.
"The Least-Heralded Bull Market in History," *Forbes*, 37-38 (Oct. 13, 1980).
"Wilshire 5000 Fundamental Characteristics," wilshire.com/home/products/w5stats.htm, visited Aug. 15, 1997.
"Wilshire Indexes" www.wilshire.com/indexes/all_descriptions.htm, visited Oct. 18, 1999.

Wilshire Small-Cap Index

A measurement of performance by stocks with a market capitalization of about $1,000 million.

The stocks of 250 companies with an average market capitalization of about $1,000 million each are selected. At the end of the trading day, the price per share of each stock is multiplied by the number of shares listed to give the market value of that stock. The market values of all 250 stocks are then summed, and the total is divided by the market value on the base date. This quotient is then multiplied by the base value of the index. The resulting value is expressed in billions of dollars rounded to two decimal places. Nonprice effects are eliminated by adjustments to the base-date market value. Monthly values are averages of daily values.

Used as a measure of the value of the U.S. equity marketplace for firms with small capitalizations and as a measure of portfolio performance. Also used as the basis for stock-index options.

Published daily by Wilshire Associates as a news release.

Source	Frequency	Extent	Form	Medium
Barron's	d, w	c	t	p
Business Week	h	c	t	e
CBS	h	c	t	e
CheckFree	d	c	t	e
StockMaster	d	c, h	g, t	e
USA Today	h	c	t	e

Bibliography
"Wilshire Small Cap Index," wilshire.com/home/products/wsxdesc.htm, visited Aug. 15, 1997.

Workweek
[See Average Manufacturing Workweek]

World Series Predictor
[See Appendix A. Nonquantitative Indicators]

Yield Curve
[See Treasury Yield Curve]

APPENDIXES

Appendix A:
Nonquantitative Indicators

Bad Guess Theorem

A nonquantitative predictor of stock market trends based on the inverse of the sentiments expressed by the advisory services.

The sentiments of the leading investment-advisory services are surveyed by the user. A cynical attitude towards those advisory services is adopted, and an investment strategy opposite to that recommended by the clear majority of the services is selected.

Used as a contrary indicator of future market performance. When the ratio of bull-to-bear sentiments of that coterie of experts is more than two, the market is expected to go down. When the ratio of sentiments is less than two-to-one, the market is expected to rise.

Bibliography

Russell, James, "Surly Waiters and Other Stock Predictors," *Miami Herald*, 1F ff. (Dec. 20, 1982).

Big Mac Index

A comparator of foreign-exchange rates that bypasses the effects of trade deficits and the interventions of central banks.

This index originated in 1984 and is attributed to Georg Grimm of Germany. It is regularly calculated and displayed by *The Economist* and displayed on its website at www.economist.com. With the index, the prices of Big Mac sandwiches in different locales are compared to the price in New York City. The comparison easily shows the strength or weakness of a currency or the relative cost of living (and relative earning power) of an area. Calculated across time, it can be used as a measure of inflation and as an indicator of real earnings. *The Economist* claims that it publishes the index "to make exchange-rate theory more digestible."

Used to compare the purchasing power of wages in dissimilar economies.

Bibliography
Banks, Howard, "The Big Mac Index," *Forbes* 110-112 (July 2, 1984).
Berlin, Howard M., *The Handbook of Financial Market Indexes, Averages, and Indicators*, Dow Jones-Irwin, Homewood, Ill., 1990.
"Big Mac Index," *Parade Magazine*, p. 14 (May 18, 1997).
"The Big Mac Index," http://www.economist.com/0ycgbLsm/editorial/freeforall/focus/bigmac.html, visited Jan. 5, 1999.

Brokerage House Rule

A nonquantitative and irreproducible predictor of near-term stock-market trends.

A cynical attitude about the forecasting and planning abilities of brokerage firms is adopted by the user. Advertising by those firms for sales trainees, contracts awarded by those firms for remodeling or expansion of their physical plants, and expansions of the labor forces of those firms are surveyed. If any of these conditions are noted, preparations are made for a sharp decline in the market.

Used as a contrary indicator of the stock market's future performance.

Bibliography
Russell, James, "Surly Waiters and Other Stock Predictors," *Miami Herald*, 1F ff. (Dec. 20, 1982).

Christmas Price Index

A melodic measure of inflation.

Each November since 1984, the PNC Asset Management Group of the PNC Bank Corp. in Pittsburgh has calculated the current cost of the gifts named in the song, "The Twelve Days of Christmas." They contact a nursery for the price of pear trees, a cleaning service for the daily rate for maids, the Pennsylvania Ballet Company for lordly leapers, etc. They take the costs for partridges, pear trees, doves, hens, songbirds, gold rings, geese, swans, maids, lady dancers, male ballet dancers, pipers, and drummers and multiply each by the number specified in the lyrics of the song. The results are summed and expressed as a percentage of the previous year's Christmas price. In addition, a total cost of Christmas and its percentage change from the previous year are calculated by using the number of items mentioned as all of the rounds of the song are sung.

Used as a predictor of inflation's influence on after-Christmas bills.

Bibliography
"PNC 1997 Christmas Price Index Up Slightly at $13,343.86," http://www.prnewswire.com/cgi-bin/stories...5&STORY=/www/story/11-18-97/362250&EDATE=, visited Nov. 20, 1997.

Coca-Cola Map

An assessment of global economics as viewed through the bottom of a Coca-Cola bottle.

As a side order to the Big Mac Index, *The Economist* serves up the Coca-Cola Map on its website at www.economist.com. Coca-Cola sales are graphed against geographic distribution, Gross Domestic Product, the United Nations Human Development Index, and political freedom. Consumption of Coca-Cola is seen to be correlated with wealth, quality of life, and democracy.

Used to underscore the slogan that "Things go better with Coke."

Bibliography

"Coca-Cola Map: Next Year, the French-Fry Index," http://www.economist.com/0ycgbLsm/editorial/freeforall/20-12-97/coca.html.

Color Index

A subjective predictor of consumer confidence based on the colors that women wear.

Ben Gaynes, Jr., of Advest, Inc., in Hartford, Conn., surveys clothing racks at local retail shops and notes what colors predominate. "Happy colors" like yellow and rosy pink indicate a positive consumer mood. Earth tones and other more-somber colors indicate troubled times ahead.

Used to predict consumer outlook, consumer purchasing, stock market, and general business cycles.

Bibliography

Solomon, David J., "And We Thought That Hemlines Were the Best Economic Indicators," *Wall Street Journal*, 33 (May 27, 1987).

Cost of Laughing Index

A leading humor indicator comparing the punch line to the bottom line.

Malcolm Kushner, a humor consultant in Santa Cruz, Calif., uses a market basket of eighteen items that Americans purchase to laugh and uses this indicator to gauge economic performance. The wholesale price of gag items like rubber chickens, Groucho glasses, and arrows-through-the-head; the newsstand price of Mad Magazine; and the price of comedy club tickets make up the market basket. Their prices are totaled and adjusted for inflation to determine the humor scale. The index is released on April Fool's Day.

Used to judge an important component of the cost of living.

Bibliography

Hodges, Bill, "Laughter Is Costing More," *Knoxville News-Sentinel*, A12 (Apr. 3, 1988).

Darts Average

An off-the-wall (literally) gauge of the perspicacity of investment professionals and of the relevance of the Dow Jones Industrial Average.

Once a month, the staff of *The Wall Street Journal* invites four leading equity-investment experts to each pick a stock whose price they feel will increase significantly in the following six months. Each month, two of this select panel are new, and two are prognosticators who had finished first and second in a previous round of this contest. After each of these experts has picked a favorite equity issue, the staff of the paper pin the stock pages on the wall and throw four darts at them. The four stocks struck by the darts are recorded. Six months later, the investment gains posted by the experts' stocks are averaged, and that average is compared with the average gain posted by the dartboard portfolio. The darts' average is also compared with the percentage change in the Dow Jones Industrial Average during the same period. The results are reported monthly in *The Wall Street Journal* as part of the column Your Money Matters.

Used in a spirit of light-hearted fun as an opportunity to embarrass top brokerage-house professionals and to question the import of Dow Jones's own flagship indicator.

Bibliography
Jasen, Georgette, "Darts Again Beat Wall Street Pros," *The Wall Street Journal*, C1, C22 (Jan. 15, 1998).

Discomfort Index
[See Misery Index]

Dom Perignon Champagne New Year's Celebration Index

A spinoff of the Moet Annual Market Basket (see below).

The Celebration Index is based on a market basket of essentials for celebrating New Year's Eve in New York City. The current costs of a bottle of Dom Perignon champagne, a one-night stay at the presidential suite at the Plaza Hotel, 10 minutes of fireworks by the Grucci Brothers, a rental of an Armani tuxedo, a limousine rental, and a make-up job for the big night from Elizabeth Arden are summed and compared to the cost for the same items a year ago, all expressed as a percent change.

Used as a gauge of the effects of inflation on the cost of the year's first headache.

Bibliography
"The Cost of Partying Remains the Same This Year," http://bspaa.com/wirelessnews/wf121896.html, visited Feb. 5, 1998.

Drinking Couple Count

A nonquantitative and irreproducible descriptor of current stock-market conditions and a predictor of near-term market trends.

The user surveys the evening crowds at cocktail lounges frequented by participants in the stock market and counts the number of drinking couples. The ratio of drinking couples to individuals drinking alone or with someone of the same sex is calculated.

Used as a direct indicator of present market performance. When the ratio of drinking couples is low, the market is depressed, and traders wish to drink alone. A rise in the market is to be expected shortly. When the ratio is high, market performance is considered to be good enough to brag about.

Bibliography

Russell, James, "Surly Waiters and Other Stock Predictors," *Miami Herald*, 1F ff. (Dec. 20, 1982).

Early Warning Barometer

A predictor of stock-market performance. It states that the stock market's directional change during the first five trading days of the year indicates the direction the stock market will go for the rest of the month and the rest of the year.

The value of the Dow Jones Industrial Average or the Standard & Poor's Composite Index at the close of the first trading day of January is compared with the value at the close of business on the fifth trading day of that same month. The direction of change is indicative of the direction the market will follow during the ensuing month and perhaps year.

Used as a gross predictor of direction of prices on the stock market.

Bibliography

Colby, Robert W., and Thomas A. Meyers, *The Encyclopedia of Technical Market Indicators*, Dow Jones-Irwin, Homewood, Ill., 1988.
Koshetz, Charles, "Barometers to Watch," *USA Today*, p. 1B (Jan. 2, 1986).

Elves' Forecast

An estimation of the general movement of the stock market in the near term.

Each week, ten panelists (elves) on the television show Wall $treet Week are asked to guess where the Dow Jones Industrial Average will be three months hence. The elves are given three choices: bullish (the DJIA will have risen 5% or more), neutral (the DJIA will be within 5% of where it currently is), and bearish (the DJIA will have fallen off 5% or more). The Forecast is calculated by throwing out the neutrals and subtracting the minuses from the pluses.

Used as a general consensus of whether the prudent investor should buy, sell, or hold.

Announced each week on Wall $treet Week and on the Wall $treet Week with Louis Rukeyser website.

Bibliography

"The Elves' Forecast," www.mpt.org/wsw/elves.html, visited Dec. 9, 1998.

First-of-the-Month Uptick

A prediction that the prices of blue-chip stocks will rise on the first trading day of each month.

The prices of blue-chip stocks are predicted to rise on the first trading day of the month because institutional investors, particularly managers of 401(k) and other retirement plans, tend to place their capital in the market on a periodic basis, usually at the beginning of the month. This coincident purchasing produces a temporary swell in the demand for securities (particularly for the blue-chip issues favored by these investors) and pushes up prices, resulting in an increase in market-price indicators like the S&P 500 and the Dow Jones Industrial Average.

Used as a predictor of the direction of prices of blue-chip stocks on particular days.

Bibliography
Associated Press, "Blue Chip Stocks Soar Early Each Month," *Knoxville News-Sentinel*, Oct. 6, 1996, p. D8.

Full-Moon Theory

A pseudopredictor of the Dow Jones Industrial Average.

The phases of the moon are observed and kept track of. A trough in the Dow Jones Industrial Average can be expected a day before the full moon to three days after; the Dow Jones Industrial Average will then rise from the fifth day before the new moon to three days after, according to Toronto stock analyst Ian McAvity.

Used to anticipate swings in the prices of stocks.

Bibliography
Lewyn, Mark, "Is There a Stock Theory for You?" *USA Today*, p. B1 (Jan. 2, 1985).

GM Indicator

A mechanical indicator of the direction of the stock market; the future direction of that market is presumed to be the same as the current direction of the price of General Motors common stock.

The trend of price of General Motors' common equity is observed. A rise is taken as an indicator that the market as a whole will rise. A four-month period in which no new high of GM stock occurs is taken as an early warning of a reverse in the market. In a declining market, a four-month period in which no new low is recorded by GM shares is taken as an indicator that the general market is about to reverse and to rally.

Used as a predictor of the direction of the stock market in the near to intermediate term.

Bibliography
Stovall, Robert, "Market Comments: A Survey of Indicators," *Financial World*, **154** (7), 54 (Mar. 20–Apr. 2, 1985).

Hemline Index
[See Short-Skirt Index]

High Life Inflation Index
[See Moet Annual Market Basket]

Incumbent President Theory

A predictor of stock-market performance.

This theory holds that the Dow Jones Industrial Average will decline when an incumbent president loses a reelection bid; of limited use because of the intervals between presidential elections. It complements the view that markets move in response to the presidential election cycle.

Similar to the Superbowl Predictor and the World Series Predictor (see below), only on a political plane.

Used to predict future stock-market direction.

Bibliography

Antilla, Susan, "Series: Market Forecaster?" *USA Today*, B1-B2 (Oct. 8, 1984).

Colby, Robert W., and Thomas A. Meyers, *The Encyclopedia of Technical Market Indicators*, Dow Jones-Irwin, Homewood, Ill., 1988.

January Indicator

A predictor of stock-market performance. It states that the stock market's directional change (as measured, for example, by the Standard & Poor's 500) in January is representative of the qualitative change that will occur in the market during the rest of the calendar year.

The value of the Dow Jones Industrial Average or the Standard & Poor's Composite Index at the close of the first trading day of January is compared with the value at the close of business on the last trading day of that same month. The direction of change is indicative of the direction the market will follow during the ensuing eleven months. A variation on the theme has been noted by The Hirsch Organization of Old Tappan, N.J.; it uses the trend of the first five days in January to indicate the general direction of the market throughout the coming year.

Used as a gross predictor of direction of prices on the stock market.

Also called the January Barometer; not to be confused with the January Effect, the tendency of smaller stocks to outperform larger ones during the month of January.

Bibliography

Colby, Robert W., and Thomas A. Meyers, *The Encyclopedia of Technical Market Indicators*, Dow Jones-Irwin, Homewood, Ill., 1988.

Currier, Chet, "Inexact Science: Is Wall Street Saying Recession Is Over?" *Knoxville News-Sentinel*, p. D7 (Feb. 2, 1992).

Koshetz, Charles, "Barometers to Watch," *USA Today*, p. 1B (Jan. 2, 1986).

Laubscher, Harry W., "The January Barometer," *Financial World* **56**, 69 (1987).
Lewyn, Mark, "Is There a Stock Theory for You?" *USA Today*, p. B1 (Jan. 2, 1985).
Martinich, Joseph S., "The January Indicator: A Nonrandom but Unprofitable Walk," *Mid-South Business Journal* **4**, 10-13 (1984).
Norris, Floyd, "Are Small Stocks Set to Rebound?" *New York Times*, p. C8 (Dec. 12, 1989).
Stovall, Robert, "Market Comments: A Survey of Indicators," *Financial World*, **154** (7), 54 (Mar. 20-Apr. 2, 1985).

Magazine Cover Indicator

A contraindicator of the future performance of a market.

Attributed to Paul Macrae Montgomery, this technique calls for a content analysis of the covers of magazines to gain insight into the near-term performance of a market, such as the stock market in general, individual stocks, or commodity futures. When a topic, person, product, company, or industry associated with business or finance is featured on the cover of a magazine, this is a warning sign of a turning point about a month hence for the subject of the cover story. Indeed, according to the proponents of this contraindicator, 11 months after the appearance of the cover, the situation will be just the opposite of that described in the magazine.

An explanation of this contraindicator is that research about a trend (e.g., in the stock market) or about an industry or personality takes so long that, by the time the story is published, (1) the sentiments expressed are outdated and (2) change is imminent. General-interest weekly news magazines (such as *Time* and *Newsweek*) are felt to provide better signals than do business periodicals that feature a financial story every issue (such as *Business Week*, *Forbes*, and *Futures*).

Used as a contrary indicator of a trend or condition of a market or of a stock associated featured in a magazine cover story.

Bibliography
Burke, Gibbons, "How to Tell a Market by Its Covers," *Futures: The Magazine of Commodities and Options* **22** (4), 30-31 (1993).

Misery Index
[Also called the Discomfort Index]

A nonempirical estimation of the condition of the general economy as it affects the general public.

The nationwide unemployment rate (expressed as a percentage) is added to the year-to-year change in the Consumer Price Index (expressed as a percentage). The resulting Misery Index is also expressed as a percentage. The origin of the index is popularly ascribed to the late Arthur Okun, a member of the President's Council of Economic Advisers. An alternative formulation adds the prime rate to the equation.

Used as a gauge of the broad political reaction to be expected as a result of current economic conditions. These conditions are assumed to be closely associated with the economic policies (and policymakers) under which they have occurred. A high Misery Index is viewed as an indicator of failure of economic policies (specifically governmental policies) and as a harbinger of the replacement of elected officials.

Bibliography

Asher, Martin A.; Robert H. Defina; and Kishor Thanawala, "The Misery Index: Only Part of the Story," *Challenge* **36** (2), 58-62 (1993).

Berlin, Howard M., *The Handbook of Financial Market Indexes, Averages, and Indicators*, Dow Jones-Irwin, Homewood, Ill., 1990.

Chandrasekhar, Ashor, "Gauging Living Standards in '84," *Wall Street Journal*, p. 62 (July 24, 1984).

Colby, Robert W., and Thomas A. Meyers, *The Encyclopedia of Technical Market Indicators*, Dow Jones-Irwin, Homewood, Ill., 1988.

"Misery as an Indicator," *New York Times*, p. 18F (May 23, 1982).

"Misery Index Doesn't Feel Our Pain," *The Arizona Republic*, p. A19 (Feb. 11, 1996).

Wiseman, Clark, "More on Misery: How Consistent Are Alternative Indices?" *American Economist* **36** (2), 85-88 (1992).

Moet Annual Market Basket

A measure of the rate of inflation for those living high on the hog.

The prices of 12 luxuries in New York City (less taxes, freight, and other add-on charges) are used to calculate the change from year to year in each of them expressed as a percentage. The 12 percentages are then averaged, and the average percent change is compared with the domestic Consumer Price Index-derived cost of living index for the same period. The compilation is performed by Moet and Chandon.

The commodities in the market basket include Beluga caviar, a Rolls-Royce convertible, a Rolex watch, a round-trip ticket to Paris on the Concorde, Dom Perignon champagne, Hennessy cognac, a ticket to "Cats," a hairdo, a mink coat, a day's maid service, a limo rental, and chocolate truffles.

Used to judge the cost of living for a specific class of consumers.

Bibliography

Berlin, Howard M., *The Handbook of Financial Market Indexes, Averages, and Indicators*, Dow Jones-Irwin, Homewood, Ill., 1990.

Pentafilia Paradigm

An theory that the Dow Jones Industrial Average will rise during years ending with the number five.

Years that end in five (2005, 2015, 2025, etc.) are expected to be years during which the stock market as a whole and the Dow Jones Industrial Average in particular will perform amazingly well.

Used as a gross predictor of direction of prices on the stock market.

Bibliography
Stovall, Robert, "Market Comments: A Survey of Indicators," *Financial World*, **154** (7), 54 (Mar. 20–Apr. 2, 1985).

Quasimodo Principle

Succinctly put: I back my hunches.

A tenet characteristic of those in the higher ranges of investor confidence. This approach to investing (or research or life in general) reflects an extraordinarily high belief in one's own perceptions, analyses, and decisions.

Used as a defense against nagging doubts induced by arcane technical analyses, contemporary but transient negative market trends, and investment-advisory-service opinions (which, according to the Bad Guess Theorem, are wrong, anyway).

Bibliography
"Non-Ivory Tower Research," *Mini-Annals of Improbable Research* (electronic journal), Issue 1996-06 (June 1996).

Santa Claus Rally

Pseudopredictor of stock market trends.

It holds that, if the Standard & Poor's 500 posts a gain of 0.8% or more in the first seven trading days following Christmas, the stock market will be strong during the new year. In actuality, the rally frequently occurs because of end-of-year realignment of portfolios for tax purposes. Proceeds from tax-loss selling are put to work by reinvestment in the market, thus driving up the demand for and price of stocks, producing the Christmas-time rally.

Used by some to predict market direction for the new year.

Bibliography
Koshetz, Charles, "Barometers to Watch," *USA Today*, p. 1B (Jan. 2, 1986).
Rynecki, David, "Strong 'Santa Claus Rally' Is Coming to Stocks," *USA Today*, p. 1B (Dec. 28, 1998).

Short-Skirt Index
[Also called the Hemline Index]

A nonquantitative predictor of stock-market performance.

The average height of hemlines of women's skirts shown by international fashion designers is observed and calculated by the user.

Used as a near-term to midterm predictor of future stock market performance. When hemlines are high, the market is expected to rise. When they are low, the market is expected to decline.

Bibliography

Russell, James, "Surly Waiters and Other Stock Predictors," *Miami Herald*, 1F ff. (Dec. 20, 1982).
Shapiro, Joshua, "The New Science of Hemlines," *Institutional Investor* 28 (5), 196 (1994).
"Watch the Grasshopper: Some Gurus Find Market Predictors in Astrology, Hemlines, and Insect Cycles," *Wall Street Journal*, R28 (Dec. 2, 1988).
"You Can Also Use Tea Leaves," *Business Week*, 120 ff. (Nov. 17, 1962).

Sotheby Index

A cost-of-living indicator based on a market basket of slightly more pricey objects than are used in calculating the Consumer Price Index.

Formerly the Sotheby Art Index, it tracks price trends in 12 categories of *objets d'art* and antiques. Each category has a fixed market basket of 25 to 65 representative types of art. A value for each item is determined from sales prices. These items are chosen to represent the types of things that come on the market frequently. Periodically, the market baskets are reappraised by teams of experts at Sotheby's Auction House in light of recent auctions, private sales, exhibitions, and prevailing market conditions. About 95% of the revaluations are based on auction sales, an open market. Each category is weighted according to its dollar-value portion of Sotheby's business, and the 12 adjusted values are summed and compared with a base value (1975 = 100). The categories include impressionist and postimpressionist paintings, old-master paintings, 19th century European paintings, modern paintings, Chinese ceramics, English furniture, continental furniture, continental silver, English silver, American furniture, American paintings, and continental ceramics.

Used as a surrogate for the common cost of living (or cost of common living) calculations to reflect market activities in a specialized segment of the economy.

Bibliography

Berlin, Howard M., *The Handbook of Financial Market Indexes, Averages, and Indicators*, Dow Jones-Irwin, Homewood, Ill., 1990, pp. 239-241.
Mahon, Gigi, "Unveiling Sotheby's Art Index," *Barron's*, Nov. 9, 1981, pp 4+.
Tucker, Michael; Walter Hlawischka; and Jeff Pierne, "Art as an Investment: A Portfolio Allocation Analysis," *Managerial Finance* 21 (6), 16-24 (1995).

Superbowl Predictor

A pseudopredictor of the gross change in the stock market for the following year based on the winner of the Superbowl.

The winning of the Superbowl by one of the original National Football League teams signifies an up year for the stock market as measured by the Standard

& Poor's 500 Index, the Dow Jones Industrial Average, or other market indicator. The winning of the Superbowl by one of the newer teams (those franchised since 1963, including all AFC teams and any NFC expansion teams) indicates a decline of the market as a whole during the following year.

Used to predict the overall performance of the stock market for the months from February to January.

Bibliography

Berlin, Howard M., *The Handbook of Financial Market Indexes, Averages, and Indicators*, Dow Jones-Irwin, Homewood, Ill., 1990.

Koshetz, Charles, "Barometers to Watch," *USA Today*, 1B (Jan. 2, 1986).

Lewyn, Mark, "Is There a Stock Theory for You?" *USA Today*, p. B1 (Jan. 2, 1985).

Russell, James, "Surly Waiters and Other Stock Predictors," *Miami Herald*, 1F ff. (Dec. 20, 1982).

Stovall, Robert, "Market Comments: A Survey of Indicators," *Financial World*, **154** (7), 54 (Mar. 20-Apr. 2, 1985).

Stovall, Robert, "The Play from Pasadena (Super Bowl and the Stocks)," *Financial World* **156**, 70 (Jan. 28-Feb. 10, 1987).

Surly Waiter Index

A nonquantitative indicator of the current performance of the stock market.

The user dines in three- and four-star restaurants and observes the behavior of the waiters. The graciousness (or lack thereof) of the waiters is graded on an arbitrary scale for comparison across a time series.

Used as a counter-cyclical coincident indicator. When the market is depressed, waiters will be as accommodating as possible to maximize tips and supplement their major incomes, which are presumed to be derived from playing the market. When the market is rising rapidly (and due for a sharp reverse), no such accommodating nature is needed or proffered.

Bibliography

Russell, James, "Surly Waiters and Other Stock Predictors," *Miami Herald*, 1F ff. (Dec. 20, 1982).

World Series Predictor

Pseudopredictor of election results and market direction.

According to William LeFevre of Purcell Graham & Co., an American League victory in the World Series indicates a Republican victory at the polls, while a National League victory indicates a Democratic victory. In the month after a Republican win, stocks tend to rise; while after a Democratic victory, stocks tend to fall.

Used to predict election results and future market direction.

Bibliography

Antilla, Susan, "Series: Market Forecaster?" *USA Today*, B1-B2 (Oct. 10, 1984).

Appendix B:
Key to Printed Sources

Abbreviated names, full names, publishers, and addresses for the printed sources of indicators (places where the values can be found) that are cited in the main text.

ABA Banking Journal
ABA Banking Journal
American Bankers Association
Order Processing Department
Suite 343
1120 Connecticut Ave., NW
Washington, DC 20036

Aerospace Facts and Figures
Aerospace Facts and Figures
Aerospace Industries Assoc. of America
1250 Eye St., NW
Washington, DC 20005

Aerospace Industry
Aerospace Industry
U.S. Department of Commerce
Bureau of the Census
Customer Services Branch
Washington, DC 20233

Agricultural Income and Finance
Agricultural Income and Finance
U.S. Department of Agriculture
Economic Research Service

Information Services Division
1800 M St., NW
Washington, DC 20036
Order from: ERS-NASS
5285 Port Royal Rd.
Springfield, VA 22161

Agricultural Outlook
Agricultural Outlook
U.S. Department of Agriculture
Economic Research Service
Information Services Division
1800 M St., NW
Washington, DC 20036
Order from: ERS-NASS
5285 Port Royal Rd.
Springfield, VA 22161

Agricultural Prices Annual Summary
Agricultural Prices Annual Summary
U.S. Department of Agriculture
National Agricultural Statistics Service
Washington, DC 20250-2000
Order from: ERS-NASS
5285 Port Royal Rd.
Springfield, VA 22161

Agricultural Prices Monthly Report
Agricultural Prices Monthly Report
U.S. Department of Agriculture
National Agricultural Statistics Service
Washington, DC 20250-2000
Order from: ERS-NASS
5285 Port Royal Rd.
Springfield, VA 22161

Agricultural Statistics
Agricultural Statistics
U.S. Department of Agriculture
National Agricultural Statistics Service
Washington, DC 20250-2000
Order from: Superintendent of Documents
USGPO

Washington, DC 20402
www.usda.gov/nass/pubs/agstats.htm

AHAM Fact Book
AHAM Fact Book
Association of Home Appliance Manufacturers
20 Wacker Dr., Suite 1231
Chicago, IL 60606

Air Carrier Industry Scheduled Service Traffic Statistics Quarterly
Air Carrier Industry Scheduled Service Traffic Statistics Quarterly
U.S. Department of Transportation
Bureau of Transportation Statistics
Customer Service
400 7th St., SW, Room 3430
Washington, DC 20590

Air Carrier Traffic Statistics Monthly
Air Carrier Traffic Statistics Monthly
U.S. Department of Transportation
Bureau of Transportation Statistics
Customer Service
400 7th St., SW, Room 3430
Washington, DC 20590

Air Transport
Air Transport Facts and Figures
Air Transport Association of America
1301 Pennsylvania Ave., Suite 1100
Washington, DC 20004-7017

AMEX Fact Book
American Stock Exchange Fact Book
American Stock Exchange
86 Trinity Pl.
New York, NY 10006

AMT Industry Estimates
AMT Industry Estimates
The Association for Manufacturing Technology
7901 Westpark Drive
McLean, VA 22102
www.mfgtech.org

Annual Capital Expenditures Survey
Annual Capital Expenditures Survey
U.S. Department of Commerce
Bureau of the Census
Customer Services Branch
Washington, DC 20233

Annual Energy Review
Annual Energy Review
U.S. Department of Energy
Energy Information Administration
National Energy Information Center
EI-20, MS 1F048
1000 Independence Ave., SW
Washington, DC 20585

Annual Statistical Digest (FRB)
Annual Statistical Digest
Board of Governors of the Federal Reserve System
Publications Services, MS-127
Washington, DC 20551

Annual Statistical Report (AISI)
Annual Statistical Report
American Iron and Steel Institute
1101 17th St., NW, 13th Floor
Washington, DC 20036-4700

Automotive News Market Data Book
Automotive News Market Data Book
Crain Automotive Group
965 E. Jefferson
Detroit, MI 48207-3185

Balance of Payments Statistics Yearbook (IMF)
Balance of Payments Statistics Yearbook
International Monetary Fund
Publication Services
700 19th Street, NW
Washington, DC 20431
www.imf.org

Bank Rate Monitor
Bank Rate Monitor
P.O. Box 88888
North Palm Beach, FL 33408-8888

Barron's
Barron's National and Financial Weekly
Dow Jones & Company, Inc.
22 Cortland St.
New York, NY 10007

Basic Petroleum Data Book
Basic Petroleum Data Book
American Petroleum Institute
1220 L Street, Northwest
Washington, DC 20005

Blue Chip Economic Indicators
Blue Chip Economic Indicators
Blue Chip Newsletters
Customer Service
FULCO
P.O. Box 3000
Denville, NJ 07834-9272

Bob Nurocks Advisory
Bob Nurocks Advisory
Investor's Analysis, Inc.
P.O. Box 460
Santa Fe, NM 87504-0460

Bond Buyer, The
The Bond Buyer
1 State St. Plaza, 26th Floor
New York, NY 10004-1549

Builder
Builder
National Assoc. of Home Builders
1201 15th St., NW
Washington, DC 20005

Business Executives' Expectations
Business Executives' Expectations
The Conference Board
845 3rd Ave.
New York, NY 10022

Business Failure Record
The Business Failure Record
Dun & Bradstreet
P.O. Box 1861
Grand Central Station
New York, NY 10163-1861

Business Statistics
Business Statistics of the United States
Bernan Press
4611-F Assembly Drive
Lanham, MD 20706-4391

Business Week
Business Week
McGraw-Hill Publishing Co.
1221 Avenue of the Americas, 40th Floor
New York, NY 10020-1095

Chain Store Age
Chain Store Age
Lebhar-Friedman, Inc.
425 Park Ave., 6th Floor
New York, NY 10022-0212

Changing Times
Kiplinger's Personal Finance Magazine
The Kiplinger Washington Editors, Inc.
1729 H Street
Washington, DC 20006

Characteristics of New Housing
Characteristics of New Housing
U.S. Department of Commerce
Bureau of the Census
Customer Services Branch
Washington, DC 20233

Chemical Week
Chemical Week
Chemical Week Associates
888 7th Ave., 26th Floor
New York, NY 10106-0001
www.chemweek.com

Commercial Carrier Journal
Commercial Carrier Journal
201 King of Prussia Road
Radnor, PA 19089
www.ccjmagazine.com

Commodity Yearbook
The CRB Commodity Yearbook
Bridge Commodity Research Bureau
30 S. Wacker Dr., Suite 1810
Chicago, IL 60606-7404

Compensation and Working Conditions
Compensation and Working Conditions
U.S. Department of Labor
Bureau of Labor Statistics
Information Office
Postal Square Bldg.
2 Massachusetts Ave., NW
Washington, DC 20212
Order from: Superintendent of Documents
USGPO
Washington, DC 20402
www.access.gpo.gov/su_docs/sale.html

Conference Board
Conference Board
The Conference Board
845 3rd Ave.
New York, NY 10022

Construction Outlook
Construction Outlook
F. W. Dodge
148 Princeton-Heightstown Rd.
South-2
Heightstown, NJ 08520

Construction Review
Construction Review
U.S. Department of Commerce
Bureau of the Census
Customer Services Branch
Washington, DC 20233
Order from: Superintendent of Documents
USGPO
Washington, DC 20402
www.access.gpo.gov/su_docs/sale.html

Consumer Confidence Survey
Consumer Confidence Survey
The Conference Board
845 3rd Ave.
New York, NY 10022

Consumer Credit
Consumer Credit
Board of Governors of the Federal Reserve System
Publications Services, MS-127
Washington, DC 20551

Consumer Credit Delinquency Bulletin
Consumer Credit Delinquency Bulletin
American Bankers Association
Order Processing Department
Suite 343
1120 Connecticut Ave., NW
Washington, DC 20036

Consumer Installment Credit
Consumer Installment Credit
Board of Governors of the Federal Reserve System
Publications Services, MS-127
Washington, DC 20551

Consumer Price Index
Consumer Price Index
U.S. Department of Labor
Bureau of Labor Statistics
Information Office
Postal Square Bldg.
2 Massachusetts Ave., NW

Washington, DC 20212
Order from: Superintendent of Documents
USGPO
Washington, DC 20402
www.access.gpo.gov/su_docs/sale.html

Consumer Price Index Detailed Report
Consumer Price Index Detailed Report
U.S. Department of Labor
Bureau of Labor Statistics
Information Office
Postal Square Bldg.
2 Massachusetts Ave., NW
Washington, DC 20212
Order from: Superintendent of Documents
USGPO
Washington, DC 20402
www.access.gpo.gov/su_docs/sale.html

Conventional Home Mortgage Rates
Conventional Home Mortgage Rates
Federal Housing Finance Board
1777 F St., NW
Washington, DC 20066

CRB Commodity Yearbook, The
The CRB Commodity Yearbook
Bridge Commodity Research Bureau
30 S. Wacker Dr., Suite 1810
Chicago, IL 60606-7404

Daily Treasury Statement
Daily Treasury Statement
U.S. Department of the Treasury
Financial Management Service
Funds Control Branch
Public Affairs
401 14th Street, SW
Washington, DC 20227
www.fms.treas.gov

Debits and Deposit Turnover at Commercial Banks
Debits and Deposit Turnover at Commercial Banks
Board of Governors of the Federal Reserve System

Publications Services, MS-127
Washington, DC 20551

Economic Handbook of the Machine Tool Industry
Economic Handbook of the Machine Tool Industry
The Association for Manufacturing Technology
7901 Westpark Drive
McLean, VA 22102
www.mfgtech.org

Economic Indicators
Economic Indicators
Joint Economic Committee
U.S. Congress
Washington, DC 20510
Order from: Superintendent of Documents
USGPO
Washington, DC 20402
www.access.gpo.gov/su_docs/sale.html

Economic Report of the President
Economic Report of the President
Council of Economic Advisors
New Executive Office Building
Washington, DC 20806
Order from: Superintendent of Documents
USGPO
Washington, DC 20402
www.access.gpo.gov/su_docs/sale.html

Electric Power Annual
Electric Power Annual
U.S. Department of Energy
Energy Information Administration
National Energy Information Center
EI-20, MS 1F048
1000 Independence Ave., SW
Washington, DC 20585

Electric Power Monthly
Electric Power Monthly
U.S. Department of Energy
Energy Information Administration
National Energy Information Center

EI-20, MS 1F048
1000 Independence Ave., SW
Washington, DC 20585

Electrical World
Electrical World
McGraw-Hill Companies, Inc.
11 West 19th Street, 2nd Floor
New York, NY 10011

Electronic Business
Electronic Business
Cahners Business Information
275 Washington St.
Newton, MA 02458-1630

Employment & Earnings
Employment and Earnings
U.S. Department of Labor
Bureau of Labor Statistics
Information Office
Postal Square Bldg.
2 Massachusetts Ave., NW
Washington, DC 20212
Order from: Superintendent of Documents
USGPO
Washington, DC 20402
www.access.gpo.gov/su_docs/sale.html

Employment Cost Index
Employment Cost Index
U.S. Department of Labor
Bureau of Labor Statistics
Information Office
Postal Square Bldg.
2 Massachusetts Ave., NW
Washington, DC 20212

Employment Situation, The
The Employment Situation
U.S. Department of Labor
Bureau of Labor Statistics
Information Office
Postal Square Bldg.

2 Massachusetts Ave., NW
Washington, DC 20212

ENR
Engineering News-Record
McGraw-Hill Publishing Co.
1221 Avenue of the Americas, 40th Floor
New York, NY 10020-1095

FAA Statistical Handbook
FAA Statistical Handbook of Aviation
Federal Aviation Administration
Public Inquiry Center (APA-420)
800 Independence Ave., SW
Washington, DC 20590
Order from: Superintendent of Documents
USGPO
Washington, DC 20402
www.access.gpo.gov/su_docs/sale.html

Farm Labor
Farm Labor
U.S. Department of Agriculture
National Agricultural Statistics Service
Washington, DC 20250-2000
Order from: ERS-NASS
5285 Port Royal Rd.
Springfield, VA 22161

FDIC Annual Report
FDIC Annual Report
Federal Deposit Insurance Corporation
550 Seventeenth St., NW
Washington, DC 20429-9990

FDIC Quarterly Banking Profile
FDIC Quarterly Banking Profile
Federal Deposit Insurance Corporation
550 Seventeenth St., NW
Washington, DC 20429-9990

Federal Reserve Bulletin
Federal Reserve Bulletin
Board of Governors of the Federal Reserve System

Publications Services, MS-127
Washington, DC 20551

Final Monthly Treasury Statement of Receipts and Outlays of the US Government
Final Monthly Treasury Statement of Receipts and Outlays of the US Government
U.S. Department of the Treasury
Financial Management Service
Funds Control Branch
Public Affairs
401 14th Street, SW
Washington, DC 20227
www.fms.treas.gov

Finance Companies (FRB Stat Rel G.20)
Finance Companies
Board of Governors of the Federal Reserve System
Publications Services, MS-127
Washington, DC 20551

Financial Data
US Financial Data
Federal Reserve Bank of St. Louis
P.O. Box 442
St. Louis, Mo. 63166
www.stls.frb.org/publications/usfd/

Financial Digest
Financial Digest
Chase Manhattan Corp.
P.O. Box 932
New York, NY 10008

Flow of Funds Accounts
Flow of Funds Accounts
Board of Governors of the Federal Reserve System
Publications Services, MS-127
Washington, DC 20551

Forbes
Forbes
Forbes, Inc.
60 5th Ave.
New York, NY 10011-8882

Forecast
Forecast
First Interstate Economics
633 West Fifth St.
Los Angeles, CA 90071
Discontinued in 1996

Foreign Exchange Rates
Foreign Exchange Rates
Board of Governors of the Federal Reserve System
Publications Services, MS-127
Washington, DC 20551

Fortune
Fortune
Time Publishing
1271 Avenue of the Americas
Rockefeller Center
New York, NY 10020-1393

Gold: Mineral Industry Surveys
Gold: Mineral Industry Surveys
U.S. Geological Survey
Books and Open Field Reports Section
Box 25425
Federal Center
Denver, CO 80225

Government Finance Statistics Yearbook
Government Finance Statistics Yearbook
International Monetary Fund
700 19th St., NW
Washington, DC 20431

H&Q Weekly Review
H&Q Weekly Review
Hambrecht & Quist
One Bush Street
San Francisco, CA 94104

Historical Statistics
Historical Statistics of the United States
Superintendent of Documents
USGPO

Washington, DC 20402
www.access.gpo.gov/su_docs/sale.html

Home Appliance Newsline
Home Appliance Newsline
Association of Home Appliance Manufacturers
20 Wacker Dr., Suite 1231
Chicago, IL 60606

Housing Starts
Housing Starts
U.S. Department of Commerce
Bureau of the Census
Customer Services Branch
Washington, DC 20233

Housing Units Authorized by Building Permits
Housing Units Authorized by Building Permits
U.S. Department of Commerce
Bureau of the Census
Customer Services Branch
Washington, DC 20233
www.census.gov/pub/const/www/C40/c40text.html

Industrial Production and Capacity Utilization
Industrial Production and Capacity Utilization
Board of Governors of the Federal Reserve System
Publications Services, MS-127
Washington, DC 20551

Industry, Trade, and Technology Review
Industry, Trade, and Technology Review
U.S. International Trade Commission
Office of Industries
500 E St., SW
Washington, DC 20436

Industry Week
Industry Week
Penton
Penton Plaza
1111 Chester Ave.
Cleveland, OH 44114

International Economic Review
International Economic Review
U.S. International Trade Commission
Office of Industries
500 E St., SW
Washington, DC 20436

International Economic Scoreboard
International Economic Scoreboard
The Conference Board
845 3rd Ave. ·
New York, NY 10022

International Financial Statistics
International Financial Statistics Yearbook
International Monetary Fund
700 19th St., NW
Washington, DC 20431

International Petroleum Statistics Report
International Petroleum Statistics Report
U.S. Department of Energy
Energy Information Administration
National Energy Information Center
EI-20, MS 1F048
1000 Independence Ave., SW
Washington, DC 20585

International Trade Statistics Yearbook
International Trade Statistics Yearbook
U.N. Statistical Office
U.N. Publishing Division
New York, NY 10017

Investor's Business Daily
Investor's Business Daily
12655 Beatrice St.
Los Angeles, CA 90066

Journal of Commerce
Journal of Commerce
110 Wall St.
New York, NY 10005

Lumber Production and Mill Stocks
Lumber Production and Mill Stocks
U.S. Department of Commerce
Bureau of the Census
Customer Services Branch
Washington, DC 20233
blue.census.gov/

Major Household Appliances
Major Household Appliances
U.S. Department of Commerce
Bureau of the Census
Customer Services Branch
Washington, DC 20233
blue.census.gov/

Manufacturers' Shipments, Inventories, and Orders
Manufacturers' Shipments, Inventories, and Orders
U.S. Department of Commerce
Bureau of the Census
Customer Services Branch
Washington, DC 20233
www.census.gov/ftp/pub/indicator/www/m3/index.htm

Minerals Yearbook
Minerals Yearbook
U.S. Geological Survey
Minerals Information
988 National Center
Reston, VA 20192
Order from: Superintendent of Documents
USGPO
Washington, DC 20402
minerals.usgs.gov/minerals/pubs/commodity/myb/

Money
Money
Time-Warner, Inc.
Magazine Group
Time and Life Building, Room 2132
1271 Avenue of the Americas
New York, NY 10021

Monthly Business Failures
Monthly Business Failures
Dun & Bradstreet
99 Church St.
New York, NY 10007

Monthly Energy Review
Monthly Energy Review
U.S. Department of Energy
Energy Information Administration
National Energy Information Center
EI-20, MS 1F048
1000 Independence Ave., SW
Washington, DC 20585

Monthly Labor Review
Monthly Labor Review
U.S. Department of Labor
Bureau of Labor Statistics
Information Office
Postal Square Bldg.
2 Massachusetts Ave., NW
Washington, DC 20212
Order from: Superintendent of Documents
USGPO
Washington, DC 20402
www.access.gpo.gov/su_docs/sale.html

Monthly Retail Trade Sales and Inventories
Monthly Retail Trade, Sales, Accounts Receivable, and Inventories
U.S. Department of Commerce
Bureau of the Census
Customer Services Branch
Washington, DC 20233
Order from: Superintendent of Documents
USGPO
Washington, DC 20402
www.access.gpo.gov/su_docs/sale.html

Monthly Statement of the Public Debt of the US
Monthly Statement of the Public Debt
U.S. Department of the Treasury
Bureau of the Public Debt
999 E St., NW

Washington, DC 20226
www.publicdebt.treas.gov/

Monthly Statistical Report (API)
Monthly Statistical Report
American Petroleum Institute
1220 L Street, Northwest
Washington, DC 20005

Monthly Wholesale Trade Sales and Inventories
Monthly Wholesale Trade Sales and Inventories
U.S. Department of Commerce
Economic Statistics Administration
Bureau of the Census
Customer Services Branch
Washington, DC 20233
Order from: Superintendent of Documents
USGPO
Washington, DC 20402
www.access.gpo.gov/su_docs/sale.html

Moody's Bond Record
Moody's Bond Record
Moody's Investors Service
99 Church St.
New York, NY 10007

Moody's Credit Survey
Moody's Credit Survey
Moody's Investors Service
99 Church St.
New York, NY 10007

Moody's Handbook of Common Stocks
Moody's Handbook of Common Stocks
Moody's Investors Service
99 Church St.
New York, NY 10007

Mortgage Banking
Mortgage Banking
Mortgage Bankers Association of America
1125 15th St., NW
Washington, DC 20005

Mortgage Market Trends
Mortgage Market Trends
Office of Thrift Supervision
1700 G St., NW
Washington, DC 20552

Motor Vehicle Facts and Figures
Motor Vehicle Facts and Figures
Motor Vehicle Manufacturers Association
320 New Center Building
Detroit, MI 48202

Mutual Fund Fact Book
Mutual Fund Fact Book
Investment Company Institute
Membership Department
1401 H St., NW, Suite 1200
Washington, DC 20005-2148

Mutual Funds Update
Mutual Funds Update
Wiesenberger
1455 Research Blvd.
Rockville, MD 20850

NASDAQ Factbook
NASDAQ Factbook
NASDAQ
1735 K St., NW
Washington, DC 20006

National Delinquency Survey
National Delinquency Survey
Mortgage Bankers Association of America
1125 15th St., NW
Washington, DC 20005

National Income and Product Accounts of the US
National Income and Product Accounts of the United States
U.S. Department of Commerce
Bureau of Economic Analysis
Information Services Division
1441 L St., NW
Washington, DC 20230

Order from: Superintendent of Documents
USGPO
Washington, DC 20402
www.access.gpo.gov/su_docs/sale.html

National Transportation Statistics
National Transportation Statistics
U.S. Department of Transportation
Bureau of Transportation Statistics
Customer Service Program
400 7th St., SW, Room 3430
Washington, DC 20590

New Business Incorporations
New Business Incorporations
Dun & Bradstreet
P.O. Box 1861
Grand Central Station
New York, NY 10163-1861

New One Family Houses Sold (CCR C25)
New One Family Houses Sold
U.S. Department of Commerce
Bureau of the Census
Customer Services Branch
Washington, DC 20233
Order from: Superintendent of Documents
USGPO
Washington, DC 20402
www.access.gpo.gov/su_docs/sale.html

New York Times
The New York Times
The New York Times Co.
229 W 43rd St.
New York, NY 10036

NYSE Fact Book
New York Stock Exchange Fact Book
11 Wall St.
New York, NY 10005

Outlook
Standard & Poor's Outlook
Standard & Poor's Corp.

25 Broadway
New York, NY 10004

Paper, Paperboard, and Wood Pulp
Paper, Paperboard, and Wood Pulp
American Forest and Paper Association
1111 19th St., NW
Washington, DC 20009

Pensions and Investments
Pensions and Investments
Crain Communications
77 Franklin St.
Boston, MA 02110-1510
Order from: Subscriber Services
P.O. Box 07937
Detroit, MI 48207-9903

Petroleum Supply Annual
Petroleum Supply Annual
U.S. Department of Energy
Energy Information Administration
National Energy Information Center
EI-20, MS 1F048
1000 Independence Ave., SW
Washington, DC 20585

Petroleum Supply Monthly
Petroleum Supply Monthly
U.S. Department of Energy
Energy Information Administration
National Energy Information Center
EI-20, MS 1F048
1000 Independence Ave., SW
Washington, DC 20585

Precious Metals: Mineral Industry Surveys
Precious Metals: Mineral Industry Surveys
U.S. Geological Survey
Books and Open Field Reports Section
Box 25425
Federal Center
Denver, CO 80225

Preliminary Scheduled Passenger Traffic Statistics
Preliminary Scheduled Passenger Traffic Statistics
Air Transport Association of America
1301 Pennsylvania Ave., NW, Suite 1100
Washington, DC 20004-1707

Primary Mortgage Market Survey Results
Primary Mortgage Market Survey Results
Federal Home Mortgage Corp.
1770 G St., NW
Washington, DC 20552

Producer Price Index Report
Producer Price Indexes
U.S. Department of Labor
Bureau of Labor Statistics
Information Office
Postal Square Bldg.
2 Massachusetts Ave., NW
Washington, DC 20212
Order from: Superintendent of Documents
USGPO
Washington, DC 20402
www.access.gpo.gov/su_docs/sale.html

Productivity and Costs
Productivity and Costs
U.S. Department of Labor
Bureau of Labor Statistics
Information Office
Postal Square Bldg.
2 Massachusetts Ave., NW
Washington, DC 20212
Order from: Superintendent of Documents
USGPO
Washington, DC 20402
www.access.gpo.gov/su_docs/sale.html

Quarterly Business Failures
Quarterly Business Failures
Dun & Bradstreet
Economic Analysis Department
P.O. Box 1861
Grand Central Station, NY 10163

Quarterly Coal Production
Quarterly Coal Report
U.S. Department of Energy
Energy Information Administration
National Energy Information Center
EI-20, MS 1F048
1000 Independence Ave., SW
Washington, DC 20585

Railroad Facts
Yearbook of Railroad Facts
Association of American Railroads
50 F Street, NW
Washington, DC 20001

Railway Age
Railway Age
Simmons Boardman Publishing Co.
345 Hudson St.
New York, NY 10014

Rates and Terms on Conventional Home Mortgages
Rates and Terms on Conventional Home Mortgages
Federal Housing Finance Board
1777 F St., NW
Washington, DC 20066

Real Earnings
Real Earnings
U.S. Department of Labor
Bureau of Labor Statistics
Information Office
Postal Square Bldg.
2 Massachusetts Ave., NW
Washington, DC 20212
Order from: Superintendent of Documents
USGPO
Washington, DC 20402
www.access.gpo.gov/su_docs/sale.html

Real Estate Outlook
National Association of Realtors
430 N. Michigan Ave.
Chicago, IL 60611
www.realtor.com

Recession Recovery Watch
Recession Recovery Watch
Center for International Business Cycle Research
Foundation for International Business and Economic Research
122 E. 42nd St., Suite 1512
New York, NY 10168

Report on Business
NAPM Report on Business
National Association of Purchasing Management
2055 E. Centennial Cir.
P.O. Box 22160
Tempe, AZ 85285

S&P Basic Statistics
S&P Basic Statistics
Standard & Poor's Statistical Service
Standard & Poor's Corp.
25 Broadway
New York, NY 10004

S&P Credit Week
Standard & Poor's Credit Week
Standard & Poor's Corp.
25 Broadway
New York, NY 10004

S&P Current Statistics
S&P Current Statistics
Standard & Poor's Statistical Service
Standard & Poor's Corp.
25 Broadway
New York, NY 10004

S&P Outlook
Standard & Poor's Outlook
Standard & Poor's Corp.
25 Broadway
New York, NY 10004

S&P Security Price Index Record
S&P Security Price Index Record
Standard & Poor's Corp.
25 Broadway
New York, NY 10004

SEC Annual Report

SEC Annual Report
Securities and Exchange Commission
Office of Public Information
450 5th St., NW
Washington, DC 20549
Order from: Superintendent of Documents
USGPO
Washington, DC 20402
www.access.gpo.gov/su_docs/sale.html

Securities Industry Trends

Securities Industry Trends
Securities Industry Association
Research Department
120 Broadway, 35th Floor
New York, NY 10271-0080

Securities Industry Yearbook

Securities Industry Yearbook
Securities Industry Association
Research Department
120 Broadway, 35th Floor
New York, NY 10271-0080

Selected Interest Rates

Selected Interest Rates
Board of Governors of the Federal Reserve System
Publications Services, MS-127
Washington, DC 20551

Selected Interest Rates: A Weekly Series of Charts

Selected Interest and Exchange Rates: Weekly Series of Charts
Board of Governors of the Federal Reserve System
Publications Services, MS-127
Washington, DC 20551

Sindlinger Report, The

The Sindlinger Report
Sindlinger Inc. Forecasts
405 Osborne Lane
Wallingford, PA 19086

Social Security Bulletin
Social Security Bulletin
Social Security Administration
Office of Research, Evaluation, and Statistics
6401 Security Blvd.
Baltimore, MD 21235
Order from: Superintendent of Documents
USGPO
Washington, DC 20402
www.access.gpo.gov/su_docs/sale.html

Statistical Abstract
Statistical Abstract of the United States, National Data Book, and Guide to Sources
U.S. Department of Commerce
Bureau of the Census
Customer Services Branch
Washington, DC 20233
Order from: Superintendent of Documents
USGPO
Washington, DC 20402
www.access.gpo.gov/su_docs/sale.html

Statistical Yearbook of the Electric Utility Industry
Statistical Yearbook of the Electric Utility Industry
Edison Electric Institute
EEI Publications
P.O. Box 266
Waldorf, MD 20604

Statistics of Paper, Paperboard, and Wood Pulp
Statistics of Paper, Paperboard, and Wood Pulp
American Forest and Paper Association
1111 19th St., NW
Washington, DC 20009

Survey of Current Business
Survey of Current Business
U.S. Department of Commerce
Bureau of Economic Analysis
Information Services Division
1441 L St., NW
Washington, DC 20230
Order from: Superintendent of Documents

USGPO
Washington, DC 20402
www.access.gpo.gov/su_docs/sale.html

Transportation Statistics in the US
Transportation Statistics Annual Report
U.S. Department of Transportation
Bureau of Transportation Statistics
Customer Service
400 7th St., SW, Room 3430
Washington, DC 20590

Treasury Bulletin
Treasury Bulletin
U.S. Department of the Treasury
Public Affairs Office
15th and Pennsylvania Ave., NW
Washington, DC 20226
Order from: Superintendent of Documents
USGPO
Washington, DC 20402
www.access.gpo.gov/su_docs/sale.html

Trends: Weekly Traffic of Major Railroads
Trends: Carloadings of Major Railroads
Association of American Railroads
Policy, Legislation, and Communications Department
50 F St., NW
Washington, DC 20001-1564

Unemployment Insurance Claims
Unemployment Insurance Claims
U.S. Department of Labor
Employment and Training Administration
601 D St., NW, Room 10426
Washington, DC 20213

Unemployment Insurance Weekly Claims Report
Unemployment Insurance Weekly Claims Report
U.S. Department of Labor
Employment and Training Administration
601 D St., NW, Room 10426
Washington, DC 20213

United Nations Statistical Yearbook
United Nations Statistical Yearbook
United Nations Publications
801 U.N. Plaza
New York, NY 10017

USA Today
USA Today
1000 Wilson Blvd.
Arlington, VA 22229

US Automobile Industry, The
US Automobile Industry
U.S. International Trade Commission
500 E St., SW
Washington, DC 20436
Discontinued in March 1997

US Budget
Budget of the United States Government
Office of Management and Budget
Publications Unit, Rm. 4236
New Executive Office Bldg.
Washington, DC 20503

US Farm and Farm-Related Employment
US Farm and Farm-Related Employment
U.S. Department of Agriculture
National Agricultural Statistics Service
Washington, DC 20250-2000
Order from: ERS-NASS
5285 Port Royal Rd.
Springfield, VA 22161

US Financial Data
US Financial Data
Federal Reserve Bank of St. Louis
P.O. Box 442
St. Louis, MO 63166
www.stls.frb.org/publications/usfd/

US Foreign Trade Highlights
US Foreign Trade Highlights
International Trade Administration

Office of Public Affairs
Washington, DC 20230

Value Line Investment Survey, Part 2: Selection and Opinion
The Value Line Investment Survey, Part 2: Selection and Opinion
Arnold Bernhard & Co.
711 3rd Ave.
New York, NY 10017

Value of New Construction Put in Place (CCR C30)
Value of New Construction Put in Place
U.S. Department of Commerce
Bureau of the Census
Customer Services Branch
Washington, DC 20233

Wall Street Journal
The Wall Street Journal
Dow Jones & Company, Inc.
22 Cortland St.
New York, NY 10007

Weekly Coal Production
Weekly Coal Production
U.S. Department of Energy
Energy Information Administration
National Energy Information Center
EI-20, MS 1F048
1000 Independence Ave., SW
Washington, DC 20585

Weekly Statistical Bulletin (API)
Weekly Statistical Bulletin
American Petroleum Institute
1220 L Street, Northwest
Washington, DC 20005

World Financial Markets
World Financial Markets
Morgan Guaranty Trust Co. of New York
23 Wall St.
New York, NY 10015

World Motor Vehicle Data
World Motor Vehicle Data
1401 H. St., NW, Suite 900
Washington, DC 20005

Appendix C:
Compilers of Indicators

ABC News
77 W. 66th St.
New York, NY 10023-6201

Aerospace Industries Association of America
1250 Eye St., NW
Washington, DC 20005

Air Transport Association of America
1301 Pennsylvania Ave., Suite 1100
Washington, DC 20004-7017

American Automobile Manufacturers Association
1401 H. St., NW, Suite 900
Washington, DC 20005

American Bankers Association
1120 Connecticut Ave., NW
Washington, DC 20036

American Council of Life Insurance
1001 Pennsylvania Ave., NW
Washington, DC 20004-2599

American Forest and Paper Association
1111 19th St., NW
Washington, DC 20036

American Iron and Steel Institute
1101 17th St., NW
13th Floor
Washington, DC 20036-4700

American Railway Car Institute
700 N. Fairfax St.
Alexandria, VA 22314

American Society for Quality
611 E. Wisconsin Ave.
P.O. Box 3005
Milwaukee, WI 53201-3005

American Stock Exchange
86 Trinity Pl.
New York, NY 10006

Association for Manufacturing Technology
Publications
7901 West Park Dr.
McLean, VA 22102

Association of American Railroads
50 F St., NW
Washington, DC 20001

Association of Home Appliance Manufacturers
20 N. Wacker Dr., Suite 1231
Chicago, Il. 60606

E. W. Axe & Co.
400 Benedict Ave.
Tarrytown, NY 10591

Bank of Tokyo-Mitsubishi, Ltd.
1251 Avenue of the Americas
New York, NY 10020-1104
www.btmny.com

BanxQuote
362 Fifth Ave., Suite 901
New York, NY 10001
www.banx.com/about.asp

Barron's National and Financial Weekly
Dow Jones & Co.
200 Liberty St.
New York, NY 10281

Board of Governors of the Federal Reserve System
Twentieth St. and Constitution Ave., NW
Washington, DC 20551

E. H. Boeckh
2885 S. Calhoun Rd.
P.O. Box 510291
New Berlin, WI 53151-0291

Bond Buyer
Newsletter Division
1 State St. Plaza
New York, NY 10004
www.bondbuyer.com

Business Week
McGraw-Hill Publishing Co.
1221 Avenue of the Americas
New York, NY 10020
www.businessweek.com

Cahners Business Information
275 Washington Street
Newton, MA 02458-1630
www.cahners.com

Center for International Business Cycle Research
Foundation for International Business and Economic Research
122 E. 42nd St., Suite 1512
New York, NY 10168

Chartcraft, Inc.
30 Church St.
New Rochelle, NY 10801

Chicago Board Options Exchange
400 S. LaSalle
Chicago, IL 60605

CNN America
One CNN Center
P.O. Box 105366
Atlanta, GA 30348-5366

Commodity Research Bureau
30 S. Wacker Dr., Suite 1820
Chicago, IL 60606

The Conference Board
845 3rd Ave.
New York, NY 10022

Crain Communications
965 E. Jefferson
Detroit, MI 48207-3185

F. W. Dodge Group
McGraw-Hill Information Systems Co.
1221 Avenue of the Americas
New York, NY 10020

Dow Jones & Co.
22 Cortland St.
New York, NY 10007

Dun & Bradstreet Information Services
Economic Analysis Department
P.O. Box 1861
Grand Central Station
New York, NY 10163-1861

Federal Home Loan Mortgage Corp.
1770 G St., NW
Washington, DC 20066

Federal Housing Finance Board
1777 F St., NW
Washington, DC 20006
Federal Reserve Bank of New York
33 Liberty St.
New York, NY 10045

FINEX
4 World Trade Center
New York, NY 10048

Forbes, Inc.
60 5th Ave.
New York, NY 10011

Frank Russell Co.
909 A St.
Tacoma, WA 98402
russell.com

Hambrecht & Quist, Inc.
One Bush St.
San Francisco, CA 94104
www.hambrecht.com

IBC/Donoghue, Inc.
P.O. Box 91004
Ashland, MA 01721-9104

International Monetary Fund
700 19th St., NW
Washington, DC 20431
www.imf.org

Investment Company Institute
1401 H St., NW, 12th Floor
Washington, DC 20005-2148

Investor's Business Daily
P.O. Box 661750
Los Angeles, CA 90066-8950

Lehman Brothers
3 World Financial Center
New York, NY 10285
www.lehman.com

Lincoln Institute of Public Opinion Research
453 Springlake Rd.
Harrisburg, PA 17112
www.lincolninstitute.org

McGraw-Hill Economics
1221 Avenue of the Americas
New York, NY 10020

McGraw-Hill Information Systems Co.
1221 Avenue of the Americas
New York, NY 10020

Media General Financial Services
P.O. Box 85333
Richmond, VA 23293
www.mgfs.com/

Merrill Lynch
World Financial Center
North Tower
New York, NY 10281-1332
www.ml.com

Moody's Investors Service
99 Church St.
New York, NY 10007-0300

Morgan Guaranty Trust
Economic Research
P.O. Box 495
Church Street Station
New York, NY 10260

Mortgage Bankers Association
1125 15th St., NW
Washington, DC 20005

National Association for Purchasing Management
2055 E. Centennial Circle
P.O. Box 22160
Tempe, AZ 85285-2160
www.napm.org/

National Association of Homebuilders
1201 15th St., NW
Washington, DC 20005

- National Association of Realtors
  430 N. Michigan Ave.
  Chicago, IL 60611

National Association of Securities Dealers (NASD)
1735 K St., NW
Washington, DC 20006-1506

National Conference of States on Building Codes and Standards
505 Huntmar Park Dr., Suite 210
Herndon, VA 20170

National Forest Products Association
1111 19th St., NW
Washington, DC 20036

National Quality Research Center
University of Michigan Business School
701 Tappan St.
Ann Arbor, MI 48109-1234

New York Mercantile Exchange
1 North End Ave.
World Financial Center
New York, NY 10282

New York Stock Exchange
11 Wall St.
New York, NY 10005

Office of Management and Budget
Publications Unit, Rm. G236
New Executive Office Bldg.
Washington, DC 20503

Philadelphia Stock Exchange
1900 Market Street
Philadelphia, PA 19103-3584
www.phlx.com

Ryan Investment Strategies
45 Broadway Atrium
21st Floor
New York, NY 10006
ryanlabs.com

Saloman Brothers
388 Greenwich St.
New York, NY 10013

Schroders Wertheim
787 Seventh Ave.
New York, NY 10019

Sindlinger Inc. Forecasts
405 Osborne Lane
Wallingford, PA 19086

Society of Industrial and Office Realtors
700 11th St., NW, Suite 510
Washington, DC 20001-4511

Sotheby's
1334 York Ave.
New York, NY 10021

Standard & Poor's Corp.
25 Broadway
New York, NY 10004

Survey Research Center
University of Michigan Business School
701 Tappan St.
Ann Arbor, MI 48109-1234

Technical Data Group
Thomson Financial Services
22 Thomson Place
Boston, MA 02210
www.tgmarkets.com

TheStreet.com
2 Rector St., 14th floor
New York, NY 10006
www.thestreet.com

United Nations
Statistics Division
Department for Economic and Social Information and Policy Analysis
New York, NY 10017
www.un.org/depts/unsd/

U.S. Department of Agriculture
Economic Research Service
Information Services Division
Washington, DC 20005-4788

U.S. Department of Agriculture
ERS-NASS Publications
341 Victory Drive
Herndon, VA 22070

U.S. Department of Agriculture
National Agricultural Statistics Service
Washington, DC 20250-2000

U.S. Department of Commerce
Bureau of Economic Analysis
Information Services Division
1441 L Street, NW
Washington, DC 20234

U.S. Department of Commerce
Bureau of the Census
Customer Service Branch
Washington, DC 20233

U.S. Department of Commerce
International Trade Administration
Office of Publis Affairs
Washington, DC 20230

U.S. Department of Energy
Energy Information Administration
National Energy Information Center
EI-20, Mail Station 1F048
1000 Independence Ave., SW
Washington, DC, 20585

U.S. Department of Housing and Urban Development
Publication Service Center
Rm. B-258
Washington, DC 20410

U.S. Department of Labor
Bureau of Labor Statistics
Information Office
Postal Square Building
2 Massachusetts Ave., NW, Rm. 4110
Washington, DC 20212

U.S. Department of Labor
Employment and Training Administration
Room 10426
601 D St., NW
Washington, DC 20213

U.S. Department of Transportation
Bureau of Transportation Statistics
Room 2104
400 7th St., SW
Washington, DC 20590

U.S. Department of Transportation
Federal Aviation Agency
Public Inquiry Center (APA-420)
800 Independence Ave., SW
Washington, DC 20591

U.S. Department of the Treasury
Public Affairs Office
15th and Pennsylvania Ave., NW
Washington, DC 20220

U.S. News & World Report
2300 N St., NW
Washington, DC 20037

Value Line
711 3rd Ave.
New York, NY 10017
Also 220 E. 42nd St.
New York, NY 10017 for Online Services

Ward's Communications, Inc.
28 W. Adams St.
Detroit, MI 48226

WEFA
800 Baldwin Tower
Eddystone, PA 19022
www.wefa.com

Wilshire Associates
1299 Ocean Ave., Suite 700
Santa Monica, CA 90401-1085

Appendix D: Key to Electronic Sources

Abbreviated names, sponsoring organizations, and universal resource locators for the electronic sources of indicators (places where the values can be found) that are cited in the main text.

AAMA
American Automobile Manufacturers Association
www.aama.com

American Banker
American Banker magazine
www.americanbanker.com/mmxx.html

Bank of America
Bank of America
www.bankamerica.com/capmkt/brief_us.html

Bank of Tokyo-Mitsubishi
Bank of Tokyo-Mitsubishi
www.btmny.com/cgi-bin/comment-reports.pl

Bank Rate Monitor
Bank Rate Monitor newspaper
www.bankrate.com/brm/rate/avg_natl.asp

Bankinfo
Thomson Financial Publishing
www.bankinfo.com/stats-aag/stats.html

BCI
Business Cycle Indicators/Global Exposure
www.globalexposure.com/index.html

BEA
Bureau of Economic Analysis, U.S. Department of Commerce
www.bea.doc.gov/bea/glance.htm

Bloomberg
Bloomberg L.P.
www.bloomberg.com/markets/america.html

BLS
Bureau of Labor Statistics, U.S. Department of Labor
stats.bls.gov

Bond Buyer, The
The Bond Buyer newspaper
www.bondbuyer.com/

Bridge
Bridge Information Systems
www.bridge.com

Business Week
Business Week magazine
www.businessweek.com/quote.htm

CBS
CBS and Data Broadcasting Corporation
cbs.marketwatch.com/data/dbcfiles/indext.htx?source=htx/http2_mw

Cents
Cents Financial Journal
lp-llc.com/cents/current/home.htm

Chain Store Age
Chain Store Age magazine
www.chainstoreage.com

CheckFree
CheckFree Investment Services
farstar.secapl.com/cgi-bin/mw

Chicago Mercantile Exchange
Chicago Mercantile Exchange
www.barchart.com/cme/cmeint.htm

CNN
Cable News Network
www.cnnfn.com/markets/

Conference Board
The Conference Board
www.conference-board.org

Conference Board/BCI
The Conference Board and Business Cycle Indicators/Global Exposure
www.tcb-indicators.org

Dow Jones
Dow Jones and Company
averages.dowjones.com/home.html

Economic Indicators
U.S. Government Printing Office and University of California
www.gpo.ucop.edu/catalog/econ_latest.html

Economic Report of the President
Council of Economic Advisers/University of Missouri–St. Louis
www.umsl.edu/services/govdocs/

EIA
Energy Information Agency, U.S. Department of Energy
www.eia.doe.gov/oil_gas/petroleum/pet_frame.html

Electronic Business
Electronic Business magazine
www.eb-mag.com/

Federal Reserve Board
Board of Governors of the Federal Reserve
www.bog.frb.fed.us/releases/

First Union
First Union Corporation
www.firstunion.com/library/econews/indicator.html

Fortune
Fortune magazine
cgi.pathfinder.com/fortune/

FRB Atlanta
Federal Reserve Bank of Atlanta
www.frbatlanta.org/econom/index.html

FRB Chicago
Federal Reserve Bank of Chicago
www.frbchi.org/econinfo/welcome.html

FRB Dallas
Federal Reserve Bank of Dallas
www.dallasfed.org/

FRB Minneapolis
Federal Reserve Bank of Minneapolis
woodrow.mpls.frb.fed.us/economy/

FRB New York
Federal Reserve Bank of New York
www.ny.frb.org/pihome/statistics/

FRED
Federal Reserve Bank of St. Louis
www.stls.frb.org/fred/

Handbook of International Economic Statistics (CIA)
U.S. Central Intelligence Agency/University of Missouri–St. Louis
www.umsl.edu/services/govdocs/

IBC Financial Data
IBC Financial Data
www.ibcdata.com/index.html

ICSC
International Council of Shopping Centers
www.icsc.org

JP Morgan
J.P Morgan & Co.
www.jpmorgan.com/cgi-bin/Indices

Lincoln Institute
The Lincoln Institute
www.lincolninstitute.org/SINDCOMP/Sindcomp.htm

Lipper
Lipper
www.lipperweb.com

Media General
Media General Financial Services
www.mgfs.com/barom/latest.htm

Money
Money magazine
pathfinder.com/money/money30/

NASD
National Association of Security Dealers and the Nasdaq Stock Market
www.nasdaq.com

New York Times
New York Times newspaper
www.nytimes.com

Northeast Louisiana University
Center for Business and Economic Research, Northeast Louisiana University
leap.net1.nlu.edu/mrkfin.htm

NYSE
New York Stock Exchange
www.nyse.com/public/

PCQuote
PC Quote
www.pcquote.com

Philadelphia Exchange
Philadelphia Stock Exchange
www.phlx.com/index.stm

Quote.com
Quote.com
www.quote.com/index.html

Retail Trends
Convenience.Net
www.c-store.com/retailtrend.htm

Stat-USA
U.S. Department of Commerce
www.stat-usa.gov/stat-usa.html

Statistical Abstract
U.S. Department of Commerce, Bureau of the Census
www.census.gov/statab/www/freq.html

StockMaster
Marketplace.net
www.stockmaster.com/index.html

Survey of Current Business
Bureau of Economic Analysis, U.S. Department of Commerce
www.bea.doc.gov

The Bond Buyer
The Bond Buyer newspaper
www.bondbuyer.com/

TheStreet.com
TheStreet.com
www.thestreet.com

US Census Bureau
Bureau of the Census, U.S. Department of Commerce
www.census.gov/econ/www/

USA Today
USA Today newspaper
www.usatoday.com/

Appendix E:
General Reading

This bibliography lists books, journal articles, and serials on the general topic of economic indicators and includes a section on global economic indicators. Many of these sources have been cited in the bibliographies of individual indicators in the body of this book. The list is compiled here for those who desire to do further reading on the subject and is intended to guide the beginning of that search. Where available, the call numbers assigned by the Library of Congress are included.

Books

Allison, Elisabeth, and Penelope Mathews, *Economy Watching: A Guide to Current Numbers*, Data Resources, Lexington, Mass., 1982. HC103.A44 1982

Anderson, Victor, *Alternative Economic Indicators*, Routledge, New York, 1991. HC79.I5 A5 1991

Bry, Gerhard, *The Average Workweek as an Economic Indicator*, Occasional Paper No. 69, National Bureau of Economic Research, New York, 1959. H11.N2432 no. 69

Cagan, Phillip, and Geoffrey H. Moore, *The Consumer Price Index: Issues and Alternatives*, American Enterprise Institute Studies in Economic Policy No. 325, American Enterprise Institute, Washington, D.C., 1981. HB225.C33

Carnes, W. Stansbury, and Stephen D. Slifer, *The Atlas of Economic Indicators: A Visual Guide to Market Forces and the Federal Reserve*, HarperBusiness, New York, 1991. HC59.C28 1991

Carson, Carol S., *GNP: An Overview of Source Data and Estimating Methods*, Bureau of Economic Analysis Methodology Papers, U.S. National Income and Product Accounts No. 4, U.S. Department of Commerce, Bureau of Economic Analysis, USGPO, Washington, D.C., 1987. HC110.I5 C36 1987

Darnay, Arsen J., Ed., *Economic Indicators Handbook: Time Series, Conversions, Documentation*, 2nd ed., Gale Research, Detroit, 1994. HC103.E26 1994

Diodato, Virgil Pasquale, *Where to Find Business and Economic Indexes*, V. Diodato, Milwaukee, Wis., 1994. Z7165.U5 D56 1994

Dovring, Folke, *Productivity and Value: The Political Economy of Measuring Progress*, Praeger Publishers, New York, 1987. HC79.I52 D68 1987

Economic Research Service, *Agricultural and Rural Economic and Social Indicators,* Agricultural Information Bulletin No. 667, U.S. Department of Agriculture, Economic Research Service, Herndon, Va., 1993. HS21.A74 no. 667

Economist, The, *The Economist Guide to Economic Indicators: Making Sense of Economics*, 3rd ed., John Wiley, New York, 1997. HB137.E296 1997

Eichhorn, Wolfgang, Ed., *Measurement in Economics: Theory and Applications of Economic Indices*, Springer-Verlag, New York, 1988. HB135.M42 1988

Fisher, Kenneth L., *The Wall Street Waltz: 90 Visual Perspectives: Illustrated Lessons from Financial Cycles and Trends*, Contemporary Books, Chicago, 1987. HG4916.F47 1987.

Folbre, Nancy, and the Center for Popular Economics, *The New Field Guide to the U.S. Economy: A Compact and Irreverent Guide to Economic Life in America*, rev. ed., New Press and W. W. Norton, New York, 1995. HC106.5.F565 1995

Frumkin, Norman, *Guide to Economic Indicators*, 2nd ed., M. E. Sharpe, Armonk, N.Y., 1994. HC103.F9 1994

Frumkin, Norman, *Tracking America's Economy*, 3rd ed., M. E. Sharpe, Armonk, N.Y., 1998. HC106.8.F78 1998

Gramlich, Edward M., *Fiscal Indicators*, Working Papers No. 80, Organisation for Economic Cooperation and Development, Department of Economics and Statistics, Paris, 1990. HJ192.G7 1990 P

Grant, John, *A Handbook of Economic Indicators*, University of Toronto Press, Toronto, 1992. HC113.G72 1992

Hildebrand, George, *Business Cycle Indicators and Measures: A Complete Guide to Integrating the Key Economic Indicators*, Probus Publishing Co., Chicago, 1992. HB3730. H54 1992

Hoel, Arline Alchian, Kenneth W. Clarkson, and Roger LeRoy Miller, *Economics Sourcebook of Government Statistics*, Lexington Books, Lexington, Mass., 1983. H106.8.H63 1983

Horn, Robert Victor, *Statistical Indicators for the Economic & Social Sciences*, Cambridge University Press, New York, 1993. HB137.H627 1993

Klein, Philip A., Ed., *Analyzing Modern Business Cycles: Essays Honoring Geoffrey H. Moore*, M. E. Sharpe, Armonk, N.Y., 1990. HB3711.M59 A53 1990

Lahiri, Kajal, and Geoffrey H. Moore, Eds., *Leading Economic Indicators: New Approaches and Forecasting Records,* Cambridge University Press, New York, 1991. HB3711.L43 1991

Lehmann, Michael B., *The Irwin Guide to Using the Wall Street Journal*, 6th ed., Irwin, Chicago, 1999. HB3743.L44 1999

Moore, Geoffrey Hoyt, *The Anatomy of Inflation*, Bureau of Labor Statistics Report No. 373, U.S. Bureau of Labor Statistics Washington, 1969. HD8051.A7876 no. 373

Moore, Geoffrey Hoyt, *Business Cycles, Inflation, and Forecasting*, 2nd ed., National Bureau of Economic Research Studies in Business Cycles No. 24, Ballinger Publishing, Cambridge, Mass., 1983. HB3711.M59 1983

Moore, Geoffrey Hoyt, *Improving the Presentation of Employment and Unemployment Statistics*, National Commission on Employment and Unemployment Statistics Background Paper No. 22, USGPO, Washington, D.C., 1978. HD5711.M662

Moore, Geoffrey Hoyt, *Leading Indicators for the 1990s*, Dow Jones-Erwin, Homewood, Ill., 1990. HC106.8.M66 1990

Moore, Geoffrey Hoyt, and Melita H. Moore, *International Economic Indicators: A Sourcebook*, Greenwood Press, Westport, Conn., 1985. HC59.M62 1985

Morrison, Catherine J., *A Microeconomic Approach to the Measurement of Economic Performance: Productivity Growth, Capacity Utilization, and Related Performance Indicators*, Bilkent University Lecture Series, Vol. 3, Springer-Verlag, New York, 1993. HC79.I52 M67 1993

Nelson, Charles R., *The Investor's Guide to Economic Indicators*, Wiley, New York, 1987. HN38 1987

Niemira, Michael P., and Gerald F. Zukowski, *Trading the Fundamentals: The Trader's Complete Guide to Interpreting Economic Indicators & Monetary Policy*, McGraw-Hill, New York, 1998. HG4521.N477 1998

Office of Federal Statistical Policy and Standards, *1980 Supplement to Economic Indicators: Historical and Descriptive Background*, USGPO, Washington, D.C., 1980. HC101.A186 1980

Oppenländer, Karl Heinrich, Ed., *Business Cycle Indicators*, Avebury, Brookfield, Vt., 1997. HB3711.B938 1997

Plocek, Joseph E., *Economic Indicators: How America Reads Its Financial Health*, New York Institute of Finance, New York, 1991. HB3743.P66 1990

Renshaw, Edward, Ed., *The Practical Forecasters' Almanac: 137 Reliable Indicators for Investors, Hedgers, and Speculators*, Business One Irwin, Homewood, Ill., 1992. HD30.27.P73 1992

Rogers, R. Mark, *Handbook of Key Economic Indicators*, 2nd ed., McGraw-Hill, New York, 1998. HC103.R64 1998

Ruggles, Richard, *Employment and Unemployment Statistics as Indexes of Economic Activity and Capacity Utilization*, National Commission on Employment and Unemployment Statistics Background Paper No. 28, USGPO, Washington, D.C., 1979. HD5724.R823

Shim, Jae K., Joel G. Siegel, and Jonathan Langer, *100 & One Investment Decision Tools: Barometers, Instruments, and Keys (Where to Find Them and How They're Used)*, International Publishing, Chicago, 1994. HG4515.9.S55 1994

Stock, James H., and Mark W. Watson, Eds., *Business Cycles, Indicators, and Forecasting*, National Bureau of Economic Research Studies in Business Cycles No. 28, University of Chicago Press, Chicago, 1993. HB3730.B8457 1993

Tainer, Evelina M., *Using Economic Indicators to Improve Investment Analysis*, Wiley, New York, 1998. HG4529.T34 1998

Zarnowitz, Victor, *Business Cycles: Theory, History, Indicators, and Forecasting*, National Bureau of Economic Research Studies in Business Cycles No. 27, University of Chicago Press, Chicago, 1992. HB3711.Z37 1992

Journal Articles

Anon., "User's Guide to BEA Information: National Economics," *Survey of Current Business* 73 (1), 50-57 (Jan. 1993).

Duncan, Joseph W., "Understanding Statistics," *D&B Reports* 40 (5), 8 (Sept./Oct. 1992).

Duncan, Joseph W., "When to Trust a Survey," *D&B Reports* 42 (4), 6 (July/Aug. 1993).

Eugeni, Francesca, Charles Evans, and Steven Strongin, "Making Sense of Economic Indicators: A Consumer's Guide to Indicators of Real Economic Activity," *Economic Perspectives* 16 (5), 2-32 (Sept./Oct. 1992).

Hershey, Robert D., "U.S. Is Considering a Large Overhaul of Economic Data: Business and Government Say Statistical Measures Could Be Distorting the View," *New York Times*, A1 ff (Jan. 16, 1995).

Levitan, Donald, "How To Read the Economy: A Primer," *Government Finance Review* 9 (2), 25-27 (April 1993).

Moore, Geoffrey H., "Following the Indicators," *American Economist* 39 (1), 15-19 (Spring 1995).

Portas, Carole, "Using Economic Indicators," *American Printer* 210 (2), 44-46 (Nov. 1992).

Serials

Blue Chip Economic Indicators, Capitol Publications, Alexandria, Va. HC10.B6

Business Cycle Indicators: A Monthly Report from the Conference Board (continues the Business Cycle Indicators section of *Survey of Current Business*), The Board, New York. HC101.B875

Conference Board Briefing Charts, The Board, New York. HC106.8.C663

Economic Indicators, USGPO, Washington, D.C. HC101.A186

Economic Indicators of the Farm Sector: Production and Efficiency Statistics, U.S. Department of Agriculture, Economics and Statistics Service, Washington, D.C. HD1751.A5

International Financial Statistics, International Monetary Fund, Washington, D.C. HG3881.I626

Global Economic Indicators

Economist, The, *The Economist Book of Vital World Statistics*, 1st U.S. ed., Times Books, New York, 1990. HC59.W634 1990

Economist, The, *The Economist Guide to Global Economic Indicators*, Wiley & Sons, New York, 1994. HB3711.E43 1994.

Economist, The, *World Business Cycles*, Economist Newspaper Ltd., London, 1982. HC59.W632 1982

Freeman, Michael J., *Atlas of the World Economy*, Routledge, New York, 1991. HC59.F734 1991

International Monetary Fund, *International Financial Statistics: Supplement on Economic Indicators*, Supplement Series No. 10, International Monetary Fund, Washington, D.C., 1985. HG3881.I626 no. 10

Jones, Mark, and Ken Ferris, *Market Movers: Understanding and Using Economic Indicators from the Big Five Economies*, McGraw-Hill, New York, 1993. HB137.J66 1993

Klein, Philip A., and Geoffrey Hoyt Moore, *Monitoring Growth Cycles in Market-Oriented Countries: Developing and Using International Economic Indicators*, National Bureau of Economic Research Studies in Business Cycles No. 26, Ballinger Publishing Co., Cambridge, Mass., 1985. HB3711.K58 1985

Roman, Jean Claude, *Europe, United States, Japan, 1970-86: Main Indicators of Economic Accounts*, Studies of National Accounts No. 9, Office for Official Publications of the European Community, Luxembourg, Belgium, 1986. HC241.2.R557 1986

Note: Eurostat, the European Community's statistical agency, maintains a website at europa.eu.int/eurostat.html that contains a calendar of release dates for reports of indicators for the European economy. It appears as the Eurostat Release Calendar in the Eurostat Press Releases section of the website.

INDEX

Subject Index

About the Authors

F. M. O'HARA, JR., is a private consultant in technical communication in Oak Ridge, Tennessee. He has written books on economics, edited reports on energy efficiency, set up computerized library management systems, and compiled bibliographies on the effects of the rain forests on global climate. He is currently editor of *Global Climate Change Digest.*

F. M. O'HARA, III, is a librarian, anthropologist, and archaeologist. He is currently Associate Librarian and Archivist at the Museum of Northern Arizona.